Crime, Justice, and Society

Crime, Justice, and Society

Second Edition

CALVIN J. LARSON
AND
GERALD R. GARRETT

A General Hall Book

ALTAMIRA PRESS

A Division of
ROWMAN & LITTLEFIELD PUBLISHERS, INC.
Walnut Creek • Lanham • New York • Oxford

This AltaMira Press edition of *Crime, Justice, and Society: Second Edition* is an unabridged republication of the edition first published in New York in 1996 by General Hall, Inc.

A GENERAL HALL BOOK

ALTAMIRA PRESS
A Division of Rowman & Littlefield Publishers, Inc.
1630 North Main Street, #367
Walnut Creek, CA 94596
www.altamirapress.com

Rowman & Littlefield Publishers, Inc.
A Member of the Rowman & Littlefield Publishing Group
4501 Forbes Boulevard, Suite 200
Lanham, MD 20706

PO Box 317
Oxford
OX2 9RU, UK

First AltaMira Press paperback edition 2003
Composition: *Graphics Division*, General Hall, Inc.

Library of Congress Catalog Card Number: 95-82131

ISBN: 978-1-882289-25-7

Printed in the United States of America

™ The paper used in this publication meets the minimum requirements of American National Standard for Information Sciences—Permanence of Paper for Printed Library Materials, ANSI/NISO Z39.48–1992.

Dedicated to

Edith Mary
CJL
Helen Nevitt Day
Teacher, Activist, and Mother
GRG

Contents

Introduction

The aim of this revised and expanded edition is the same as that of the first edition: to provide the undergraduate with a highly readable general introduction to basic criminological subjects and knowledge about criminology and criminal justice. The expanded coverage is largely the result of the contributions of coauthor Gerald Garrett. His expertise in the field of corrections generally and the relationship between substance abuse and crime in particular are most evident in the chapters on these subjects.

In keeping with the first edition, initial emphasis is placed on putting crime into historical perspective. This is necessary for a number of reasons, perhaps mainly because of the need to assess crime trends fairly, when they indicate a departure from the past and when they do not. For example, during the late 1970s and early 1980s, official announcements were generally reported as indicating a more radical departure from earlier periods than was warranted. Frequently overlooked was the fact that the relatively low and stable rate of crime during preceding decades, notably the years from the mid-1930s through the 1950s, reflected a period unusually free of domestic conflict and turmoil. Consequently, effort is devoted to the identification of various factors historically associated with social upheaval and the rise and fall of crime rates — in particular, industrialization, urbanization, and population growth.

Additionally, the book gives special attention to major problems and issues of both longstanding and more recent concern to students of crime and criminal justice. These include the quality of official crime data, biological versus social and psychological causation, substance abuse and crime, sentencing reform, prison overcrowding and alternative sentencing, community policing, and community corrections.

The reader will find that topics and issues are occasionally discussed in "boxed" material, a new feature of the second edition. Used throughout the book, these "boxes" allow us to explore in greater detail topics of special interest not possible in the main text. The boxes, which are titled, vary widely in content, from first-person and eyewitness statements to definitions and explanations of concepts and subjects. Regardless of their content, the boxes are intended to provide a different slant or to supplement important chapter ideas and subjects.

The book is divided into four parts. Part I examines the nature of the crime problem in the United States, some of its more basic types, and the connection between substance abuse and crime. The first chapter has two objectives: to provide a historical overview of crime in the United States and to put the problem in cross-national perspective. The second chapter deals with the complex relationship between substance abuse, crime and criminality, as well as focusing on drug laws, drug trafficking and the criminal justice agencies involved in policing drug law violations. Chapter 3 examines topics of current and evolving concern: child abuse, terrorism, and environmental crimes. Chapters 4 and 5 discuss two major kinds of crimes: white collar crime, ranging from employee pilferage to corporate and organizational illegality, and "organized" crime, the activities of groups such as La Cosa Nostra, outlaw motorcycle gangs, the triads of Asia and the yakuza of Japan.

Part II outlines the field of criminology and its major theoretical perspectives. Chapter 6 relates the emergence of modern criminology to the industrialization and urbanization of Europe and the United States. The primary concern is to detail the evolution of criminological theory from its beginnings to the present. Chapters 7 and 8 discuss the range of problems studied by criminologists and students of criminal justice and the difficulties encountered in constructing particular theories of criminality.

Part III scrutinizes the American criminal justice system. Chapter 9 charts the historical development of policing in the United States. Topics studied include the complexity of the police role, the police subculture, and approaches to community policing. Chapter 10 examines offender processing from arrest through sentencing. The use of bail and other forms of pretrial release, the nature and extent of plea bargaining, and sentencing and sentences are some of the major subjects of concern. Chapter 11 provides a broad overview of the field of corrections and the evolution of the correctional system in the United States. Topics include jails, their functions and organization (formal and informal), prisons (their growth and development and stated functions and effectiveness), prisonization and the inmate social system (the manner in which prisoners adapt to imprisonment and the patterns, roles and statuses revealed by incarcerated offenders), rehabilitation and treatment programs, halfway houses, and community corrections. Attention is also given to the problem of the diverse and conflicting aims of corrections.

Part IV, Chapter 12, is an effort to gauge the future of crime in the United States. The chapter begins with a discussion of estimates of future crime rates in relation to major economic and demographic possibilities, unemployment rates, the nature and the extent of the underground economy, and future employment needs in terms of technological expertise and education. It next examines the bearing of future crime and criminality on the future of policing and corrections. Topics of key concern include the influence of "hackers" and "cyberpunks" on the nature and type of possible future computer crime, future rates of incarceration, and the likely expansion of alternatives to traditional incarceration, such as intensive probationary supervision via electronic monitoring.

In summary, the overall goal of this Second Edition is to provide a general introduction to major topics in criminology and criminal justice. The intention is to provide a book that can be used in a single semester or quarter to acquaint the student with basic subjects and knowledge. We hope the addition of the "boxes" will stimulate interest in and lively discussion of a variety of important acknowledged and emerging problems and issues.

We have accumulated numerous debts in the course of writing the second edition. We are very indebted to Professor Carolsue Holland, Troy State University Europe, for her important contributions to the section on terrorism contained in Chapter 3, and to Albert P. Cardarelli for assistance on the section in Chapter 3 dealing with child abuse and crime. Christoph Arroll, Anthony Ferdaise, James Greer, Paul Clayton, and Rus Smith have our gratitude for their generous technical assistance at various stages of preparing the manuscript. We also appreciate valuable comments on selected chapters provided by Professors Charlie Souris of North Shore Community College, Don Melisi of Middlesex Community College, and Greg Pierce of Blue Mountain Community College. To Gail Boucher, Tricia Lucek, Lauren McDonald, and David Hughes, assistants in the Graduate Program in Applied Sociology at the University of Massachusetts at Boston, we extend our sincere thanks for helping amass relevant material and attending to a variety of details.

Also, a special note of thanks is extended to Benjamin Marte, M.D., Medical Center Hospital of Vermont, and to James Day for their generous assistance in preparation of the final manuscript.

Finally, we are indebted to the University of Massachusetts at Boston for supporting our work and to our students in Boston and at Washington State University Spokane for their insightful comments on materials used in this textbook. As always, we extend our sincere thanks to Anne Foxx, our departmental officer manager, and to Kathy Evelyn and Carolyn Dunn for their help in every aspect of this book proiect.

PART I

The Crime Problem

Chapter 1

Crime in the United States: A Historical Overview

The study of crime in the United States is particularly challenging because of its prevalence, diversity, and complexity. No so-called modern society approaches the documented extent of crime in the United States. No other Western society is as racially and ethnically heterogeneous. And no other society is comparable in pitting its citizens against one another in a relatively open economic system that encourages all—regardless of race, ethnicity, and social class—to seek upward social mobility and the attainment of the highest socioeconomic status and political power. That intense competition and goal striving within an individualistically oriented, freedom emphasizing social context should breed amounts of frustration and aggression conducive to a variety of interpersonal problems should not be surprising. That the nation does not experience even higher rates of crime, violence, mental illness, and so on may well be the most surprising fact of all.

However one might approach the study of crime in the United States, it is important to note that Americans, from colonial times to the present, have thought of themselves as having a crime problem. "Virtually every generation since the founding of the Nation...has felt itself threatened by the spectre of rising crime and violence" (Graham 1969, 464). But, because impression and fact have not always coincided, the expressed degree of public concern with crime may not be an accurate indication of its prevalence. To understand the extent to which crime was and is a problem, it is necessary to identify the factors that influence perception of the extent of crime apart from its measured prevalence. While this subject is an integral part of the discussion, the essential aim of the chapter is to document, as much as available information permits, the extent of the crime problem in the United States. Is crime increasing? Are Americans more violent than other people? These are some of the important questions to be pursued.

The Colonial Period

Unfortunately, systematically collected national crime statistics date only from the 1930s. And as the first census of the population was not conducted until 1790, one must rely on the results of local and regional studies for information concerning crime during the colonial era. Even so, and as historian Douglas

Greenberg points out, "although there are many excellent studies of the development of law in colonial America, few historians have attempted the sort of sustained, comprehensive, and in-depth analysis of crime and law enforcement which has been emerging in studies of early modern European societies" (1976, 10). Greenberg's study of colonial New York is a major exception. Before examining his work, however, we begin where colonial institutions early took root, the colony of Massachusetts Bay.

The Massachusetts Bay Colony

The Puritan settlers of the Boston-area colony encountered deviance in their ranks before their ships reached the new land. Governor John Winthrop's *Arabella* witnessed a rash of punishable minor offenses, from petty theft to unauthorized consumption of what was then referred to as "strong water" and "hott waters." The *Talbot*, which arrived in 1629, reported incidents of sodomy, a capital offense in England and later in the Bay Colony.

These acts came as no surprise to the Puritans. Their London Backers advised Winthrop's predecessor, Captain John Endecott, to expect some religious "libertines," "swearers," excessive users of "strong waters," and those with "other sinns" (Powers 1966, 45–6). More important, they believed that God had made a covenant with them. In exchange for His protection in their hazardous venture, they were to punish sin wherever and whenever encountered. "To keep their solemn covenant with God," notes Edwin Powers, "the Puritan leaders of the Bay Colony were forever vigilant in suppressing sin and inflicting on evildoers 'such punishment as their offences shall deserve'" (1966, 45).

Table 1.1 shows the most frequent crimes and their penalties for the years 1630 to 1683, as indicated by court records for the settled areas of Boston, Plymouth, and Salem. It should be noted that the number of penalties invariably exceeds the number of reported cases because crimes often received multiple penalties. Available data indicate that the leading crimes were fornication, drunkenness, and stealing; the main punishments were fining and whipping.

Even though the data are not sufficient to provide an accurate estimate of the volume of crime for the period, they do convey a picture of a society highly concerned with identifying and punishing a broad range of deviance. Criminal offenses included card playing, calling one's wife a "whore," allowing shuffleboard in a tavern, pushing one's wife, living alone, keeping unringed swine, scoffing at religion, calling a man a "rogue," idleness, lying, and uttering blasphemy. Behavior was carefully observed, and people (not only the "authorities") expected one another to practice self-restraint and lead a morally and ethically disciplined life. In Kai Erikson's words: "Puritan discipline was largely a matter of community vigilance, and each citizen, no matter what his official

Table 1.1

The Most Common Crimes and Their Punishment in Colonial Massachusetts, as Indicated by Court Records, 1630-83

	No. of Cases	Fine	Whip-ping	Bond of good behavior	Fine or Whipping	Restit-ution	Admoni-tion	Stocks and Pillory	Prison	Banish-ment	Burn on Shoulder	Disenfran-chisement	Wear Placard	Public Acknowl-edgment	Death	Other
Fornication	129	18	32	5	65		1	11	3	1				4		3
Drunkenness	117	72	15	2	1		2	11	1			1	2	1		4
Stealing	106	29	38	2	8	45	5	3	2							6
Lewd, lascivious, wanton behavior	76	15	36	12	1	1	2	3	1	3	2		3			10
Villifying authorities	76	37	16	12	3		2	6	6	6		2		1		4
Assault and battery	62	45	11	7	9	1	3									2
Liquor law violations	61	51		8			3									2
Lord's Day violations	47	19	2	6			20	1					1			1
Breach of Peace	41	39		3												1
Swearing	31	15	1	3	2		3	3	2							2
Avoiding jury duty	22	22														
Burglary	16	1	9	4		5	1		1							3
Murder	15														12	3
Miscellaneous	249	119	32	13	10	16	28	10	5	13		1	1	1	1	25
Total	1,048	482	192	77	99	68	70	48	21	24	4	4	7	7	13	66

Source: Edited from tables 1 through 5 in Edwin Powers, Crime and Punishment in Early Massachusetts 1620-1692 (Boston: Beacon Press, 1966), pp. 404-8.

function in the control apparatus, was expected to guard the public peace as carefully as he would the peace of his own household" (1966, 169).

Such a social order is conducive to the stability one associated with a constant rather than a fluctuating crime rate. Erikson's analysis of court data for 1651 to 1680 supports this interpretation. He examined the offender rate (the number of individuals found guilty of a crime) for five-year periods and found only a slight variation, from a low of 3.5 per 100 population between 1656 and 1660 to a high of 3.64 between 1661 and 1665 and 1671 and 1675.

However stable the rate of crime might appear in retrospect, witnesses throughout the Puritan period expressed fear of rising crime. For example, in 1642 Governor William Bradford of Plymouth observed that

> [marvilous it may be to see and consider how some kind of wickedness did grow & breake forth here, in a land where the same was so much witnessed against, and so narrowly looked into, & severly punished when it was knowne. And yet all this could not suppress the breaking out of sundrie notorious sinns, especially drunkenness and unclainnes; not only incontinencie between persons unmarried but some maried persons allso. I say it may justly be marveled at, and cause us to fear & tremble at the consideration of our corrupte natures. (Bradford 1898, 459)]

Notwithstanding the influence of the prevailing conception of humankind (to be discussed below) on Governor Bradford's view of the situation, it is also true that the Massachusetts settlements did at times manifest "crime waves." In this context it is important to consider Erikson's point that a crime wave is not always measurable in terms of the number of offenders involved or the volume of crime committed. In reference to the Puritans, Erikson uses the term to refer "to a rash of publicity, a moment of excitement and alarm, a feeling that something needs to be done" (1966, 69). As he sees it, a crime wave may reflect change or the threat of change in the boundaries of established norms, beliefs, and practices. Three such crime waves occurred during the Puritan era in Massachusetts: the antinomian controversy, the Quaker "invasion," and the witchcraft hysteria.

The antinomian controversy became a public issue in 1636 when the population, swollen by new arrivals from England, began to spread and create new settlements. The established social order was based on a conception of the state as an extension of government by church congregation—"that the bible could serve as a competent instrument of law and that the ministers could act as the final moral authority in civil as well as spiritual matters" (Erikson 1966, 72).

Some, Anne Hutchinson in particular, began to question the authority of ministers to decide who was and was not conforming to accepted moral precepts. After all, a key tenet of the Puritan rebellion was the separation of church and salvation, that is, salvation was held to be determined by God, not by a church or any human agency. The Puritans also believed in original sin, but modified it with the doctrine of predestination. A few, some Puritan leaders estimated the proportion to be one in five, were believed to be saved, and the vast majority damned. No one knew or could know whether he or she was one or the other. But all were compelled to behave as if among the elect. Faith was to be demonstrated by a lifetime of devoted work. Puritans were, as Max Weber put it, worldly rather than monastic ascetics. They practiced their religion by subjecting themselves to the temptations of everyday life, as opposed to worship in an isolated retreat. The question was, was the state of grace a matter of individual attitude and feeling or community judgment? Was it a private matter or a public issue? Did a select few have the moral obligation to evaluate the conduct of all by praise or punishment?

What the Puritans were encountering was the difficulty of reconciling religious principles and private freedoms on the one hand with political necessities and public responsibilities on the other. The experience gained in opposing one social order was not adequate preparation for building another. As long as the colony remained small and homogeneous, this limitation was not a great drawback. Its effects became apparent in the wake of population increase via immigration and the addition of people less interested in religious than economic freedom.

A new form of government had to be devised. From the vantage point of the established powers, this meant the creation of a political institution separate from, but at a crucial point subordinate to, religious authority. To become an eligible voter, one was required to have demonstrated to ministerial satisfaction a deep and abiding conversion experience. Eschewing the growing problem of governance in favor of fundamental religious belief, Anne Hutchinson and her followers questioned the authority of any minister to determine the fact of conversion or validly judge anyone's state of grace. "The danger of Mrs. Hutchinson's position," notes Erikson, "was that she did not want to give the ministers the authority they needed to use the covenant of grace as a political instrument" (1966, 86–7). In time, her teachings became intolerable. She was brought to trial in 1637 and eventually banished from the colony. Her supporters in authoritative positions were dismissed from their posts, and some seventy-five others were disarmed of their weaponry.

The Quaker invasion began in 1656. The term "invasion" refers to the manner in which the Puritan authorities viewed and reacted to the landing in 1656 of two Quaker women aboard the *Swallow*. As soon as the ship docked, officers went aboard and arrested them in order to halt a possible "invasion." The Quakers threatened the Puritans for essentially the same reason as the antinomians. The Quakers believed in the possibility of direct communication with God by means of an "inner light." They referred to themselves as "the Society of Friends," and as Powers states, they "repudiated the authority of an ordained ministry and saw no need for creed or ritual, prayer book, or baptism" (1966, 322). They were called Quakers because of the "agitated manner" in which they appeared to express themselves at religious meetings.

The antinomian controversy and the Quaker challenge differed in a subtle but important respect. While the antinomians threatened established political authority by challenging the competency of ministers to determine anyone's state of grace, the Quakers threatened the prevailing emphasis on a unified orthodox community by demanding freedom of religion as a civil right (Erikson 1966, 108). The Quaker cause was abetted by a worldwide mood of increasing toleration for diversity of religious viewpoints.

During the civil war in England, immigration and other means of contact with the outside world were severely curtailed. Cromwell's eventual victory buoyed the colonial Puritans, but not for long. Cromwell's soldiers had become more intolerant of religious orthodoxy and tolerant of religious diversity. The New England colony began to be seen as a regressive rather than a progressive experiment. Repudiated by their English brethren, the Puritans were made to doubt their very purpose and identity. Their backs to the wall, they were in no mood to tolerate any further challenge to their position. The more militant Quakers knew this and were encouraged. From their position, the enemy was at bay, flushed into the open and vulnerable. This is not to suggest that the Quakers were an organized social movement. "There is little evidence of organization anywhere in [their] ranks, aside from the efforts of a few experienced missionaries" (Erikson 1966, 115). Basically, their aim was to resist at all costs a social structure that made religion something compelled rather than voluntary. The more aggressive provoked the reaction sought, punishment so severe as to turn public opinion against established authority.

In the fall of 1657, the Massachusetts Bay Colony's General Court increased penalties for Quaker violations. It was announced that "after they have once suffered what the lawe requireth," a male Quaker would "for the first offence, have one of his eares cutt off, and be kept at worke in the howse of correction till he cann be sent away at this owne charge." A second conviction would lead to the loss of his other ear; and for a third conviction he would have his tongue "bored through with a hot iron" (Powers 1966, 328).

The threat and the fact of such punishment had little deterring effect. Banished Quakers returned to the colony, claiming their return violated no English law. Their authority challenged to the limit, the Puritans invoked the death penalty and promptly hanged two Quakers. Throughout the colony, Quaker households were set upon and destroyed, their property confiscated, and individuals publicly and brutally flogged. This continued until roughly 1665 when King Charles II urged the colony to adopt a policy of "freedom and liberty of conscience" for all. Combined with a more tolerant public mood, this led to a reduction in the harsh treatment accorded Quakers, but not to the end of their persecution.

Erikson found court records to indicate that the Massachusetts Bay Colony experienced a rise in crime between 1656 and 1670. Over these years, he identified fifty-one offenders sympathetic to the Quaker cause. These individuals accounted for 383 convictions—in effect, the "crime wave."

The years between the Quaker challenge and the witchcraft hysteria were fraught with difficulties in the Bay Colony. King Philip's War broke out in 1675 (King Philip was the native American chief Metacomet; he led his tribes in the massacre of hundreds of colonists between 1675 and 1676), and King Charles II intervened increasingly in colonial affairs. In 1676, he ordered the establishment of an Anglican church in Boston. These and a variety of other factors created a general air of pessimism and fear among the Puritans—fear that their charter might be revoked and fear that God was punishing them for having sinned by compromising their beliefs by becoming more tolerant of those who disagreed with them. It was in this atmosphere that the witchcraft mania erupted in the fall of 1691.

In the Bay Colony and Plymouth, the legal definition of a witch referred to "a person who had a 'familiar spirit,' or consulted with one, and was thus in direct communion with the Devil and bound by a solemn oath to carry out his evil designs" (Powers 1966, 455). Belief in the devil and witches was pervasive. All segments of society feared the presence of witches and felt bound by God's command that "thou shalt not suffer a witch to live." In 1648, 1656, and 1688, before the Salem outbreak, three women had been tried and executed as witches. But these incidents did not threaten the populace the way the outbreak in Salem did.

The origin of the problem was traced to the home of a local minister, one Samuel Parris. It had become the practice of several young girls and women to meet daily in the minister's kitchen with Tituba, a slave women from Barbados who practiced black magic. The session that sparked the episode was concerned with an experiment to determine what the occupations of future husbands might be. The Reverend John Hale described the results as follows:

> I fear some young persons, through a vain curiosity to know their future condition, have tampered with the Devil's tools so far that hereby one door was opened to Satan....I knew one of the afflicted persons who (as I was credibly informed) did try with an egg and a glass to find her future husband's calling, till there came up a coffin, that is, a specter in likeness of a coffin. And she was afterwards followed with diabolical molestation to her death, and so died a single person. Another, I was called to pray with, being under sore fits and vexations of Satan. And upon examination I found that she

> had tried the same charm, and after confession of it and manifestation of repentance for it, and our prayers to God for her, she was speedily released form those bonds of Satan. (Hansen 1969, 55–6)

The cured girl was the Reverend Mr. Parris's nine-year-old daughter. The less fortunate of the two was his eleven year-old niece. Their illness also befell Ann Putnam (age twelve), Mary Warren (twenty), Mercy Lewis (nineteen), Mary Walcott (sixteen), and Elizabeth Hubbard (seventeen). After the victims were taken to several doctors, one finally diagnosed them as having been bewitched. Shortly thereafter, they named Tituba and two old women of "dubious repute," Sarah Good and Sarah Osburn, as the source of their affliction. The three women were quickly brought before the magistrates, but only Tituba confessed to witchcraft.

When asked if she had ever seen the Devil, Tituba answered by saying that the devil had come to her and asked that she serve him. Chadwick Hansen describes her confession as follows:

> The Devil has come to her in the shape of a man-a tall black man, with white hair. Other times he had come in the shape of an animal. He had shown her a book. There were nine marks in the book, and two of them had been made by Good and Osburn. Sometimes the black man had brought four witches with him-Good and Osburn and two women from Boston whose names she did not know-and they had forced her to go with them and afflict the children. Both Good and Osburn had familiars. Sarah Good had a cat and a yellow bird, and the bird sucked her "between the fore-finger and long-finger upon the right hand." Sarah Osburn had a thing with "wings and two legs and a head like a woman." (1969, 63–4)

Tituba's confession had a dramatic effect. Many left the scene looking over their shoulders. Yet to be identified were the two witches from Boston and the seven others who had made marks in the Devil's book. More important, the young "victims" were regarded as seers. They were asked for and subsequently provided the names of other witches. The witchhunt had begun.

Fifty individuals eventually confessed to the practice of witchcraft. Nineteen of them, thirteen women and six men, were executed. The last execution occurred September 22, 1692, roughly a year after the initiation of the episode.

Popular impression has it that the American Puritans were unusually brutal in their treatment of deviants, and the execution of the so-called witches is invariably cited to prove the point. But the comparative evidence does not substantiate this interpretation. Hansen refers to New England's record as "surprisingly good": "While Europe hanged and burned literally thousands, executions in New England were few and far between" (1969, 34). Powers states that during the fifteenth, sixteenth, and seventeenth centuries, "thousands of witches, including many children, were hanged or burned to death, the latter a penalty never exacted in New England" (1966, 456). Powers claims that Scotland executed some 3,400 witches and the continent of Europe approximately a half-million.

Overall, and comparatively speaking, the punishment meted out by the Puritans to deviants of all sorts (branding, the stocks and the pillory, mutilation, flogging, and hanging) was not as severe as it may appear. What made Puritan punishment so terrifying was not so much its fierceness as its cold-blooded righteousness. In its application, emotion and the offender's motives and personality traits were irrelevant considerations. Puritan justice was administered mechanically and inexorably. The law was derived from the Bible which required literal adherence.

Nevertheless, the Puritans were strong advocates of civil rights. In 1641, the Reverend Nathaniel Ward, a barrister before entering the ministry, presented to the General Court of Massachusetts a "Body of Liberties." It was in the nature of a bill of rights, and most of its articles were enacted into law. Due process, equal protection of the law, the prohibition of torture to extract a confession, the right to bail, and nearly every other basic principle of the American legal system can be traced to the "Body of Liberties."

If forced to choose a word to describe the thinking and actions of the Puritans, one would be hard pressed to improve upon *paradoxical.* James Russell Lowell described them as "a strange hybrid." "The earth," he said, "never before saw such mystic-practicalism, such niggard-geniality, such calculating fanaticism, such cast-iron enthusiasm, such sour-faced humor, such close-fisted generosity" (cited in DeWolf 1975, 71).

Although incapable of reconciling their paradoxical notions and attributes, the Puritans were not unaware of the problems this created for them. At a certain level, for example, they acknowledged the incompatibility of their humanitarian convictions and the enforcement of laws taken literally from the Pentateuch. A common theme of sermons was the absence of a determined legal effort to eradicate immorality. L. Harold DeWolf claims that we have inherited the Puritan predicament. "The United States," he says, "holds to sharply contrasting norms with unusual tenacity and not only fails to resolve the resulting tensions but ardently promotes opposing ideals as moral obligations" (DeWolf 1975, 78).

We also have ideals that clash with norms. We believe strongly in individualism and freedom, which we expect to be tempered by norms of self-restraint and social responsibility. Unfortunately, we, like the Puritans, have difficulty specifying where one side of the equation ends and the other begins.

Considering the broad sweep of American history, everyday norms of self-restraint and social responsibility seem to have yielded more to the pressure of ideals regarding individual rights and freedom of expression than vice versa. We have consistently resisted and challenged the forces of constraint (family, church, and community) more than we have questioned the meaning of ideals such as freedom and liberty. Periodically, inevitably when people believe themselves to be in the midst of a crime wave, agents of law and order are called on to assert themselves; but it is nonetheless the case that we have evolved in the direction of greater freedom and fewer constraints.

Immigration has undoubtedly contributed mightily to this long-term trend. The increasing social and cultural heterogeneity of the population encourages unity about the country's ideals more than any set of group norms. Freedom, liberty, and equality can be grasped immediately by most anyone; but it takes time to develop everyday norms that facilitate communication and mutual respect and understanding. The colony most influenced by social and cultural heterogeneity as a result of immigration was New York. Its rate of crime was much higher than that of the Massachusetts Bay Colony.

The Colony of New York

Unlike the Massachusetts Bay Colony, colonial New York contained a variety of religious groups. In 1687, Governor Thomas Dongan wrote: "Here bee not many of the Church of England; few Roman Catholicks; abundance of Quaker preachers men and women especially' Singing Quakers, Ranting Quakers; Sabbatarians; Antisabbatarians; Some Anabaptists; some Independents; some Jews; in short of all opinions there are some, and the most part none at all" (cited in Greenberg 1976, 26). At this time, the population of the colony was approximately 5000. Although the largest contingent was English, there also were sizable numbers of individuals of Dutch, German, French, Irish, and Scots-Irish descent. Added to this mix was the largest slave population north of Maryland.

Members of the English majority often expressed their uneasiness about the diversity of the colony's population. In a letter written to the Royal Society in 1692, one Charles Lodwick stated that "our chiefest unhappyness here is too great a mixture of Nations" (cited in Greenberg 1976, 33). Most colonials, whatever their ethnic heritage, shared a mood of doubt about the tenability of the situation. As Greenberg says, "New York was an extraordinarily heterogeneous society in an environment which held heterogeneity to be politically disruptive, socially untenable, and potentially revolutionary" (1976, 123).

The fears of citizens were greatly exacerbated when English convicts began to be regularly transported to the colonies after 1717. Transported felons were blamed for the prevalence of all manner of deviance. Interestingly enough, however, two-thirds of the 30,000 felons transported to eighteenth-century America went to Virginia and Maryland. None of the other colonies, including New York, received more than a small number of the remaining one-third.

Even though New Yorkers misperceived the extent to which transported felons accounted for deviance. they were correct in attributing a disproportionate amount to those of English extraction. Nearly three-fourths (73.4 percent) of the 5297 court cases for 1691 to 1776 analyzed by Greenberg were accounted for by those of English heritage.

Greenberg's data suggest that colonial New York had a relatively high rate of crime. In 1723, for example, New York's crime rate was estimated at 150 prosecutions per 100,000 population; in 1725, the comparable statistic for Massachusetts was 12.5 per 100,000.

During the eighteenth century, the colonies experienced steady economic development, population growth, and urbanization. There was an ever increasing exchange of people, ideas, and goods from all areas, and this gave rise to common social problems, including crime.

Although the volume of crime rose throughout the eighteenth century, the colonies did not generally evidence a higher rate of crime because population growth kept pace with the amount of crime being committed. A good deal of the rise in the amount of crime was the consequence of the French and Indian Wars (1689–1763). Increases in property crime (burglary, robbery, theft) were related to the movement of people driven off the land to major population centers such as Boston, Charles Town, New York, and Philadelphia. Theft was the prevailing offense, and according to Carl Bridenbaugh, "Boston suffered most from this crime, both because of its size and wealth, and because hundreds of people flocked there during the wars to increase the number of what [Samuel] Sewall [one who lived through the period] called the 'disorderly poor'" (Bridenbaugh 1968, 220).

Crimes of violence also became more prevalent. Bridenbaugh claims that "the Mayor's Court at New York had continually to deal with cases of assault and battery" and that "citizens of Philadelphia seem to have been continually running afoul of drunken sailors and getting themselves beaten up" (1968, 223).

The wars attracted a sizable English military presence. Members of England's armed forces had a significant impact on the crime problem. Greenberg describes as extraordinary "the range of crimes committed by military men," but particularly violent crimes such as assaults, rapes, and murders (1976, 120–22).

While townspeople deeply resented and felt threatened by the British armed forces for violating their laws, they felt even more endangered by the possibility of widespread social disruption on the part of blacks. In New York the situation gave rise to the so-called Negro Conspiracy of 1741. The details of the event are reminiscent of the witchcraft hysteria in Massachusetts. As Bridenbaugh tells it,

> John Hughson, a white man of evil repute, kept a dramshop much frequented by Negroes, where it was suspected black orgies took place and stolen goods were profitably disposed of. A series of

> robberies in February, 1741, were ascribed to Hughson's disreputable customers. [T]error of violence from the Negro disclosures of Mary Burton, a white servant girl, who coined "wild and impossible stories" of a Negro conspiracy, further terrified the already hysterical populace. Militia had to be called out, and hundreds of people fled in fear of a black uprising. (1968, 379–80)

Many blacks were quickly jailed and punished. Two slaves were summarily burned at the stake, and Hughson and his wife were hanged. All told, thirteen blacks were burned to death, eight were hanged, and seventy-one were deported. According to Bridenbaugh, "the whole 'conspiracy' probably originated in the terrified imagination of the mob, for even the prosecutor later declared that there was no plot at all" (1968, 380).

Despite such incidents (similar events occurred in Newport in 1737 and Charles Town in 1738), crimes of violence in the colonies increased more after than before 1750. In New York City, for example, prosecutions for acts of personal violence (primarily assaults and robberies) represented 12.5 percent of all cases between 1691 and 1749 and 27.6 percent between 1750 and 1776. In rural areas, acts of personal violence showed little change, but violations of public order involving violent behavior rose from 27 percent of all prosecutions in the former period to 34 percent in the latter.

The different rural and urban patterns in New York have been attributed primarily to the effects of accelerated population growth. Between 1698 and 1771, the colony's population grew by a factor of 8.3 (from 18,067 to 168,007) and New York City's by 3.43 (from 4,937 to 21,863). It is argued that the city's growth rate yielded a higher population density and that this was conducive to increased interpersonal contact and crimes involving theft and violence.

In rural areas of colonial New York, population dispersion occurred rapidly after 1750 as the threat of war lessened. But the effect was to make obsolete the existing structure of capabilities of county government, on the one hand, and exacerbate landowner-tenant relationships, on the other. In the absence of effective local government to resolve issues and disputes, rural people participated in a variety of "antirent riots," "land disturbances," "land riots," and "tenant rebellions."

Under such circumstances it is not surprising to uncover a gap between expressions of the fear of crime as opposed to its apparent fact. Exaggerations of the fear of crime stem from the unpredictability of behavior in an unstable social order. In the absence of clearly defined norms and laws and effective means of enforcing them, people might be expected to approach one another with a certain amount of circumspection, misinterpret motives and actions, and overreact to perceived threat. Not to be overlooked are the additive effects of an increasingly competitive way of life. All these elements came to a head in nineteenth century

America, and any attempt to comprehend the crime problem must take them into account.

The Nineteenth Century

While Industrialization in America began in the 1830s, it was most "strikingly evident," points out geographer David Ward (1971, 32), in the 1840s and 1850s. It was made possible by population growth and rapid urbanization. Between 1800 and 1850, the nation's population increased by a factor of 3.37 (from 5.3 million to 23.1 million) and that of its urban areas by a factor of 10 (from 322,000 to 3.5 million). Between 1850 and 1900, while the country's population grew by a factor of 2.28 (from 23.1 million to 75.9 million), the urban population expanded by a factor of 7.51 (from 3.5 million to 30.1 million).

As cities grew, so did the fear and fact of crime. As in the case of contemporary America, expressions of the fear of crime were generally pervasive. For example, Charles Silberman tells us that "in 1844, a Philadelphian wrote that people were arming themselves because experience taught them not to expect protection from the law" (1978, 22).

Silberman claims that law-and-order problems were more prevalent in the West than the more populated and urban East. Over a fifteen month stretch in the 1850s, Los Angeles, with a population of roughly 8000, reported forty-four murders. This amounts to a murder rate forty to fifty times higher than the city's current rate. In the 1860s, San Francisco had gangs of juveniles that routinely robbed, raped, and tortured the Chinese population. In 1868, a Chinese fisherman was dragged under a wharf by a youth gang, which proceeded to rob and beat him, brand him with hot irons, and slit his ears and tongue (Silberman 1978, 23).

In frontier areas criminal behavior could be even more of a problem than it was in the cities. "Outlaws-singly or in gangs-headed for the new areas and took every advantage they could of the social disorganization stemming from the newness of settlement and the weakness of the traditional institutions of state, society and church" (Brown 1969, 166). Inadequate law enforcement, an ineffective, easily corrupted judicial system, and a dearth of jails created an intolerable void filled by vigilantism. As the historian Richard Maxwell Brown puts its, vigilantism in America is "indigenous" and a response to "a typical American problem," namely, "the absence of effective law and order in a frontier region" (1975, 96).

In the early decades of the nineteenth century, the two major frontier crimes were horse theft and counterfeiting. Vigilante groups formed to deal with these and other crimes varied in size from twelve to fifteen members to as many as 8000. Vigilantes sought, caught, tried, and punished offenders as quickly as possible. Looking backward, a former vigilante observed: "Punishment was swift, sure and certain" (cited in Brown 1969, 167).

At first, whipping and expulsion were the main forms of punishment. But eventually lynching became the norm. Between 1767 and 1849, vigilante groups executed at least 88 persons; another 105 were put to death between 1849 and 1859; and from 1860 to 1909, at least 511 killings were the result of vigilante justice.

Just as some might overly emphasize the association between cities and crime, others might overly stress the bearing of the frontier experience on the prevalence of violence and crime in America from the past to the present. The historian Roger McGrath's study of Aurora, Nevada, and Bodie, California, frontier mining towns, suggests that lawlessness and violence were not as generally pervasive as might be assumed.

Aurora had its boom period in the 1860s and Bodie in the 1870s. Although the populations of both were predominantly young males, they were ethnically and racially mixed. Many were foreign born (from Canada, China, England and Wales, France, Germany, Ireland, Mexico, Norway, and Sweden). Homicides were frequent, but they resulted primarily from conflicts between young males. Neither town could be described as essentially lawless. As McGrath summarizes his findings:

> The kind of crime that pervades American society today has little or no relation to the kind of lawlessness that occurred on the frontier if Aurora and Bodie are at all representative of western communities. Robbery of individuals, burglary, and theft occurred only infrequently and rape seems not to have occurred at all. Racial violence and serious juvenile crime were absent also. The homicides that occurred almost invariably resulted from gunfights between willing combatants. The old, the weak, the innocent, the young, and the female were not the targets of violent men. There simply is no justification for blaming contemporary American violence and lawlessness on a frontier heritage. (1989, 141–42)

The best evidence indicates that America experienced an overall rising rate of crime in the first half of the nineteenth century that declined during the Civil War years. After 1865, however, the crime rate went sharply upward. With the end of the Civil War, the exploitation of the nation's natural resources was undertaken as never before. In the three decades between 1870 and 1900, nearly 12 million immigrants came to the United States to fuel economic expansion. This number is more than one and a half times as many as came during the preceding five decades. Most went to the cities.

Life in too many nineteenth century immigrant urban neighborhoods was squalid and mean. Immigrants were disproportionately represented among the ranks of the inner-city poor. By 1860, nearly 90 percent of New York City's paupers were immigrants. The journalist Jacob Riis states that in eight years during the 1880s,

> 135,595 families in New York were registered as asking for or receiving charity. For five years past one person in every ten who dies in this city was buried in the potter's field. These facts tell a terrible story. The first means that in a population of a million and a half, very nearly, if not quite, a half a million persons were driven, or chose, to beg for food, or to accept it in charity at some period of the eight years, if not during the whole of it. (Cordasco 1968, 86)

In the poorest tenement sections of New York City, population density was extremely high. A visitor to a tenement described it as "a dark cellar filled with smoke, there sleep, all in one room, with no kind of partition dividing them, two men with their wives, a girl of thirteen or fourteen, two men and a large boy of about seventeen years of age, a mother with two more boys, one about ten years old, and one large boy of fifteen; another woman with two boys, nine and eleven years of age-in all, fourteen persons" (Cordasco 1968, 54–5).

Such conditions were the natural breeding ground of alcohol abuse and crime. According to historians Charles Glaab and A. Theodore Brown,

> although the immigrant in poorer areas of cities was often arrested for inconsequential crimes that might be ignored elsewhere, there is little doubt that a life of desperation and the ready availability of alcohol contributed to a high rate of serious crime among immigrants, particularly among the Irish. (1967, 95–6)

In 1870, 65 percent (32,322 of 49,423) of those in New York's city prisons were foreign born. Of the foreign born, 68 percent were from Ireland (Brace 1880, 35).

The crime for which the most reliable information is available in the past and present is homicide or murder. From 1850 to 1860, homicide in major urban centers disproportionately involved young immigrant males, particularly those of Irish descent. The historian Eric Monkkonen states that in the 1860s "young Irish and German males were slaughtering each other in New York City, homicide was an ethnic problem" (1989, 91). In Philadelphia, the historian Roger Lane found homicide arrests to be particularly high for those of Irish but not German descent because of the influential presence among the latter of those referred to as the "Pennsylvania Dutch" (pacifically inclined American-born people of German descent, see Lane, 1979).

According to Gurr, "the effects of Irish emigration and post-war disruption on homicide seem to have dissipated by the last two decades of the century"

(1989, 37). Studies of trends in major urban areas such as Boston, Philadelphia, and New York showed declines in homicide arrests and indictments of as much as 50 percent. Interestingly enough, the decline occurred despite continued large-scale European immigration. Various reasons have been proposed to account for the change, among them the formalization of agents of social control or the establishment of police departments.

As the nineteenth century progressed, people became increasingly concerned with the crime problem and the need to institute strong countermeasures. An important reason for this was the prevalence of urban riots. During the 1830s, 1840s, and 1850s, a number of confrontations occurred between the residents of inner-city immigrant enclaves and so-called native Americans. Richard Maxwell Brown believes that this may have been "the era of the greatest urban violence that America has ever experienced" (1969, 50). These years witnessed thirty-five major riots in four cities: Baltimore (12), Philadelphia (11), New York (8), and Boston (4). There were labor riots, election riots, antiabolition riots, antiblack riots, and anti-Catholic riots. Urban rioting subsided by the 1860s and 1870s.

The riots led to the establishment of police forces in all the major cities. New York City's police force was organized in 1844, Philadelphia's in 1850, Boston's in 1854, and Baltimore's in 1857.

The fact of the urban riots notwithstanding, Roger Lane believes that the demand for the formalization of criminal justice mainly reflected the emergence of higher standards of behavior rather than worsening social conditions: "Really violent crime brought more severe retribution than formerly; the same offenses which had earned 2–year sentences in the 1830s were punished by 3 to 4 years or more in the state penitentiary" (1969, 451). He attributes the increased concern with law and order to the systematization of life demanded by industrial employment and urban living. As he sees it,

> The factory demanded regularity of behavior, a life governed by obedience to the rhythms of clock and calendar, the demands of foreman and supervisor. In the city or town, the needs of living in closely packed neighborhoods inhibited many actions previously unobjectionable. (Lane 1969, 452–53)

While agreeing with Lane on the positive influence of rapid and extensive industrialization on the rate of serious crime, geographer John Schneider offers an important qualification. In his view it was not so much the growth of higher standards of behavior as an improving standard of living and ever broadening economic opportunity that was crucial. In his view,

> to a large degree, crime has always been a way for persons who cannot be employed by society to obtain some of the material rewards jobs would offer. In short, crime is meant to be remunerative. As industrialization proceeded in the nineteenth century it provided more and more people with the noncriminal economic opportunities they might earlier have been denied. In the process, crime declined. (Schneider 1980, 135)

Schneider argues that an overlooked factor in the effort to account for the declining rate of crime in the latter decades of the nineteenth century is urban sprawl. In analyzing Detroit, he makes the case for the idea that "spatial dispersion," the movement of people from inner-city neighborhoods to newly created dwelling areas outside traditional city limits separated those who had competed as well as those newcomers most likely to compete for access to limited living space.

Whatever their differences, most scholars are well aware that their retrospective positive assessment of late nineteenth century crime trends was not shared by the general citizenry of the day. They were more inclined to believe that the situation was worsening than improving. But as far as Lane is concerned, "the degree of public concern has never been, nor is it now, an accurate index of the degree of criminal activity" (1969, 457).

As relevant a point as this may be, it also should be stated that experts have been known to underestimate public concern as an indicator of rising crime and overestimate their own powers of discernment. In the early 1960s, public perception of rising street crime, particularly crimes of violence, was consistently portrayed as invalid by criminologists. As Fred Graham (1969, 464) notes. it was not until the 1967 publication of the results of a highly regarded special presidential crime commission (*The President's Commission on Law Enforcement and Administration of Justice*) that the scholarly community generally came to agree with the public that street crime was indeed on a dangerous upward spiral. The skepticism of criminologists stemmed not only from doubts about the reliability of public perception but also a lack of confidence in the accuracy of the best source of available official data at the time: *the Uniform Crime Reports* (UCRs). The nature of the data supplied by this measure and its limitations are an integral part of the discussion concerning recent crime trends.

The Twentieth Century

Crime in the United States has followed a general pattern. It has risen in periods of prosperity and peace and either fallen or remained steady in times of economic decline. The years between the turn of the century and World War I were marked by intense economic growth. A clear indication of this fact is the number of immigrants admitted to the country: 8.8 million between 1901 and 1910 and 5.7 million between 1911 and 1920. Expansion of the industrial labor force led to a number of confrontations between workers and employers. One of the most violent occurred in Ludlow, Colorado, in 1914 after coal miners went on strike against the Colorado Fuel & Iron Company. In the first five weeks of the strike, eighteen people were killed in armed battles. Soon after, a fifteen-hour battle resulted in the burning of the strikers' tents and the deaths of two mothers and eleven children. This led to a ten-day rebellion, which was terminated only by the intervention of federal troops (Brown 1969, 69).

As can be seen in Table 1.2, the nation's homicide rate rose steadily from 1901 to 1935. Although the rate peaked during the early years of the Great Depression (1931–5), it steadily dropped thereafter for the five-year periods ending in 1960. After 1960, the rate steadily rose over the next two decades (reaching an all-time high of 9.3) and began to drop slightly over the course of the 1980s.

Such data rely heavily on the vagaries of local reporting methods, particularly up to 1930. During the 1920s, the International Association of Chiefs of Police, recognizing the need for systematic data collection on crime in the nation, formed a committee to develop a method for accomplishing the aim. A plan was completed in 1929, and in 1930 some 400 cities in forty-nine states began contributing to what became the Uniform Crime Report Program. Today, law-enforcement agencies representing nearly the entire population of the country contribute to the program, which is administered by the Federal Bureau of Investigation (FBI).

The *Uniform Crime Reports* provide two kinds of information: crimes known by law-enforcement agencies to have been committed and arrests. The primary subject of each is seven crimes: the violent crimes of murder and non-negligent manslaughter, forcible rape, robbery, and aggravated assault, and the property crimes of burglary, larceny-theft, and motor vehicle theft. Box 1.1 contains the definitions used in the FBIs Crime Index. In 1979 arson was added to the list, but data on this crime are yet to be reported alongside the others. The eight crimes compose what the FBI refers to as the Index of Crime, an indicator or measure of trends in serious crime. Thus Table 1.3 contains recent data on the Index of Crime in the United States.

As one notes, decade crime rates fluctuated somewhat. Considering the Crime Index total, the rate increased between 1974 and 1975, declined from 1975 to 1977, increased from 1977 to 1980, decreased from 1980 to 1984, and increased steadily from 1984 to 1991. From 1991 to the most recent year for which data were available, (1993) one notes a decreasing trend. The same basic pattern holds for property crime. This is to be expected as property crimes generally account for some 87 percent of the Crime Index total. And two

Table 1.2
Homicides in The United States, 1901–90 (per 100,000 people)

Year	Homicides Number	Rate
1986–90	106,330	8.7
1981–85	100,510	8.6
1976–80	101,960	9.3
1971–75	97,310	9.3
1966–70	72,042	7.2
1961–65	47,342	5.0
1956–60	39,708	4.6
1951–55	38,342	4.8
1946–50	42,250	5.8
1941–45	36,983	5.5
1936–40	45,565	7.0
1931–35	56,350	9.1
1926–30	47,485	8.5
1921–25	38,482	8.1
1916–20	26,002	6.7
1911–15	16,846	5.8
1906–10	8,887	4.5
1901–05	1,470	1.4

Sources: for the years 1900–1970, *Historical Statistics of the United States, Colonial Times to 1970* (Washington, D.C.: Government Printing Office, 1975); for the years 1971 to 1990, *Uniform Crime Reports, 1975, 1986, 1991* (Washington, D.C.: Government Printing Office).

crimes (larceny-theft and burglary) account for most of the property crime total. In 1993, the two accounted for 75 percent of the Crime Index total and 87 percent of all property crime.

Violent crime evidenced a slightly different, more fluctuating pattern than property crime. It too increased from 1974 to 1975 and has declined from 1991 to 1993. Between 1975 and 1991, it decreased twice and increased three times.

Rates for the most frequent violent crime, aggravated assault, followed a different, less fluctuating course. It increased steadily from 1974 to 1980, declined from 1980 to 1983, increased steadily from 1983 to 1992, and declined slightly from 1992 to 1993. At +51.7 percent, aggravated assault registered the largest increase of all Crime Index offenses between 1984 and 1993.

Box 1.1 Crime Index Offenses Defined

Criminal homicide: *a.* Murder and nonnegligent manslaughter; the willful (nonnegligent) killing of one human being by another. Deaths caused by negligence, attempts to kill, assaults to kill, suicides, accidental deaths, and justifiable homicides are excluded. Justifiable homicides are limited to (1) the killing of a felon by a law-enforcement officer in the line of duty; and (2) the killing of a felon by a private citizen. *b.* Manslaughter by negligence: the killing of another person through gross negligence. Traffic fatalities are excluded. [M]anslaughter by negligence is not included in the Crime Index.

Forcible rape: The carnal knowledge of a female forcibly and against her will. Included are rapes by force and attempts or assaults to rape. Statutory offenses (no force used, victim under age of consent) are excluded.

Robbery: The taking or attempting to take anything of value from the care, custody, or control of a person or persons by force or threat of force or violence and/or by putting the victim in fear.

Aggravated assault: An unlawful attack by one person on another for the purpose of inflicting severe or aggravated bodily injury. This type of assault usually is accompanied by the use of a weapon or by means likely to produce death or great bodily harm. Simple assaults are excluded.

Burglary-breaking or entering: The Unlawful entry of a structure to commit a felony or a theft. Attempted forcible entry is included.

Larceny-theft: (except motor vehicle theft): The unlawful taking, carrying, leading, or riding away of property from the possession or constructive possession of another. Examples are thefts of bicycles or automobile accessories, shoplifting, pocket-picking, or the stealing of any property or article that is not taken by force and violence or by fraud. Attempted larcenies are included. Embezzlement, "con" games, forgery, worthless checks, etc., are excluded.

Motor vehicle theft: The theft or attempted theft of a motor vehicle. A motor vehicle is self-propelled and runs on the surface and not on rails. Specifically excluded from this category are motorboats, construction equipment, airplanes, and farming equipment.

Source: *Uniform Crime Reports for the United States* Government Printing Office (Washington, D.C.: 1991), 237.

As precise as it may appear, such data must be regarded cautiously as much more crime occurs than is either reported to or discovered by law-enforcement agencies. To shed light on the "dark figure" of crime in the United States, the U.S. Department of Justice Statistics introduced what it refers to as the National Crime Survey (NCS) in 1973. Administered by the U.S. Department of the Census, the NCS annually reports interviews with all individuals twelve years of

Table 1.3

Index of Crime, United States, 1974-1993

Population	Crime Index Total	Violent crime	Property crime	Murder and nonnegligent man-slaughter	Forcible rape	Robbery	Aggravated assault	Burglary	Larceny-theft	Motor vehicle theft
	Number of Offenses									
Population by year:										
1974-211,392,000	10,253,400	974,720	9,278,700	20,710	55,400	442,400	456,210	3,039,200	5,262,500	977,100
1975-213,124,000	11,292,400	1,039,710	10,252,700	20,510	56,090	470,500	492,620	3,265,300	5,977,700	1,009,600
1976-214,659,000	11,349,700	1,004,210	10,345,500	18,780	57,080	427,810	500,530	3,108,700	6,720,800	966,000
1977-216,332,000	10,984,500	1,029,580	9,955,000	19,120	63,500	412,610	534,350	3,071,500	5,905,700	977,700
1978-218,059,000	11,209,000	1,085,550	10,123,400	19.560	67,610	426,930	571,460	3,128,300	5,991,000	1,004,100
1979-220,099,000	12,249,500	1,208,030	11,041,500	21,460	76,390	480,700	629,480	3,327,700	6,601,000	1,112,800
1980-225,349,264	13,408,300	1,344,520	12,063,700	23,040	82,990	565,840	672,650	3,795,200	7,136,900	1,131,700
1981-229,146,000	13,423,800	1,361,820	12,061,900	22,520	82,500	592,910	663,900	3,779,700	7,194,400	1,087,800
1982-231,534,000	12,974,400	1,322,390	11,652,000	21,010	78,770	553,130	669,480	3,477,100	7,142,500	1,062,400
1983-233,981,000	12,108,600	1,258,090	10,850,500	19,310	78,920	506,570	653,290	3,129,900	6,712,800	1,007,900
1984-236,158,000	11,881,800	1,273,280	10,608,500	18,690	84,230	485,010	685,350	2,984,400	6,591,900	1.032,200
1985-238,740,000	12,431,400	1,328,800	11,102,600	18,980	88,670	497,870	723,250	3,073,300	6,926,400	1,102,900
1986-241,077,000	13,211,900	1,489,170	11,722,700	20,610	91,460	542,780	834,320	3,241,400	7,257,200	1,224,100
1987-243,400,000	13,508,700	1,484,000	12,024,700	20,100	91,110	517,700	855,090	3,236,200	7,499,900	1,288,700
1988-245,807,000	13,923,100	1,566,220	12,356,900	20,680	92,490	542,970	910,090	3,218,100	7,705,900	1,432,900
1989-248,239,000	14,251,400	1,646,040	12,605,400	21,500	94,500	578,330	951,710	3,168,200	7,872,400	1,564,800
1990-248,709,873	14,475,600	1,820,130	12,655,500	23,440	105,560	639,270	1,054,860	3,073,900	7,945,700	1,635,900
1991-252,177,000	14,872,900	1,911,770	12,961,100	24,700	106,590	687,730	1,092,740	3,157,200	8,142,200	1,661,700
1992-255,082,000	14,438,200	1,932,270	12,505,900	23,760	109,060	672,480	1,126,970	2,979,900	7,915,200	1,610,800
1993-257,908,000	14,141,000	1,924,190	12,216,800	24,530	104,810	659,760	1,135,100	2,834,800	7,820,900	1,561,000
Percent change: number of offenses:										
1993/1992	-2,1	-.4	-2.3	+3.2	-3.9	-1.9	+.7	-4.9	-1.2	-3.1
1993/1989	-.8	+16.9	-3.1	+14.1	+10.9	+14.1	+19.3	-10.5	-.7	-.2
1993/1984	+19.0	+51.1	+15.2	+31.2	+24.4	+36.0	+65.6	-5.0	+18.6	+51.2

Table 1.3

Index of Crime, United States, 1974-1993 (Continued)

Population	Crime Index Total	Violent crime	Property crime	Murder and nonnegligent man-slaughter	Forcible rape	Robbery	Aggravated assault	Burglary	Larceny-theft	Motor vehicle theft
	Rate per 100,000 Inhabitants									
Year: 1974	4,850.4	461.1	4,389.3	9.8	26.2	209.3	215.8	1,437.7	2,489.5	462.2
1975	5,298.5	487.8	4,810.7	9.6	26.3	220.8	231.1	1,532.1	2,904.8	473.7
1976	5,287.3	467.8	4,819.5	8.8	26.6	199.3	233.2	1,448.2	2,921.3	450.0
1977	5,077.6	475.9	4,601.7	8.8	29.4	190.7	247.0	1,419.8	2,729.9	451.9
1978	5,140.3	497.8	4,642.5	9.0	31.0	195.8	262.1	1,434.6	2,747.4	460.5
1979	5,565.5	548.9	5,016.6	9.7	34.7	218.4	286.0	1,511.9	2,999.1	505.6
1980	5,950.0	596.6	5,353.3	10.2	36.8	251.1	298.5	1,684.1	3,167.0	502.2
1981	5,858,2	594.3	5,263.9	9.8	36.0	258.7	289.7	1,649.5	3,139.7	474.7
1982	5,603.6	571.1	5,032.5	9.1	34.0	238.9	289.2	1,488.8	3,084.8	458.8
1983	5,175.0	537.7	4,637.4	8.3	33.7	216.5	279.2	1,337.7	2,868.9	430.8
1984	5,031.3	539.2	4,492.1	7.9	35.7	205.4	290.2	1,263.7	2,791.3	437.1
1985	5,207.1	556.6	4,650.5	7.9	37.1	208.5	302.9	1,287.3	2,901.2	462.0
1986	5,480.4	617.7	4,862.6	8.6	37.9	225.1	346.1	1,344.6	3,010.3	507.8
1987	5,550.0	609.7	4,940.3	8.3	37.4	212.7	351.3	1,329.6	3,081.3	529.4
1988	5,664.2	637.2	5,027.1	8.4	37.6	220.9	370.2	1,309.2	3,134.9	582.9
1989	5,741.0	663.1	5,077.9	8.7	38.1	233.0	383.4	1,276.3	3,171.3	630.4
1990	5,820.3	731.8	5,088.5	9.4	41.2	257.0	424.1	1,235.9	3,194.8	657.8
1991	5,897.8	758.1	5,139.7	9.8	42.3	272.7	433.3	1,252.0	3,228.8	659.0
1992	5,660.2	757.5	4,902.7	9.3	42.8	263.6	441.8	1,168.2	3,103.0	631.5
1993	5,482.9	746.1	4,736.9	9.5	40.6	255.8	440.1	1,099.2	3,032.4	605.3
Percent change: rate per 100,000 inhabitants:										
1993/1992	-3.1	-1.5	-3.4	+2.2	-5.1	-3.0	-.4	-5.9	-2.3	-4.1
1993/1989	-4.5	+12.5	-6.7	+9.2	+6.6	+9.8	+14.8	-13.9	-4.4	-4.0
1993/1984	+9.0	+38.4	+5.4	+20.3	+13.7+24.5	+51.7	-13.0	+8.6	+38.5	

Source: Uniform Crime Reports for the United States Government Printing Office (Washington, D.C.: 1994), 58.

age or older in systematically sampled households. The latest report contains the results of interviews with 97,000 people in some 48,000 housing units.

Data from the NCS and UCRs are not strictly comparable mainly because of differences in crimes of concern in each. The essential differences between the nation's two official crime measures are contained in Box 1.2. As is apparent, for example, homicide is excluded from the NCS; the NCS deals with both aggravated and simple assault; and whereas the UCRs measure both commercial and household burglary, the NCS measures only household burglary. As expected, NCS data reveal quite a different picture of the amount of crime and crime trends from that shown by the UCRs.

Table 1.4 includes NCS data from 1973 to 1992. It should be noted that figures in the table refer to the nation as a whole and are based on statistical estimates calculated from the information supplied by those interviewed. The estimation procedure is explained in an appendix included in the annual NCS report.

In 1992, some 33.6 million victimizations are estimated to have occurred. In that year, the UCRs reported a Crime Index total of approximately 14.4 million (see Table 1.3). As the NCS figure is approximately 2.5 times larger that of the UCRs, it might be said that the best official national evidence indicates that at least twice as much crime may occur as is reported to or detected by law-enforcement agencies.

With the exception of 1991, Table 1.4 indicates a general decline in victimization rates for each of the three categories of crime between 1981 and 1992 and most years in between. Between 1981 and 1990, violent crime victimizations declined by 16.3 percent, personal theft victimizations by 25 percent, and household victimizations by 28.8 percent. The general decline is most evident between 1981 and 1986. All three 1987 rates are higher than those for the previous year. And while steady declines appear after 1987 for both personal theft and household crimes, the violent crime victimization rate holds rather steady.

Contrary to NCS data, UCR violent crime data indicate an overall rise—a 23 percent increase between 1981 and 1990. The UCR data indicate a fall in violent crime between 1981 and 1983, a rise between 1983 and 1986, a fall between 1986 and 1987, a steady increase from 1987 to 1991, and a steady decline from 1991 to 1993.

Trends for property crime reported in the UCRs also followed a different course. Thus, whereas NCS household property crime victimization levels have generally declined (with the major exceptions of 1987 and 1989), property crime rates reported in the UCRs, as noted above, steadily increased from 1983 to 1991. Part of the explanation for this trend is suggested by NCS data indicating a greater willingness of victims to report incidents to law-enforcement agencies. From 1973 to 1992, the percentage of victims saying that they reported incidents to

Box 1.2 How do UCR and the NCS Compare?

The National Crime Victimization Survey	The Uniform Crime Reports
Using stable data collection methods since 1973, the NCVS has the following strengths: *It measures both reported and unreported crimes. *It is not affected by changes in the extent to which people report crime to police or improvements in police record-keeping technology. *It collects information that is not available when the initial police report is made including contacts the victim has with the criminal justice system after the crime, extent and costs of medical treatment, and recovery of property. *It collects detailed information about victims and characteristics of the victimization including who the victims are, what their relationship is to the offender, whether the crime was part of a series of crimes occuring over a 6-month period, what self-protective measures were used and how the victims assess their effectiveness, and what the victim was doing when victimized. *On occasion, it includes special supplements about particular topics such as school crime and the severity of crime.	The UCR program measures police workload and activity, has the Local police departments voluntarily report information to the FBI including the numbers of crimes reported to police, arrests made by police and other administrative information. The UCR program has the following strengths: *It can provide local data about States, counties, cities and towns. *It measures crimes affecting children under age 12, a segment of the population that experts agree cannot be reliably interviewed in the NCVS. *It includes crimes against commercial establishments. *It collects information about the number of arrests and who was arrested. *It counts the number of homicides (murders and non-negligent manslaughters), crimes that cannot be counted in a survey that interviews victims. UCR also collects detailed information about the circumstances surrounding homicides and the characteristics of homicide victims.

Source: *Criminal Victimization in the United States, 1992*. Government Printing Offices (Washington, D.C., March 1994), 9.

Table 1.4
Victimization Levels for Selected Crimes, 1973–1992

	Number of victimizations (in 1,000's)			
Year	Total	Violent crimes	Personal theft	Household crimes
1973	35,661	5,350	14,970	15,340
1974	38,411	5,510	15,889	17,012
1975	39,266	5,573	16,294	17,400
1976	39,318	5,599	16,519	17,199
1977	40,314	5,902	16,933	17,480
1978	40,412	5,941	17,050	17,421
1979	41,249	6,159	16,382	18,708
1980	40,252	6,130	15,300	18,821
1981	41,454	6,582	15,863	19,009
1982	39,756	6,459	15,553	17,744
1983	37,001	5,903	14,657	16,440
1984	35,544	6,021	13,789	15,733
1985	34,864	5,823	13,474	15,568
1986	34,118	5,515	13,235	15,368
1987	35,336	5,796	13,575	15,966
1988	35,796	5,910	14,056	15,830
1989	35,818	5,861	13,829	16,128
1990	34,404	6,009	12,975	15,419
1991	35,497	6,587	12,885	16,025
1992	33,649	6,621	12,211	14,817
1981–92*	–18.8%[a]	.6%	–23.0%	–22.1%

*Total victimizations peaked in 1981.

[a]The difference is statistically significant at the 95% confidence level.

Source: Criminal Victimization in the United States, 1992. Government Printing Office (Washington, D.C., March, 1994), 4.

authorities slowly but steadily increased from 28 to 37 percent for personal crimes and 38 to 41 percent for household crimes.

As to which of the two measures is the most reliable and best indicator of the nature and extent of crime in the United States, it is important to emphasize that each sheds light on the problem from a different angle, and both have important shortcomings. Just as the accuracy and significance of the findings of the *Uniform Crime Reports* have been severely criticized (see, e.g., the analyses of Skogan 1974 and Savitz 1978), so too have the findings of the National Crime Surveys. According to James Levine (1976), for example, if there are grounds for suspecting that at least twice as much crime occurs as is reported, there also are reasons for suspecting that about half as much crime occurs as is reported in victim surveys. Summarily put, the problem of underreporting in the one may be matched by overreporting in the other.

Whatever their deficiencies and differences, the two crime measures share important points in common. Both indicate that serious crime in the United States is prevalent and enduring and that the volume of property crime far exceeds that of violent crime. Further, as Reid (1991, 60) indicates, and in terms of frequency, the rank order of crimes common to both measures is the same and is as follows: larceny-theft, burglary, motor vehicle theft, aggravated assault, robbery, forcible rape.

Gender and Crime

Crime is a disproportionately male activity. In 1992, for example, 77.9 percent of those arrested for Crime Index offenses were men. The percentage of arrests for such crimes accounted for by women increased three percent between 1981 and 1992 (from 19.1 percent in 1981 to 22.1 percent in 1992).

Arrest data make it clear that women are much more likely than men to be arrested for property than violent crimes. In 1992, 85 percent of female arrests for Crime Index offenses were for property crimes. The comparable figure for men was 71 percent. The percentage of women arrested for Crime Index property offenses rose from 21.4 percent in 1981 to 25.4 percent in 1992. The major gain was in larceny-theft (primarily shop-lifting) which experienced a three percent gain (from 29.1 percent to 32.1 percent). Burglary was a close second registering a 2.9 percent increase.

Women did, however, slightly increase their share of arrests for Crime Index violent offenses (from 10.1 percent in 1981 to 12.5 percent in 1992). Arrests for aggravated assault increased the most (from 12.6 to 14.8 percent).

Considering non-Crime Index offenses, the proportion of arrests for prostitution and commercialized vice accounted for by females declined from 73.4 percent in 1981 to 65.3 percent in 1992. The one crime where women come closest to approaching equality with men is fraud ("obtaining money or property by false pretenses" as by means of "confidence games and bad checks, except forgeries and counterfeiting"). In 1992, 42.1 percent of those arrested for fraud were women (in 1981, the comparable figure was 41.2 percent).[7]

International Crime Rates

To put all the above data in larger perspective, it is useful to examine how crimes rates in the United States compare with those of other nations. Unfortunately, it must be emphasized that there is a dearth of useful and accurate cross-national crime information. No international equivalent of the Bureau of Justice Statistics (BJS) has been created and assigned the task of collecting and annually disseminating basic crime statistics on world nations. Reasons for the situation include the absence of an international commitment to the systematic collection of comparative crime data and national differences in crime definition and crime data collection procedures (for more on this subject, see Archer and Gartner 1984). The most recent BJS report (May 1988) on the subject contains information from the three available sources: the United Nations (UN), the World Health Organization (WHO), and the International Police Organization, or Interpol, for 1980 and 1984. The aim was to amass comparative crime data on sixty-two countries for six crimes most likely to be similarly defined (homicide, forcible rape, robbery, burglary, theft, and auto theft). As it turned out, only forty-one countries reported crime data to at least one of the above three sources. Table 1.5 contains the crime rate data reported on the six crimes. In the table, Europe includes Austria, Belgium, Denmark, England and Wales, Finland, France, Germany (FRG), Greece, Hungary, Ireland, Italy, Luxembourg, the Netherlands, Northern Ireland, Norway, Portugal, Scotland, Spain, Sweden, and Switzerland.

The table shows that United States crime rates are substantially higher than those of the others with one exception–1984 Interpol data show that the burglary rate in Canada, Australia, and New Zealand is highest. Worthy of particular attention, however, is the fact that on all three measures of violent crime (homicide, rape, and robbery), the United States rates are unrivaled.

A recent report by the U.S. Senate Judiciary Committee based on 1990 *Uniform Crime Report* data concluded that the United States is "the most violent and self-destructive nation on earth" (Weiner 1991, 3). The report, according to Weiner, claims that Americans kill, rape, and rob one another at rates which greatly exceed those of all other industrialized nations regularly recording crime statistics. The report is said to indicate that the U.S. homicide rate is more than twice that of strife-torn Northern Ireland, four times greater than Italy's, nine times greater than England's, and eleven times greater than Japan's.

The U.S. forcible rape rate is said to be eight times more than France's, fifteen times more than England's, twenty-three times more than Italy's, and twenty-six times more than Japan's.

For robbery, the U.S. rate is said to be six times more than England's, seven times more than Italy's, and almost 150 times more than Japan's.

"When viewed from the national perspective," says Weiner, "these crime rates are sobering, [but] when viewed from the International perspective, they are truly embarrassing" (1991, 3).

Table 1.5
International Crime Rates, 1980 and 1984
Number of crimes per 100,000 population

Crimes by source	United States	Europe	Canada Australia, and New Zealand[a]
Homicide			
WHO 1980	10.5	1.4	1.5
UN 1980	10.1	1.3	N.A.
Interpol 1980	10.0	1.8	2.3
Interpol 1984	7.9	1.5	2.2[b]
Rape			
UN 1980	36.0	5.0	N.A.
Interpol 1980	36.0	4.2	10.5
Interpol 1984	35.7	5.4	14.1[c]
Robbery			
UN 1980	240.9	25.4	N.A.
Interpol 1980	244.0	38.4	56.4
Interpol 1984	205.4	49.1	63.8
Burglary			
Interpol 1980	1,669.0	893.1	1,498.4
Interpol 1984	1,263.7	1,055.3	1,806.0
Theft			
UN 1980	5,262.2	2,086.8	N.A.
Auto theft			
Interpol 1980	495.0	233.8	418.0[d]
Interpol 1984	437.1	221.8	444.8[d]

Source: International Crime Rates, Special Report. (Washington, D.C.: Bureau of Justice Statistics, Government Printing Office, May 1988), 2.

[a]Rates represent averages for reporting countries; Interpol data for 1980 and 1984 are not directly comparable since identical sets of countries did not report for both years.

[b]Does not include Australia

[c]Does not include Canada

[d]Does not include New Zealand

Summary and Conclusion

Over the years, crime rates in the United States have risen and fallen. They rose at the end of the eighteenth century and increased well into the nineteenth century. From the middle of the nineteenth to the middle of the twentieth century, the overall rate of crime declined. In the early 1960s, crime rates began a rise that did not abate until the early 1980s. From 1984 to 1990, the property crime rate steadily rose and the violent crime rate fluctuated. Between 1981 and 1990, however, the property crime rate decreased by 3.3 percent and the violent crime rate increased by 23.1 percent.

Victimization survey data present a less negative picture of recent crime trends. Between 1981 and 1990, the total victimization rate declined 17 percent, violent crime victimizations declined 8.7 percent, personal theft victimizations declined by 18.2 percent, and household crime victimizations declined 18.9 percent. Nevertheless, the number of reported criminal victimizations is in excess of 34 million, a figure at least twice as large as the number of crimes reported to or known by law-enforcement agencies.

When compared to other nations, crime rates in the United States, particularly those for violent crime, are exceptionally high. The reasons for this important and troubling fact remain to be precisely determined.

A factor that must be considered in accounting for the high rate of crime in the United States is that individuality and social change in other industrial nations appear to be much more constrained by traditional institutions (community, family, social class). The American way of life is based heavily on limiting, if not eliminating, such ties toward the end of making future individual possibilities as unlimited as possible. The emphasis on unlimited aspirations and the inevitable experience of limitations must be assumed to provoke considerable frustration, resentment, and a level of aggression conducive to crime, deviance, and violence. Exactly how these forces will be played out during a period of substantial economic stagnation and decline as well as increasing racial polarization remains to be determined, but the signs are not hopeful. Chief among the indicators of concern are the escalation of criminal violence and the prevalence of illicit drug dealing and substance abuse throughout the nation, but especially in the poorer sections of major urban areas. The nature and prevalence of substance abuse and its bearing on crime in America are detailed in the next chapter.

References

Archer, Dane, and Rosemary Gartner. 1984. *Violence and Crime in Cross-National Perspective*. New Haven: Yale University Press.

Bastian, Lisa D., and Marshall M. DeBerry, Jr. 1991. *Criminal Victimization 1990.* Government Printing Office, Bureau of Justice Statistics, Washington D.C.

Brace, Charles Loring. 1980. *The Dangerous Classes of New York.* New York: Wynkoop & Hallenback.

Bradford, William. 1898. *Of Plimoth Plantation.* Boston: Wright & Potter.

Bridenbaugh, Carl. 1968. *Cities in the Wilderness.* New York: Knopf.

Brown, Richard Maxwell. 1969. "The American Vigilante Tradition."

In *Violence in America* edited by Hugh D. Graham and Ted Robert Gurr. New York: Signet Books, 144–205.

—, Richard Maxwell. 1977. *Strain of Violence.* New York: Oxford University Press.

Bureau of Justice Statistics. 1988. *Report to the Nation on Crime and Justice.* 2nd edition Government Printing Office, Washington D.C.: U.S. Department of Justice.

Cordasco, Francesco, (ed.). 1968. *Jacob Riis Revisited.* New York: Doubleday.

DeWolf, L. Harold. 1975. *Crime and Justice in America.* New York: Harper & Row.

Erikson, Kai T. 1966. *Wayward Puritans.* New York: Wiley.

Glaab, Charles N., and A. Theodore Brown. 1967. *A History of Urban America.* New York: Macmillan.

Graham, Fred P. 1969. "A Contemporary History of American Crime." In *Violence in America* edited by Hugh D. Graham and Ted Robert Gurr. New York: Signet Books, 460–78.

Greenberg, Douglas. 1976. *Crime and Law Enforcement in the Colony of New York.* Ithaca: Cornell University Press.

Gurr, Ted Robert, (ed.). 1989. *Violence in America Volume 1, The History of Crime.* Newbury Park, Calif.: SAGE.

Hansen, Chadwick. 1969. *Witchcraft in Salem.* New York: New American Library.

Lane, Roger. 1969. "Urbanization and Criminal Violence in the 19th Century: Massachusetts as a Test Case." In *Violence in America* edited by Hugh D. Graham and Ted Robert Gurr. New York: Signet Books, 445–59.

Levine, James P. 1976. "The Potential for Crime Overreporting in Criminal Victimization Surveys." *Criminology* 14 307–30.

McGrath, Roger D. 1989. "Violence and Lawlessness on the Western Frontier." In *Violence in America Vol.1, The History of Crime* edited by Ted Robert Gurr. Newbury Calif.: SAGE.

Monkkonen, Eric H. 1989. "Diverging Homicide Rates: England and the United States, 1850–1875." In *Violence in America, Vol.1, The History of Crime* edited by Ted Robert Gurr. Newbury Park.: SAGE.

Powers, Edwin. 1966. *Crime and Punishment in Early Massachusetts.* Boston: Beacon Press.

Reid, Sue Titus. 1991. *Crime and Criminology*, 6th edition. Fort

Worth: Holt, Rinehart and Winston.

Riis, Jacob. 1968. *Jacob Riis Revisited*, edited by Francesco Cordasco. New York: Doubleday.

Savitiz, Leonard D. 1978. "Official Police Statistics and Their Limitations." In *Crime in Society* edited by Leonard D. Savitz and Norman Johnston. New York: Wiley, 69–81.

Schneider, John C. 1980. *Detroit and the Problem of Order, 1830–1880.* Lincoln: University of Nebraska Press.

Silberman, Charles. 1978. *Criminal Violence, Criminal Justice.* New York: Random House.

Skogan, Wesley G. 1974. "The Validity of Official Crime Statistics: An Empirical Investigation." *Social Science Quarterly* 55 25–38.

Ward, David. 1971. Cities and Immigrants, New York: Oxford University Press.

Weiner, Tim. 1991. "Senate Unit Calls U.S. 'Most Violent' Country on Earth." *Boston Globe*, March 13.

Chapter 2

Alcohol, Drugs And Crime

> By the time the squad car arrived at the crime scene in New York's Bowery District, a small crowd had already gathered on the opposite side of Houston Street. A homeless man was staggering in delirium along the curbside, bleeding from serious stab wounds to the chest, throat and stomach. He died moments before the Emergency Medical Team arrived. Witnesses told police officers that no one dared to offer the dying man help. "The man who stabbed him," explained a teenage boy who witnessed the attack, "was like crazy. He was high on something, screaming, 'The scum tried to steal my bottle and make off with my stash!' . . . Screaming, again and again, and jabbin' at the air with his knife" (Garrett and Heubner 1988).

> John W. is in jail at a California correctional center, currently serving out sentences for embezzlement, check forgery, and theft. According to John W., his troubles began when his cocaine habit got out of control: "After I graduated from college, I got a job with a brokerage firm. For the first time in my life, I was making money—in fact, a lot of money—after only a few years with the company. I used drugs, coke especially—and I liked it a lot! Things got out of hand. I fell in with a 'fast crowd,' you might say, and my habit took over my life. Some weeks I'd blow $1,000 or more on coke, and with all the other high livin' expenses, I took advantage of 'certain' opportunities."

Although neither a Bowery homicide nor the case of John W. can capture the magnitude and complexity of alcohol- and drug-related crimes in America, they illustrate as well as any crime scenarios obvious links between substance abuse and criminal behavior. And while this relationship is not fully understood, by either criminologists or substance-abuse experts, the assumption that alcohol and drugs are linked to crime at the user level is central to present-day efforts to control crime through law enforcement and through alcohol/drug prevention and treatment programs (Gropper 1985).

The link between alcohol, drugs, and crime is complicated. Nevertheless, it is important that students of criminology and criminal justice have a fundamental understanding of this relationship. First, while America has been suffering through dramatic increases in the rates of drug abuse over the past twenty years, the number of drug-involved offenders has steadily increased. Between 1974 and 1986, for example, the proportion of state prisoners who reported being under the influence of an illegal drug at the time of offense grew from 25 percent to 35 percent, and more than half (54 percent) reported being under the influence of drugs or alcohol or both. In fact, those under the influence of cocaine at the time of arrest increased from 1 to 11 percent over this period (Bureau of Justice Statistics [BJS] 1991), becoming the most prevalent drug used among the majority of arrestees for felonies in many major cities (National Institute Justice [NIJ] 1992). And while recent declines in cocaine use have been noted in some cities, overall data from the 1990s show that cocaine remains the most prevalent drug among the arrestees for felonies, reaching as high as two of every three arrested offenders in Philadelphia and New York (NIJ, 1992). No less alarming are the statistics showing that drug or alcohol use is highest among violent offenders, especially those who victimize strangers. As many as two of every three state prison inmates serving time for violent offenses—homicide, rape, aggravated assault, for example—reported that either they or their victims were under the influence of drugs or alcohol at the time of the offense (BJS, 1991). In sum, the sheer volume of drug-related crimes makes it mandatory that criminologists give special attention to offenses linked to alcohol and drug factors (see Box 2.1).

It is also important to appreciate the nature and volume of crime generated by the illegal drug industry. The drug business involves both international and domestic trafficking, constituting a multibillion-dollar industry. In addition to crimes directly related to the manufacture, trafficking, and distribution of these drugs, this industry is associated with political corruption and the deterioration of inner-city districts, as well as with organized crime organizations, and with private, otherwise legal, businesses, that eventually "launder" drug money in the local economy. Even terrorist organizations have been linked to the drug industry; reports show that drug trafficking is used to generate revenues to purchase weapons for terrorist causes. At the local level, police in many cities have seen street gangs wage violent warfare in their communities, such as the Jamaican posses that operate in at least seventeen U.S. cities (McGuire 1988) and the Los Angeles Crips, a gang that controls the drug market in several western cities. Thus, the illicit drug industry has a direct and indirect impact on the very fabric of our social, economic and political life.

This chapter focuses on these key topics: (1) alcohol problems and crime; (2) other drug problems and crime; and (3) drug trafficking and drug enforcement. Treatment approaches and recovery programs for drug-involved offenders are discussed in Chapter 11.

Box 2.1 How Are Drugs and Crime Related?

Drugs and crime are closely related. Those who use or distribute drugs are subject to criminal prosecution. Even crimes that do not directly involve drugs can result from illegal drug use or distribution, such as those who resort to prostitution to support a drug habit or those who commit robbery or larceny for money to buy drugs. In addition, drug use and crime can become common features of a deviant lifestyle. Thus, drug users who must negotiate the drug market come into frequent contact with a criminal element that offers opportunities to commit other crimes. In these circumstances, drug use cannot be seen as a simple cause of crime, because the drugs and other criminal activities reinforce one another. The table shown here summarizes the relationship between drugs and crime.

Drug & Crime Relationship	Definition	Examples
Drug-defined offenses	Violations of law prohibiting or regulating the possession, use, distribution,	Drug possession or use. Marijuana cultivation. Meth- or manufacture of illegal drugs amphetamine, production. Cocaine, heroin or marijuana sales.
Drug-related offenses	Offenses in which a drug's pharmacologic effects contribute; offenses motivated by user's need for money to support continued use; offenses connected with drug distribution itself.	Violent behavior resulting from drug effects. Steal to get money to buy drugs. Violence against rival drug dealers.
International circumstances	Drug use and crime are common aspects of a deviant lifestyle. The likelihood and frequency of involvement in illegal activity is increased because drug users and offenders are exposed to situations that encourage crime.	A life orientation with an emphasis on short-term goals supported by illegal activities. Opportunities to offend resulting from contacts with offenders and illegal markets. Criminal skills learned from other offenders.

Source: Adapted from BJS 1992, 2.

Alcohol and Drug Abuse: The Fundamentals

Although alcohol and other drug abuse are not new problems unique to modern times, substance abuse has had a dramatic and unparalleled impact on contemporary America. A brief overview of alcohol and other drug problems offers insights as to why this is so.

Alcohol Problems

Over the past few decades, public opinion polls have gathered extensive information about alcohol problems. Although the overall proportion of U.S. residents who report that they are drinkers has remained fairly constant (65 percent admit to drinking alcohol in their lifetime; 51 percent are current users), and in some age groups has even declined somewhat (National Institute on Drug Abuse [NIDA] 1991), those indicating an alcohol problem in their immediate family has steadily increased. In 1972, for example, only about 12 percent of respondents reported a family problem with alcohol. By 1978, this figure rose to one out of every four (24 percent); and in the mid–1980s, as many as 38 percent indicated a problem with alcohol in their family (Kinney and Leaton 1991).

How many people actually are problem drinkers? Although the polls provide only a partial picture, a 1990 report on alcohol and health to the U.S. Congress indicates that about 20.4 million Americans—or about 10 percent of the total adult population—are problem drinkers (National Institute on Alcohol Abuse and Alcoholism [NIAAA] 1990). That is, they attribute at least one personal problem—work, health, family, interpersonal or others—to alcohol abuse. The complexity of personal problems becomes even more complicated among those who are alcoholics, involving a configuration of social, psychological and medical problems (see Box 2.2).

Still other statistics about alcohol leave no room for doubt that America's drinking problems come with a heavy price tag. In 1990 the federal government estimated that alcohol use cost America $136.3 billion, and that by 1995 this figure increased to $150 billion. Reduced productivity in the workplace and home carries the highest price tag ($64.7 billion), followed by alcohol-related motor vehicle accidents ($13.2 billion); crimes linked to alcohol produce a bill totaling $8.1 billion (Kinney and Leaton 1991). All this, of course, says nothing of the personal costs suffered through impairment, oftentimes permanent, to interpersonal and family relations, especially to children raised in an alcoholic family; damage to our social institutions that erodes public trust and morale; and the actual loss of life through alcohol-related homicides, suicides, accidents, and illnesses.

Although alcoholic beverages can play important roles in convivial, ritualistic, and religious circumstances, as well as have medicinal uses, all forms of beverage alcohol contains ethanol, which is one of several alcohols. Less toxic than other alcohol substances, such as methyl or "wood" alcohol, ethanol is a highly addictive substance that can create chemical dependence and impairment if consumed in excess. This characteristic of ethanol has led some to call it a "drug" in the same sense as cocaine or heroin. Of course, ethanol is never consumed in its pure state; it is ingested from beer (5 percent or less ethanol), wine (13 percent), or such spirits, as gin, whiskey, and vodka (40–60 percent).

In whatever form Americans consume alcoholic beverages, one thing is clear: The alcohol beverage industry is a significant factor in the nation's economy, taking in approximately $70 billion per year. Statistically, the "average American" consumes yearly about 2 gallons of liquor, 3.1 gallons of wine, and nearly 30 gallons of beer. Kinney and Leaton (1991), however, point out that since about one-third of adult Americans do not drink at all and still others drink

Box 2.2 The Disease of Alcoholism

No one knows better than children raised in a family with parental alcoholism that alcoholics typically create problems for themselves and for others. This can make for miserable family circumstances, especially for children. The alcoholic is also likely to suffer from psychological problems: The loss of a job, friends, and not infrequently family through divorce or separation; injuries due to accidents; alcohol-related illnesses; and legal and criminal problems.

For those who suffer the direct consequences of an alcoholic's misbehavior, it is often hard to accept a disease concept of alcoholism. Even professionals have trouble with the disease concept, some arguing that it is scientifically flawed and that it mitigates responsibility for one's misbehaviors (Wilbanks 1989). Nevertheless, public acceptance of alcoholism as a disease has grown steadily since the 1940s, and more than 80 percent of Americans now regard alcoholism as a sickness (Kinney and Leaton 1991, 57).

The work of E. M. Jellinek (1946, 1968) laid the groundwork for defining alcoholism as a chronic disease. Jellinek (1946) studied more that 2000 chronic alcoholics, analyzing the symptoms, patterning, and phases of alcoholism. He identified four phases of the disease process of alcoholism. In the prealcoholic phase, the drinker gradually learns to associate the relief of stress with drinking. The drinker comes to enjoy drinking, most likely in social or convivial situations. Gradually tolerance to alcohol begins to increase, which means that it takes more and more alcohol to achieve the same level of well-being.

At some point, the drinker typically experiences the first alcoholic palimpsest, or "blackout," wherein behavior on the surface seems normal, yet later the drinker has no memory of what has happened. This amnesialike event marks the onset of what Jellinek called the prodromal phase of alcoholism—the beginning of active symptoms of a drinking pathology. Other suspect behaviors surface, such as a preoccupation with alcohol, gulping the first few drinks, and sneaking drinks out of view of others.

The major turning point comes when the drinker loses control over alcohol consumption, that is, once drinking begins, it becomes a compulsive behavior that cannot be stopped so long as alcoholic beverages are available. Known as the "loss of control" syndrome, it is the hallmark of what Jellinek called the crucial phase of alcohol addiction. Alcohol-related misbehaviors occur: drunk driving and auto accidents, aggressive behaviors, and occasionally even assault. Alcoholics often try to control their drinking by making changes in their living and drinking circumstances (e.g., periods of abstinence, known as "going on the water wagon"; changing their drinking habits or choice of beverages; changing jobs; avoiding stress), but these efforts always fail. Jellinek notes that the "morning drink," that is, having a drink as soon as one gets up in the morning, is observable evidence that one is becoming a chronic alcoholic.

In the chronic phase, symptoms continue to worsen as more of the alcoholic's life becomes alcohol-centered. What used to be frequent episodes of drunkenness now turn into "benders" —prolonged periods of drunkenness, punctuated by periods of sobriety, followed by an extended episode of drunkenness. Social standards, morals, and ethics deteriorate, which often relocates the alcoholic to vastly different social circumstances than seen in the prealcoholic years. Significant physical changes also occur. Tolerance for alcohol diminishes dramatically, so that one or two drinks is sufficient to make the alcoholic drunk, if not stuporous. Alcohol-related illnesses occur, pancreatitis and cirrhosis of the liver in particular. Other behaviors are symptomatic of organic brain damage: hallucinations, delusions, and psychomotor difficulties. Perhaps the most dreaded symptom comes when the alcoholic has not been drinking at all: delirium tremens (DTs). Although medical management of withdrawal symptoms has reduced the risks and mortalities associated with DTs, every chronic alcoholic agrees that the DTs are serious business!

George Vaillant published an important work, *The Natural History of Alcoholism* (1983), in which he offers several studies that help to confirm, even expand our appreciation of alcoholism as a progressive disease process. Although Vaillant found that the patterning of symptoms is not as orderly as described by Jellinek, his overall results suggested essentially two outcomes of alcoholism: recovery through abstinence or death.

Sources: Jellinek 1946, 1968; Kinney and Leaton 1991; Wilbanks 1989; Vaillant 1983.

very little, about 30 percent of the population consume 80 percent of the beverage alcohol manufactured each year. Moreover, they calculate that less than 7 percent of the entire population consumes up to 50 percent of all alcohol (Kinney and Leaton 1991). It is among this group that alcohol-related misbehaviors are most closely associated with criminal conduct.

Other Drug Problems

Although alcohol remains America's number-one drug problem, heroin, amphetamines, barbituates, and especially cocaine are sources of even greater public concern. In fact, national surveys report that as many as four of every ten Americans consider drug abuse as the most significant social problem today, and that even more, nearly six of every ten, cite drugs as the factor most responsible for crime in the United States (BJS 1991). These findings are hardly surprising. Stories of major "drug busts" are almost daily media events; gang wars over drug trafficking are not uncommon in many American cities; and news of international drug lords who command supply routes to the United States is common knowledge. Perhaps the most visible reminder is the unavoidable drug addicts working the streets of urban America.

That America is a drug-oriented culture is especially evident in the amount of money generated by illegal drugs, which some experts estimate to be upwards of $90 billion a year (Witters et al. 1992), compared to approximately $18 billion spent on prescription drugs (Payne et al. 1991). Given this lucrative industry, to what extent do Americans consume illegal drugs? (See Box 2.3)

Box 2.3 Glossary of Drugs and Drug Terminology

Here are some of the more common drugs and drug terms found in professional or research literature.

Amphetamines: drug substances, such as Benzedrine or certain diet pills that stimulate the central nervous system; this form of drug action is similar to naturally occurring adrenaline.

Analgesics: drugs such as narcotics, which reduce pain without a loss of consciousness.

Barbituates: depressant drugs, such as phenobarbital, Tuinal, and Seconal; among the most frequently prescribed drugs to induce sedation and sleep.

Cannabis: the hemp plant; in the United States, marijuana refers to the cannabis plant.

Codeine: a natural narcotic derived from opium; has antitussive properties; used in many prescription cough medicines.

Cross tolerance: a condition where tolerance to one drug can result in tolerance to other drugs.

Depressants: class of drugs such as barbituates, methaqualone, and alcohol (the most widely used depressant) that act on the central nervous system; slow mental and physical processes.

Designer drugs: analogs (slightly altered compounds) of illegal drugs so as to fall outside the specifications of controlled substances. Example: MDMA. *DOM*: known also as STP; hallucinogenic amphetamine; 100 times more potent than mescaline.

Hallucinogens: a category of drugs that produce distortions of reality, auditory and visual.

Hallucinogenic amphetamines: synthetic hallucinogens, a "designer" drug that resembles both mescaline and amphetamine. Examples: DOM, MDA, and MDMA.

Hashish: dried and smokable resin from the flower and leaves of marijuana plants.

LSD: the abbreviation of the German expression for lysergic acid diethylamide; a hallucinogen that can create dramatic distortions of reality, auditory or visual hallucinations. Often called "acid" on the street.

Mescaline: an LSD-like hallucinogen extracted from the peyote cactus.

Methadone: an analgesic that produces effects similar to morphine or heroin; a synthetic narcotic used widely in treatment of heroin addicts.

MDMA: *(methylenedioxymethamphetamine)*: hallucinogenic amphetamine similar but more potent that mescaline; both are considered designer drugs; MDMA also known as "ecstasy."

Morphine: a natural narcotic derived from opium; has important medical uses in relieving pain.

Narcotic: refers to opium, opium derivatives, and synthetic substitutes; produces numbness, sedation, and relief of pain. Examples: heroin, morphine, codeine.

Opium: a primary psychoactive substance extracted from the oriental poppy.

PCP: *(phencyclidine)*: hallucinogenic drug that in moderate amounts produces a sense of detachment, distance, strength, and invulnerability; developed for use as an anesthetic in veterinary medicine. PCP can induce psychotic states almost indistinguishable from schizophrenia.

Polydrug use: use of two or more drugs at the same time.

Psychoactive drugs: drugs that alter mood, sensory perceptions, thought processes, or behavior.

Stimulants: drugs that act on the central nervous system, producing excitation, sense of strength, and alertness. Examples: cocaine, crack cocaine, amphetamines, caffeine, and nicotine.

THC: (tetrahydrocannabinol): the primary active compound found in marijuana.

Data to answer this question come from the National Institute on Drug Abuse, which has conducted national surveys on drug abuse since 1971. Despite trends that show a decrease in drug use among certain groups, as well as results from a two-decade-long "war on drugs," research findings demonstrate that drug abuse remains a serious problem. A capsule of the 1991 results shows the following (NIDA 1992):

—More than 75 million Americans (or 37 percent of the population, age 12 or older) have tried cocaine, marijuana, or other illicit drugs at least once in their lifetime.

—Nearly 13 percent, or 26 million people, have used cocaine, marijuana, or other illegal drugs at least once in the past year.

—The highest percentage of users is young adults (18–25 years old), nearly one-third of whom admit to using drugs at least once in past year and better than 15 percent at least once in the past month.

—One-third of the population has used marijuana at least once in their life and nearly 20 million Americans report they have used marijuana at least once a week.

—Although the number of past-year and past-month cocaine users has decreased significantly since the 1985 survey, more than 6 million Americans have used cocaine in the past year. An actual increase has occurred in the number of those who use cocaine at least once a week.

—Within the past year, 1 million people used crack cocaine at least once, the highest rates found among young adults (ages 18–25).

No less alarming are research data showing that the drugs remain relatively accessible to many segments of the population. In a nationwide survey of high school seniors, the vast majority reported that they could obtain drugs fairly easily or very easily, including cocaine and crack, marijuana, amphetamines, LSD, and heroin (BJS 1991). NIDA's 1992 reports confirm that easy access to illicit drugs is also true of other groups. For example, 44 percent of the population say that access to cocaine is fairly easy or very easy. Among African Americans, this percentage increases: Nearly two-thirds report access to cocaine if they want it. Partly because they are less widely used, heroin, LSD, and PCP were considered easy to get, though by less than 30 percent of the population (NIDA 1992). Thus, while the war on drugs has enjoyed wide visibility and undoubtedly has had impact on the so-called drug epidemic, present-day studies suggest that both drug trafficking and illicit consumption remain a major social problem and a centerpiece of the American crime problem.

Alcohol and Crime

Several approaches have been used to explore the link between alcohol and crime. The first and perhaps the simplest of these is to ascertain evidence that directly links alcohol to specific crimes at the user (and/or victim) levels. A second, albeit related, approach is to examine a population of offenders, such as prison inmates, to see how many of them evidence alcohol problems or alcoholism. Third, it is also possible to study the criminal histories of chronic alcoholics.

In addition to these approaches, some studies have used experimental methods in laboratory settings, examining the effect of drinking on various misbehaviors, such as aggression. That alcohol facilitates aggression in some circumstances appears to be firmly established in research literature (Taylor et al. 1975, 1976, 1979, 1983; Fagan 1990). Although this approach can yield insightful findings, these studies lack all the natural elements present in real crime (Cordilia 1985), and it becomes difficult to generalize results to criminal behavior per se. Still other research involves the use of aggregate data, instead of examining information about specific users. Thus, trends in alcohol consumption have been shown to correlate with trends in crime rates. Similarly, trends in the rates of specific crimes, such as homicide and aggravated assault, can be correlated with changes in the availability of alcohol beverages, such as the number of sales outlets and price increases (Cordilia 1985). Since the first three approaches are most relevant to understanding the alcohol-crime link, they deserve special attention.

Alcohol Use by Type of Crime

Research evidence documenting the presence of alcohol as a factor in specific felonies is extensive. Some important studies surfaced as early as the 1940s and 1950s. Shupe (1954), for example, took blood and urine samples just after the arrests of 882 felons. Although his study presumed guilt, his findings revealed blood-alcohol levels, often indicative of heavy drinking, in better than nine of every 10 arrested for crimes of violence. For property crimes, this percentage was about 60 percent.

Early studies on alcohol-related homicides are fairly consistent. A Cincinnati study observed that 44 percent of a sample of homicide victims had blood-alcohol levels over 0.15, a level that indicates intoxication (Cleveland 1955). In Texas, a time study of homicides found that nearly 30 percent of all homicides occurred in public places where alcohol was served (Bullock 1955). Still other early studies show that homicide offenders are typically under the influence of alcohol at the time of their crimes. Results from an Ohio study (Shupe 1954) revealed that 43 percent of homicide offenders had been drinking; an even higher percentage (87 percent) was reported by Spain (1951).

Yet the hallmark study of alcohol-related homicide was conducted by Wolfgang and associates (1958), who examined 588 homicides in Philadelphia. Of these, alcohol was present in 64 percent of the cases, linked either to the offender, the victim, or both. In 44 percent of these cases , alcohol was linked to both offender and victim. As Wolfgang and others have observed, the presence of alcohol in such a high number of victims raises the issue of victim-precipitated homicide, in which alcohol-influenced conduct by the victim plays in varying degrees a causal role in the dynamics of the homicide. Though conducted in the 1950s, Wolfgang's study is unusual in that he also gathered criminal history information about offenders and victims, noting that relatively high proportions of both had histories of crimes against persons.

Although the crime picture may be far more complex in the 1990s than it was during the time of these early studies, research reviews and studies on alcohol-related crime report very similar results (Roizen and Schneberk 1977; Cordilia 1985; Brain 1985; Abadinsky 1989; NIAAA 1990; BJS 1991). Similar to Wolfgang's study thirty years earlier, Smith (1986) reported that alcohol can be linked to the offender, the victim, or both in more than 60 percent of homicides. In sexual assaults against women, alcohol use by the offender is reported in about two of every three cases (Smith 1986), which parallels findings from earlier reports on forcible rape and other violent crimes (Amir 1971; Brain 1985; Gross 1983; Collins 1981). Rada (1975) reports evidence that approximately half of a sample of rapists were drinking at the time of the crime, and Mayfield (1976) found that nearly six of every ten of a sample of murderers had been under the influence when they committed homicide. These findings are not unlike those reported in recent federal studies (BJS 1991) from the 1980s, which predictably show higher numbers of cases linking both alcohol and drugs to crime. For example, more than half (54 percent) of state prison inmates report that they were under the influence of alcohol, drugs, or both at the time of committing their offenses. Among those committing violent crimes, this percentage increases to nearly two-thirds (64 percent).

Asking victims of crimes whether or not the offender was under the influence yields slightly different results, probably because these are based on perceptual data rather than more objective evidence. Nevertheless, information gathered from victims of crimes is illuminating: alcohol (or drugs and alcohol) is present in nearly one-third of all violent crimes, including rape, armed robbery, and simple and aggravated assaults.

Finally, if alcohol is closely linked to violent offenses in general, it evidently has an even stronger involvement in family violence. Royce (1989), for example, reports alcohol involvement in 67 percent of child beatings, 80 percent of spouse batterings, and up to 90 percent of incest cases. It should be added that crimes involving abusive conduct in the family are among the most difficult criminal cases to investigate.

In sum, available studies demonstrate that alcohol is highly linked to a variety of criminal offenses, and the link seems highest among crimes of violence. Some authorities estimate that about half of those arrested on any charge in the United

States are under the influence of alcohol when they are taken into custody (Glaser 1978).

Alcohol Problems among Criminal Offenders

Still another group of studies focuses specifically on criminal offenders to ascertain the extent of their histories of problem drinking or alcohol abuse. This approach assumes that high numbers of offenders with histories of drinking problems offer clues about how drinking and alcohol abuse influenced their criminal behaviors. Typically inmate populations in prisons and county or municipal jails served as the study groups. Since data are gathered after their incarceration, these studies rely on the truthfulness of respondents in reporting details of both their drinking and their criminal histories.

As before, both early and contemporary findings show a remarkable consistency. One of the most instructive of the early studies examined more than 2300 new male inmates in California prisons during the 1960s. Not only did their histories show high involvement with alcohol, but also slightly under one-third claimed that alcohol abuse was the major problem in their lives. A similar percentage reported that they had been intoxicated at the time of their crimes (half of which were for auto theft and over one-third for crimes of violence). Nearly twice as many problem drinkers as nonproblem drinkers had prior criminal histories (Blum 1967).

Still other studies (Guze et al. 1962; Whalen 1962), including those using female inmate samples (Cramer and Blacker 1967), report essentially the same results, each claiming to ascertain higher rates of problem drinking among convicted offenders than would be found in comparable nonoffender populations. This outcome is even more true of findings on homeless populations, who as a special population evidence substantially higher prevalence of alcohol abuse and alcoholism than other groups. Data from these studies suggest that about half or more of all homeless subjects with jail and prison records also have confirmed histories of serious alcohol problems (Garrett and Heubner 1989).

Even more instructive are the self-report data collected from male and female arrestees in twenty major U.S. cities by the National Institute of Justice Drug Use Forecasting (DUF) Program. It found that virtually all male and female subjects had consumed alcohol at one point in their lives, most taking their first drink in early- to mid-adolescent years. Among male subjects, the percentage of those indicating alcohol dependence ranged from a low of 6 percent in Miami and New Orleans to between one-fifth to nearly one-third in Indianapolis, Kansas City, Omaha, Los Angeles, and Phoenix. Half or more of all male respondents indicated that they had used alcohol within the past forty-eight hours, and the vast majority had consumed alcohol within the past thirty days (NIJ/DUF 1990).

For women in the DUF research data, percentages were slightly lower for alcohol dependency (ranging from 4 percent in New Orleans to 23 percent in Detroit). A majority of women in the city samples had consumed alcohol within the past thirty days, and from one-quarter to one-half had drunk alcohol within the past forty-eight hours NIJ/DUF 1990).

Criminal Histories of Alcoholics

Special attention has also been given to examining the criminal histories of chronic alcoholics. Typically this approach involves studying alcoholic populations in prisons or jails, clinics and other institutions, particularly those on Skid Row or serving homeless clientele, to learn about their criminal behaviors. Prior to the 1970s, researchers were particularly interested in chronic police-case inebriates, since in most major cities these offenders represented as many as two-thirds of all arrests over a year's time. Even though public intoxication has since been decriminalized in many jurisdictions, instead treating inebriates as a public health problem, homeless alcoholics continue to cycle through the criminal justice system, typically for misdemeanors or for criminal offenses committed during a drunkenness episode (Garrett and Heubner 1988).

Available studies report that while chronic alcoholics in jails and prisons, detoxification facilities, clinics, and Skid Row appear to have somewhat more extensive criminal histories than nonalcoholics, only about one-third commit serious criminal offenses (Blacker 1959;Blum 1967; Garrett and Heubner 1988). Pittman and Gordon's (1962) classic study of 187 chronic drunkenness recidivists in New York State probably best illustrates the criminal careers of chronic alcoholics. Their results revealed that about one-third committed only alcohol-use offenses; another one-third committed relatively minor offenses; and the remaining third had histories of serious offenses, including violent crimes. Findings from this and similar studies are not altogether surprising, since chronic alcoholism typically involves serious, debilitating consequences that detract from the skills needed to commit many kinds of felonies (see also Box 2.4).

Box 2.4 The Homeless Alcoholic

No group of offenders has been more bothersome to police than homeless alcoholics. These offenders have accounted for up to two-thirds of all arrests, usually for crimes of public intoxication and drinking-related misdemeanors, which have eaten up police time and clogged court dockets and city jails at enormous cost to taxpayers (President's Commission 1967). Jacqueline Wiseman's *Stations of the Lost* (1970) also chronicles the saga of homeless alcoholics and their stops on a loop of institutions, consisting of alcoholic and psychiatric wards in city and county hospitals, police farms, homeless shelters, Skid Row missions, and jails.

The passage of the Uniform Alcoholism Treatment Act of 1971, commonly called the Hughes Act, establishes detoxification ("detox") centers as alternatives to jailing public inebriates, and so stints in jails for these alcoholics are now less frequent than in past decades. Yet at least one study of the act (Fagan and Mauss 1978) concludes that detoxification centers do little more than replace jails for public inebriates. Another report (Wright et al. 1987, 3), citing a case study of a thirty-nine-year-old subject, documents as many as 480 admissions to "detox" over nine years!

How much time do public inebriates spend in public and private agencies? A study conducted on New York's Bowery in the 1970s found that about half of a sample of 57 alcoholic women spent more than 275 days each year in shelters, hospitals and residential care facilities. "It's what keeps me alive," said one respondent. "The shelter is my home," remarked one 63-year old alcoholic, "and it is the only way I can have my 'cake and bottle', too!" (Garrett 1974).

A study on chronic recidivist alcoholics prepared by the Minnesota Institute of Public Health (Neuner and Schultz 1986) reported data on networking of private and public agencies by chronic alcoholics and the estimated cost of providing services. The case of "Nick" illustrates a common pathway for many alcoholics:

Hennepin County Detox	115 days
Ramsey County Detox	69 days
Out-of-state Detoxes	10 days (min.)
Court Appearances	5 days
Bell Hill	13 days
Adult Correctional Facility	49 days
Hennepin County Medical Center	24 days
Salvation Army	1 day
Adult Detention Center	3 days
Shelters and/or Drop-ins	20 days
	317 days

How much did all these services cost? Of the 43 chronic recidivist alcoholics in their sample, the annual cost to the public system exceeded $22,800 per client. The authors conclude that "based on an estimated population size of 425 active chronic clients, the total expenditure... is $9,707,829 per annum."

Sources: Garrett and Schutt 1987; Neuner and Schultz 1986.

Overall evidence shows a relatively strong link between alcohol and crime, some suggesting that alcohol may be a factor in 50 percent of all crimes. This link is especially pronounced in crimes of violence. This conclusion seems all the more convincing in view of findings that show that alcohol use is also a significant factor as a victim characteristic in some violent crimes.

Although this evidence has a natural appeal to our intuition about alcohol as a cause of crime, for a number of reasons the research is by no means definitive. First, many studies rely on subjects who are in detention or in jails or prisons, which raises the possibility that alcohol may be as much related to getting caught as it is to committing criminal offenses. Second, if alcohol increases the probability of committing criminal offenses, it may also be true that the stress of crime causes drinking problems. Third, it is very difficult to evaluate the extent to which alcohol (or any drug substance) affects motivation or contributes to a sequence of events that results in criminal behavior. Thus, while these studies show that alcohol is linked to several kinds of crime, that high percentages of jailed inmates have had drinking problems, and that some (but far from all) alcoholics commit serious felonies, they provide only a statistical relationship, failing to explain how alcohol interacts with criminal motivation. Put another way, the studies shed little light on how alcohol use (or abuse) interacts with other personal or situational factors involved in the dynamics of criminal behavior.

Alcoholism and Criminal Responsibility

Common sense tells us that people who commit crimes while they are drunk must be held accountable for their acts. But what if the person who commits a crime is both drunk and a chronic alcoholic? Since current definitions of alcoholism as a disease enjoy widespread credence, is it not incumbent on the law to regard these crimes as outcomes of a disease process over which the alcoholic has no control? Are not alcoholics better off in hospitals receiving appropriate treatment rather than being punished for illegal acts they probably would not otherwise have committed?

For more than a century the criminal responsibility of chronic alcoholic has been the subject of numerous court cases. In decisions rendered between 1850 and 1900, for example, numerous alcoholic defendants argued that their drinking was involuntary and that they should not be punished for criminal acts resulting from it. This defense rested on a well-established common-law rule that involuntary behavior cannot be punished as criminal. Unfortunately for the defendants, the courts ruled against them, contending that alcoholism offered a viable defense only when it amounted to insanity. In commenting on these cases, Hutt (1967, 110) points out that "In order for the courts to reconcile this result with the involuntary behavior rule, the courts resorted in these early decisions to a legal fiction." Thus, all drinking by chronic alcoholics was declared, as a matter of law rather than fact, voluntary!

In 1869, however, this ruling was rejected in *State v. Pike*. In this decision, the New Hampshire Supreme Court held that if the defendant, who was charged with murder, could prove that alcoholism was a disease and the crime was a product of his alcoholism, he could not be held criminally responsible.

The *Pike* decision stood as an isolated case in this regard for nearly a century. But beginning in the 1960s, growing public acceptance of the disease concept served as an impetus to several landmark decisions. In *Robinson v. California* (1962), the U.S. Supreme Court held that drug addiction was not a punishable offense if the drug user was "diseased and lacked volition in regard to drug use." This enabled two important arguments to be exercised: the cruel and unusual punishment doctrine contained in the Eighth Amendment and the precept that "a person cannot be punished for an involuntary act" (Garrett 1992).

In 1966, two important decisions *Easter v. District of Columbia* and *Driver v. Hinnant*,favored the defendants. While these cases involved the unimportant crimes of public intoxication, these decisions signaled a significant reversal in assigning criminal responsibility to crimes committed by alcoholics. In the *Easter* decision, which applied only to the District of Columbia, the Circuit Court of Appeals ruled unanimously that alcoholism is a permissible defense in cases involving public drunkenness. And, since alcoholism involved a "loss of control" syndrome, Easter, a longstanding alcoholic, could not be held responsible for his crime (Garrett 1989).

In *Driver v. Hinnant*, rendered by the U.S. Court of Appeals, Fourth Circuit, the court reasoned that Hinnant, a Skid Row alcoholic, should be exempted from criminal sanctions (Garrett 1992). To punish Driver for criminal misbehaviors due to his alcoholism would violate the prohibition against cruel and unusual punishment (Hutt 1967).

Since these decisions, the courts have been less generous in ruling in favor of the alcoholic defendant. The U.S. Supreme Court did not rule in favor of the defendant in *Powell v. Texas*, which specifically addressed the disease concept of alcoholism. The Court acknowledged, however, that their ruling was largely based on testimony on behalf of the defendant that was "utterly inadequate." Nevertheless, the case is significant in that four of the five justices who upheld Powell's conviction agreed that since there is no known effective treatment for alcoholism and a deficiency of treatment facilities, a jail sentence outweighs the benefit of an indeterminate civil commitment for treatment (Garrett 1992).

The *Easter* and *Driver* decisions were important benchmarks in the 1960s movement to decriminalize public intoxication. These cases laid the groundwork for the Uniform Alcoholism Treatment Act, passed by Congress in 1971, which helped establish public detoxification centers as an alternative to jail for public inebriates (Garrett 1992).

Since then, using alcoholism as an excuse for misconduct, whether or not it is criminal in nature, has largely been rejected by the courts. But it is not uncommon strategy. In the late 1980s, Michael Deaver, a former official in President Reagan's administration indicted by a grand jury investigating illegal lobbying activities, claimed that his misstatements of fact were due to his alcoholism. In the 1988 case, veterans claimed that alcoholism had prevented them from taking advantage of educational benefits from the Veterans Administration (VA). The U.S. Supreme Court upheld the VA's position that denied the plaintiffs an extension of benefits, since alcoholism was a form of willful misconduct (Maisto et al. 1991). In sum, these and other cases demonstrate that however accepted the disease concept of alcoholism may be, it is far from settled in the legal arena.

Other Drugs and Crime

The connection between drugs and crime seems obvious. In all U.S. jurisdictions possession, trafficking, and sales of contraband drug substances are violations of criminal statutes. Yet, as with alcohol, the causal relationship between drugs and crime is complicated, since it is difficult to ascertain how drug use specifically influences motivation and criminal conduct. That drug abusers and addicts are prone to crime is clear, and it is instructive to review studies and data that provide evidence of this link (see Box 2.5).

Box 2.5 Sources of Data on Drug Use and Crime

A variety of data sources shed light on the relationship between drug use and crime, the most important sources being the following:

—Urine testing of arrestees to ascertain recent drug use.

—Research surveys of offender populations, especially jail and prison inmates, that inquire about their drug use.

—Criminal justice system records of arrests, convictions, incarcerations, and other sanctions or penalties imposed on drug offenders.

—Research surveys of drug users, particularly those in treatment, that ascertain their criminal activities.

Source: BJS 1992:3.

Heroin Addiction

Often the term narcotics is used by the lay public to refer to all illegal drugs. In its medical context, however, narcotics refer to opium and its derivatives (e.g., codeine, morphine, or heroin) or to synthetic substitutes such as methadone. Narcotics are indispensable to medicine, since they are the most effective agents for relieving intense pain (see Box 2.6).

Box 2.6 Drug Talk

Almost everyone knows that drug addicts and sometimes even occasional users have a special language organized around their drug activities and street life. For heroin addicts, heroin is often "scag," "horse," or the "white lady." In New York, "black tar," which gets its name from its appearance, refers to a chunk of heroin. "Dynamite" refers to a mixture of cocaine and heroin. A "cooker" is a spoon for heating heroin until it dissolves, whereas a "rig" is a syringe or needle.

Cocaine, too, has collected synonyms: "snow," "blow," or just "coke." To "chase the dragon" is to smoke cocaine; to be "strung out" is to be heavily addicted to a drug; to "crash" is to experience a "hard" letdown or depression after a drug high. For pill junkies, a "fruit salad" is taking a variety of pills, often with an alcohol chaser; "double trouble" is a sedative, known as Tuinal.

Special lingo used by members of a subculture or "insider group" is not unique to drug addicts. Police officers have a special language riddled with slang words for different kinds of offenders, duty assignments, policing methods, and especially acronyms for different kinds of police work. Correctional staff and prison inmates have their own language, too.

Although the terms are constantly changing, this language becomes an integral part of the lifestyles of those who move inside the subculture. Sociologically, this language functions to create social boundaries that separate the subculture from the larger society, differentiating insiders from outsiders. This promotes a sense of identity and social solidarity among members of the subculture. Fluency in the argot of a subculture also conveys certain privileges: Drug addicts often refer to their own kind as "cokeheads" and "crack freaks," yet they resent being so labeled by outsiders.

One of the many challenges for undercover police and DEA officers in penetrating the drug subculture is to gain a fluency in drug talk. As one Boston officer explains: "You have to know how to hang with the junkies, and if you can't speak their language you're a dead giveaway—and sometimes you're just plain dead!"

But no other group of drugs is more closely associated with crime than narcotics, especially heroin. Heroin's link to crime in part rests with the cost of supporting a heroin habit—a cost that continues to rise as heroin dependence increases and/or market conditions inflate street values. The economics of heroin addiction can be staggering; in some cases, it requires as much as $100,000 per year to support a heroin habit (Witters et al. 1992).

Far more modest are the findings of a New York City study (Johnson et al. 1985), which reports that the average daily heroin user consumes over $17,000 worth of heroin each year. Comparing daily users with other users, it is not surprising that daily users commit about twice as many robberies and burglaries as regular users and five times as many as occasional users. According to researchers, returns on the crimes of heroin addicts are not great, averaging about $41 per crime and totaling slightly more than $11,000 annually. This figure increases to about $18,000 considering the economic value of drugs obtained without cash payments (Johnson et al. 1985). Thus, considering the cost of supporting a heroin habit, it is no wonder that the stereotypical image of the "junkie" involves a never-ending and frantic search to score drugs (see, for example, Box 2.7).

Box 2.7 Scoring Dope

We were on a real heavy run. It was colder than the tail end of an iceberg, right in the dead of winter, and we're sleeping in the car parked out in the street because the cops were looking for me at my apartment. . . .

This night we've got fifteen dollars between us. And we have to decide should we get a hotel room for the night and get down, man, or should we wait until six o'clock in the morning? If we get a room at six we can hold on to it for twenty-four hours, till the following day at six. So we're arguing this and it's cold and we're sick. But we just got enough bread to score once and we're trying to hold off. But it gets to be too much, so we finally decide, "No, to hell with it, we have to get down."

I mean, we have to fix; we have to get down. Not for the fun of getting loaded, but just to keep from getting sicker. . . . "Okay, we'll go to a connection and score." This is two o'clock in the morning and it is in the middle of winter, and all I have on is a long-sleeved white shirt that I must have been wearing for over two weeks. No undershirt, no sweats, no coat. Just a thin, dirty, white shirt. And we're walking all over the neighborhood. . . . We run into this other dope fiend who's looking to score. And he says he thinks he knows somebody who's holding the bag. So we walk all the way across town... in the damn cold, in the middle of the night. We get to the connection and he has the dope so we score. . . .

My brother went first and got down. When you're watching someone else fix and you're sick, and you're watching someone else cook the stuff and you get that sulfur smell up your nose, y'know, what a hell of a sensation.... You start gettin' cramps because the stuff is so close but you haven't got it in your arm yet. And finally, when my turn came, boy, I hit it! Y'know, and everything was smoother'n silk and real fine. I mean, man, I was dirty, I hadn't had a bath or a change of clothes for weeks. [But] . . . I just fixed heroin and I felt like a million dollars cash.

Reprinted from Rettig, Torres, and Garrett 1977, 11–13, by permission of the authors.

Research on the crime habits of heroin addicts produces a complex profile, which does not altogether support the belief that heroin addicts are on a perpetual crime rampage. There is some evidence that heroin addicts do not generally have high rates of violent crime, such as homicide, rape, or aggravated assault (Johnson et al. 1985; Gropper 1985). This would be expected, considering the narcotic- and sleeplike state produced by heroin consumption. On the other hand, while property crime such as robbery, theft, fencing, or burglary plays an important role in producing income for heavy heroin users, drug distribution crimes, such as drug sales, "steering," and "touting," are by far the most common offenses (Johnson et al. 1985). In addition, among criminal addicts, some evidence indicates that their involvement in crime preceded their heroin addiction (Inciardi 1981). In sum, while heroin is the drug most associated with crime, particularly street crime, its link to criminal behavior patterns is complex. (see also Box 2.8.)

Box 2.8 In the Words of a Heroin Addict

There is something fantastic and fatal about heroin, and no nonuser can ever dig it. Like, it's the ultimate tranquilizer. It anesthetizes the whole damn ugly world. All your troubles become forgotten memories, lost on another dimension, when you're in the nod. And you don't ever consider that it will soon wear off and the gentle nod will turn into a screaming want. And the nose-dripping, crawling wormy feel of need a fix always follows the mellowest nod. . . .

You have no values. There's no such thing as values for a dope fiend, none at all. The only livin' thing that counts is the fix. That's all that counts, nothing' else means a shit.

Like, I would steal off anybody—anybody at all, my own mother gladly included if it meant the difference between a fix and no fix. I would do anything for money to fix. I would con, I would beg, I would cry; I would break bad and threaten. I would do anything at all to get enough money to fix. If I hadn't of been so skinny and ugly I'd of sold my ass for dope.

I had a lot of friends at one time. But I burned all my friends for dope. And that's not all, I'd of killed them too, for heroin, if that'd been necessary. . . .

Listen, a dope fiend has to have this "I don't care" attitude. Just to survive out there in that jungle when you're on a long run it is going to cost you. . . . Now, there ain't no other way to con or steal that much bread but to have the confidence that you can do it. . . . Every day he has to get his hands on 150 bucks . . . every single day, 365 days per year. You cannot miss. You need it every day.

Reprinted from Rettig, Torres, and Garrett 1977, 13–15, by permission of the authors.

Cocaine and Other Stimulants

Stimulants constitute a class of drugs that acts on the central nervous system, producing varying degrees of euphoria and increased alertness. Nicotine, contained in tobacco, and caffeine, the active ingredient in coffee, tea, and some bottled soft drinks, are by far the most widely consumed stimulants. Cocaine and amphetamines are the two most potent forms of stimulants. Two derivatives of these drugs that have received special attention by drug-enforcement personnel because of their devastating effects on users are "crack" and "ice."

"Crack" a derivative of cocaine, costs a fraction of the street price for cocaine. Produced by mixing cocaine powder with sodium bicarbonate (baking soda), heating it into a paste, then drying and chipping it into "rock crystals," crack is smoked typically in a glass pipe, which produces a crackling sound that gives crack its name. What makes crack so devastating to its users is not the intense high and euphoria it creates, which lasts from five to ten minutes or more; instead, recreational use of crack quickly progresses to compulsive use—a craving for more of the drug—within a matter of days or weeks. As a crack addict who supports her habit as a prostitute along New York's Eighth Avenue explained it, "It took hold of me. I wanted more the first time I did crack and look at me now. I am down to 80 pounds." (Schutt and Garrett 1992,153; see also Box 2.9.)

Box 2.9 "Crackstitutes"

It is often said that there is "honor among thieves": they do not steal from one another; they observe the unwritten code that prohibits thieves from "ratting" on other thieves; and they respect the "turf" or territory of other thieves. Although there is a grain of truth to this, the rise of big-time drug trafficking and the proliferation of drug addicts have probably wiped out whatever traces of honor remain in the contemporary criminal subculture. "It ain't like it was in the 30s, the 40s, or even the 50s," explained a well-known criminal now serving a 20-year sentence for armed robbery in a Massachusetts institution. "The kids I see here today are punks—they been strung out on drugs, dope, junk! They got no class, no manners, no standards, no honor. ...They're not your professionals."

Yet, if drugs have rearranged the stratification system of today's prison populations, they have also had an impact on prostitution. According to a longtime prostitute in Las Vegas, where prostitution has been legalized: "Drugs, that's the problem—it's all but ruined this business for the working girl. These are filthy whores on junk who've lowered standards, made it risky business, and spread disease." Even on the streets, traditional prostitutes have made efforts to separate themselves from those involved with drugs. In New York, professional prostitutes who long worked the streets of Times Square have moved into brothels, to other neighborhoods, even across the Hudson to Jersey City, to escape the crack epidemic and the cut-rate prices of drug-addicted prostitutes. While this has left fewer prostitutes working the streets of New York, many that do are frail and sick, painfully thin and filthy, often bruised, even some with open sores. According to a *New York Times* report (Nieves 1992), 70 percent of New York's estimated 5000 street prostitutes are crack addicts. Moreover, of 3000 women prostitutes tested by the Foundation for Research in Sexually Transmitted Diseases in New York City, some 30 percent are HIV positive, with crack addicts the fastest-growing group (Nieves 1992). As for traditional prostitutes, who despise the crack addicts, the word on the streets is: Stay clear of the "crackstitutes!"

Source: Adapted in part from Nieves 1992.

"Ice" is a synthetic drug that is one of the most powerful stimulants in the amphetamine group. Ice derives its name from its appearance—translucent crystals, which resemble ice or rock candy. Sold in white powder form, it goes by the street name of "crank." In the United States, ice first appeared in Hawaii, where it is still a common street drug, later spreading to California and other West Coast states. To date it has not become a major drug nationwide. Apart from obvious medical dangers, including a high risk of overdose, ice can precipitate an "amphetamine psychosis" that can bring out aggressive, if not violent, behavior in the user.

Although research on the relationship of crime to cocaine and amphetamines is not as extensive as that for alcohol, heroin, and other drugs, data from the National Institute of Justice clearly show that cocaine is the single most prevalent drug among the majority of arrestees in major U.S. cities (NIJ/DUF 1992).

Cocaine reached its peak in the mid–1980s, when statistics showed major cities with prevalence rates of 50 percent or higher among all arrestees. In New York, for example, as many as three of every four tested positive for cocaine or its derivatives. Follow-up data suggest that while the overall percentage of arrestees linked to cocaine use has decreased in New York and elsewhere, this decline is not uniform across all major urban areas. In fact, some cities have had actual increases in the percentages of arrestees testing positive for cocaine (NIJ/DUF 1992).

Data collected in state prisons offer additional evidence connecting cocaine and amphetamine use to the drug histories of convicted offenders. Of those reporting using illegal drugs at some time in their lives, 38 percent cited they had used cocaine and 32 percent had taken amphetamines. One in ten of these inmates reported a cocaine dependency (NIJ 1992).

McBride and Swartz (1990) conclude that cocaine, and especially crack cocaine, is highly correlated to increasing rates of violence. In data collected in New York and Miami, McBride and associates observed that cocaine was the most frequently identified illegal drug in the corpses of homicide victims, which confirms findings from other studies on the relationship between assaults and cocaine use (McBride and Swartz 1990). Although extensive data on crack use and violent crime are not available, what evidence there is leads the authors to suggest that the crack trade and use may promote more violent criminality than any other drug.

Hallucinogens and Marijuana

Hallucinogens, both natural and synthetic, are substances that distort the perception of reality by acting on the central nervous system. Depending on the drug, they manifest alterations of mood, typically euphoric, but sometimes promoting severe depression. The most widely known hallucinogens are peyote and mescaline, PCP (phencyclidine, or "angel dust"), and LSD (a German abbreviation for lysergic acid diethylamide). Though often discussed separately as "cannabis," marijuana, too, is a hallucinogen, containing THC, a psychoactive chemical contained in cannabis. For most who use it, marijuana has relatively mild effects.

The abuse of hallucinogens in the United States reached a peak in the 1960s and increased again in the late 1970s; after another decline, the use of hallucinogens has begun to increase again, according to recent drug surveys, particularly the use of PCP among teenagers and young adults (NIDA 1992). Although prevalence rates of the abuse of hallucinogens are not high in comparison to other drugs, they nevertheless remain of interest to drug-enforcement personnel, partly because hallucinogens can induce unpredictable, sometimes wild and even violent behavior, and because of the underground production of analogs of hallucinogens.

Analogs, commonly called designer drugs, are manufactured by amateur chemists, who change the chemical structure of an illegal drug so that it is legally unrestricted. This change also alters its potency and toxicity, making the drug potentially very dangerous to those who use it. Designer drugs have been linked to at least one epidemic of overdoses (Abadinsky 1989). Three of the more widely known designer drugs are DOM (better known by its nickname, STP), MDA, and MDMA (commonly called "ecstasy"). Provisions contained in the Anti-Drug Abuse Act of 1986 define any analog of a controlled substance as an illegal drug (DEA 1988).

Over the years, public concern about the widespread use of marijuana and its connection to crime has generated countless articles in newspapers and other media. In fact, during the 1930s, concern about marijuana and its presumed relationship to violence, "pervert" crime, and moral decay was sufficient so that the government produced a feature film, entitled *Reefer Madness*. In 1937 Congress passed the Marijuana Tax Act to help curb this perceived menace.

Despite these fears, marijuana's link to criminal conduct has not been substantiated. In fact, no study has been able to demonstrate a causal link between the use of marijuana and criminal activity (Bartol and Bartol 1986). On the contrary, some studies (Tinklenberg and Woodrow 1974; Blumer et al. 1967) report that drug users who consume principally marijuana are less inclined to aggressive or violent behavior than those who use other drugs. After an extensive survey of research literature on marijuana, a national commission in the mid–1970s concluded that there was no persuasive evidence that marijuana use leads to criminal, delinquent, violent or aggressive conduct and that users who exhibited this conduct were probably predisposed to do so, irrespective of marijuana (Bartol and Bartol 1986). Nevertheless, marijuana is still by far the most extensively used illicit drug in America, and survey results from clients admitted to drug-abuse treatment facilities in the mid-1980s found that marijuana was second only to heroin (NIDA 1991).

Drug Trafficking

The drug trade is big business, generating as much as $90 billion annually. This would make the illegal drug industry second only to Exxon, but ahead of both General Motors and Mobil, in annual revenues (Witters et al. 1992). Thus, despite concerted efforts by federal, state, and local agencies to eradicate the demand for drugs and shut down the drug supply, it is no wonder that drug trafficking continues to flourish.

According to the DEA (1988), foreign traffickers account for an estimated 80 percent of the illegal drugs consumed in the United States, most of it heroin, cocaine and marijuana. The domestic production of drugs is principally, but not wholly, confined to LSD, methamphetamines, PCP, and other designer drugs, together with increasing amounts of marijuana. Since the international and domestic production and trafficking of drugs differ markedly, it is worthwhile to discuss each separately.

The International Drug Trade

The illicit drugs imported into the United States come from a variety of locations, the most active being South America, Asia, Mexico, and the Caribbean. In addition to production locations, other regions and cities often serve as pass-through or transshipment centers for drugs.

Cocaine is imported almost exclusively by foreign drug networks located in South America, where the coca shrub, the leaves of which are made into a coca paste, is grown in the Andes region. Although Colombia dominates the South American cocaine industry, much of this production comes from coca paste smuggled out of Peru and Bolivia, typically by small aircraft. Smaller production laboratories in Ecuador, Paraguay, Uruguay, and northern Argentina have also been identified. Colombia, however, continues to be the major source of cocaine on the world and United States markets, partly because of its geographic positioning to countries where the coca shrub flourishes and partly because of its convenient transportation routes to the U.S and other countries. An estimated twenty major drug organizations are in Colombia, three of the largest in Medellin, which make up the so-called Medellin Cartel. Ironically, American chemical manufacturers supply as estimated 90 percent of the ethyl ether, acetone, and other chemicals needed to produce cocaine in South American laboratories. Not until the late 1980s was special attention given to this problem by U.S. authorities (Lyman and Potter 1991).

Heroin has three principal origins, two of them in Asia and the other in Mexico, which supplies as much as one-third of the heroin consumed in the United States (Lyman and Potter 1991). Better known for its cultivation and production of high-potency marijuana, Mexico became a major source of heroin following the demise in the early 1970s of the so-called French Connection, an enormous heroin trafficking operation between Marseilles in the south of France and New York City. Brown heroin and more recently "black tar," an especially potent form of heroin, originate in Mexico (DEA 1986a). Because of the easy access to U.S. borders, where heroin supplies can be transported by car, boat, and small aircraft—even on foot—drug trafficking out of Mexico poses a major problem for law-enforcement authorities, especially in the southwestern states.

In Asia, heroin originates in two principal regions where growing conditions for the opium poppy are ideal. The first of these, often called the Golden Triangle, consists of the mountainous region of Asia, containing parts of Thailand, Laos, and Burma. Commanding as much as one-third of the American heroin market, heroin production in this region has flourished, especially in Burma, where production in 1983 alone reached 600 tons. Drug traffickers from Burma transport the opium harvest to refineries in Thailand and Laos by horse, mule, wagons, and by foot. The finished product is routed out of Thailand for smuggling to the United States, much of it through India, China, and Hong Kong (Lyman and Potter 1991).

The second of the Asian sources is known as the Golden Crescent, a region of southwest Asia composed of Iran, Afghanistan, and Pakistan, which produces an estimated 60 percent of the heroin on the world market (DEA 1986b). Although the history of opium consumption and opium production in the Middle East is long and complex, the collapse of the Shah's regime in Iran created political chaos ideal for stepping up heroin trafficking operations to the West, initially to Germany. Drug traffickers in Turkey were able to take advantage of the enormous numbers of Turkish guest workers in Germany, which later promoted routes into other European markets and elsewhere (Lyman and Potter 1991).

Although there are other supply sources of illicit drugs than those summarized here, (e.g., Hong Kong, China, Turkey, and the Caribbean), this discussion illustrates the global nature of drug trafficking. That efforts to shut down international trafficking of illicit drugs to America complicates U.S. foreign policy should be evident.

Domestic Drug Trafficking

There are three important domestic sources of illegal drugs: cultivation of marijuana, diversion of legally manufactured drugs into the illegal drug market, and underground laboratories (Lyman and Potter 1991).

Although enormous amounts of marijuana are illegally imported from Mexico and South America, marijuana is in fact found in all fifty states and is easily cultivated in large quantities in "underground greenhouses." The DEA estimates that 12 percent or more of the marijuana consumed in the United States is grown here. Much of the cultivation of marijuana is in rural regions that are less heavily policed and are more difficult to keep under surveillance.

Underground or clandestine laboratories have become increasingly more common as federal interdiction efforts achieve greater success in preventing illegal drugs from entering the United States by international traffickers. Although clandestine laboratories, typically operated by amateur chemists, are perhaps most known for producing designer drugs, in actuality Lyman and Potter (1991) identify three basic manufacturing operations. Extraction labs produce illegal drugs by extracting elements from one substance to create another. This method is used in producing methamphetamines ("ice," "crystal," or "crank"). Conversion labs take certain illegal drugs and create a hybrid substance by adding new ingredients, as in crack, which is made by mixing sodium bicarbonate with cocaine. Synthesis labs chemically alter drug compounds to create a different, often more potent, drug substance, which is how designer drugs, such as MDMA, MDA, and DOM are manufactured. The chemical needed to complete this process can be legally obtained from chemical manufacturers (Lyman and Potter 1991).

Drug Enforcement and the Law

Efforts at the federal level to control drugs and deal with drug abuse in America have evolved principally in the past thirty years. As David Musto (1987, ix) points out in his chronicle of the history of drug abuse and the origins of narcotics control, there is little to suggest "that the drug problem can be easily controlled or solved by some simple formula." Brief discussions of drug laws, legislation, and drug-enforcement agencies are useful in understanding how the government has traditionally approached the problem of drug abuse.

Drug Legislation

State laws concerning the possession and sale of drug substances vary widely in their definitions and penalties imposed for criminal violations of drug statutes. Take marijuana, for example: Possession of up to 2.2 lb. of marijuana carries a penalty of up to one year in jail and $1,000 fine in Alabama. Up to a mere ounce in Arkansas and Georgia will get you one year in prison and a $1,000 fine. In California and Colorado (in private circumstances), however, there is no jail sentence and the fine drops to $100. Meanwhile, in Alaska, possession of marijuana is legal for use in the home, but is subject to a fine of up to $100 in other contexts. Among the fifty states, criminal penalties for cultivation and sale of marijuana bring possible jail sentences of mere days to as many as fifteen years, as well as hefty fines (Payne et al. 1991).

Federal statutes concerning narcotics and other drug substances are, of course, enacted by Congress, thus enjoying a uniformity that is not the case across the fifty states. Even at the federal level, however, congressional acts have been changed or amended for a number of reasons, such as practical difficulties in enforcing a ban on a specific drug or because the government could generate tax revenues from legal sales.

Although state efforts to control drug abuse, such as the Tennessee Narcotic Act of 1913 (which involved registration of opiate addicts to get refills of opiate prescriptions), precede legislation at the federal level (Musto 1987, 100), the first significant step taken by Congress came in 1914, when it passed the Harrison Act. This act was designed to regulate and control the production, importation, sale, purchase, and distribution of addictive drug substances. Though initially focused specifically on opium and its derivatives, the Harrison Act served as a foundation for subsequent federal legislation concerning drugs and drug abuse. The following list constitutes only a sampling of some of the more important federal laws enacted over the past eighty years:

—*Harrison Act* (1914): Regulates and controls production, importation, sale, purchase, and free distribution of opium and its derivatives.

—*Narcotic Drug Import and Export Act* (1922): Legislation with the intent to ban the use of narcotics except for medical and other legitimate uses.

—*The Heroin Act* (1924): This act makes it illegal to manufacture heroin.

—*Marijuana Tax Act* (1937): Comparable to the Harrison Act, this law places controls on marijuana. This act did not actually ban marijuana (cannabis); instead, it placed taxes on the grower, distributor, seller, and buyer to a degree that it became prohibitive to become involved with marijuana in any way.

—*Boggs Amendment to the Harrison Act* (1951): Created harsh, mandatory penalties for convictions on narcotics charges.

—*Narcotics Control Act* (1956): The intent of this legislation is to impose severe penalties on narcotics and marijuana charges.

—*Drug Abuse Control Amendments* (1965): Creates controls over barbituates, amphetamines, LSD, and similar drug substances; also includes provisions for adding other substances, as needed.

—*Narcotic Addict Rehabilitation Act* (1966): Establishes treatment as an alternative to jail in handling drug addicts. In 1972 the Drug Abuse Office and Treatment Act allocated more than $1 billion for combating drug abuse and to create treatment programs for drug addicts.

—*Comprehensive Drug Abuse Prevention and Control Act* (1970): Replaces (or updates) previous laws on narcotics and other dangerous drugs

—*Heroin Trafficking Act* (1973): Creates harsher penalties for drug traffickers; establishes strict bail procedures.

—*Drug Enforcement Administration* (1973): Creates the Drug Enforcement Administration (DEA) by reconfiguring the Bureau of Narcotics and Dangerous Drugs.

—*Drug Abuse Education Amendments* (1978): Coordinates alcohol and drug abuse educational efforts at the state and federal levels; establishes the

Office of Alcohol and Drug Abuse Education within the U.S. Department of Education

—*Drug Offenders Act* (1984): Establishes special treatment program for drug offenders.

—*Controlled Substances Analogue Enforcement Act* (1986): Establishes controls for drug enforcement of the so-called designer drugs, such as MDMA, MDA and other synthetic drugs.

—*Anti-Drug Act* (1988): Creates the Office of National Drug Control Policy; oversees federal policies on control of drug abuse and research.

Drug Abuse and the Law

Historically, addiction to drugs has not been defined as a crime. In fact, in 1962 the Supreme Court ruling in *Robinson* v. *California* struck down a state law that would have made addiction to drugs a crime (President's Commission 1967). Thus, drug laws have been comparatively lenient with users and in some eras almost compassionate and sympathetic to those suffering from drug addiction. Leniency extends only so far, however; if addicts commit specific crimes—and previous sections of this chapter show this very often to be the case—they can expect prosecution. Moreover, many users are also drug dealers, making it increasingly difficult to distinguish between those who use and those who sell drugs. In any case, drug laws are largely focused on those who manufacture, distribute, and/or sell illegal drugs, rather than on those who use them.

Two basic models have emerged in the overall effort to respond to dangerous drug substances: the public health model and the legal-moral model (Abadinsky 1989, 9–10). The first of these, the public health model, defines both alcohol and other drug abuse as diseases that can be prevented and treated, similar to other public health problems. Earlier sections of this chapter explained the disease concept of alcoholism, and though comparable literature focusing on other drugs is not so abundant, there is strong consensus among treatment professionals that this concept is no less relevant to addiction to drugs such as heroin or cocaine. In fact, the assumption that alcohol and drug dependency are diseases has guided the research, educational services, and funding activities of such agencies as the National Institute of Drug Abuse, the National Institute on Alcohol Abuse, the National Center for Substance Abuse Treatment (successor of the Office for Treatment Improvement), and the National Center for Substance Abuse Prevention (known earlier as the Office for Substance Abuse Prevention), as well as state public health agencies concerned with alcohol and other drug abuse. Although health-care professionals have been strong advocates of a public health approach to drug abuse, the AIDS epidemic, which is associated with one of the major risk groups (intravenous drug users), adds new significance to treating drug addiction as a genuine public health problem. (See Chapter 11 for a discussion of treatment approaches for drug-involved offenders.)

A second, and by far the dominant, approach is what Abadinsky (1989) and others call the moral-legal model, in which alcohol and other drugs are defined as legal or illegal. This model emphasizes controlling availability through penalties, often very harsh. As Abadinsky (1989) points out, there are three approaches to controlling potentially dangerous drug substances: (1) regulation, which restricts the sale of certain substances by heavy taxation (such as on tobacco or alcoholic beverages) and by requiring licenses to restrict the manufacture, distribution, and sales; (2) medical auspices, such as in morphine, codeine, or barbituates, which must be prescribed and/or administered by medical professionals; and (3) law enforcement, which assigns police powers to designated agencies to enforce drug statutes, including cutting off supply routes into the United States (see Box 2.10).

Box 2.10 The War on Drugs

Beginning with President Richard Nixon in the 1970s, America has been at war with drugs; in fact, a war has been redeclared by every President until 1993, when the Clinton Administration dropped the war rhetoric. Nevertheless, the impact of past drug policies will continue to shape American attitudes about combatting the drug problem. Among the many events in this twenty-year war have been a steady flow of federal legislation, together with subsequent amendments to this legislation; new federal agencies to deal with drug issues and occasional reconfigurations or mergers of these same agencies; and, in the 1988 Omnibus Drug Act (which also amends or adds to the earlier Controlled Substance Act), a cabinet-level position, director of National Drug Control Policy, more commonly referred to as a "drug czar," to keep track of and coordinate all federal efforts involved in waging the war against drugs.

This war on drugs has not been cheap for taxpayers. For example, in 1990, $8.8 billion was requested by the President; in 1991, this figure was upped to $10.6 billion. Approximately two-thirds of this budget is dedicated to law enforcement; the remaining one-third is divided between treatment and prevention efforts.

How was this money to be spent? A few examples from the early 1990s show how Americans waged war on drugs: foreign aid (to South American nations to eradicate coca plant production); public housing (to curb drug dealing and enhance security in housing projects); local law-enforcement efforts; judiciary (to increase the number of courts and judges); corrections (to increase the number of prosecutors and prisons and expand prison capacity by 85 percent); national-international law (to improve border enforcement, the collection of intelligence information, and prevent money laundering between national and international banks); and treatment and education. That these budget categories are heavily weighted in favor of law enforcement and criminal justice agencies is obvious. According to the Office of National Drug Control Policy, for example, the war on drugs for 1991 alone cost government agencies nationwide $24 billion, $15.9 billion of which was devoted to criminal justice activities, such as police salaries and incarceration costs of processing and housing drug offenders. Broken down on a per capita basis, the overall pricetag for the "war on drugs" amounts to $64.08 per resident (UCSD 1994b)!

Based on the belief that "a government should not declare war on its own people" and the reality that jails and prisons are overcrowded with persons sentenced to drug-related offenses, President Clinton in 1993 began to shift drug policies to reflect greater emphasis on prevention, education, and treatment, thereby reducing the demand for drugs. The hallmarks of this strategy include: (1) an aggressive drug treatment strategy with hard-core drug use; (2) provisions for drug treatment as a component in national health care legislation; (3) renewed emphasis on alcohol and drug education, especially among children; and (4) reducing drug use in the workplace. In sum, the overall approach defines drug abuse as a public health problem and makes drug control policies a cornerstone of Clinton's domestic policies. In addition, community policing will play an instrumental role in continued efforts to control drug trafficking within communities (UCSD 1994a).

The legal basis for federal drug law violations derives from the Comprehensive Drug Abuse Prevention and Control Act of 1970, commonly called the Controlled Substances Act (CSA). This act classifies drugs into five categories based on the degree of their potential abuse and their use in medical and clinical practice. Thus, Schedule I substances have a high potential for abuse and no approved medical use; Schedule II drugs have a high potential for abuse, but have approved medicinal uses and can be prescribed under strict guidelines (DEA 1988).

The Controlled Substances Act (CSA)

There are four basic parts of this federal statute insofar as it governs control and enforcement: (1) mechanisms for reducing the availability of controlled substances; (2) procedures for bringing substances under control; (3) criteria for determining control requirements; and (4) the obligations incurred by international treaty arrangements.

Administered and enforced by the Drug Enforcement Administration (DEA), this act provides for nine major control mechanisms imposed on the manufacturing, purchasing and distributing of drug substances listed under the CSA: (1) registration of handlers; (2) recordkeeping requirements; (3) quotas on manufacturing; (4) restrictions on distribution; (5) restrictions on dispensing; (6) limitations on imports and exports; (7) conditions for storing these drug substances; (8) reports of transactions to the government; and (9) criminal, civil, and administrative penalties for illegal acts.

The CSA sets forth criteria for classifying drugs into one of five schedules or categories. Both criminal penalties and regulatory requirements are tied to these five schedules.

Schedule I

A. The drug or other substance has a high potential for abuse.

B. The drug or other substance has no currently accepted medical use in treatment in the United States.

C. There is a lack of accepted safety for use of the drug or other substance under medical supervision.

Schedule II

A. The drug or other substance has a high potential for abuse.

B. The drug or other substance has a currently accepted medical use in treatment in the United States or a currently accepted medical use with severe restrictions.

Schedule III

A. The drug or other substance has a potential for abuse less than the drugs or other substances in Schedules I and II.

B. The drug or other substance has a currently accepted medical use in treatment in the United States.

C. Abuse of the drug or other substance may lead to moderate or low physical dependence or high psychological dependence.

Schedule IV

A. The drug or other substance has a low potential for abuse relative to the drugs or other substances in Schedule III.

B. The drug or other substance has a currently accepted medical use in treatment in the United States.

C. Abuse of the drug or other substance may lead to limited physical dependence or psychological dependence relative to the drugs or other substances in Schedule III.

Schedule V

A. The drug or other substance has a low potential for abuse relative to the drugs or other substances in Schedule IV.

B. The drug or other substance has a currently accepted medical use in treatment in the United States.

C. Abuse of the drug or other substances may lead to limited physical dependence or psychological dependence relative to the drugs or other substances in Schedule IV.

The CSA, together with other legislation, also provides a legal foundation for arresting and prosecuting those who commit or conspire to commit a number of drug-related offenses: manufacture, importation, distribution, possession, or sale. Prosecution can also be made for failure to pay legally mandated taxes on illegal income obtained from the manufacture, distribution, and sale of controlled drug substances.

Several federal agencies are involved in drug enforcement, some confined to very specific roles, such as the Internal Revenue Service; the Bureau of Alcohol, Tobacco, and Firearms; and the Postal Inspection Service. Since law enforcement plays such an important role in the federal strategy to combat dangerous drugs, students should be familiar with the more important of these agencies.

Drug Enforcement Administration (DEA)

The sole purpose of the DEA is to enforce federal statutes concerning controlled substances, including regulation of legal drugs, such as codeine, morphine, and barbituates through nine major control mechanisms, such as enforcing restrictions on distribution, auditing records of drug sales, and monitoring quotas on manufacturing (DEA 1988).

In addition to these functions, the DEA is probably most famous for its undercover approach in apprehending drug law violators: Make a buy, then the "bust." More preferable is to make progressively larger buys, gain access to drug bosses, then make the arrest and seizure of drugs, money, and other relevant evidence.

The DEA also has an international presence, working with police in countries where drugs are processed and manufactured or in overseas cities that are "pass-through" points for drugs destined for the United States. Although this work is often portrayed as glamorous, it is also highly dangerous. Among the major goals of DEA agents working internationally are to train local police in drug enforcement, to disrupt and shut down major supply routes, to assist in convicting major drug traffickers and in dismantling international drug organizations, and to uncover national and international bank money-laundering methods. (See also Chapter 9 for a discussion of the DEA.)

Federal Bureau of Investigation (FBI)

In 1982 President Reagan reorganized the federal effort to combat drug trafficking and organized crime. Part of this reorganization involved expanding the scope of the FBI by giving it concurrent jurisdiction with the DEA in investigating and enforcing drug trafficking laws. In effect, the FBI inherited overall responsibility for coordinating and supervising drug-enforcement activities and policies. (See also Chapter 9 for a discussion of the FBI.)

Customs Service and Immigration and Naturalization (INS)

Both the Customs Service and INS play important roles in reducing the supply of drugs and drug smuggling, and discovering currency violations that are often part of the laundering schemes used by organized crime. Specifically, the INS is mandated to prevent illegal entry of persons into the United States, and its officers have the power to arrest those transporting illegal drugs.

The Customs Service, on the other hand, frequently works with transportation carriers, such as U.S. and overseas airlines, so that they are not unwittingly involved in drug smuggling and trafficking. Efforts by the Customs Service to uncover illegal drugs are not specifically restricted by Fourth Amendment rights; that is, Customs agents need neither "probable cause" nor search warrants to search for and confiscate drugs and other contraband. Search and seizure is vested in the authority of the Customs Service to protect the United States from importation of illegal or contraband substances, according to laws passed by Congress. (See also Chapter 9 for a discussion of the Customs Service and INS.)

Coast Guard

The U.S. Coast Guard plays a significant role in drug interdiction efforts along the seacoasts of the United States. Utilizing both surface patrols and surveillance aircraft, the Coast Guard has intensively patrolled routes traversed by drug traffickers in the Caribbean and the Bahamas, the Gulf of Mexico, and the Atlantic and Pacific coastal regions. Although Coast Guard personnel are bona fide law-enforcement officers, they are not required to establish probable cause or to secure search warrants in order to board a vessel suspected of drug smuggling.

Department of Defense (DOD)

Although the involvement of DOD and the U.S. military in drug-enforcement efforts has evolved over the years, though not without controversy, its role was greatly expanded in the early 1980s. For example, the DOD has had a close working relationship with law-enforcement personnel in collecting and sharing intelligence information, transporting civilian drug-enforcement personnel, and especially in surveillance of carriers suspected of smuggling illegal drugs. The U.S. Air Force has played an important role in surveillance of coastal areas, and the U.S. Army, working in cooperation with the DEA and local authorities in overseas locations, has helped destroy drug manufacturing organizations.

Summary and Conclusion

That alcohol and other drug abuse is linked to crime at the user level is certainly true. Collectively, studies reviewed in this chapter help to substantiate this assertion, showing that alcohol, drugs, or both are linked to a significant proportion of crimes, particularly homicide, violent domestic crimes, and other forms of violent conduct. What is not so clear is how alcohol and drugs influence actual criminal behavior and whether or not correlating alcohol and drugs to crime amounts to a cause.

Some of the evidence reviewed in this chapter suggest that despite high prevalence rates of substance abuse among incarcerated criminals, many of these offenders had criminal records before the onset of their substance-abuse problems. Moreover, drug use among some people can be seen as part of a deviant lifestyle, in which obtaining drugs places users in the circumstances of a criminal element, which offers them opportunities to commit other crimes.

Whatever the connection between alcohol or drug use and crime, it is clear that drug trafficking is big business—in fact, a global business. Drug use surveys also show that substance-abuse rates continue to remain exceptionally high in the United States despite generous yet costly interdiction and law-enforcement efforts by an array of federal, state, and local agencies. It seems clear that drug trafficking is market driven, and available evidence from drug surveys, though mildly encouraging in user categories, does not suggest that the market demand for drugs will disappear anytime in the near future. Whether or not interdiction and law-enforcement efforts can eliminate the demand for drugs without increasing government commitment to more drug prevention, education, and treatment is a matter to be seen. Meanwhile, alcohol and other drug abuse remains a significant social problem of this era.

References

Abadinsky, H. 1989. *Drug Abuse*. Chicago: Nelson-Hall.

Amir, R. 1971. *Patterns of Forcible Rape*. Chicago: University of Chicago Press.

Bartol, C., and A. Bartol. 1986. *Criminal Behavior: A Psychosocial Approach*. Englewood Cliffs, N.J.: Prentice Hall.

Blacker, E. 1959. "The Incidence and Significance of Crime in the History of the Chronic Drunkenness Offender." *Proceedings of the Tenth Annual Meeting of the North American Association of Alcoholism Programs*, Boston.

Blum, R., and L. Braunstein. 1967. "Mind-altering Drugs and Dangerous Behavior: Alcohol." In President's Commission on Law Enforcement and the Administration of Justice, *Task Force Report: Drunkenness*, 29–49. Washington, DC: Government Printing Office.

Blumer, H., et al. 1967. *ADD Center Project Final Report: the World of Youthful Drug Use*. Berkeley: University of California Press.

Brain, P., ed. 1985. *Alcohol and Aggression*. Dover, N.H.: Croon Helm.

Bullock, H. 1955. "Urban Homicide in Theory and Fact." *Journal of Criminal Law and Criminology* 45:565–75.

Bureau of Justice Statistics (BJS). 1991. *Drugs and Crime Facts, 1990*. Washington, D.C.: Government Printing Office.

———. 1992. *Drugs, Crime, and the Justice System*. Washington, D.C.: Government Printing Office.

Cleveland, F. 1955. "Problems in Homicide Investigations IV: The Relationship of Alcohol to Homicide." *Cincinnati Journal of Medicine* 36:28–30.

Collins, J., ed. 1981. *Drinking and Crime: Perspectives on the Relationships between Alcohol Consumption and Criminal Behavior*. New York: Guilford Press.

Cordilia, A. 1985. "Alcohol and Property Crime: Exploring the Causal Nexus." *Journal of Studies on Alcohol* 46(March):161–71.

Cramer, M., and E. Blacker. 1967. "Early and Late Problem Drinkers Among Female Prisoners." *Journal of Health and Human Behavior* 4:282–90.

Drug Enforcement Administration (DEA). 1986a. "Black Tar Heroin." Special Report. Washington, D.C.: U.S. Department of Justice.

———. 1986b. *Intelligence Trends Special Report: From the Source to the Street*. Washington, D.C.: U.S. Department of Justice.

———. 1988. *Drugs of Abuse*. Washington, D.C.: Government Printing Office.

Fagan, J. 1990. "Intoxication and Aggression." In *Drugs and Crime*, edited by M. Tonry and J. Wilson. Chicago: University of Chicago Press.

Fagan, R., and A. Mauss. 1978. "Padding the Revolving Door: An Initial Assessment of the Universal Alcoholism and Intoxication Treatment Act in Practice." *Social Problems* 46:232–47.

Garrett, G.R. 1974. "Drinking on Skid Row: The Case of the Homeless Woman." Paper presented at the Annual Meetings of the American Sociological Association, New York. August.

———. 1989. "Alcohol Problems and Homelessness: History and Research." *Contemporary Drug Problems* 16(Fall):301–32.

———. 1992. "Homelessness, Alcohol, and Other Drug Abuse: Research Traditions and Policy Responses. *New England Journal of Public Policy* 8(Spring-Summer):353–69.

Garrett, G.R. and R. Heubner. 1988. "Alcohol, Drugs, and the Crisis of Homelessness: Challenge for the Criminal Justice System." Presented at the annual meetings of the Academy of Criminal Justice Sciences, Washington, D.C., March.

Garrett, G.R., and R. Schutt. 1987. "Networking by the Homeless Alcoholic." *Alcohol, Health and Research World* 11(Spring):58–59.

Glaser, D. 1978. *Crime in our Changing Society*. New York: Holt, Rinehart and Winston.

Gropper, B. 1985. "Probing the Links Between Drugs and Crime." *Research in Brief*, National Institute of Justice. February.

Gross, L. 1983. *How Much Is Too Much? The Effects of Social Drinking*. New York: Random House.

Guze, S., et al. 1962. "Psychiatric Illness and Crime with Particular Reference to Alcoholism." *Journal of Nervous and Mental Diseases* 134:512–21.

Hutt, Peter Barton. 1967. "The Recent Court Decision on Alcoholism: A Challenge to the North American Judges Association and Its Members." In President's Commission on Law Enforcement and the Administration of Justice, *Task Force Report: Drunkenness*, 109–19. Washington: Government Printing Office.

Inciardi, J. 1981. "Crime and Alternative Patterns of Substance Abuse." In *Drug and Alcohol Abuse*, edited by S. Gardner. Rockville, Md.: National Institute on Drug Abuse.

Jellinek, E. M. 1946. "Phases in the Drinking History of Alcoholism." *Quarterly Journal of Studies on Alcohol* 7:1–88.

———. 1968. *The Disease Concept of Alcoholism*. New York: National Council on Alcoholism.

Johnson, B., et al. 1985. *Taking Care of Business: The Economics of Crime by Heroin Abusers*. Lexington, Mass.: Lexington Books.

Kinney, Jean, and Gwen Leaton. 1991. *Loosening the Grip: A Handbook on Alcohol Information*. 4th ed. St. Louis: Mosby Year Book.

Lyman, M., and G. Potter. 1991. *Drugs in Society: Causes, Concepts and Control*. Cincinnati: Anderson.

Maisto, S., et al. 1991. *Drug Use and Misuse*. Fort Worth: Holt, Rinehart and Winston.

Mayfield, D. 1976. "Alcoholism, Alcohol, Intoxication and Assaultive Behavior." *Diseases of the Nervous System* 37:288–91.

McBride, D., and J. Swartz. 1990. "Drugs and Violence in the Age of Crack Cocaine." In *Drugs, Crime and the Criminal Justice System*, edited by R. Weisheit. Cincinnati: Anderson.

McGuire, P.C. 1988. "Jamaican Posses: A Call for Cooperation Among Law Enforcement Agencies." *Police Chief*, January, 20–27.

Musto, D. 1987. *The American Disease: Origins of Narcotic Control*. New York: Oxford University Press.

National Institute on Alcohol Abuse and Alcoholism (NIAAA). 1990. *Seventh Special Report to U.S., Congress on Alcohol and Health*. Washington, D.C.: Government Printing Office.

National Institute on Drug Abuse (NIDA). 1992. *National Household Survey on Drug Abuse*. Rockville, Md.: NIDA.

National Institute of Justice (NIJ). 1990. *1988 Drug Use Forecasting Annual Report*. Washington, D.C.: U.S. Department of Justice.

———. 1992. "Fact Sheet: Drug Use Trends." *Drugs and Crime Data* Washington, DC: U.S. Department of Justice. May.

Nieves, E. 1992. "For Better Business, Prostitutes Leave Manhattan for Jersey City." *New York Times*, September 1992,B1,6.

Neuner, R., and D. Schultz. 1986. *Borrow Me a Quarter*. Anoka, Minn: Minnesota Institute of Public Health.

Payne, W., D. Hahn, and R. Pinger. 1991. *Drugs: Issues for Today*. St. Louis: Mosby Year Book.

Pittman, D., and C.W. Gordon. 1962. "Criminal Careers of the Chronic Drunkenness Offender." In *Society, Culture and Drinking Patterns*, edited by D. Pittman and C. Snyder. New York: Wiley.

President's Commission on Law Enforcement and the Administration of Justice. 1967. *Task Force Report: Narcotics and Drug Abuse*. Washington, DC: Government Printing Office.

Rada, R. 1975. "Alcoholism and Forcible Rape." *American Journal of Psychiatry* 121:776–83.

Rettig, R., M. Torres, and G.R. Garrett. 1977. *Manny: A Criminal-Addict's Story*. Boston: Houghton Mifflin.

Roizen, J. and D. Schneberk. 1977. "Alcohol and Crime." In *Alcohol, Casualties and Crime*, edited by M. Aaren et al., 283–465. Berkeley: Social Research Group.

Royce, James E. 1989. *Alcohol Problems and Alcoholism: A Comprehensive Survey*. New York: Free Press.

Schutt, R. and G. R. Garrett. 1992. *Responding to the Homeless*. New York: Plenum.

Shupe, L. M. 1954. "Alcohol and Crime. A Study of Urine Alcohol Concentration Found in 882 Persons Arrested During or Immediately After the Commission of a Felony." *Journal of Criminal Law and Criminology* 44:661–64.

Smith, D. 1986. "Cocaine-alcohol Abuse: Epidemiological, Diagnostic and Treatment Considerations." *Journal of Psychoactive Drugs* 18:117–29.

Spain, D., et al. 1951. "Alcohol and Violent Death." *Journal of the American Medical Association* 146:334–35.

Taylor, S., et al. 1975. "Effects of Type and Dose of Alcohol on Human Physical Aggression." *Journal of Personality and Social Psychology* 32:169–75.

———. 1976. "Aggression as a function of the Interaction of Alcohol and Threat." *Journal of Personality and Social Psychology* 34:938–941.

———. 1979. "The Effects of Alcohol and Extreme Provocation on the Use of Highly Noxious Shock." *Motivation and Emotion* 3:73–81.

———. 1983. "Alcohol and Human Aggression." In *Aggression: Theoretical and Empirical Reviews.* Vol. 2., edited by R. Geen and E. Donnerstein. New York: Academic Press.

Tinklenberg, J., and K. Woodrow. 1974. "Drug Use Among Youthful Assaultive and Sexual Offenders." In *Aggression*, edited by S. Frazier. Baltimore: Williams and Wilkins.

Tonry, M. 1990. "Research on Drugs and Crime." In *Drugs and Crime*, edited by M. Tonry and J.Q. Wilson, 1–8. Chicago: University of Chicago Press.

UCSD Extension Program. 1994a. "New Drug Strategy Drops War Rhetoric." *Prevention File: Alcohol, Tobacco and Other Drugs* (Spring):15–17.

———. 1994b. "The Costs of War." *Prevention File: Alcohol, Tobacco and Other Drugs* (Spring): 21

Vaillant, G.E. 1983. *The Natural History of Alcoholism*. Cambridge: Harvard University Press.

Whalen, R., and J. Lyons. 1962. "Medical Problems of 500 Prisoners on Admission to a County Jail." *Public Health Report* 77:497–502.

Witters, W., P. Venturelli, and G. Hanson. 1992. *Drugs and Society* 3rd ed. Boston: Jones and Bartlett.

Wilbanks, W. 1989. The Danger of Viewing Addicts as Victims: A Critique of the Disease Model of Addiction." *Criminal Justice Policy Review.* Thematic issue edited by G. R. Garrett: "Alcohol, Drugs and Criminal Justice Policy" 3:407–22.

Wiseman, J. 1970. *Stations of the Lost.* Englewood Cliffs, N.J.: Prentice Hall.

Wolfgang, M. 1958. *Patterns in Criminal Homicide*. Philadelphia: University of Pennsylvania Press.

Wright, J., and E. Weber. 1987. *Homelessness and Health.* New York: McGraw-Hill.

Chapter 3

Crime Today: Special Focus

As Chapter 1 pointed out, crime statistics and crime trends are mainstream to the study of criminology and criminal justice. Yet statistics alone cannot capture the impact that crime has on the moral order of society, the extent of fear that it instills in people, and how crime intrudes on daily living patterns, even for people who have not been immediately victimized.

Although American mass media sometimes make theater out of crime-impact stories, with sensational headlines of shocking crimes and human-interest features about citizen fear of crime, nonetheless these stories are salient reminders that criminal justice institutions—the police, courts, and corrections—must also understand crime in terms of how it affects the sociological fabric of the community if they are to fulfill their obligations to the public they serve. Thus, some felonies should be understood as much more than "just a felony," in that they inflict deep social wounds to the community at large. Take "hate crimes," for example, where special groups are singled out by bigots, hooligans, or organizations with social and political agendas to be victims by reason of their social characteristics. Racial, ethnic, linguistic, and religious minorities or gays and lesbians are among the many groups victimized by acts of hate in the form of property destruction, assault, and even murder. In reality, of course, the damage inflicted by hate crimes goes well beyond the immediate victims, striking lethal blows to constitutional freedoms and common standards of decency.

This chapter pays special attention to three diverse kinds of crimes: child abuse, terrorism, and environmental crimes. Crime patterns in each of these categories are unrelated. But, as with hate crimes, the sociological impact on the community and society extends well beyond the immediate victims. Although these crimes are not traditional topics discussed in criminology and criminal justice textbooks, nonetheless they are relevant domains of study of growing importance to the field.

Child Abuse

Crimes that involve children as victims are the most difficult to take. It is hard to understand how even the most heartless person could victimize children, who are probably the most defenseless and certainly the most innocent of any victims.

Even more difficult to comprehend is the abuse of a child at the hands of parents and family members, who ironically are statistically the most likely to be the abusers.

Regardless of the abusers, child abuse itself is not easily defined for a number of reasons, the most obvious being the age factor. The upper range of childhood poses the problem. Until what age are children no longer children? Age definitions vary across research studies and by legal jurisdictions, ranging from 12–16 years of age in some instances and as high as 18–21 years old in others. This may seem a trivial issue, yet a lack of clarity on "who are children" complicates gathering uniform information about child victims and assessing the degree to which child abuse is a social and criminal problem (Whitcomb 1992).

But if age definitions are problematic, so too are judgments about what constitutes abuse. Some child protection advocates insist that *any* kind of intentional physical punishment with children as victims constitutes abuse; others disagree, asserting that abuse is the intentional, nonaccidental use of force specifically aimed at hurting or destroying the child. Still others omit the intention factor altogether and define abuse as any conduct that carries ill consequences for the child. This definition also implies the inclusion of emotional and sexual abuse as dimensions of child abuse (Garbarino 1989).

Then there is the matter of neglect—the omission of parental or guardian obligations to children—and the debate over when child neglect becomes child abuse. To complicate this matter further, many researchers insist that it is important to consider community norms of how children should be treated before reaching judgments about these phenomena. Thus, some communities have greater tolerance (and preference) for physical punishment of children for their misbehaviors ("spare the rod and spoil the child"); in other communities, physical force of any variety is not acceptable.

Considering these and other variations in defining child abuse, it is not surprising that legal definitions of child abuse can also contain ambiguities, which make it difficult to obtain firm statistics on the prevalence of child abuse. Garbarino (1989, 220) points out that "child maltreatment" is probably the most accurate term to use; this can be defined as "acts of omission or commission by a parent or guardian that are judged by a mixture of community values and professional expertise to be inappropriate and damaging." (See also Box 3.1.)

However child abuse is defined, maltreatment of children in any form has immediate and far-reaching effects on personality development and behavior, according to countless psychological and clinical studies (e.g., Wyatt and Powell 1988; Finkelhor 1986; Gomes-Schwartz et al. 1990). In their extensive review of the literature on child abuse, Lusk and Waterman (1986) and Browne and Finkelhor (1986) identified several clusters of effects on children: (1) affective problems, such as guilt, shame, fear, depression, hostility; (2) physical effects, which included sexually transmitted diseases, genital injuries, pregnancy, and somatic complaints; (3) cognitive effects, specifically concentration problems or short attention spans; (4) behavioral symptoms such as antisocial conduct, withdrawal, and aggression; (5) self-destructive behaviors, such as suicide attempts and self-multilation; (6) psychopathology in the form of character disorders, psychotic symptoms, neurotic behaviors, and multiple personalities; and (7) sexualized behaviors, including excessive masturbation, atypical sexual knowledge, or repetition of sexual acts.

Box 3.1 Utah's Bill of Rights for Children

Utah Code Crime Procedure 77–37–4. In addition to all rights afforded to victims and witnesses under this chapter, child victims and witnesses shall be afforded these rights:

1. Children have the rights to protection from physical and emotional abuse during their involvement with the criminal justice process.
2. Children are not responsible for inappropriate behavior adults commit against them and have the right not to be questioned, in any manner, nor to have allegations made, implying this responsibility. Those who interview children have the responsibility to consider the interests of the child in this regard.
3. Child victims and witnesses have the right to have interviews relating to a criminal prosecution kept to a minimum. All agencies shall coordinate interviews and ensure that they are conducted by persons sensitive to the needs of children.
4. Child victims have the right to be informed of available community resources that might assist them and how to gain access to those resources. Law enforcement and prosecutors have the duty to ensure that child victims are informed of community resources, including counseling prior to the court proceedings, and have those services available throughout the criminal justice process.

Source: Reprinted from Whitcomb/NIJ 1992, 51.

Thus, child abuse robs children of their childhood, impairing personality development that will encumber personal functioning as adults. In fact, available evidence from studies conducted on adults from backgrounds of childhood abuse suggests that they have substantially higher risks of exhibiting violent behaviors that result in arrest. For example, in a study sponsored by the National Institute of Justice, 908 substantiated cases of childhood abuse or neglect processed through courts from 1967 to 1971 were tracked over a fifteen- to twenty-year period. A comparison group with similar demographic characteristics, but from nonabusing backgrounds, was tracked for the same period. Results provided convincing evidence: Coming from a background of childhood abuse or neglect increased the chance of arrest as a juvenile by 53 percent, as an adult by 38 percent, and for a violent crime by 38 percent (Widom 1992).

Prevalence of Abuse

There is no single source of information on child abuse or crimes committed against children. With the exception of murder, the *Uniform Crimes Reports* does not contain data on crimes against children. In 1991, 1075 children under the age of fifteen years were victims of homicide. Unfortunately, these data do not permit inferences about the relationship between child homicide and child abuse. Nevertheless, the National Committee for Prevention of Child Abuse estimated that of the 1698 children murdered in 1988, 1225 were child-abuse-related (Whitcomb 1992).

Instead of having precise data, knowledge about the incidence and prevalence of child abuse is derived from large-scale surveys and smaller studies of specific communities. Thus, for example, a National Incidence Study conducted in 1986 estimated that more than 1.5 million children were endangered because of abuse or neglect (Whitcomb 1992). In addition, other data showed that the rate of child neglect (15.9 per 1000 children) is nearly three times that of child physical abuse (5.7 per 1000) and about five times higher than child sexual abuse (2.5 per 1000) (Widom 1992; see also Figure 3.1.).

Sexual Abuse

Probably no form of child abuse provokes public outrage more than child sexual abuse. Like other forms of abuse, sexual exploitation can dramatically impair personality development of children, as well as present serious problems in their personal functioning as adults. Evidence of the lasting effects of child sexual abuse is abundant in clinical literature on adults who were victims of childhood abuse (Wyatt and Powell 1988; see also Box 3.2).

Numerous studies provide information about the incidence of child sexual abuse. For example, the National Incidence Study of 1986 estimated that more than 155,000 children were endangered by sexual abuse committed by parents or caretakers. Not all children, however, are abused by parents. In Whitcomb's (1992) review of studies spanning four decades that included data on child sexual abuse, she finds that from 10 to 50 percent of reported cases are committed by people outside the family. Women report high victimization rates in all these studies, ranging from 12 to 38 percent of all women. For males, findings showed a range of 3 to 16 percent. In yet another study on nonincarcerated pedophiles, commonly called "child molesters," Abel (1987) reports that incest pedophiles

Figure 3.1
Perpetrators of Abuse and Neglect.

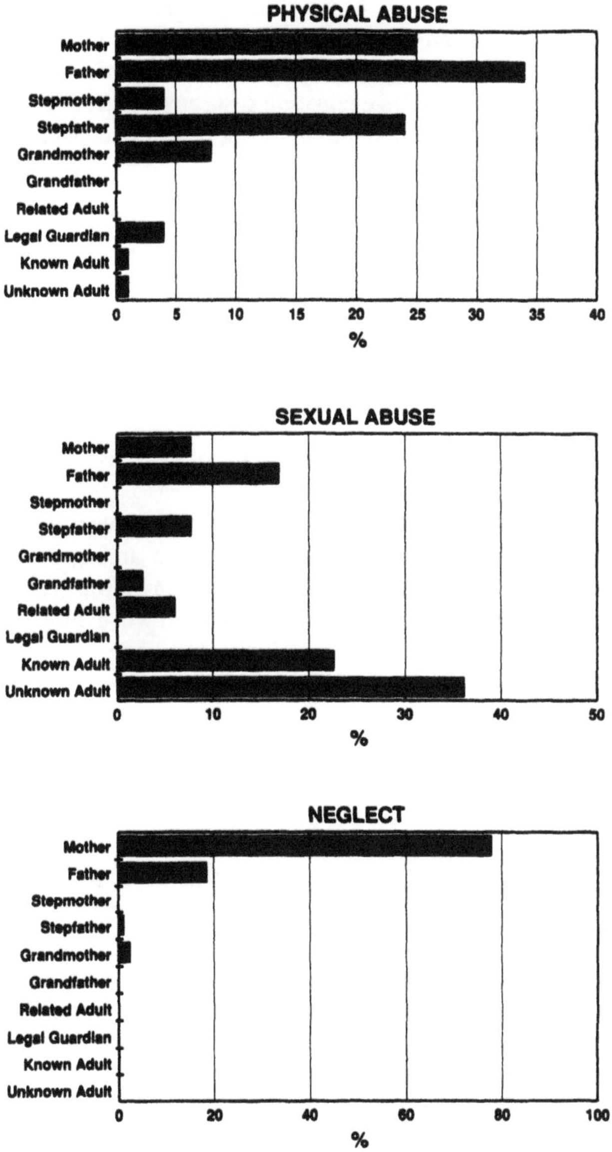

Based on 1575 substantiated cases of childhood abuse, 1967–71. From Widom/National Institute of Justice 1992, 3.

Box 3.2 Sexually Abused Children

Early attempts to describe a "sexually abused child" syndrome were quickly discarded as lacking foundation in empirical research. Today, however, some of the leading researchers and clinicians in this field are moving toward consensus on behavioral indicators of child sexual abuse. The results of a nationwide survey of professionals experienced in evaluating suspected child sexual abuse reveal high levels of agreement around the following factors (Conte et al. 1989):

—Age-inappropriate sexual knowledge.
—Sexualized play.
—Precocious behavior.
—Excessive masturbation.
—Preoccupation with genitals.
—Indications of pressure or coercion exerted on the child.
—The child's story remains consistent over time.
—The child's report indicates an escalating progression of sexual abuse over time.
—The child describes idiosyncratic details of the abuse.
—Physical evidence of abuse.

It is important to recognize, however, that these indicators represent a broad constellation of behaviors that are frequently seen among sexually abused children as a group. Because sexual abuse takes many forms (e.g., a long-term incestuous relationship or a single event), each child will exhibit a different set of behaviors. Thus, who experienced single abusive incidents may well be consistent with over time. Conversely, children who experienced several years of abuse by close relatives may seem to contradict their stories over time, depending on the attitudes expressed by family members or the manner in which they are questioned. In other words, *there is no single arrangement of behavior indicators that will definitively identify a sexually abused child.*

Source: Reprinted in part from Whitcomb/NIJ 1992, 20.

commit from thirty-five to forty-five acts against one or two children. Nonincest pedophiles commit one or two acts of sexual abuse on an astounding number of children, averaging 20 female or 150 male victims per pedophile! Many of these cases never come to the attention of law-enforcement or children's agencies. Probably one of the most extraordinary examples of underreporting of child sexual abuse surfaced in the trial of a former Catholic priest, James Porter. Convicted on multiple counts of child sexual assault in Massachusetts in December 1993, Porter may have molested well over 200 children.

Procedural Reforms

Intense media coverage has helped generate considerable public outrage over the way child protection and criminal justice systems process child abuse cases. Among the issues of greatest concern are how children witnesses are questioned in the courtroom (e.g., the use of "leading questions," the child as a competent witness, the use of reliable hearsay evidence, speedy trials with limitations on continuances, and extending the statute of limitations for prosecuting those accused of child abuse).

According to Whitcomb (1992, 47), there appears to be a consensus among experts around four initiatives to improve justice processing of child abuse cases. First, obtaining children's testimony using closed-circuit television or videotape would help reduce the trauma that many children experience in the courtroom, as well as potentially improve the quality of relevant testimony supplied by the child witness. Second, the use of anatomically correct dolls would help children in communicating information about sexual or physical activities relevant to the case. At the same time, this technique remains sensitive to the immaturity of small children when it comes to discussing sexual acts. Although there are potential legal issues involved in using dolls to solicit testimony, this technique has already been implemented in a number of jurisdictions (Freeman and Estrada-Mullaney 1988). Third, employing a team approach to investigate and prosecute child abuse cases would not only better protect child victims, but also yield greater success in conviction rates. Investigating child cases can be especially difficult. Thus a team approach would enhance the efficiency of the investigation process and enable prosecutors to establish relevant facts on which to base a prosecution (see also Box 3.3). Fourth, the use of specialized victim assistance or advocacy programs can be invaluable in providing children with emotional support during judicial proceedings and in linking the child victims to mental health and medical services.

Terrorism

To many, if not most, Americans, terrorism is senseless violence perpetrated by unscrupulous fanatics in faraway places. Yet the average American probably has very little understanding of the nature of terrorism and its relationship to political ideology. Of course, the lack of awareness partly reflects inexperience with dramatic acts of terrorism on American soil. Compared to countries in the Near and Middle East, Latin America, and Western Europe, the United States has been relatively free of violent, terrorist-related acts. Even the bombing of Pan American Flight 103 in December 1988, which claimed the lives of every passenger and crew member on board, mostly Americans, took place over Lockerbie, Scotland, not in the United States.

Box 3.3 Investigating Child Abuse Reports

Essentially, there are two "gatekeepers" in the child protection system. First is the intake worker, who receives the initial report, typically on a telephone hotline, and determines whether the report deserves further investigation. Second is the investigative caseworker, who follows up on reports that survive the first level of screening to determine whether the reported child is at risk. Many reports are screened out at each gate.

Nonetheless, occasional accounts of children abruptly removed from their homes by social workers after minimal investigation and without notifying the parents have stimulated intense debate over the mandate to report suspected child abuse and the child protection agencies' ability to respond appropriately. Acting on the premise that these agencies are overwhelmed by inappropriate reports, to the extent that resources are seriously depleted and unavailable for true cases of maltreatment (Besharov 1988a), some commentators argue strongly that reportable "child abuse and neglect" should be redefined (Besharov 1988b).

And, in fact, in recent years a majority of states have adopted guidelines intended to narrow the types of reports that are accepted for formal investigation.... The most common criteria for screening out reports include the following:

—The reporter is involved in a custody dispute.

—The reporter has made repeated unfounded allegations.

—The child is reported for truancy or educational neglect.

—The reporter provided incomplete information.

—There is no indication of harm or risk of harm.

—The reporter failed to mention a specific incident or pattern of incidents.

—The case involved maltreatment by a non-caretaker (Wells et al. 1989).

More reports are screened out after investigation, often because there is insufficient information to determine whether abuse occurred or to identify the perpetrator.

Source: Reprinted from Whitcomb/NIJ 1992, 5.

But in 1993 terrorist violence hit home dramatically when New York City's massive World Trade Center was bombed, allegedly by Muslim terrorists, causing extensive structural damage to one of its towers and injuring scores of people. Although fatalities were few in number, the Trade Center bombing publicized terrorism in a way rarely seen in America and offered convincing evidence that the United States is indeed vulnerable to international terrorism inside its own boundaries, not just in foreign lands.

Later in 1993, the mass media gave Americans a front-row seat at a standoff at the Branch Davidian complex outside Waco, Texas, where law-enforcement authorities ultimately attacked the compound, resulting in a fiery death to scores of Branch Davidians, including the children of cult members. Because the Branch Davidians were known to be stockpiling weapons, there were suspicions that they were planning terrorist activities. Nevertheless, shocking as the death toll was, many observers were no less dismayed at what appeared to be inept law-enforcement tactics and ill-advised decision-making that led to a military-like assault of the cult's compound.

Dramatic though the New York bombing and Branch Davidian tragedy were, terrorism in the United States reached a new level with the 1995 bombing of the Murrah Federal Building in Oklahoma City. More than 165 lives were lost, many of them children at a day-care center, making it the single-most devastating act of terrorism on U.S. soil. Investigation of the blast site later revealed that the explosion had been caused by a massive fertilizer-based bomb consisting of ammonium nitrate. Although law enforcement authorities were swift in making arrests, one of them Timothy McVeigh, who along with a second suspect, Terry Nichols, were later indicted, the Murrah bombing put America on notice that domestic terrorism is an ongoing threat to public safety. And, unlike the 1960s and 1970s, when many left-wing groups were regarded as capable of violence, evidence from the Oklahoma City bombing clearly pointed to political motivations of right-wing origins and to the so-called "right-wing militia" groups.

Although these instances of terrorism are far more dramatic, they are by no means isolated incidents of terrorism involving Americans, either as perpetrators or as victims. Smith (1994), for example, provides extensive documentation of terrorist-related crimes, using data culled from records in national archives and federal courts about the men and women investigated for acts of terrorism throughout the 1980s. Over this same period, American casualties resulting from terrorist acts, most of them in foreign countries, have also accumulated. According to the Department of State (1992), 580 Americans have lost their lives and 609 have been wounded as a result of acts of international terrorism over the past eleven years. Although these casualty figures are low by comparison to countries in the Near and Middle East, nevertheless they speak to the vulnerability of Americans to terrorist acts.

Over the past decades, the hijacking of aircraft, both domestic and international, has been a favorite target of international terrorists. None was more dramatic than the TWA hijacking out of Athens, Greece, in the mid-1980s. According to the Federal Aviation Administration (DOT/FAA 1990), American carriers suffered forty-three actual hijackings and averted fourteen attempted hijackings from 1983 to 1990. Bomb threats to airlines or airport facilities add up to even higher figures. Over this same period, 3,363 threats to bomb air carriers and 1,955 threats to airports were made (Maguire/NIJ 1993).

Results from airline-passenger screening offer further evidence of the vulnerability of airlines to hijacking and potential violence. For example, of the more than 1.1 billion passengers screened at U.S. airports in 1990, 1337 were arrested for carrying either firearms or explosives. In the same year, just under 3000 weapons, mostly handguns, were detected by X-ray inspection or physical search of passengers and carry-on items. Figures were even higher during most of the 1980s, peaking in 1986 and 1987. Although these data reveal nothing of the motives of those carrying weapons, they must be regarded as having the potential to manifest violent acts.

Because terrorist acts sometimes involve much more than violations of criminal statutes, students of criminology and criminal justice would do well to understand terrorism in a broader sociopolitical context. And since traditional criminological and sociological theories of crime have little to say about terrorism, we must look to scholarship in political science and international relations. Understanding the nature of terrorism as a form of political violence, however, is very relevant to developing and enhancing strategies for prevention and policing.

Terrorism and Criminal Violations

Terrorism as a form of political violence is certainly criminal in virtually every jurisdiction on the globe. Treating it as a political crime or as a felonious assault on people and property is differentiated by the law of the land where it occurs. In the United States, however, neither the federal government nor the fifty states categorize political crimes separately from other criminal offenses. Thus the terrorist aspects of these events are media theater, *not* legal issues.

Research findings from studies in political violence have little impact on the prosecution of terrorists because terrorism, per se, is not defined as a crime. Instead, *what the terrorists do is criminal.* If they are apprehended and indicted, they are tried for murder, kidnapping, hijacking, willful destruction of property, and other felonies. The political aspects of their crime, while they may anger the public, fall on deaf ears in the courtroom. Consequently, while public interest in the World Trade Center and the Oklahoma City bombings is piqued by details of the police investigation, the procedures trying those who have been indicted deal with criminal law, not terrorism.

The "system" and how to change it legally lies at the heart of what titillates public interest in terrorism. Laqueur (1977, 206) comments, "Seldom in history has so much been written about so few and so little." The political aspects of the violence done by terrorists are directed primarily toward winning significant concessions from a government in power by holding it hostage to dramatic events. Terrorists substitute violence for legal ways to change the system.

Individually or in groups, they perceive themselves powerless to gain legitimate access to the legal mechanisms by which economic, social, or political change can be accomplished. Although the perception of political powerlessness as an incentive to terrorism was identified by Hacker as early as 1976, few observers of terrorism have realized how important a component it becomes in the determination of whether some political violent event is terrorism or something else.

As actual or threatened violence to gain attention and create alarm, which in turn will cause people to exaggerate the strength of the group and the importance of the cause, terrorism intimidates or victimizes a random, incidental target population (Holland 1989). Since terrorists see themselves as powerless to bring about change by any other means, their violence is deliberately shocking. They are less concerned about winning sympathizers than they are about destablizing the legal authority and holding public attention hostage to their antics.

Therefore, terrorism is carefully choreographed to attract the media, especially television, to monitor widely exposed confrontations with the authorities. Terrorists target a viewing audience. As theater, terrorism seeks to break down the confidence people have in their government. Unlike other forms of political violence, such as insurgency or revolutionary warfare, terrorism does not necessarily reflect a particular ideology.

Whether terrorists are rightists, leftists, Marxists or fascists, those who use insurrectional strategies to maneuver the authorities into situations in which the powerless hold the powerful at bay practice terrorism. Laqueur (1977, 3) points out: "The title 'urban guerrilla' is in fact a public relations term for terrorism; terrorists usually dislike being called terrorists, preferring the more romantic guerrilla image."

Definition and Typology of Terrorism

As a topic of interest to law enforcement, criminologists, and political scientists, contemporary terrorism came on the scene in the early 1970s when Wilkinson (1973) raised "Three Questions on Terrorism." Since the definition of "terrorism" remains controversial, its attributes have been classified over and over again. Although numerous books and more than eight hundred periodicals about terrorism have tried to establish definitive parameters, terrorism has been treated differently from other political conflict studies, especially if the writer uses theoretical perspectives in trying to define the concept (Reid 1984).

Among the many experts, Laqueur's (1977, 1987) and Wilkinson's (1987) definitions of terrorism by typology appear to be the longest lived. Both subsume terrorism as a subcategory under political violence, and both emphasize that terrorism assumes different forms according to the intended audience. While both scholars gloss over Hacker's (1976) claim that terrorism in any form comes about because its perpetrators perceive themselves as powerless to effect legitimate political change, their typologies explain the concept of Hacker's notion of political powerlessness.

Terrorism can be *international* or *domestic*. Some of the specific labels within these categories are confusing because it could be expected that *state terrorism*, for instance, is a form of domestic terrorism. Even though it is terrorism waged by the government of a state, the key to understanding state terrorism is recognizing that the government perceives itself powerless to realize national self-interest by a legitimate pursuit of international affairs. Any means other than the use of violence would be self-defeating, so the government channels its efforts into a domestic campaign to replicate a "a nation in arms." Like Libya's Qaddaffi, who ordered the bombing of a Berlin disco in 1986, those in power, believing that the state is militarily weak in comparison with other states, choose terrorism instead of war. To obtain their goals, they gain the attention of an international audience by carrying out outrageous acts of violence (see Box 3.4).

Other forms of international terrorism include the terrorism carried out by zealots who hijack airplanes, bomb aircraft and airports, take hostages, or kill or maim outside the territorial area of authority they target. Moreover, international terrorism occurs in places where the perpetrators retain neither immediate political interest nor residency.

An example of this "*fundamentalist terrorism*," as it has been defined by Wilkinson and Stewart (1987, xiii), is the Pan American Flight 103 bombing over Lockerbie, Scotland, in December 1988, by Muslim terrorists. Yet another example is the World Trade Center bombing. If the investigation of the bombing uncovers a conspiracy of Middle East religious fanatics supporting the perpetrators of the crime, a more striking example of international fundamentalist terrorism inside the United States will be documented. But knowledge that fundamentalist terrorists committed the crimes changes nothing about the way the American criminal justice system deals with the adjudication of the matter.

In Germany and Italy, where terrorism is labeled as criminal activity, the accused stand trial as terrorists whether their terrorism is international or domestic. Why terrorism has been labeled as a crime may derive from experiences during the more than thirty years that domestic terrorists targeted the governing authority.

In general, three types of terrorism can be identified as domestic. First is the *anarchic-nihilist* type, exemplified by the Red Brigades in Italy and the Red Armée Faction-Baader Meinhof gang in Germany, which sought to tear down the structure of order and the rule of law during the 1970s and 1980s (Iviansky 1977). Because these terrorists believed there was no other way to influence existing government authority to make changes in a political system they rejected, they intimidated the population by waging campaigns of terror to make it appear that the police were incapable of keeping public order. Like the Tupamoros, a terrorist group in Uruguay, they saw themselves as "urban guerrillas" who used domestic terrorism to bring down the state by destroying the routines of compliance by which the day-to-day functions of state authority operate. Even though their locus of operation is the countryside rather than urban areas, Sendero Luminoso (Shining Path) in Peru is another example of anarchist-nihilist terrorism.

National liberation terrorism, the early post-World War II form that successfully forced the British to leave Cyprus and Palestine, was first used to justify the idea that "one man's terrorist was another man's freedom fighter." As the second form of domestic terrorism, it is still used by local activists to justify violence to end what is deemed colonial exploitation. The difference now is that what might be the sources of the so-called economic exploitation have shifted from the colonialist state to international market dynamics dominated by multinational business interests. Moreover, the PIRA (Provisional Irish Republican Army), which claims to represent national liberationists, appears to have reorganized to fight the British as insurgents, not terrorists. In other words, the PIRA members see themselves as rising up in revolt against British authority, rather than as terrorists seeking to establish a new social order.

The third form of domestic terrorism, *system terrorism*, sets up terrorists as unwitting transgressors against the public authority for reasons known only to the secret cabal that manipulates a political system via terrorism. In other words, those doing the violence become "fall-guys," operating against targets identified by members of the conspiracy whose role in the action remains secret and far removed from the acts of terrorism. Examples of this terrorism can be seen in the operations of the Black Hand in Bosnia that precipitated World War I, or the "death squads" in many Latin American countries that still operate today. If the Ku Klux Klan operated outside the United States, it would clearly fulfill the criteria of a system terrorist movement. But since terrorism is not a crime in the United States, Klan violence of any kind is labeled otherwise by criminal statutes of the jurisdiction in which it occurs.

Early in 1993, the Branch Davidians appeared to be preparing for some kind of system terrorism by accumulating an arsenal of weapons and sealing themselves off from contacts with neighboring people. While their religious fanaticism suggested to outside observers all the hallmarks of system terrorism, if the police and federal authorities were to charge them, they first required some indication that the lifestyle and practices broke criminal laws in Texas and the United States. Thus, Americans learned during extraordinary media coverage of the standoff of allegations of child sexual abuse made against the Branch Davidians. Similarly, jurisdictions in Idaho and the State of Washington had experiences with groups of religious zealots, the Aryan People's Nation, which terrorized local populations and made law enforcement very difficult. But since the U.S. government characterizes as international what it specifies as terrorism against American citizens, system terrorism is not an issue in American jurisprudence.

Box 3.4 A Typology of Contemporary Terrorism

Terrorist activity of any type expresses the perpetrators' perception of being powerless to change the system it seeks to destabilize by any legitimate means, including war. This is true of both international and domestic terrorism.

International	*Domestic*
State-sponsored terrorism	Fanatic virgule single-issue terror ism
Fundamentalist terrorism	Anarchist–nihilist terrorism
Emigré terrorism	System terrorism
Terrorism targeted against U.S flag carriers and. transnational business	National liberation terrorism
	Insurgent or tactical terrorism

Recently the term "narco-terrorism" has been used to label transnational activities dealing with illicit drugs (see Chapter 2). Nevertheless, it is a misnomer. The U.S. Department of State (1992, 1) defines terrorism as premeditated, politically motivated violence perpetrated against non-combatant targets by subnational groups or clandestine state agents, usually intended to influence an audience. International terrorism is terrorism involving citizens or territory of more than one country. Accordingly, the U.S. government disqualifies international drug trafficking as "narco-terrorism." Inconsistencies between the legal position taken on terrorism by U.S. authorities and the notion that the activities of people such as General Manuel Noriega of Panama or now-deceased Colombian drug lord Pablo Escobar are narco-terrorists have confused public perceptions of prosecution as well as law enforcement in narcotics cases when there is an international dimension.

Consequently, a useful typology recognizes that terrorism is one among other forms of political violence. Just because some terrorists target their activities to specific governments does not mean that they are exclusively domestic or international. The locus of activity, as well as the purpose for the terrorism, intervenes in the classification. Thus, single-issue fanatics about animal rights, antiabortionists, and antinuclear extremists are terrorists if the jurisdictions in which they operate define terrorism as a crime. Should these groups restrict their activities to the United States, law enforcement emphasizes the criminal, not the terrorist, aspect of their operations, even though they may be an arm of a larger international movement.

Conversely, there are *émigré nationalist movements* seeking to realize political self-determination at the expense of the government that exercises authority over territory they covet. The Armenians and the Palestinians, as represented by the Palestine Liberation Organization (PLO), conduct much of their terrorism from bases in exile. How does one classify the Basque ETA military in border areas in France who cross the frontier into Spain to practice terrorism? Yet, while there is an overriding domestic focus to their operations, even by U.S. definition, nationalists' terrorism falls into the category of international, not domestic, terrorism.

Finally, limited terrorism against purely political targets has been employed effectively in recent history as a tactic by insurgent movements and revolutionaries who genuinely seek to win the hearts and minds of the population in whose name they aim to overthrow the sitting regime. Hence the classification of domestic types should include a category called *insurgent* or *tactical* terrorism.

The Investigation of Terrorism

Investigating terrorism in the U.S. is technically the responsibility of any relevant law-enforcement agency, including local police agencies, when criminal statutes are violated within their jurisdictions. On issues of importing contraband or illegal substances into the United States or violations of U.S. immigration laws, both the ***U.S. Customs Service* and *Immigration and Naturalization Service*** (INS) could become involved. Even ***U.S. Postal Service Inspectors*** can play a significant role in investigating terrorist activities, that is, to the extent that these violate postal regulations. In the past few decades, letter and package bombs have been favorite techniques of terrorists, both in the U.S. and in Europe.

The ***Department of Defense*** (DOD) has a very important role in surveillance and policing of terrorist activities. The ***Defense Intelligence Agency*** (DIA), for example, provides the Joint Chiefs of Staff with intelligence information, mostly gathered from ordinary media and information sources, such as radio or print journalism. These data are also shared with other federal agencies, such as the ***Central Intelligence Agency*** (CIA) and the ***Federal Bureau of Investigation*** (FBI). And the DOD's ***Intelligence and Security Command*** (INSCOM) not only gathers intelligence information but assists the FBI in espionage and counterespionage activities involving the U.S. Army.

Traditional police functions are also exercised by all branches of the military service, such as the ***U.S. Army's Military Police Command*** (MPC) and the

Office of Security Police in the U.S. Air Force (USAF). Investigative branches also operate to protect military bases, such as the ***USAF's Office of Special Investigations*** (OSI), the ***U.S. Army's Criminal Investigation Command***, or the ***U.S. Navy's Naval Investigation Service***. During the 1970s and 1980s, both traditional and investigative commands in all services were kept busy on Army and Air Force bases in Europe, especially in Western Germany, because of the blitz of terrorist activities during this period. U.S. bases became prime targets for terrorist action, and a dramatic bombing of the Officer's Club at Rhein Main Air Force Base located near passenger terminals at Frankfurt Airport.

Probably the most important agency involved in investigating terrorist activities is the FBI, which is called in to investigate virtually every serious crime within the U.S. when there is evidence of a connection to terrorism. Their efficiency in tracking down terrorists suspected of serious and violent crimes was especially evident following the New York Trade Center bombing, when suspects were arrested within a remarkably short period of time.

Although the ***Central Intelligence Agency*** (CIA) is limited to conducting intelligence and counterintelligence activities outside the United States in support of U.S. interests and policies, it often works in cooperation with the FBI on domestic cases, especially when terrorism is suspected. Depending on circumstances, the ***Bureau of Alcohol, Tobacco, and Firearms*** may work in cooperation with the FBI, as may, in international drug trafficking, the ***Drug Enforcement Agency*** (DEA).

Finally, the ***International Criminal Police Organization***, better known as *INTERPOL*, provides assistance to its 150 member countries in conducting investigations of criminal offenses that go beyond international borders. Headquartered in France, INTERPOL created an antiterrorist unit in 1987 that enables member countries to use its resources and data bases for tracking suspected terrorists wanted for crimes committed in one of the member nations, including the U.S. Contrary to common beliefs, INTERPOL does not itself operate field agents or conduct investigations.

Environmental Crime

Environmental crimes are among the most insidious of law violations. Unlike conventional crimes, where there are usually immediate consequences, crimes against the environment are not always visible and are sometimes very difficult to detect. Nevertheless, environmental offenses have serious cumulative costs to the environment and human life, including injury, illness, and even death. Illegal disposal of toxic wastes, for example, can pollute soil and groundwater that contaminates the ecological system and the food chain, ultimately causing disease and death to humans and other organisms. Thus, serious environmental contamination, when it eludes detection for an extended period, becomes a "time release" death sentence for the environment and for those who come into contact with its hazards.

Historically, environmental crime has not been a traditional subject examined by students of criminology and criminal justice. In fact, despite diligent efforts by local "watchdog" groups and dedicated environmentalists, such as the Sierra Club and Greenpeace, the general public has not usually shown long-term concern over environmental problems or crimes. When it has, public agitation over environmental issues is confined to local "NIMBY" (not-in-my-back-yard) concerns, such as the construction of an atomic energy facility. Moreover, many community groups regard some environmentalists more as enemies of the public than as advocates for a safe environment and the preservation of natural resources. For example, conflict between environmental protection policies and the public at large was particularly evident in Oregon during the early 1990s, when government officials and environmental protectionists were in a pitched battle with the lumber and building industry, involving local residents who depend on logging for their livelihoods, to preserve the forest habitat of the spotted owl. Although the dispute was eventually resolved through a compromise plan that permitted limited logging of timber-rich forest lands, this example, among others, shows that environmental laws and policies are not always popular with the general public.

Nevertheless, public commitment to solving environmental problems and prosecuting violators of environmental laws is increasing. Catastrophic events during the 1980s did much to arouse public concern about environmental affairs such as the emergency shutdown of the atomic energy plant at Three Mile Island in Pennsylvania, the nuclear disaster at Chenobyl in the former Soviet Union, and especially the massive *Exxon Valdez* oil spill on Prince William Sound in Alaska (see Box 3.5),

Box 3.5 The Exxon Valdez Oil Spill

Shortly after midnight on March 29, 1989, the supertanker *Exxon Valdez* struck a reef and ran aground in Prince William Sound, off the coast of Alaska, spilling 11 million gallons of crude oil, the largest oil spill in U.S. history. The spilled oil spread to more than 1200 miles of Alaska's coastline, which is rich in fish and wildlife. The spill killed and injured large numbers of many wildlife species....

During 1989, state and federal agencies focused on containing and cleaning up the spill and rescuing oiled wildlife. Although winter storms helped in cleaning many beaches, additional cleanup was needed in 1990 and 1991....

Both Alaska and the federal government filed claims against Exxon seeking to recover damages for injuries to and the restoration of natural resources. In

October 1991, the U.S. District Court for the District of Alaska settled the claims against Exxon for civil damages and criminal charges. Under the major terms of the civil settlement, Exxon (1) agreed to pay the federal government and the state of Alaska a total of $900 million in 11 annual payments... beginning in December 1991 and ending in September 2001 and (2) might be liable for up to an additional $100 million between 2002 and 2006 for projects to restore populations, habitats, or species that had suffered a substantial loss or decline not anticipated on the effective date of the settlement.

Exxon pleaded guilty to four criminal charges arising from the oil spill and was fined $150 million, the largest fine ever imposed for an environmental crime. In addition, Exxon agreed to pay $100 million ($50 million to the federal government and $50 million to the state of Alaska) as remedial and compensatory (restitution) payments to be used exclusively for the restoration of natural resources damaged by the oil spill.

Despite fines and restitution payments, however, the Exxon Valdez case again captured national headlines on June 13, 1994, when a federal jury convicted Valdez Captain Joseph Hazlewood of negligence on grounds that he was drunk at the time the supertanker struck the reef. This conviction opens the door for potential law suits against Exxon.

Source: Adapted from GAO 1993, 12–13.

Notwithstanding efforts by environmentalists to educate the public, catastrophic events have brought environmental issues and crimes into the public arena in ways not seen in past decades. Findings from national surveys show that the public is becoming increasingly intolerant of violations of environmental laws. In the 1980s, a Bureau of Justice Statistics survey reported that Americans believed that some environmental crimes were more serious than such traditional crimes as robbery, auto theft, and burglary (Celebrezze 1990; BJS 1984). By 1991, survey results suggested that public opinions about environmental crimes were even more harsh, showing that 84 percent of Americans believed that damaging the environment was a serious crime. Moreover, three out of every four study participants said that corporate officers should be held *personally* responsible for violations of environmental law committed by their firms (Hammett and Epstein 1993a).

Because environmental crimes are not likely to disappear in the future, criminologists and criminal justice professionals must become more interested in and literate on environmental laws and violations. As laws become more stringent, making it more costly for industries and businesses to comply with regulatory standards, the prevalence of environmental crimes is also likely to increase. Thus criminal prosecution should be viewed as an important option in efforts to control and deter violations.

Environmental Laws

Because of pervasive statutory inconsistencies, both within and across jurisdictions, defining environmental crime is no simple matter. What constitutes an environmental crime in one state may not be defined as a crime in another. Some states seek only civil damages for violations, while others pursue both civil damages and criminal prosecution. Inconsistency among the fifty states offers environmental criminals opportunities to move their operation across state lines to evade conviction for environmental violations (Hammett and Epstein 1993b).

At the federal level, however, environmental statutes derive from congressional legislation. In 1970 Congress established the Environmental Protection Agency (EPA) to administer environmental programs and assure compliance with federal statutes on environmental affairs. Thus, much of the work of the EPA is regulatory in nature, such as *prohibition* and *permitting* of regulated activities, notice requirements (e.g., *before* a regulated act takes place, such as asbestos or *after* the act, such as release of hazardous materials), or labeling requirements.

Environmental laws are less understood by the public than criminal statutes, especially because violations of environmental laws rarely enjoy high visibility in the mass media, that is, unless they are major disasters. Neither are they policed in quite the same way as conventional crimes.

Nevertheless, violations of environmental laws can carry both civil and criminal penalties. Depending on the extent of damage, civil penalties in the form of fines can be very high. Under certain circumstances, criminal penalties can also be imposed on individuals deemed to be directly responsible for violations of environmental laws.

The Environmental Protection Agency administers federal environmental programs and implements and enforces laws associated with these programs. Although environmental laws existed prior to the formation of the EPA, the most important environment laws were developed principally in the 1970s or later, many by congressional amendments to existing laws. A dozen major statutes form the legal basis for EPA programs:

—*The Pollution Prevention Act* seeks to prevent pollution through reduced generation of pollutants at their point of origin.

—*The Clear Air Act* requires the EPA to set mobile source limits, ambient air-quality standards, hazardous air-pollutant-emission standards, standards for new pollution sources, and significant deterioration requirements; and to focus on areas that do not attain standards.

—*The Clean Water Act* establishes the sewage treatment construction grants program and a regulatory and enforcement program for discharges of wastes into U.S. waters.

—*The Ocean Dumping Act* focuses on the regulation of the intentional disposal of materials into ocean waters and authorizes related research.

—*The Safe Drinking Water Act* establishes primary drinking water standards, regulates underground injection disposal practices, and establishes a groundwater control program.

—*The Solid Waste Disposal Act* and *Resource Conservation and Recovery Act* provide regulation of solid and hazardous waste, while the *Comprehensive Environmental Response, Compensation, and Liability Act*, better known as the "Superfund" Act, establishes a fee-maintained fund to clean up abandoned hazardous waste sites or oil or hazardous substance spills. The Superfund is supported by monies collected from industries.

—*The Emergency Planning and Community Right-to-Know Act* requires reporting of compilation on toxic releases and encourages response for chemical releases.

—*The Toxic Substances Control Act* regulates the testing of chemicals and their use, and the *Federal Insecticide, Fungicide, and Rodenticide Act* governs pesticide products and their use.

—*The Environmental Research and Development Demonstration Act* authorizes all EPA research programs; and the *National Environmental Police Act* requires, EPA to review environmental impact statements (Lee 1993; GAO 1993).

In addition to performing regulatory functions, the EPA maintains a criminal investigations unit, since violations of federal environmental statutes contain provisions for both civil and criminal penalties. Criminal penalties have become increasingly stiff in the past decades because of the perception that existing laws are not sufficient to prevent environmental crimes (see Box 3.6).

Criminal Violations

Because the short-term effects of violations of environmental laws are sometimes negligible, affixing responsibility for violations can be complicated. Despite the absence of a "smoking gun" at the time of the crime, environmental criminals can become murderers because of birth defects, cancers, and other medical problems caused by their crimes that do not appear until years later. Hammett and Epstein (1993b, 7) provide examples of how mishandling chemical substances commonly used in industries and even in small businesses, such as dry cleaners, can have serious health consequences:

> Exposure to many common industrial solvents can cause severe damage to every human organ system. Prolonged exposure to xylene, for example, can damage the central nervous system, liver, and heart. Inhaling or handling methyl ethyl ketone can cause severe irritation to the skin, eyes, and throat. Significant dose exposure to ethyl benzene can produce pulmonary edema, a fluid buildup in the lungs that can be fatal. Where 1,1,1 trichloroethane has leaked into groundwater, it is suspected of causing birth defects. In short, these and other common pollutants are extremely dangerous substance whose mishandling can cause serious harm to persons and to the natural environment.

Box 3.6 Hazardous Waste Violations: A Snapshot

It is instructive to observe how regulatory requirements and criminal penalties are configured into environmental laws. Because hazardous waste violations constitute the bulk of environmental investigations and prosecutions, it is a particularly good example to use.

> Any person who knowingly transports or causes to be transported hazardous waste to an unpermitted facility or treats, stores, or disposes of hazardous wastes without a permit or in knowing violation of a material condition or requirement of a permit or interim status regulations or standards may be guilty of a class D felony. The maximum term of imprisonment under this section of the act is five years, while the maximum fine for an individual is $50,000 per day, or $250,000, or twice the wrongdoer's gain or society's loss from the illegal activity, whichever is greater. The maximum fine for a corporation is $50,000 per day, or $500,000, or twice gain or loss, whichever is greater. For a subsequent violation, a class C felony, the maximum term of imprisonment is 10 years, and the maximum fine can go as high as $100,000 per day or $500,000 for an individual or $1,000,000 for a corporation to twice the gain or loss, whichever is greater.

Source: Adapted and reprinted from Hammett and Epstein 1993b, 4

Although there are no precise figures on the extent of environmental crimes, violations can be separated into three basic categories. In the first category are violations of permit conditions or other illegal acts committed by firms or individuals already included in the regulatory system. An example of this violation would be a waste hauling company that is properly permitted under the Toxic Substances Control Act (TSCA) but improperly disposes of toxic substances while invoicing the generators as if proper disposal methods had been used. Still another example is an industry that is properly permitted yet bypasses wastewater treatment required by the Clean Water Act.

The second category of environmental crime is committed by individuals or firms outside the regulatory scheme of the EPA and/or the state's environmental agency. An example of this type of crime would be a firm that stores or disposes of hazardous wastes without obtaining a permit required by the Resource Conservation and Recovery Act (RCRA) (see Box 3.6).

The third type of environmental crime involves violations that are illegal whether or not they are within the regulatory scheme. The classic example of this crime is the "midnight dumper," that is, environmental criminals who discard toxic wastes along highways and in abandoned warehouses (Hammett and Epstein 1993b).

Despite technical problems in gathering national data on the extent of environmental crimes, a look at the most common crime—the illegal disposal of hazardous waste—is instructive. According to studies reviewed by Hammett and Epstein (1993b), in cooperation with the National Institute of Justice, an estimated 247 to 275 million metric tons of hazardous wastes were illegally disposed of each year during the mid-1980s. Moreover, as environmental laws on hazardous waste disposal become more stringent, violations are likely to increase, since higher regulatory standards involve higher costs to business. Hammett and Epstein (1993b, 9) explain why:

> Firms that dispose of their wastes illegally, and thereby avoid the high costs of legal disposal, can gain a competitive advantage. In industries where legal disposal costs are large relative to profits, this advantage may be so signficant that legal disposers cannot compete. Take, for example, a small dry cleaning business for which the cost of legal disposal of its monthly output of perchloroethylene (perc) sludge is $200 per month. This represents a substantial portion of the cleaner's $2,000 per month net revenue.

Thus, as industries and businesses struggle to remain competitive, and as costs to meet new disposal standards rise, incentives to use legal methods may decline. This principle also applies to other environmental statutes, such as the Clean Air Act and the Clean Water Act. For this reason, criminal enforcement is becoming increasingly important as a deterrent to violating environmental laws.

Box 3.7 Toxic Tickets

Traffic tickets have long been the centerpiece of police strategies to enforce traffic laws and promote safe driving. Depending on the number and severity of the violations, offenders can face fines, license suspension, and even jail confinement if they fail to answer to traffic court.

Borrowing on this strategy, California has developed a 1993 pilot program in selected counties to issue tickets—"Toxic Tickets"—for lesser environmental violations. These tickets serve a function similar to traffic tickets and involve a similar process of disposition. Ticketing violations enable health officers to take immediate action on minor hazardous waste and other environmental violations. These tickets also have a deterrent value. Taking action on a minor violation may prevent a small problem from developing into a major environmental hazard, and the tickets are particularly suitable for violations committed by small businesses.

Source: Adapted from Hammett and Epstein 1993a.

Criminal Prosecution

During the 1980s state and federal governments expanded criminal-enforcement programs of environmental laws, even though the actual numbers of cases referred for criminal prosecution, cases filed, and convictions obtained are modest compared to figures for conventional crimes. At the federal level, however, the EPA referred 318 matters to the U.S. Department of Justice for prosecution from 1982 to 1989. This resulted in the conviction of 351 defendants. (A single case often has more than one defendant.) In fiscal year 1989, seventy-six defendants were convicted, twenty-four of them for criminal violations of the Resource Conservation and Recovery Act (hazardous waste violations) and thirty for violations of the Clean Air Act (Hammett and Epstein 1993b:13) (see Box 3.7).

There are many reasons for such modest figures. First, criminal prosecution for environmental crimes is still in its infancy. Thus, most local prosecutors feel unprepared to take on environmental crimes, which are often perceived as enormously complicated and difficult to win. At the judicial level, many federal and state judges are not particularly versed in environmental laws. Still others are insensitive to the seriousness of environmental crimes or believe that such violations are more appropriately handled as civil cases. Juries, too, can be obstacles to successful prosecution of environmental criminals, since they may be reluctant to convict business leaders (who, after all, employ members of the community) unless the alleged crime has serious public health consequences.

Nevertheless, the federal government and several states have implemented very aggressive environmental prosecution policies and have achieved strong conviction records. The investigation and prosecution process is typically labor-intensive, time-consuming, technical, and almost always costly.

Stage 1 is the detection phase, wherein information about the environmental offense or the intent to commit an offense is gathered. *Stage 2* is the equivalent of a "criminal rap sheet," in this case an "environmental rap sheet," in which investigators check out the history of the suspect, such as prior convictions or previous investigations conducted for environmental offenses. In *stage 3*, the suspect is under surveillance, similar to that used in conventional criminal cases. Depending on the circumstances, surveillance activity can take many forms, such as the classic "stakeout," monitoring garbage or sewage discharge, or the use of video cameras. *Stage 4* involves collecting relevant documents, samples potentially useful as evidence, and conducting interviews with key personnel connected to the crime. In some cases, a search warrant may be needed to collect specific evidence. In *stage 5* laboratory analysis of samples and evidence is conducted. This stage is especially critical, since results must show that the evidence meets the legal requirements to warrant prosecution. In addition, careful attention at this stage is given to safeguarding the chain of evidence so that it will be admissible in court. Depending on local rules for criminal procedure, *stage 6* involves filing charges by indictment or information. In *stages 7 and 8*, the case is adjudicated or settlement is reached and compliance with the ruling and sentence of the court is implemented (Hammett and Epstein 1993b).

Environmental cases are very diverse and may not involve all of the outlined investigation and prosecution stages. Whatever the diversity, however, current trends suggest that the criminal justice system must be prepared in the near future to deal with both the technicalities of these cases and with increasing numbers of defendants accused of environmental crimes.

Prosecuting Environmental Crime: A Case Study

Regulatory agencies to monitor business and industry for compliance with federal and state environmental laws and standards are not always enough to protect the public and environment. Thus, federal, state, and local governments have increasingly moved to assign criminal penalties for violations of environmental laws, making "environmental criminals" subject to virtually the same process as conventional criminals. This involves the stigma of criminal indictment and, depending on the severity of the crime, even incarceration. Advocates of this approach argue that in addition to civil sanctions and fines, criminal penalties are needed to add teeth to the deterrent value of environmental laws. In so doing, local prosecutors become equal partners with regulatory agencies, which have primary responsibility for enforcing environmental laws (Hammett and Epstein 1993a).

Probably no urban region in the country has environmental problems as severe as Southern California. Thus, among the first to create an innovative team approach to environmental crime prosecution was Los Angeles County. Known as the LA County Environmental Crimes Strike Force, it entails a cooperative arrangement among state, county, and city governments that includes agencies within each, such as the County District Attorney for Environmental Crimes and the Fire Department's Hazardous Materials Control Program of the Fire Department; the City of Los Angeles, including the LAPD, the City Sanitation Enforcement Division and the City Attorney's Environmental Protection Section; the State's Highway Patrol Environmental Crimes Unit, among others; and agencies in other cities within the county—nineteen in all.

What makes this coalition approach nearly unique among local efforts is that it contains all the essential elements needed to enforce environmental laws: law enforcement organizations to conduct criminal investigations; technical components with a capacity to gather evidence or samples at the scene of alleged violations and conduct health risk assessments; and a laboratory unit to do analyses of samples, safeguard the chain of evidence, and provide expert testimony at trials.

Because all components are coordinated, the LA Strike Force can work with incredible efficiency, much like police organizations investigating conventional crimes. Prosecutors view serious violations as "crimes of violence against the environment" and ultimately against the public. Here's how the process works:

—In addition to monitoring businesses and industries for compliance with environmental laws, the Strike Force depends on tips from informants to learn about possible violations. In this respect it operates in much the same way as any ordinary law-enforcement officers.

—Investigations proceed by collecting samples, gathering relevant evidence, and assessing the damage to public health and to the environment.

—A decision to prosecute the case as a criminal offense (as opposed to a civil matter) depends on the seriousness of the violation, the intent of the violator, the amount of toxicity of the substances involved, and the environmental record of the individual or firm.

—Attorneys typically pursue criminal prosecution when justified, since the desired outcome is the remediation of the problem, and the threat of a prison sentence is effective in motivating the defendant to act.

Since 1987, the Strike Force has had remarkable success in their criminal prosecutions. Many of these criminal cases, had they occurred only a decade ago, would have no criminal penalties and possibly would have escaped detection altogether. Because of the success of the LA Strike Force, other jurisdictions throughout the nation are adapting this model to suit their local circumstances (Hammett and Epstein 1993a).

Year	Criminal cases filed	Defendants with jail sentence	Total days jail time	Average sentence (days)	Total fines ($ millions)
1987	53	5	357	71	1.2
1988	45	6	630	105	1.4
1989	50	7	1170	169	1.5
1990	72	5	690	139	3.9
1991	38	13	3043	234	1.7
1992 (Jan.–June)	23	5	1940	388	.8

Summary and Conclusion

This chapter has focused on three crime areas: child abuse, terrorism, and environmental crimes. Although these crimes are unrelated, they share in common the potential to have enormous social impact on the general public.

Probably no crime offends our common standard of public decency more than child abuse. As evidence in this chapter has shown, however, child abuse in the form of neglect, physical maltreatment, and sexual abuse is by no means rare. Whatever the form of abuse, these crimes pose special challenges to the criminal justice system. Child abuse cases must be handled swiftly so that the child can be spared further abuse and provided with proper care as soon as possible.

Evidence reviewed in this chapter also suggests that terrorism may be a crime area that criminologists ought to study more carefully. Although there are different motives behind acts of terrorism, there are clear indications that United States citizens are more likely than ever to be victims of crimes committed by terrorists.

Finally, because environmental crimes have the potential to inflict widespread damage on both the environment and public health, they should be considered as one of the more serious crimes. What makes environmental crimes especially insidious is that the damage is long range—a time-capsuled death sentence for the environment and the people who come into contact with its hazards.

References

Abel, G.G., et al. 1987. "Self-reported Sex Crimes of Non-incarcerated Paraphiliacs." Journal of Interpersonal Violence 2:3–25.

Bresharov, D. 1988a. "The Child-abuse Numbers Game." Wall Street Journal, August.

———. 1988b. *Child Abuse and Neglect Reporting and Investigation*. Washington, D.C.: American Bar Association.

Browne, Angela, and David Finkelhor. 1986. "Initial and Long-Term Effects: A Conceptual Framework." In *Sourcebook on Child Sexual Abuse*, edited by David Finkelhor. Beverly Hills: Sage.

Bureau of Justice Statistics (BJS). 1884. "The Survey of Crime." *Bulletin*. Washington, D.C: National Institute of Justice.

Cayouette, Susan. 1990. *The Addicted or Alcoholic Batterer*. Boston: EMERGE/PCADV.

Celebrezze, A.J., et al. 1990. "Criminal Enforcement of State Environmental Laws: The Ohio Solution." *Harvard Environmental Law Review* 14:217–18.

DOT/Federal Aviation Administration. 1990. *Annual Report to Congress on the Effectiveness of the Civil Aviation Security Program, January 1–December 31, 1990*. Washington, D.C.: U.S. Department of Transportation.

Finkelhor, David. 1986. *A Sourcebook on Child Sexual Abuse*. Newbury Park, Calif.: Sage.

Freeman, K.R., and T. Estrada-Mullaney. 1988. "Using Dolls to Interview Child Victims: Legal Concerns and Interview Procedures." *NIJ Reports* No. 207 (January/February):2–6.

Garbarino, James. 1989. "The Incidence and Prevalence of Children Maltreatment." In *Family Violence*, edited by Lloyd Ohlin and Michael Tonry. Chicago: University of Chicago Press.

General Accounting Office (GAO). 1993. *Natural Resources Restoration: Use of Exxon Valdez Oil Spill Settlement Funds*. Washington, D.C.: General Accounting Office.

Gomes-Schwartz, B, J. Horowitz, and A. Cardarelli. 1990. *Child Sexual Abuse: The Initial Effects*. Newbury Park, Calif.: Sage.

Hacker, Federal J. 1976. *Crusaders, Criminals and Crazies*. New York: Norton.

Hammett, Theodore, and Joel Epstein. 1993a. *Prosecuting Environmental Crime*. Washington: National Institute of Justice.

———. 1993b. *Issues and Practices in Criminal Justice Series: Local Prosecution of Environmental Crime*. Washington, D.C.: National Institute of Justice.

Heide, Kalthleen. 1992. *Why Kids Kill Parents: Child Abuse and Adolescent Homicide*. Columbus: Ohio State University Press.

Holland, Carolsue. 1989. "The More Deadly of the Species: Relevant Scholarship Dealing with Female Terrorists," paper presented to the Wellesley College Center for Research on Women.

Iviansky, Ze'ev. 1977. "Individual Terrorism: Concept and Typology." *Journal of Contemporary History* 12 (January):43–63.

Laqueur, Walter. 1977. *Terrorism*. Boston: Little, Brown.

———. 1987. *The Age of Terrorism*. Boston: Little Brown.

Lee, Martin R. 1993. *Summaries of Environmental Laws Administered by the Environmental Protection Agency*. Washington, D.C.: Congressional Research Service, Library of Congress.

Lusk, R., and J. Waterman. 1986. "Effects of Sexual Abuse on Children." In *Sexual Abuse of Young Children*, edited by K. MacFarlane et al. New York: Guilford Press.

Maguire, Kathleen, et al. 1993. *Sourcebook of Criminal Justice Statistics, 1992*. Washington, D.C.: U.S. Department of Justice, Bureau of Justice Statistics.

Reid, Edna. 1984. "An Analysis of Terrorism Literature." In *The Use of Information in a Changing World*, edited by A. van der Laan and A.A. Winters. North-Holland: Elsevier Science.

Smith, Brent. 1994. *Terrorism in America: Pipe Bombs and Pipe Dreams*. New York: SUNY Press.

U.S. Department of State. 1992. *Patterns of Global Terrorism.* Washington, D.C.: U.S. State Department.

U.S. Department of Transportation (DOT). 1992. *Report to Congress on the Effectiveness of the Civil Aviation Security Program, January 1–December 31, 1990.* Washington: DOT/Federal Aviation Administration.

Wells, S., et al. 1989. "Screening in Child Protective Services." *Social Work* 34:45–48.

Whitcomb, Debra. 1992. *When the Victim Is a Child.* 2nd ed. Washington: National Institute of Justice

Widom, Cathy. 1992. *The Cycle of Violence.* Washington, D.C.: National Institute of Justice.

Wilkinson, Paul. 1973. "Three Questions on Terrorism." *Government and Opposition* 8 (Summer):290–312.

———. 1977. *Terrorism and the Liberal State.* New York: John Wiley.

Wilkinson, Paul, and, Alasdair M. Stewart, eds. 1987. *Contemporary Research on Terrorism.* Aberdeen, Scotland: Aberdeen University Press.

Wyatt, G., and G. Powell, eds. 1988. *Lasting Effects of Child Sexual Abuse.* Newbury Park, Calif: Sage.

Chapter 4

White-Collar Crime

White collar crime is a complex and somewhat ambiguous subject. It is important because it focuses on the criminality of those in positions of power and authority in business and government, those entrusted with protecting the integrity of the nation's laws and ideals and promoting the general interest. It is a complex subject for a number of reasons but particularly because it is even more difficult to quantify than street crime, largely because the higher the social status of the offender, the greater the access to means of concealment of wrongdoing and defense when caught.

White-collar crime is a somewhat ambiguous subject because criminologists are not in firm agreement as to its proper definition. In the absence of conceptual clarity, the significance of research findings and theoretical inferences therefrom are debatable at best and meaningless at worst. The debate about the proper way of defining white collar crime is a reflection of basic differences among criminologists as to whether or not crime is best studied as a general phenomenon or a number of discrete phenomena. Behind this problem is the absence of agreement as to whether or not the alleged different kinds of crime, for example, street crimes such as robbery and aggravated assault versus so-called suite crimes such as insider trading and price fixing, are manifestations of different causes or different manifestations of the same underlying causes? As criminologists disagree as to the best answer to this basic question, it is important to proceed by taking both possibilities into account. Thus, toward the end of outlining what is and is not known about white collar-crime, we examine both attempts to differentiate it from other crimes and efforts to interpret it as an expression of the same causes as all other crime. We begin with the initial effort to define and justify the study of white-collar crime—the work of Edwin Sutherland (1883–1950).

Defining White-Collar Crime

Sutherland's interest in white-collar crime stemmed from his concern with the prevailing assumption that crime was a consequence of economic deprivation and poverty and therefore was largely confined to the lower socioeconomic stratum. But, he thought, if crime were more pervasive than assumed, that is, if it was in fact as prevalent among the highest as the lowest social reaches, a new causal source must be sought and criminological theory revamped. To test the idea he documented as much as available sources allowed the criminal involvement of those of high social status. Accordingly, he defined white collar-crime "as a crime committed by a person of respectability and high social status in the course of his occupation" (1949, 9). As it turned out, Sutherland examined not individual white- collar offenders but the criminal activities of seventy of the nation's largest nonfinancial institutions. The results are outlined below. For the moment, it is important to discuss Sutherland's definition and the conceptual problems it has generated.

What Sutherland failed to clarify was the relative importance of focusing on the individual white-collar offender on the one hand and the nature of the offense on the other. From his definition, to quality as a white-collar crime an act must be committed by someone of high social standing in the course of his or her job. Embezzlement by a bank president would obviously seem to qualify, but embezzlement by a bank teller would seem not to. The essential problem this causes for the criminologist is that the emphasis is placed on actors rather than actions. That is, to qualify as a fit subject for criminological analysis the dependent variable, or the thing to explain, must be a crime—an act that violates the law. Thus, those who study white-collar crime from the legal side of the subject emphasize the nature of the offense, not the status of the offender. An outstanding example is Herbert Edelhertz's conception of white collar-crime.

To Edelhertz, a former chief of the Fraud Section, Criminal Division, U.S. Department of Justice,

> white-collar crime is democratic. It can be committed by a bank teller or the head of an institution. The offender can be a high government official with a conflict of interest. He can be the destitute beneficiary of a poverty program who is told to hire a work group and puts fictional workers on the payroll so that he can appropriate their wages. *The character of white-collar crime must be found in its modi operandi and its objectives rather [than] in the nature of its offenders.* (1970, 4; italics added).

Edelhertz defines white collar-crime as "an illegal act or series of illegal acts committed by nonphysical means and by concealment or guile, to obtain money or property, to avoid the payment or loss of money or property, or to obtain business or personal advantage" (1970, 3). He identifies sixty-one kinds of white-collar crime and classifies them under four major categories: (1) crimes by individuals acting on an ad hoc basis (income tax violations); (2) crimes that occur in the course of an individual's occupation (embezzlement, payroll padding); (3) crimes incidental but potentially beneficial to a business (food and drug violations, deceptive advertising); and (4) crimes that are the central activity of a business (home-improvement schemes, advance fee swindles). To Edelhertz, all white-collar crime has the following elements: intent to commit an illegal act, intent disguise, reliance on victim carelessness and naivete, unwitting victim cooperation, and concealment of illegality. In Edelhertz's opinion,

> Sutherland's definition is far too restrictive. His view provided a rational basis for the economic determinism which was the underlying theme of his analysis, but did not comprehend the many crimes committed outside one's occupation. Ready examples of crimes falling outside one's occupation would be personal and nonbusiness false income tax returns, fraudulent claims for social security benefits, concealing assets in a personal bankruptcy, and use of large-scale buying on credit with no intention or capability to ever pay for purchases. His definition does not take into account crime as a business, such as a planned bankruptcy, or an old fashioned "con game" operated in a business milieu. Though these crimes fall outside Sutherland's definition, they were considered and discussed by him. (1970, 3)

More recently, Susan Shapiro has emphasized the need to study white collar-crime as an offense of a certain type rather than something done by high-status people in the course of their occupations. In her view, "it is time to integrate the 'white-collar' offenders into mainstream scholarship by looking beyond the perpetrators' wardrobe and social characteristics and exploring the modus operandi of their misdeeds and the ways in which they establish and exploit trust" (1990, 363). To Shapiro, white-collar crimes involve violations of trust. In advanced industrial societies such as the United States, certain individuals, by virtue of their position, training, or expertise—for example, elected and non-elected government officials, bankers, corporate directors, doctors, lawyers, and accountants—have privileged access to information and resources and are entrusted with their proper care and use. Trust is part of a social setting—for example, a business or a hospital—and all social settings include, in varying degree of specificity, certain normative expectations involving trust (ethical expectations and legal obligations) and means for their enforcement (e.g., formal data access procedures and financial audits). Thus, to Shapiro the proper sociological way to study white collar-crime begins by "sampling from settings of trust—legislatures, pension funds, hospitals, labor unions, probate or surrogates' courts, charities, law enforcement agencies, wire services, purchasing departments, universities—and examine how these fiduciaries define and enforce trust norms, the structural opportunities for abuse, the patterns of misconduct that ensue, and the social control processes that respond" (1990, 362).

A general theoretical justification for thinking of white-collar crime as a certain kind of offense rather than a certain type of offender has been developed by Travis Hirschi and Michael Gottfredson. As they indicate, the emphasis given to identifying the particulars of white-collar crime has been tied to preventative policy formation. They point out, however, that seeking the identification and implementation of effective policies to control white-collar crime should not be confused with seeking its causal antecedents. And although a given crime is likely to have particular features, one may not infer that it has unique causes requiring unique theoretical interpretation. As they put it, "a finding that the employed are more likely to steal because of their employment no more justifies a unique theory of theft (white-collar crime) than a finding that the unemployed are more likely to steal justifies a theory focusing exclusively on the lower class" (1987, 954).

Hirschi and Gottfredson trace the emphasis placed on identifying types of crimes and seeking their unique causes to the displacement of classical by positivist philosophy. In classical theory (to be discussed in Chapter 6), they say, the causal source of crime is assumed to be "internal," that is, in "human nature." In positivism, the causal realm is "external" to people, as their actions (criminal and noncriminal) are viewed as determined by forces beyond their control. To the sociological positivist, the causal antecedents of crime are to be sought, for example, in the constraining and frustrating conditions of social and economic deprivation. Hirschi and Gottfredson contend that theories based on acceptance of the view that crime is a product of social pathology are noteworthy for their silence on the subject of white-collar crime. Sociological theories accepting of the idea of white collar crime, they say, moved in two directions: "toward a general theory that denied 'pathological' causes (for example, differential association) or toward theories tailed to particular crimes or types of crime" (1987, 950–51).

To avoid these problems, Hirschi and Gottfredson advocate the development of an inclusive general theory of crime. In their view, the basic elements of such a theory are to be found in the tenets of classical or eighteenth-century utilitarian theory. In classical theory people are assumed to be motivated by the pursuit of self-interest and self-interest by the pursuit of pleasure and the avoidance of pain. The difference between the law abiding and the law violating is the willingness of the latter to resort to the use of force or fraud. As they explain it, "to be maximally pleasurable,"

> events should take place immediately; pleasure is therefore enhanced by the *rapidity* with which it is obtained. [E]vents should be *certain* in outcome; force and fraud can provide more certain

> benefits than alternative means. [E]vents should require *minimal effort*; force and fraud can provide benefit with less effort than alternative means, especially when the benefit also has the properties of rapidity and certainty. White-collar crimes satisfy these defining conditions. (1987, 959)

Unfortunately, no attempt is made to specify the meaning of the concepts of *force* and *fraud.* Force, either the threat or the application of coercive means (from subtle intimidation to the infliction of grievous bodily harm), is generally associated with common street crime rather than white collar crime. Fraud, the intentional use of deception to obtain desired ends, is more associated with white-collar crime rather than everyday Crime Index offenses. Reliance on trust is commonly associated with fraudulent criminal opportunity. Senator Joseph Biden regards trust as "the most precious of commodities in a free society" (Hearings, 1986, 4). As he explains it,

> Without trust, people could not delegate the discretionary use of their funds to others. Money need only have to be kept under a mattress, not saved in banks or invested in the creation of new jobs and products, which could be a disaster for us all. Lawyers would have to become mining engineers to invest in gold. University scholars in the humanities would have to audit books themselves to invest their school's endowments. Individuals would have to create their own savings plans.

More generally, decline in the general public trust of those who lead economic and governmental decisionmaking is most certainly an integral component of the recent economic downturn. Restoration of public confidence in key governmental (the executive and legislative branches most of all) and economic institutions (financial and nonfinancial corporations) is an essential prerequisite to the correction of the problem.

Rather than close analysis of concepts such as force and fraud and their precise connection to white-collar crime, Hirschi and Gottfredson are more concerned to develop a general theory of criminality, why some individuals are more predisposed to commit crime than others. Criminality, according to Hirschi and Gottfredson, is based on an individual tendency to pursue immediate gratification by the most direct means available with little regard for possible long-range consequences. Indicators of the trait "include impulsivity, aggression, activity level, and lack of concern for the opinion of others" (1987, 959).

Hirschi and Gottfredson do not suggest that those who score high on such factors are compelled to commit crime regardless of setting. In addition to predisposing individual traits, crime, they say, requires "physical opportunity and immunity from immediate punishment" (1987: 960). Further, a variety of noncriminal alternatives may "provide the benefits of crime," namely, "drugs, alcohol, and cigarette use, sex, divorce, job quitting, and fast cars" (1987, 960).

As Hirschi and Gottfredson see it, the essential traits of the criminally predisposed are less likely to be associated with white collar than blue-collar employment. Associated with white-collar employment is the ability to practice deferred gratification, to postpone the pursuit of everyday sensual and worldly pleasures in favor of commitment to the acquisition of advanced degrees based on long-term and demanding courses of study. "In other words, selection processes inherent to the high end of the occupational structure tend to recruit people with relatively low propensity to crime" (1987, 960). White-collar crime, then, is predicted to be less frequent than common of street crimes such as robbery and burglary. Yet, because their theory of criminality is based on the premise that given the opportunity, individuals with certain character traits are more likely to commit crime than others, there should be no essential demographic differences among criminals in general. Thus, for example, the white-collar offender should not differ from his street-crime counterpart in age, sex, or race. Examination of *Uniform Crime Reports* arrest data for the presumed white collar crimes of embezzlement, forgery, and fraud and the Crime Index offense of homicide supported their prediction.Predictably, critical reaction was not long in coming.

Darrell Steffensmeier takes issue with Hirschi's and Gottfredson's predictions concerning the expected rate of white- collar as compared to other kinds of crime and the demographic comparability of all types of criminal offenders. He begins by questioning the validity of using UCR data on embezzlement, forgery, and fraud as measures of white-collar crime. He finds the evidence "conclusive" that those arrested for these crimes are not restricted to employees or persons of high social status in the course of their occupations, so they do not qualify as white collar crimes. Arrests for forgery and fraud, he says, "are not occupationally related" but individual acts involving "passing bad checks, credit card fraud, theft of services, falsification of identification, defrauding an innkeeper, fraudulent use of public transport, welfare fraud, and small con games" (1989, 347). But, he finds those arrested for embezzlement to fit what is generally regarded as white-collar crime. Those typically arrested for embezzlement include "the club treasurer or the trusted clerk, cashier, teller, or secretary who takes money from his or her organization or employer, and the amount taken is usually small" (1989, 348). Notwithstanding these limitations, Steffensmeier finds that the arrest data fail to support either of Hirschi's and Gottfredson's predictions.

Steffensmeier finds, for example, that while arrest rates by age for fraud and homicide are similar, those for fraud and burglary are quite different. As to sex and race, he finds considerable variation across the six offenses of fraud, forgery, embezzlement, homicide, robbery, and burglary. Lastly, on the relative frequency of white-collar crime, Steffensmeier states that assessments of the prevalence of white-collar crime depend on how it is defined and classified on the one hand and which crimes and groupings it is compared to on the other. "But, in general," he says, "it is not *relatively* rarer than other types of crime" (1989, 354).

In a rejoinder, Hirschi and Gottfredson point out that they did not define white-collar crime as employee related offenses and those committed by high-status people in their employed line of work. For comparative purposes, they say, they used UCR arrest statistics because "they are defined without reference to the occupational setting in which they occur" (1989, 363). On the matter of the demographic correlates of crime (age, sex, and race), they claim that studies by cited others support their predictions. As to the frequency issue, they agree with Steffensmeier that different conceptions of white-collar crime and comparisons of different groupings of white-collar and other crimes will indeed yield different results. They defend their conception of white-collar crime, their manner of grouping crimes for comparative purposes, and they show how their calculations were made and which findings support the prediction of the relatively rarity of white-collar crime (see, in particular, 1989, 366).

For a variety of reasons (ideological conviction, discomfort with theoretical approaches rooted in preconceptions concerning "human nature," commitment to one or another interactionist or structural perspective), sociologically inclined criminologists appear more inclined to adhere to some version of Sutherland's more narrowly conceived conception and approach than to accept more general alternative approaches to the study of white-collar crime, such as Hirschi's and Gottfredson's or that of others (see, for example, Coleman, 1987). There is, however, a general inclination to differentiate among three types of white collar crime: (1) crimes committed by individuals apart from their employment or any particular organizational context (income tax fraud, credit card fraud, and so on); (2) crimes committed by individuals in the course of their occupations (from the embezzlement of a bank teller to the misappropriation of an employer's data, stocks, bonds, money, goods, and services by a high-ranking business executive); and (3) organizational crime (crimes committed in furtherance of a firm's or a corporation's interests, such as price fixing and bid rigging).

Unfortunately, major data sources, especially on individual white-collar crime, do not adhere to these distinctions. For example, although the Bureau of Justice Statistics periodically publishes information on federal white-collar offending, it makes no effort to differentiate frauds committed by individuals in the course of their work from those that are not. Such drawbacks are a constant in the effort to document what is known about the nature, extent, and consequences of the three types of white-collar crime.

Individual White-Collar Crime

There is at present no systematic attempt to amass individual white-collar offenses at all comparable to the *Uniform Crime Reports* or the *National Victimization Crime Survey.* As noted earlier, the *Uniform Crime Reports* do contain arrest data on the white-collar crimes of embezzlement, fraud, and forgery but make no effort to differentiate those committed by individuals acting alone from those committed by individuals in the course of their occupation. A fourth crime, counterfeiting, is tabulated with forgery as a combined category. The four are classified by the FBI as "Part II" offenses. Fraud is defined as "fraudulent conversion and obtaining money or property by false pretenses." Embezzlement is the "misappropriation or misapplication of money or property entrusted to one's care, custody, or control." Forgery and counterfeiting are "making, altering, uttering, or possessing, with intent to defraud, anything false in the semblance of that which is true."

Of the three basic categories, arrests for fraud far outnumber the others. In 1990, there were some 291,000 arrests for fraud, 94,800 for forgery and counterfeiting, and 15,300 for embezzlement. Between 1985 and 1990, however, only arrests for fraud declined (15 percent). Embezzlement arrests increased 34 percent (from 11,400 to 15,300) and forgery and counterfeiting arrests increased 8 percent (or from 87,600 to 94,800).

Although not included in the FBI's index of serious crime, such crimes have enormously important effects, financial and otherwise. In a 1974 publication, the United States Chamber of Commerce reported that "the yearly cost of embezzlement and pilferage reportedly exceeds by several billion dollars the losses sustained throughout the nation from burglary and robbery" and that "fraud was a major contributing factor in the forced closing of about 100 banks during a 20–year period" (1974, 4). Bankruptcy fraud, consumer-related fraud, credit card and check fraud, insurance fraud, and security thefts and frauds were said to cost annually some $28 billion. Writing in the mid–1980s, Rod Willis, the managing editor of *Management Review*, reported that insurance fraud annually costs the industry some $4 billion and that the average loss to a bank from either embezzlement or fraud amounted to $42,000 (1986, 40). Willis reports that estimates of the annual cost of all types of white collar crime range from 40–to–200 million dollars.

Two of the most common types of fraud are "Ponzis" and "Pyramids." Ponzis are named after Charles Ponzi, an Italian immigrant who introduced the scheme in 1919. It is based on identifying and effectively advertising an apparently untapped investment opportunity to realize a particularly high rate of profit in a short period of time. Ponzi discovered that he could realize a profit by purchasing International Postal Reply Coupons at a low rate from countries with weak currencies and redeeming them at a higher rate in richer countries. Not satisfied with keeping the matter to himself he sought to attract investors by promising a 40 percent profit in three months. According to a joint publication of the North American Securities Administrators Association (NASAA) and the Council of Better Business Bureaus (CBBB), "by giving some of the investors the 40 percent returns promised—using the money of new participants to pay off earlier ones—he baited the trap, and he was not averse to promising new investors 50 percent returns in 90 days, and eventually 100 percent" (Cross 1988, 109). When the swindle was exposed, Ponzi was found to have "purchased less than $50 worth of International Postal Reply Coupons, most of them at the very start of the operation" (Cross 1988, 110). The investment enabled him to fleece unwary Bostonians of $10 million.

The North American Securities Administrators Association claims that the Ponzi scam "now appears to be the biggest single fraud threat confronting average American investors" (Cross 1988, 110). Their joint report with the CBBB describes a recent version in which a busboy attracted $5.7 million in 1985 by promising investors a doubling of their investment in sixty to ninety days. His scheme involved the purchase and scalping of rock concert tickets. As is the pattern in such schemes, the initial investors were paid the promised high rate of return in order to generate the necessary word-of-mouth advertisement to attract many others. Also, as customary, the scheme collapsed when the available income eventually became insufficient to pay the promised rate of return to others. Only about a $1 million of investor's money was recovered (Cross 1988, 111).

Pyramid schemes are similar to Ponzis and sometimes are used in conjunction with them. They may be initiated in the manner of a chain letter by an individual or group promising a quick and particularly high rate of profit on a promising venture for an initial outlay and by recruiting a certain number of others. A recent example is the "airplane" pyramid that appeared in New York State in 1987. As described in the joint CBBB-NASAA report,

> for an initial payment of $1,000 to $3,000, a participant becomes one of eight so-called "passengers" on a plane. Also on the imaginary plane are four flight attendants and two copilots, who pay nothing. After the pilot (in this case the promoter of the swindle) collects the money from passengers, each copilot then becomes a pilot, forming two new "airplanes" and taking half the passengers from the old group. Each passenger is then expected to recruit at least one new investor, motivated by the expectation of moving up the line, becoming a pilot, and then collecting a large sum. (Cross 1988, 115–16)

As the writers of the report point out, prosecution of such cases is especially difficult because their originators are usually "long gone" when they come to light, and those involved are unlikely to come forward because of embarrassment at being duped and awareness of little chance of getting their money back.

As widespread as they may be, there is no routinely published authoritative source on the number and variety of Ponzis, Pyramids, and other such scams committed by individuals in a given time period. The most detailed account of individual white-collar crime offenders is that periodically provided by the Bureau of Justice Statistics on federal law offenders. The most recent report contains data on those arrested for the four offenses defined above. The definitions of each are contained in Box 4.1.

Box 4.1 Definitions of White Collar Crimes

Counterfeiting: the manufacture or attempted manufacture of a copy or imitation of a negotiable instrument with value set by law or convention, or possession of such a copy without authorization and with intent to defraud by claiming the genuineness of the copy. Federal laws prohibit counterfeiting U.S. coins, currency, and securities; foreign money; domestic or foreign stamps; and official seals and certificates of Federal departments or agencies.

Embezzlement: the misappropriation, misapplication, or illegal disposal of property entrusted to an individual with intent to defraud the legal owner or intended beneficiary. Embezzlement differs from fraud in that it involves a breach of trust that existed between the victim and the offender, for example, an army supply officer who sold Government property for personal profit.

Forgery: the alteration of something written by another person or writing something that purports to be either the act of another or to have been executed at a time or place other than was in fact the case.

Fraud: the intentional misrepresentation of fact to unlawfully deprive a person of his or her property or legal rights, without damage to property or actual or threatened injury to persons. Perjury—a false statement under oath—is not included in the category of fraud.

Source: *White Collar Crime*, U.S. Department of Justice, Bureau of Justice Statistics, Special Report, Washington, DC, September 1987, 2.

Thus, between October 1, 1984, and September 30, 1985, 80,949 individuals suspected of white collar crimes were investigated by U.S. attorneys. More than half (55 percent) led to the filing of formal charges (the same as for non-white-collar offenses). The percentage of cases filed ranged from a low of 43 percent (for lending and credit fraud) to a high of 79 percent (for tax fraud). Table 4.1 shows convictions by number and percent for specified white-collar offenses.

Table 4.1
Federal White-Collar Crime Convictions, 1985

	Convictions	
Offense	Percent	Number
Fraud	100%	5,972
Tax	20	1,204
Lending and credit	9	540
Wire and mail	24	1,428
Other[a]	47	2,800
Embezzlement	100%	1,753
Bank	48	842
Government	10	173
U.S. Postal Service	18	313
Other[b]	24	425
Forgery	100%	2,014
U.S. Government documents	79	1,594
U.S. Postal Service	8	152
Securities	13	254
Other	1	14
Counterfeiting	100%	503

Source: *White Collar Crime*, U.S. Department of Justice, Bureau of Justice Statistics, Special Report, Washington, DC, September 1987, Table 1, p. 2.

[a]Includes false claims and statements; Government Program fraud; fraud concerning bankruptcy, commodities, securities, passports, or citizenship; and conspiracy to defraud.

[b]Includes labor organizations, Indian tribal organizations, and other federally protected victims.

Some 78 percent of the convictions were determined by a guilty plea (compared to 68 percent for non-white-collar defendants). Some 34 percent of those who pled not guilty were convicted (compared to 32 percent for non-white-collar defendants). Trial convictions were highest for those charged with tax fraud (63 percent) and counterfeiting (45 percent) and lowest for those charged with lending and credit fraud (25 percent) and embezzlement (26 percent).

As for sentencing, white-collar offenders were more apt to receive probation and less apt to be incarcerated than non-white- collar offenders. Fifty-six percent of the convicted received probation (compared to 31 percent for non-white-collar offenders) and 40 percent incarceration (compared to 54 percent for non-white-collar offenders). For those sentenced to incarceration the average sentence length was 29 months for white-collar offenders and 50 months for non-white-collar offenders. Of those sentenced to more than a year in prison, however, the median time served for those in both categories was the same (14 months for those with sentences of 1–2 years, 19 months for those with sentences of 25 months to 5 years, and 24 months for those with sentences of 61 months to 10 years).

Between 1980 and 1985, convictions for federal white-collar offenses rose 18 percent (compared to 43 percent for non-white- collar offenses). The "other fraud" category recorded the highest rate of increase (52 percent) and embezzlement the lowest (8 percent). There was a 1 percent change in the proportion of convicted white-collar offenders receiving incarceration (from 39 percent to 40 percent) and a five percent change in the proportion of convicted non-white-collar offenders receiving incarceration (from 49 percent to 54 percent). Lastly, while median sentence lengths imposed remained essentially unchanged for convicted non-white-collar offenders, those for white-collar offenders rose from 11 months in 1980 to 21 months in 1985 (the highest average increase was recorded by the "other fraud" category, from an average of 19 months in 1980 to 26 months in 1985).

For the two years examined (1984 and 1985), the characteristics of those charged with white-collar offenses were noticeably different from those charged with non-white-collar offenses. Overall, defendants in both categories were most likely to be male, white, non-Hispanic, under forty years of age, and unlikely to have ever attended college. The white-collar category, however, had higher proportions of females, nonwhites, and people over forty than the non-white-collar category. For specific white collar offenses, the following differences were noted:

1. Whites dominated the ranks of those charged with tax fraud (93 percent), lending and credit fraud (81%), counterfeiting (76 percent), and regulatory offenses (90 percent),

2. Females recorded higher proportionate rates for those charged with embezzlement (41 percent) and forgery (30 percent) than those charged with any white-collar offense (26 percent),
3. Those over age forty represented two-thirds of those arrested for tax fraud,
4. Those who had attended college were more likely to be charged with tax fraud, lending and credit fraud, and embezzlement than those who had not (of all those interviewed forgers were the least likely to have attended college. (1987, 7)

The same document contains information on federal regulatory offenses (individual acts in violation of the rules and regulations of regulatory agencies such as the Securities and Exchange Commission), data that shed some light on the extent of occupational white collar crime. For the most part, however, information on this type of white-collar crime must be culled from nonscholarly or journalistic sources.

Occupational White-Collar Crime

Between October 1, 1984, and September 30, 1985, U.S. attorneys investigated 1286 individuals suspected of a regulatory offense. Sixty-five percent of these led to a filing in a U.S. district court. The number and percentage of those convicted are contained in Table 4.2. As is evident, the proportion convicted was highest for import-and-export related offenses and lowest for agriculture and agricultural materials offenses.

Of all convicted white-collar offenders, regulatory offense violators were far and way the least likely to receive an incarceration sentence (at 17 percent their rate was substantially below the second lowest, the 28 percent recorded by embezzlers). Furthermore, convicted regulatory offense violators were much more likely than other white-collar violators to be fined (35 percent) only upon conviction. As stated in the report,

> The use of fines rather than incarceration for this group may reflect, among other factors, the corporate nature of these defendants. Although some statutes permit incarceration of corporate officers or placement of a corporation on probation (conditioned on restitution or other public acts), such practices are rarely used. (1987, 5)

Among federal white-collar offenders, those convicted of regulatory offense violations received the lowest imposed sentences (in 1985 the average sentence

Table 4.2
Federal White Collar Regulatory Offense Convictions, 1985

	Convictions	
Offense	Percent	Number
Total	100%	491
Import and Export[a]	26	127
Antitrust	23	114
Transportation	23	113
Food and Drug	17	84
Labor	8	37
Agriculture and agriculture materials	3	16

Source: *White Collar Crime*, U.S. Department of Justice, Bureau of Justice Statistics, Special Report, Washington, DC, September 1987, Table 1, p. 2.

[a]Includes customs violations and export of restricted defense materials and information; does not include drug offense.

imposed for all white- collar crimes was 42 months and for regulatory offense violators the average was 13 months) and served the least amount of time (in 1985 the average sentence length for regulatory offense violators was 6 months as compared to 18 months for all white collar offenses). Between 1980 and 1985, there was no discernable change in either overall average sentence length imposed (that is, including those sentenced to probation and prison) or average sentence length to incarceration imposed on those convicted of regulatory offenses. The evidence since 1985 indicates continuation of this pattern of relative leniency shown this category of white-collar crime.

Important documented occupational white-collar crimes since 1985 occurred in both government and business. In 1986, for example, eleven Boston area policemen were indicted for illegally obtaining, selling and manipulating police examinations over a period of eight years (*Boston Globe*, July 31, 1986). In 1988, two former Beech Nut executives were convicted of hundreds of counts of consumer fraud involving the marketing and selling of bogus apple juice (advertised as 100 percent pure but in reality a blend of water, sugar, and chemicals) meant for babies (*Boston Globe*, June 17, 1988).

In 1988, *Time* magazine referred to a white-collar crime wave and identified an array of incidents indicative of the claim—from a case surrounding the conviction of a U.S. congressman to a "Medicaid scam," "Pentagon payola," a "rental-car rip-off," a case of securities fraud, and a case of "insider trading." Twenty-year Congressman Mario Biaggi (a New York Democrat) was found guilty of extortion and accepting $50,000 for influencing the procurement of a defense contract by a Bronx-based firm. The Medicaid incident involved a Queens, New York physician and his father who purchased blood from poor people (including drug addicts) at 50 cents a sample and then billed Medicaid as much as $2000 each for the cost of testing the blood of alleged Medicaid patients. In the "Pentagon payola" case, some eighty-nine employees from Unisys, a computer manufacturing firm, were fired and Pentagon officials charged with procurement fraud and bid rigging. The "rental-car rip off" involved the Hertz corporation. The company pleaded guilty to overcharging customers and insurance companies for the cost of repairing damaged cars. Hertz's accident-control manager and some twenty other employees were involved in a scheme to bilk customers by charging them retail prices for car repairs made at wholesale rates and for work never done. The securities laws violators included five top officials of the investment firm of Princeton/Newport and a former employee of the Wall Street trading firm of Drexel Burnham Lambert. The six were indicted on criminal charges by a federal grand jury for tax evasion by means of fraudulent stock deals. The insider trading case involved the stealing of prepublication copies of *Business Week* magazine by sixteen individuals. "In the most fully investigated case so far, former Merrill Lynch Broker William Dillon is believed to have paid employees at a magazine printing plant in Connecticut to give him copies of *Business Week* a full day before the issue was available to the general public so he could buy stocks recommended in the 'Inside Wall Street' column before the price went up" (1988, 28). For an initial outlay of $30 per copy, Mr. Dillon was able to make profits of $2000 or more a week.

Far and away the most potentially menacing data-accessing offenses are those involving the computer. Minimum annual losses due to computer crime are estimated to be about $100 million. Rod Willis (1986, 43) identifies the following five types of computer crime: (1) computer *vandalism* or destroying or damaging computer hardware and software (motives range from acts of terrorism to efforts to destroy incriminating evidence); (2) *theft of information* (stealing an employer's data and selling it to a competitor); (3) *use of computers for personal benefit* (using an employers equipment for one's own purposes, monetary and otherwise); (4) *burglary by modem* (using the telephone lines via computer to illegally access a firm's products); and (5) *financial fraud* (creating false accounts, hiding accounts, "losing" accounts, and so on). All, some more than others, are as likely to be committed by individuals acting on an ad hoc basis or in the course of their occupation. Whatever the situation, and to paraphrase Willis, widespread access to computer hardware and software provides seemingly limitless opportunities for the criminally inclined. As he puts it (1986, 43), "equipped with a PC, a modem, a telephone, and a few passwords, a computer hacker can electronically transfer millions of dollars in less than a second to an account anywhere in the world—and then program the computer to hide the tracks." The ability to transmit funds electronically quickly over great distances played a crucial role in the most important occupationally linked white-collar crime episodes of the past decade, if not the century, namely, the insider trading and savings and loan Scandals. The immensity of the combined impact of the two on the nation's economic and general well-being are difficult to estimate but are most certainly indicative of the importance of white-collar crime.

The Inside Traders

Essentially, insider trading is "the buying and selling of stock by officers, directors, major shareholders, and other people with an ear to the boardroom door" (Boland 1985, 12). According to John Boland, a journalist who has long studied the subject, insider trading has a long history, and the wise investor is one who follows the lead of its practitioners.

Any investor would like to have accurate foreknowledge of the best time to buy and sell stocks to maximize earnings and minimize losses. Theoretically, that is, in a truly open and competitive stock market, all "players" should have equal access to generally available information prerequisite to investment decision making. In such an ideal world, goal attainment, profit making, is based on adherence to principles ensuring "a level playing field." The problem is that in the "real world" goal attainment has a way of becoming more important than means compliance. Accordingly, approximation of the ideal of fair and open competition on the athletic field or the stock market requires regulation by those obligated only to maintenance of the rules of fair play. Before the Securities Exchange Act (1934) and the subsequent creation of the Securities & Exchange Commission, securities regulation was basically nonexistent. One was expected to exploit any and all available means to accomplish desired goals. Colluding with insiders, pooling knowledge to anticipate rising and falling stock prices, was expected and sanctioned regardless of the consequences (for shareholders, company employees, uninvolved citizens, the general social and economic well-being). In a recent work on the banking empire founded by J.P. Morgan, Ron Chernow tells us that

> Morgan bank partners were in an excellent position to take advantage of insider trading, which was a common vice of the 1920s, and not illegal lax Stock Exchange rules and meager corporate reports make inside information more valuable, and investors milked their Wall Street friends for news. Inside tips didn't guarantee success_ many investors perished on Black Thursday clutching them—yet they were profitable enough to be considered a major perk of Wall Street employment. Between 1927 and 1931, the bank participated

> in more than fifty stock pools, which weren't outlawed until the New Deal. (1990, 305–6 and 7)

Pools, syndicates, cliques of one kind or another were formed not only to take better advantage of the general market but also to "gang up" on the competition. In a noted work on America's early financiers, Gustavus Myers states that Daniel Drew, James Fisk, Jr. and Jay Gould "formed a coalition against [Cornelius] Vanderbilt; they betrayed and then outgeneraled him at every turn; proved themselves of a superior cunning; sold him large quantities of spurious stock; excelled him in corruption; defrauded more than $50,000,000, and succeeded—Gould, at any rate—in keeping most of the plunder" (1936, 308). The same kind of cabalistic, the end justifies the means competition, albeit in only slightly less crude form, is apparent in the insider trading scandal of the 1980s. The forces leading to the economic collapse of the late 1980s are remarkably comparable to those leading to the economic collapse of the late 1920s. But, unlike the earlier collapse, the later one was witnessed by a regulatory agency, the Securities and Exchange Commission, whose job it is to prevent a recurrence of the problem.

The Securities and Exchange Commission (SEC) is a five-member board with an appointed chair (the first chair was Joseph P. Kennedy, President John F. Kennedy's father). The commission is empowered by law to enforce certain rules regarding the sale and distribution of securities. In particular, section 10(b) of the Securities Exchange Act of 1934 states that

> it shall be unlawful for any person, directly or indirectly, by the use of any means or instrumentality of interstate commerce or the mails, or of any facility of any national securities exchange, to use or employ, in connection with the purchase or sale of any security registered on a national securities exchange or any security not so registered, any manipulative device or contrivance in contravention of such rules and regulations as the Commission may prescribe as necessary or appropriate in the public interest or for the protection of investors.

Further, rule 10b–5 states that

> it shall be unlawful for any person, directly or indirectly, by use of any means or instrumentality of interstate commerce, or of the mails, or of any facility of any national securities exchange, (a) to employ any device, scheme, or artifice to defraud, (b) to make any untrue statement of a material fact or to omit to state a material fact necessary in order to make the statements made, in the light of the circumstances under which they were made, not misleading, or (c)

> to engage in any act, practice, or course of business which operates or would operate as a fraud or deceit upon any person, in connection with the purchase or sale of any security. (Boland, 45–6).

As useful as the fraud forbidding language was in the effort to curb securities violations generally (especially, the prohibition against the use of "any manipulative device or contrivance" in purchasing or selling securities), by 1980 many felt it needed to be reformed to target insider trading more precisely. The result was an amendment to the Securities and Exchange Act of 1934, the Insider Trading Sanctions Act of 1984. Key parts of the act are the following:

> Section 2(A) Whenever it shall appear to the Commission that any person has violated any provision of this title or the rules or regulations thereunder by purchasing or selling a security while in *possession of material nonpublic information* in a transaction (i) on or through a broker or dealer, and (ii) which is not part of a public offering by an issuer of securities other than standardized options, the Commission may bring an action in a United States district court to seek, and the court shall have jurisdiction to impose, a civil penalty to be paid by such person, or any person aiding and abetting the violation of such person. The amount of such penalty shall be determined by the court in light of the facts and circumstances, but shall not exceed *three times the profit gained or loss avoided* as a result of such unlawful purchase or sale, and shall be payable into the Treasury of the United States. Section 3. Section 32 of the Exchange Act of 1934 is amended by striking "$10,000" from subsection (a) and inserting in lieu thereof "$100,000." (U.S. Code, Congressional and Administrative News, 1984, 1264, italics added)

At present, then, the SEC says that "insider trading refers generally to the act of purchasing or selling securities in breach of a fiduciary duty or a relationship of trust or confidence, while in possession of material nonpublic information about an issuer or the trading market for an issuer's securities" (Langevoort 1987, 10). By a "breach of a fiduciary duty" is meant the breaking of a responsibility not to convey confidential monetary information by an employee, agent, or officer of a firm. "Material" information refers to data possessed by the insider about the issuer of stock that would, if made generally available to investors, likely cause "a 'revaluation' of the stock" (Langevoort 1987, 157). "Nonpublic" information is that which "is not generally available to the investing public" (Langevoort 1987, 168).

Members of the insider-trading ring exposed in the 1980s were company officers predisposed to put selfish monetary gain above adherence to fiduciary responsibility and the rules and regulations of the SEC. They came together from different levels of monetary influence.

At the lowest level was Dennis B. Levine, among the first to be caught and charged by the SEC. According to Levine, he and Robert Wilkis, later an investment banker with Lazard Freres, agreed to share privileged information for personal monetary gain early in their careers. As Levine tells it,

> Throughout my college and graduate studies, I do not believe I ever heard the word "ethics." In the big business environment of the late 70s, morality was not an issue. The liberal, radical, humanistic 60s were gone and society was veering toward materialism. Trading on the basis of inside information is wrong. Instead I thought: Here's a way I can make some extra money. (1991, 57)

When Levine was employed by Smith Barney, he accepted an assignment in Paris. The experience led to the idea of concealing illegal earnings in a confidential Swiss bank with a subsidiary in the Bahamas. Accordingly, he and Wilkis "hammered out a strategy that, if we had dared commit to paper, would have looked like this: 1. each of us will only trade on the other's information, 2. we will never share tips with other members of our family or with friends, and we will keep our activities secret even from our wives, 3. we will trade stocks only through secret foreign accounts, 4. we will share information only in person, and when we speak to each other by phone, we will refer to one another by a code name so that no one will notice our association, and 5. we will use common sense" (1991, 73). But ambition and greed soon outstripped caution and others were recruited, most notably Ilan Reich, a young lawyer and a member of a prestigious New York law firm, and Ira Sokolow, a CPA and employee of Shearson Lehman.

In time, Levine met and was recruited by arbitrageur[1] Ivan Boesky. Boesky's other noteworthy recruit was Martin Siegel, at the time an employee of the Wall Street firm of Kidder, Peabody and an expert in defending firms against hostile takeovers. Siegel also traded inside information with another arbitrageur, Robert Freeman, of the Wall Street firm of Goldman, Sachs. Siegel was later employed by Drexel Burnham Lambert and had an office next door to Dennis Levine. The major figure at Drexel was the young "junk bond"[2] tycoon Michael Milken.

Journalist James Stewart claims that at the height of his career Ivan Boesky "controlled $3 billion worth of stock purchasing power, enough to strike terror into almost any corporation with a single phone call" (1991 photograph 1). "Milken," says Stewart, "was the most powerful man in American finance—and one of the richest, with earnings in one year of $550 million" (1991 photograph 2). Milken and Boesky developed a particularly close investment relationship that included violation of SEC regulations such as those prohibiting insider trading, stock price manipulation, and stock "parking" ("Stock parking occurs when an investor disguises ownership of securities by arranging for another firm or individual to hold or trade them on the investor's behalf," *The Guide to American Law Supplement 1990*, 163).

When caught, inside trading-ring members, as part of their negotiated pleas (none pleaded not guilty and went to trial) with federal prosecutors, were expected to cooperate by implicating one another and others. The first to be treated in this manner was Dennis Levine. In May 1986 he was arrested and charged with illicitly acquiring $12.6 million by means of the insider trading of fifty-four stocks. He pleaded guilty to four felony counts, agreed to pay fines and penalties amounting to $11.6 million and received a two-year prison sentence. He completed his sentence in September 1988 and has founded a financial advisory firm, Adasar Group.

Soon after Levine's plea, Robert Wilkis, who was then with E.F. Hutton, was offered the same terms as Levine. He was able to corroborate Levine's information concerning the involvement of others, Boesky in particular. He was required to disgorge $3.3 million and received a sentence of a year and a day in prison and 5 years probation. He was released in March 1987 after serving 8 months in prison.

Ilan Reich received the same sentence as Wilkis and was fined $485,000. He entered prison with Wilkis, and they were discharged at the same time. After release, Reich entered the real estate business.

Robert Freeman pleaded guilty to one felony and was not required to cooperate with federal investigators to aid the identification or corroborate the testimony of others. He served a 4 month sentence and was released in August 1990. Unlike many of the others, he was not barred from the investment business.

Martin Siegel pleaded guilty to two felony charges of insider trading. He was required to disgorge $4.25 million and received a sentence of 2 months in prison and 5 years probation. He also signed a consent order barring him from future employment in the securities industry. He was released from prison in August 1990.

Implicated by Levine, Ivan Boesky pleaded guilty to a felony charge of conspiring to file false claims with the SEC. As part of his agreement to cooperate with federal prosecutors' investigations of others, he was barred from future employment in the securities industry and required to disgorge $50 million in profits gained by insider trading. He was also fined an additional $50 million and sentenced to 3 years in prison. In 1988, Reuters released an article under the title "Boesky in 'Country Club' Jail." The prison in question was the federal minimum-security facility in Lompoc, California. According to the Reuters release, "the prison, 150 miles north of Los Angeles, has open air television so prisoners can watch and work on their suntans at the same time, and daily deliveries of the New York Times and Wall Street Journal" (*Boston Globe*,

March 25, 1988). Boesky was released in December 1989, and a photograph shows him looking gaunt, heavily bearded, and anything like someone who has had an easy time of it. In March 1991 a federal judge approved the settlement of lawsuits against Boesky by cheated investors to the amount of $46.8 million.

At the center of so much, Boesky identified confederates and the man federal prosecutors waited until last to charge: Michael Milkin. In September 1988 the SEC filed a complaint against Milken containing such charges as stock price manipulation in collusion with Boesky, advising Boesky to purchase numerous shares in a company to aid a Drexel client's purchase of it, advising Boesky to purchase numerous shares in a company to attract prospective company buyers, advising Boesky to buy stock in a company to increase the cost of a client's transaction and thereby increase Drexel's fee, advising a friend to buy a large number of a company's stock so that Drexel could persuade it to avoid underwriting with a competitor, and having Boesky purchase a company the day after a meeting in which the bid of another prospective buyer was discussed. Milken eventually pleaded guilty to six felony counts involving "conspiracy, fraud, and assisting in filing of a false tax return" (*The Guide to American Law, Supplement 1991*, 348). Before sentencing him, Judge Kimba Wood made the following statement:

> When a man of your power in the financial world, at the head of the most important department of one of the most important investment banking houses in this country, repeatedly conspires to violate, and violates, securities and tax laws in order to achieve more power and wealth for himself and his wealthy clients, and commits financial crimes that are particularly hard to detect, a significant prison term is required in order to deter others. (Stewart 1991, 442)

She then proceeded to sentence him to 10 years in prison. He entered prison in March 1991 and was paroled in March 1993. His guilty plea also required him to pay a fine of $200 million and to disgorge $400 million to reimburse victimized investors. Although Milkin has avoided being charged with anything connected directly to the savings and loan scandal, large purchases of his junk bonds by failed institutions have been documented.

The Savings and Loan Exploiters

As with insider trading, the savings and loan scandal is a repeat product of pre-Depression circumstances. In the 1920s, savings and loans were largely unregulated. What regulation existed occurred at the state level, and many states did not have regulatory agencies. Savings and loans, or thrifts, were primarily locally owned and managed institutions concerned with attracting depositors and making mortgage loans. "In contrast with large commercial banks, operating out of skyscrapers in large cities and distant from the concerns of working people, S&Ls were grass-roots banking—a frugal way to save and to provide homeownership. That is why they are known commonly as 'thrifts'" (Waldman 1990, 15). There were more than 12,000 S&Ls in existence in the 1920s.

Box 4.2 Just Color it Criminal by Art Buchwald

There is always someone questioning the status quo. This week it was my friend Alonzo Powdama, who believes that we make a mistake by referring to many criminal activities as white-collar crimes.

"I suppose you'd say Michael Milken committed a white-collar crime?" he asked me.

"He must have," I said. "He did it in his office."

"But it was the crime of the century. People lost millions of dollars investing in his junk bonds. Many were widows and orphans," Alonzo said.

"They were greedy widows and orphans. They were always going for a higher interest rate, and then when they lost their money they cried crocodile tears."

"Why isn't stealing other people's money through an invest-ment bank, an S&L or a regular bank the same as holding them up on the street"? Alonzo wanted to know.

I replied, "The difference is in the quality of the criminal. Most stick-up men are sloppy and do not observe the dress code. They carry weapons and resort to violence. White-collar robbers are pillars of the community. They hold up their victims with calculators and computers. You can't put white-collar and blue-collar criminals on the same volleyball court."

"What about this one?" Alonzo asked. "The defense companies, including some of the largest aviation manufacturers, have been caught cheating the government on their contracts. Some did such shoddy work that it could cost the lives of pilots flying the planes. Is that a white-collar crime or first-degree murder?"

I replied, "We would have to designate it as white-collar."

Alonzo was agitated. "I'm for abolishing the use of the term white-collar crime. If you embezzle someone's pension, which he worked for all his life, it's rape."

"That's ridiculous. The reason that the legal system uses white-collar crime as a designation is that it helps the judge know where to send the wrongdoers. You can't send a white-collar criminal to a low-class prison."

"Why not?" Alonzo asked.

"Because you want the punishment to fit the crime. You have to distinguish between the sleazeballs who sell dope on the street and MBAs who launder their money in skyscrapers. White-collar criminals are different from you and me, Alonzo, and must be shown respect."

"What makes them different?" he wanted to know.

"They have better lawyers. The worst thing you could do to prevent white-collar felonies is to single out business criminals for serious punishment. If you take their tennis courts away from them at Allenwood, they'll go back to crime as soon as they come out."

Alonzo was not convinced. "What I don't like is that white-collar criminals get to plea-bargain. We had a bank in Washington where all the Hispanic people put their savings. It turned out to be a phony bank and was not insured by the U.S. Government. The people who started the bank stole them blind. Why should that be termed a white-collar crime?"

"Because," I said, "except for taking someone's life's savings, no one really got hurt."

Source: *Boston Globe*, January 17, 1991, p. 13. Reprinted by permission

During the 1920s, as in the 1980s, profitable investing seemed on a never ending upward spiral. "During the roaring Twenties speculation reached a fever as bankers sucked in deposits with high interest rates and gambled away the funds on risky or fraudulent investments" (Waldman 1990, 16). When the end came in 1929, and because accounts were uninsured, depositors were compelled to withdraw their money quickly before there was nothing left. More than 1700 thrifts failed and depositors lost an estimated $200 million.

As part of the effort to restore the economy and the viability of S&Ls, President Herbert Hoover in 1932 signed into law the Federal Home Loan Bank Act. The act created a regulatory governing structure for S&Ls. At the top of the administrative hierarchy was the Federal Home Loan Bank Board (FHLBB). Below the FHLBB were twelve regional federal home loan banks (FHLBs) and below these were the governing boards of individual S&Ls. It was optional for an S&L to be chartered by a state or the federal government. Deeming this measure insufficient, Congress sought to attract depositors by creating the Federal Savings and Loan Insurance Corporation (FSLIC), which it empowered to insure accounts up to $5000. Funding of the FSLIC was to be by member institutions rather than the federal government. For the first fifty years of its operation, the system, by all accounts, worked very well.

Problems began in the 1960s when inflation began noticeably to increase the price of homes. Congress reacted by limiting S&L deposit interest rates. "Congress' reasoning was that if S&Ls didn't have to pay too much for deposits, they wouldn't have to charge too much to the homeowners who borrowed from them" (Pizzo, Fricker, & Muolo 1989, 10). The cap on interest rates began to be a problem in the 1970s, again because of inflation. As Pizzo et al. indicate, by 1979 the inflation rate was 13.3 percent, while S&Ls were restricted to paying depositors 5.5 percent. Further, with the creation of the higher-interest rate money market and the development of electronic means to invest nationally and internationally, there was a serious drain on S&L deposits. As Pizzo et al. tell it,

> The outflow from thrifts quickly reached crisis proportions. In 1972 the nation's savings and loans had a combined worth of $16.7 billion. By 1980 that figure had plummeted to a *negative* net worth of $17.5 billion, and 85 percent of savings and loans were losing money. Regulators began to warn that if nothing were done, all thrifts would collapse by the end of 1986. (1989, 11)

In 1980, Congress reacted by passing a deregulation bill, the Depository Institutions Deregulation and Monetary Control Act, whose purpose it was to phase out restrictions on the rate of interest S&Ls could pay. Further, the insured amount on accounts was increased from $40,000 to $100,000. While these measures attracted new deposits and money available for loans, they caused a problem. A gap was created between the higher rate of interest paid on short-term loans and the lower rate of interest charged on long-term mortgage loans. This led to a S&L deficit of some $3.3 billion in the first half of 1982. To counter this problem, the Garn-St. Germain (its authors were Republican Senator Jake Garn of Utah and Democratic Congressman Fernand St. Germain of Rhode Island) Depository Institutions Act was created and signed later that year by President Ronald Reagan.

The stated purpose of the Garn-St.Germain Bill was to enable S&Ls to generate the funds necessary for financial solvency and continuous growth. It allowed thrifts (1) to invest in nonresidential real estate (up to 40 percent of their assets); (2) to lend as much as 15 percent of their capital to a single borrower; (3) not to be required to maintain a balance between the amount loaned a developer and the value of the purchased property; (4) to set their own interest rates; and (5) to offer money market accounts and withdrawals without penalty.Other regulatory changes in 1982 and 1983 allowed S&Ls to reduce the amount of their net worth in capital (from the previous 3 percent to 1 percent), to offer 100 percent financing (one could borrow without putting up a single dollar of one's own), and to be owned by single individuals or commercial firms (previously owners were local investors).

All this deregulation not only improved the ability of thrifts to exploit investment opportunities but to improve the ability of investors to exploit them. Five years after Garn-St. Germain, 500 of 3200 S&Ls were insolvent and another 500 nearly so. The cost to taxpayers to repair the damage was estimated (in 1987) as nearly $23 billion. The question is, how did the exploitation occur and who did it? The question is unlikely ever to be answered completely. But sufficient material is available to provide a more than adequate partial explanation.

To begin with, the billions lost by poorly managed thrifts indicate that deregulation enabled them to attract large sums of money. The vehicle for this was jumbo certificates of deposit (CDs). Government-insured blocks of $100,000 at competitive interest rates were created to attract wealthy investors anywhere. Brokerage houses began to pool large sums of money (not simply that of individuals but also insurance company, union, and pension funds) and transfer them to S&Ls offering the highest rate of interest regardless of who they were owned by or the quality of their management. The huge amounts of capital involved attracted a variety of people to S&L ownership and investment—from the experienced to the inexperienced, from the scrupulous to the unscrupulous.

Many attracted to S&L ownership or management after deregulation had backgrounds in real estate development. Some of the techniques used by the unscrupulous to exploit the situation include (1) *land flipping* (the buying and selling of a property by conspirators to increase its value and profitability rapidly); (2) *Time-bomb loans* (100 percent loans unlikely ever to payoff given to a developer to acquire a property in order to enable both parties to borrow more from others); (3) *cash for trash* (a thrift agrees to a loan with the proviso that the borrower purchase a repossessed property: "the borrower gets the loan; the S&L gets rid of a probably worthless piece of property, and gets to cover up the loss on its books" (Waldman 1990, 37); and (4) *straw loans* (when a borrower "fronts" for another to circumvent restrictions on allowable loan amounts to a single individual).

To date, Texas has had the greatest number of S&L failures and some of the most notorious offenders. Among the latter is Don Dixon. He gained control of Vernon Savings & Loan in 1982, and over the next four years increased its assets from $82.6 million to $1.3 billion. When regulators took possession of Vernon in 1987, its losses were estimated at $1.3 billion. In December 1991 Dixon was convicted on twenty-three counts of bank fraud. He spent millions of the firm's money on airplanes, helicopters, a beach house in California, prostitutes for clients, and sundry other items that he "wrote off" as business expenses. Despite having cost taxpayers in excess of a $1 billion, Dixon received the modest sentence of 5 years in prison. He was also fined $600,000 and required to do 500 hours of community service within two years after being released. He was paroled in December 1992. Among those with whom Dixon had dealings was Erv Hansen, the president of Centennial Savings & Loan, based in Santa Rosa, California.

Unlike Dixon, whose background qualifications were limited to real estate development, Hansen was an experienced banker. Like Dixon, he is described by Pizzo et al. as having been unscrupulously devoted to self-aggrandizement.

Soon after becoming president of Centennial in 1980, Hansen promoted Beverly Haines, a receptionist who began as a teller in 1977, to executive vice president in charge of the firm's money desk, the position through which came all large deposits from pension funds and all other brokered accounts. Additionally, Hansen befriended two ambitious developers, "Sid" Shah, an engineer employed by a heavy construction company and owner of a fledgling development company, and Nicholaas Sandmann, a Dutch investor wishing to develop the 1000-acre George Ranch site. Regulators found that loan money began circulating among the three in July 1982. Sandmann was loaned $5.4 million, and Shah's company was paid a finder's fee of $150,000. "Later the George Ranch deal would collapse in a flurry of defaults and allegations of fraud, inside deals, and kickbacks (Pizzo et al. 1989, 29).

When regulators assumed control of Centennial in 1985, its assets, at $404 million, had increased 1000 percent in thirty-two months. But over 80 percent of its deposits were in high-cost brokered jumbo CDs and more than a third of its loans in high-risk-firm or crony owned projects. Beverly Haines was charged with embezzling $1.6 million in a check-kiting scheme. To avoid a lengthy prison sentence she agreed to cooperate with investigators. Investigators met with Hansen and informed him of the pending charges against him.

> Some 26 in all were contemplated, including charges that he had embezzled at least $872,000. The investigation had revealed that Hansen had routinely used his institution's funds to fuel his own extravagant life-style, taking $20,000 here, $25,000 there, $55,000 for antiques, $137,000 for jewelry, $80,000 for his taxes, $85,000 for cars, $25,000 for art, $45,000 for a vacation. He had arrogantly used Centennial's treasury for his own personal petty cash drawer. (Pizzo et al. 1989, 55)

As fate would have it, Hansen died before formal charges could be brought against him. Beverly Haines was given a 5 year prison sentence but was released after serving only 67 days. Shah and Sandmann went uncharged. As well publicized as it was, the Centennial Savings and Loan case paled by comparison to another case involving a California thrift, the Lincoln Savings and Loan and the activities of its owner, lawyer Charles Keating.

Keating's real estate company, American Continental Corporation (ACC), acquired Lincoln Savings and Loan in 1983. At the time, Michael Milken's Drexel Burnham owned more than a 10 percent interest in ACC. According to Martin Mayer (1992, 172) this information was required by California law to be reported before the sale of Lincoln, but it wasn't. Mayer suggests that Keating acquired Lincoln as a means of funding various teetering real estate projects in Salt Lake City, Seattle, and Phoenix. "To support Keating's varied speculations," says Mayer, "Lincoln grew from about $1 billion in 1983 to almost $6 billion at the time of its seizure by the government in 1989" (1992, 173). The estimated cost to taxpayers of the thrift's failure was estimated to be $2.5 billion.

Keating, as too many others, was inclined to invest large amounts in risky ventures. He invested $100 million of his S&L's depositors' money in a Boesky owned risk-arbitrage fund. He also invested heavily in junk bonds. Mayer (1992: 185) reports that when Lincoln's junk bond holdings were examined in 1988, 77 percent were found to be in "bonds that not only were not rated as 'investment grade' securities by Moody's or Standard & Poor's—they were not rated at all!"

In 1984, concerned about the propensity of thrifts to invest so much in risky ventures such as high-yield junk bonds, SEC Chairman Ed Gray proposed limiting direct investments to 10 percent of a firm's assets or 200 percent of its net worth. Keating's efforts to block the proposal from becoming law led to a congressional lobbying effort involving many, but especially "The Keating Five": Senators John Glenn of Ohio, Alan Cranston of California, Donald Riegle of Michigan, John McCain and Dennis DiConcini of Arizona. Largely through their efforts, Chairman Gray's proposal was not accepted prior to Lincoln's seizure. When regulators seized control of the S&L in 1989, however, and found evidence of bank fraud, the ethical nature of the five senators efforts on behalf of Keating came under question. Keating's campaign contributions to the five totaled some $1.4 million. Cranston received $982,000, DeConcini $48,000, Riegle $76,000, McCain $112,000, and Glenn $200,000 (Waldman 1990. 95–6). A Senate Ethics Committee hearing held during the Gulf War tarnished the reputations of all five, but only Cranston was singled out for engaging in "impermissible conduct." In Cranston's case, the Committee found that "fund raising and official activities were substantially linked" (Carlson 1991, 69).

Of all Keating's activities, however, the one that attracted the most attention was the direct sale of some $235 million worth of unsecured notes or junk bonds to 23,000 primarily elderly customers. Customers were led to believe that the notes were insured. According to Waldman (1990, 98), an internal memorandum informed employees that the "weak, meek and ignorant are always good targets" and included the following sample customer name and address: Name: Edna Gert Snidlip, 1 Geriatric Way, Retiredville, CA 92627. When Lincoln filed for bankruptcy in 1989, the notes became worthless.

In September 1990 Keating was indicted for securities fraud. At his arraignment the judge set bail at $5 million fearing that he might flee the country. At the time, according to Waldman (1990, 135), Lincoln bondholders feared that Keating was hiding some $100 million in bank accounts in Switzerland, Panama, and the Bahamas. By July 1991 Keating's case had yet to come to trial He was, however, free, having had his bail reduced to $300,000. Claiming that he was broke upon being arrested and jailed, Keating was, nevertheless, able to make substantial mortgage payments. As to the source of the money, *Forbes* magazine (July 8, 1991) reported the following:

> Some of the money seems to be coming from Keating's son-in-law, Gary Hall, a Phoenix ophthalmologist and former director of Keating's American Continental Corp. According to informed sources, before American Continental's Lincoln Savings & Loan was seized in April 1989, hundreds of thousands of dollars were shifted from the thrift to an American Continental unit called Medema Homes of Utah, and eventually to Hall. It was Hall, apparently, who posted Keating's bail last year.

In January 1993, a federal jury found Keating guilty on 73 counts of fraud and racketeering. In July, he was sentenced to prison for twelve years and seven months. The sentence was to run concurrently with an earlier ten year sentence for violating California's securities laws (*Facts on File* July 15, 1993, 521).

The individuals identified here represent only a handful of the 250 S&Ls (the number regularly increases) that failed before enactment of bailout legislation (the Financial Institutions Reform, Recovery and Enforcement Act of 1989). The unfortunate number of unscrupulous and law violating that were attracted to S&L ownership and management as a consequence of deregulation was made possible by the absence of concern with adequate regulation of the newly achieved freedom of the thrifts. No serious thought was given to the possible negative consequences of abrupt and total deregulation. The lessons of the past, the factors that led to the banking industry's collapse in the 1920s, were ignored seemingly because of ideological commitment to replacement of New Deal control mechanisms with policies and programs more in line with laissez-faire capitalism. The consequences were undoubtedly predictable to any number of congressional lawmakers. That nothing was done until after the collapse is traceable to a number of possible factors, among the more troublesome of which is the fact that so many in Congress were recipients of thrift largess. As Waldman (1990, 60) states, "the S&L disaster couldn't have happened without a posse of thrift allies on Capitol Hill—lawmakers purchased by campaign contributions, personal gifts, entertainment, and speech fees." Corporate PACs (political action committees) are the primary source of lobby funds, and it is to the subject of organizational white collar-crime that the discussion now turns.

Organizational White-Collar Crime

The first major study of organizational white-collar crime was undertaken by Edwin Sutherland; the results were published in 1949. Because of limited resources Sutherland studied the criminal records of only seventy of the nation's largest nonfinancial corporations. His data were derived from court decisions (federal, state, and local) and the records of regulatory agencies such as the Federal Trade Commission (FTC), Interstate Commerce Commission (ICC), Securities and Exchange Commission (SEC), National Labor Relations Board (NLRB), and Food and Drug Administration (FDA). He recognized that such sources provided only an indication of the criminal actions of corporations because many decisions were not published in accessible documents: many charges were settled out of court and were not recorded; many suits, for a variety of reasons (e.g., staff and budgetary limitations), were dropped after preliminary investigation; the federal practice of not identifying offending firms by name; and an inability to identify the subsidiaries of the seventy corporations.

Despite the limitations, Sutherland found the firms to have had a great number of decisions rendered against them for violations such as restraint of trade (price fixing), misrepresentations in advertising, infringement of patents, trademarks, and copyrights, unfair labor practices, rebates, financial fraud and violations of trust, violations of war regulations, and "miscellaneous offenses." The seventy companies accounted for 980 decisions (an average of 14 each). The range was from 1 to 50. The most frequent violations were for restraint of trade (307 or 31 percent of the total) and infringement of patents, trademarks, and copyrights (22 or 23 percent of the total). Most of the decisions were rendered by courts (158 by criminal courts, 298 by civil courts, and 129 by equity courts). The remaining 397 decisions were determined by administrative actions of one sort or another.

Sixty percent of the seventy corporations had been convicted in criminal courts. These forty-two firms averaged four convictions each. "The frequency of these convictions of large corporations under criminal jurisdiction," Sutherland stressed, "might be sufficient to demonstrate the fallacy in the conventional theories that crime is due to poverty or to the personal and social pathologies connected with poverty" (1949, 25).

At the time, Sutherland's work was generally acknowledged to be a path-breaking contribution, but it did not lead to an immediate and thorough study of organizational white-collar crime. The next major study of corporate crime in America (discussed below) was not published until 1979. Between Sutherland and the 1979 study, interest in the subject can be traced to the radical critique of America's political and economic motives for involvement in the Vietnam war.

The critical sensitivities of scholars were raised by evidence of a concentration of economic power in a few multinational corporations. Federal data, for example, showed that in 1960, the 28 manufacturing firms with assets of $1 billion or more accounted for 37 percent of the net profits of all manufacturers. Less than 2 percent of the nation's manufacturing firms accounted for 89 percent of the net profits of all.

Such concentrated wealth was related to the prevalence of conglomeration, or the merging of firms engaged in unrelated lines of work. The growth of the corporate conglomerate suggested to many the impotence of antitrust laws. Mark Green (1972, 10–11), a colleague of Ralph Nader's, wryly observed that "oddly, the merger waves of the past 80 years have each followed the passage of antitrust legislation aimed at slowing them down."

In an analysis of the record of the Justice Department's Antitrust Division, law Professor Richard Posner (1970) found that between 1890 and 1969, it had instituted 693 criminal cases. Seventy percent, or 536 cases, had led to convictions. But 70 to 80 percent were the result of a *nolo contendere* plea. Such a plea amounts to an admission of guilt but allows the defendant to challenge any future allegations that may be made.

The failure of antitrust law-enforcement was most evident in the case of General Electric (GE). Jerry DeMuth (1972) pointed out that since 1911 the company had been involved in sixty-four antitrust cases. In 1911 General Electric was found guilty of price fixing and "eliminating competition with respect to light bulbs by concealing its stock ownership of ostensibly independent companies and using tie-in contracts and other arrangements" (DeMuth, 61). In 1937 the FTC ordered GE and four other companies to "cease and desist" fixing prices on turbine generators. The company was convicted of the same offense in 1960.

The 1960 case is referred to as the GE affair, but it involved virtually the entire electrical industry. General Electric and thirty other firms were indicted for conspiring to fix prices on $7 billion worth of equipment. It was learned that the conspirators regularly held clandestine meetings. As *Fortune* editor Richard Smith (1963, 107) described it,

> they had their own lingo and their own standard operating procedures. The attendance list was known as the "Christmas-card list," meetings as "choir practices." Companies had code numbers—G.E. 1, Westinghouse 2, Allis-Chalmers 3, Federal Pacific 7—which were used in conjunction with first names when calling a conspirator at home for price information ("This is Bob, what is 7's bid?"). At the hotel meetings it as S.O.P. not to list one's employer when registering and not to have breakfast with fellow conspirators in the dining room. The G.E. men observed two additional precautions: never be the ones who kept the records and never tell G.E.'s lawyers anything. Twenty-eight of the 45 defendants were convicted. Each received a 30-day jail sentence, but 23 were given suspended sentences. A total of $1,924,500 in fines was assessed—$437,000 on G.E., $372,000 on Westinghouse, and individual fines ranging from $1,000 to $12,000. The convicted were not those at the top of

the company hierarchy. They tended to be vice-presidents or division heads.

The 1979 study was led by sociologists Marshall Clinard and Peter Yeager and supported by a near quarter-million-dollar federal grant. In their view, "corporate crime actually is *organizational* crime occurring in the context of complex relationships and expectations among boards of directors, executives, and managers, on the one hand, and among parent corporations, corporate divisions, and subsidiaries, on the other" (1980, 17). They examined the illegal behavior record of the nation's 582 largest publicly owned corporations. By area they represented 477 manufacturing, 18 wholesale, 66 retail, and 21 service organizations. Excluded were firms in banking, insurance, transportation, communication, and utilities. The information obtained was based on the enforcement actions taken by the twenty-four federal regulatory agencies for the years 1975 and 1976.

Sixty percent of the 582 corporations were found to have been charged with at least one violation by a federal agency. One company, unnamed, had 62 cases initiated against it. Over the two years, the 582 companies recorded 1860 violations for an average of 3.2 each.

An important finding was that the larger corporations recorded the highest number of violations. The size measure was a firm's average assets for the years 1971–75. But when the number of violations per unit size (as indicated by "number of violations per $100 million in sales") was examined, larger corporations were found to "commit no more violations per unit size than smaller corporations" (Clinard and Yeager 1980, 130). More recently, and using total sales as the measure of size, Dan Dalton and Idalene Kesner found a strong relationship between corporation size and engagement in illegal activity (as measured by determinations of guilt in litigated cases). In their view, the results of their study "would seem to indicate that larger firms are both far more likely to engage in illegal behavior and more likely to be multiple violators than their smaller counterparts" (1988, 866). Unfortunately, empirically verified reasons for the finding have yet to be identified. Hypothesized explanations range from a cost-benefit interpretation (the idea, for example, that the larger and more affluent the firm, the greater the ability to risk illegality for gain) to an administrative interpretation (the larger and more administratively decentralized the corporation, the greater the opportunity for bureaucrats to conceal illegality).

Seven kinds of enforcement action were identified: (1) monetary penalties; (2) orders, *unilateral* (orders imposed by courts not involving the consent of the corporation), *consent* (orders where the corporation agrees to comply with court stipulations but is not required to admit guilt), and "orders not elsewhere classified" (instances when it was not possible to determine whether the consent of the corporation was or was not involved); (3) nonmonetary penalties against officers (incarceration, job suspension, probation, civil contempt); (4) actions enjoined (court injunctions requiring a corporation to halt a specified illegal act immediately); (5) warnings; (6) other sanctions (those not subsumable under the six categories); and (7) unspecified detail (actions taken but sanctions unspecified).

Between 1975 and 1976, the 582 corporations had 1,554 federal enforcement actions taken against them. Slightly more than a third (36.3 percent) had none. The 367 that had at least one sanction imposed on them averaged 4.2 each. One had 65.

Warnings, the least severe of the five sanctions, were applied most often (43.4 percent of the total). Monetary penalties ranked second (23.5 percent of the total). Overall, one is impressed with the leniency shown corporate crime. The magnitude of the effects of some violations appear not to warrant such treatment. The costs and losses estimated from known violations stagger the imagination. For example, "the Judiciary Subcommittee on Antitrust and Monopoly estimated that faulty goods, monopolistic practices, and similar law violations annually cost consumers between $174 and $231 billion" (Clinard, et al, 1979, 15).

The following explanations were given by corporations for their illegal activities:

1. All measures proposed constitute government interference with the free enterprise system.

2. The government is to blame because the additional costs of regulations and bureaucratic procedures cut heavily into profits.

3. The government is to blame because most of their regulations are incomprehensible and too complicated.

4. The government is to blame because the things being regulated are unimportant.

5. There is little deliberate intent in corporation violations; most of them are simply errors of omission, and many are mistakes.

6. Other concerns in the same line of business are violating the law, and if government cannot prevent this situation, there is no reason why other corporations cannot also benefit.

7. Although it is true, as in price-fixing cases, for example, that some corporate violations may involve millions of dollars, the damage is so diffused among a large number of consumers that individually there is little loss.

8. If there is no increase in corporate profits, a violation is not wrong.

9. Violations are due to economic necessity.

10. The corporation has changed its practices and is no longer in violation. (Clinard et al. 1979, xiv)

Corporate crime, in other words, is attributed to government, accident, and circumstances beyond anyone's control—everything but corporate structure and leadership. Whatever its validity, such a mode of rationalization seems more apt than not to encourage the continuation of illegality. That firms such as General Electric appear over and over in reported incidents of illegality suggests that recidivism is indeed prevalent among corporate offenders (Weisburd, Chayet, and Waring, 1990).

Lacking an updated systematic account of the prevalence of corporate crime, one must examine a variety of sources to obtain an estimate of the problem. Thus, in 1984, John Braithwaite published a book documenting the prevalence of crime (bribery, fraud, antitrust violations, and so on) in the international pharmaceutical industry, and in 1985 *Time* magazine published an article on white-collar crime that carried the subtitle, "a spree of corporate skulduggery raises questions and concerns" (Alexander 1985, 42). Identified corporate offenders included General Electric, General Dynamics, Bank of Boston, and E.F. Hutton. General Electric pleaded guilty to a charge of defrauding the air force of $800,000. It paid fines and penalties amounting to more than $2 million. General Dynamics too had overcharged the Pentagon some $75 million—for "overhead" charges involving personal executive costs, country club fees and transportation. "All together," noted Alexander (1985, 42), "45 of the 100 largest U.S. military suppliers are under criminal investigation."

The Bank of Boston was fined $500,000 for failing to report having sent more than $1 billion to financial institutions overseas. E.F. Hutton pleaded guilty to 2000 felony counts of mail and wire fraud. The company was fined $2 million and required to pay for government investigating costs amounting to $750,000. Hutton was caught perpetrating a massive "check-kiting" scheme. As described in Senate Judiciary Committee hearings (1986, 22–23, 24),

> Hutton's illegal conduct was a series of variations on its established "draw down" system. Hutton modified the legal draw down procedure to withdraw funds from its branch depository accounts in arbitrary amounts well in excess of either customer receipts or the collected balances in those accounts. To do this, Hutton had to "cover" or otherwise conceal the overdrafts it created by depositing into those accounts checks drawn upon other Hutton accounts. These overdrafts, in turn, were hidden from the depository banks by covering checks drafted by Hutton branch personnel and deposited into bank accounts. These checks, available in each Hutton branch office, were drawn upon "zero balance" accounts at one of two New York City banks. By agreement with these banks, Hutton was required to keep no minimum balance but rather permitted to wire transfer into accounts, on a daily basis, sufficient funds to cover all checks presented for collections that day....By overdrafting as much

> as $250 million per day from its depository accounts, Hutton both avoided the necessity to borrow extensive amounts of working capital and earned income on surplus funds.

Hutton was also required to pay interest to those victimized by its crimes.

In 1987 E.F. Hutton was again in the news. By agreement with the Commonwealth of Massachusetts's secretary of state, the company agreed to refund some $650,000 to eighty-four investors who had been sold unregistered securities by its brokers (*Boston Globe*, October 14, 1987).

In 1989, Drexel Burnham Lambert pleaded guilty to six felony counts of mail, wire, and securities fraud. The company agreed to a $650 million settlement.

In 1990, General Electric again made news when the Justice Department announced that the company had paid $20 million to settle claims of overcharging the army for such equipment as a battlefield computer. The Justice Department also reported reaching settlements with 137 unidentified companies for a variety of charges involving military contracts. Additionally, a Japanese bid-rigging cartel involving procurement of military contracts was identified and fined some $34 million (*Boston Globe*, November 27, 1990).

In 1991, the Unisys Corporation, among the nation's largest military contractors, pleaded guilty to what the *New York Times* (September 6, 1991) referred to "an array of felony and civil charges" involving "procurement fraud and bid-rigging on Pentagon contracts." The company agreed to pay a record $190 million to settle all charges.

By this point, the reader might well wonder if the sentencing pattern evident in white-collar crime has been subject to the criticism merited by its apparent leniency and ineffectiveness. Detailed assessment of the effectiveness of the sentences imposed on white collar offenders is virtually non-existent, and not for lack of interest or concern, but because of the difficulties surrounding the close scrutiny of individual's lives and business operations (for example, ethical dilemmas such as invasion of privacy and research problems such as gaining access to everyday corporate decision-making via participant observation). Nonetheless, some important research and analyses have been done and remedies suggested.

Sentencing the White-Collar Offender: How Effective Is It, What are the Alternatives?

Sentencing effectiveness in white-collar crime is a variable influenced by a number of factors. Among the most important is how a given judgment is interpreted by offenders, their colleagues, and their superiors. If the offender feels more victim than victimizer, that circumstances beyond his or her control compelled the law violation, repentance and behavioral change toward law abidance are problematical. If one's peers are doing the same thing but are not getting caught, or even if many are caught, one may deny guilt and culpability on the grounds that what was done was what everyone else was doing to survive in a particular line of work. The claim that one was caught and punished for doing what everyone else was and is doing is commonplace among certain white-collar offenders. As virtually the entire electrical industry was involved in restraint-of-trade activities in the 1960 General Electric case suggests that the claim has considerable validity. Granting this, how is society most likely to defend itself against the consequences of such behavior by means of sentencing? What combination of fines and prison terms would have the greatest deterrent effect?

Perhaps the most widely recognized response to the question has been proposed by the economist Gary Becker (1989, 22), who stresses that all corporate crime punishment should be calculated on the basis of "the harm done to individuals, other organizations, and society at large." For corporate offenses, he advocates the imposition of fines but not prison sentences. In his view, fines should not be equal to but a multiple of the harm done. "For example, "if it is known that only a third of a particular kind of security fraud is punished, those companies convicted of this kind of fraud should pay three times the damage they cause" (1989, 22). Becker recognizes that it may seem unfair to punish the firm caught for the crimes of those not caught. Nevertheless, as he sees it, perpetrators operate on the assumption that the odds favor not being caught. "Therefore, companies fined according to this formula do not overpay: In the security fraud example, guilty companies have a one-third chance of being caught and paying three times the damage they cause, and a two-thirds chance of escaping punishment and paying nothing" (1989, 22). The aim, in Becker's view, is not revenge but deterrence. And his scheme aims to deter both the caught and the uncaught.

Becker's basic argument against prison sentences for corporate officials and employees is that prisons are too costly, that their construction and maintenance punish the taxpayer as well as the offender. Only when crimes cannot be compensated for by fines or when corporate employees commit crimes such as murder does he think prison sentences are appropriate. As to deaths caused by corporate negligence, for example, by a mining firm's failure to adhere to prescribed safety standards resulting in a mine collapse and the loss of life or a pharmaceutical firm's illegally polluting the environment with substances that in time cause death by cancer, Becker does not say. The intent to kill may be lacking, but culpability is surely present. What should be the punishment to deter this kind of crime? What is the formula to determine the appropriate punishment in the light of the harm done in these cases? Financial compensation of survivors is surely not the answer.

A law professor Daniel Farber, reacting to Becker's approach, questions the effectiveness of fines as a means either of deterring corporate crime or correcting corporate offenders. Even stiff fines, he says, may in a sense "actually legitimize criminal conduct by putting a price on it" (1988, 18). Following the lead of Columbia Law School Professor Jack Coffee, Farber suggests the use of probation in corporate sentencing. The goal would be to require a company to develop an approved plan for correcting a problem and preventing its recurrence. As Farber explains it,

> like street criminals many corporate criminals are recidivists. The first condition of probation would be a complete investigation into how the crime occurred and why management allowed it. The company might then be required to prepare a "compliance plan" detailing how it intends to prevent future violations. The plan would require an independent audit committee, appointment of independent counsel or independent directors, or the use of special consultants. The idea is the same as that behind corporate fines: that it is cheaper for companies to police themselves than for Washington to police them. (1988, 18)

The U.S. Sentencing Commission has accepted new federal white collar crime sentencing guidelines calling for stiffer fines and the development of company programs to deter illegality. According to *Facts on File World News Digest* (April 26, 1991, 323),

> the guidelines called for judges to impose fines based on several factors, including the size of a company and the amount of its illicit gain. Other factors included whether top company officials had been involved in the illegal activity, whether the company had cooperated with investigators or had been previously convicted of a crime and whether the company had a program in place to try to deter illegal activity.

But there were signs that the administration saw the proposed changes as too stringent and in need of softening. In mid–1990, a Deputy Attorney General, Donald B. Ayer, was reported to have "abruptly resigned" after serving less than six months. According to a report in *Facts on File World News Digest* (May 11, 1990, 384), "Ayer's resignation came only two weeks after it was disclosed that he had been forced by [then Attorney General Richard Thornburgh] to retract support for tough sentencing guidelines for corporations convicted of criminal activity." Thornburgh denied the validity of such an interpretation and insisted that he had not "abandoned support for tougher penalties for white-collar offenders and stood second to none in pressing for nothing less than the maximum penalties that we can accommodate under the law" (1990, 384). The conflicting nature of such reports suggests that it remains an open question not only what sentencing measures are adopted but also how diligently and effectively they are likely to be implemented.

Interestingly, there is some indication of an increasing willingness on the part of local jurisdictions to prosecute corporate crime. Box 4.3 contains the most recent information available on this important trend.

Box 4.3, Local Prosecutors and Corporate Crime

Crimes committed by and for business pose a serious threat to the health, safety, and financial welfare of consumers and workers as well as to the orderly functioning of the economy and the government. Commonly known as corporate or organizational crimes, these offenses raise special problems for detection, prosecution, and sanction. Isolated efforts by individual enforcement agencies have proven inadequate against this type of crime, . . .

Historically, the federal government has assumed primary responsibility for controlling corporate crime, but in the past two decades, local prosecutors have become increasingly concerned about this problem. In 1973 the National District Attorneys Association established an Economic Crime Committee to encourage local prosecutors to enforce white-collar crime laws and to enhance their enforcement ability. By 1975, 43 district attorneys' offices were participating in the committee's Economic Crime Project.

Since the Economic Crime Project was begun nearly 20 years ago, local response to corporate white-collar crime has changed significantly. In the past, district attorneys concentrated almost exclusively on economic crimes such as consumer fraud. They are now prosecuting a wider variety of cases, including occupational safety violations and the illegal dumping of toxic waste. In nearly every state, prosecutors have sought criminal indictments against corporations, partnerships, and other business entities for noneconomic offenses.

This *Research in Brief* summarizes a National Institute of Justice study of local prosecutors' work against corporate crime. For the study, corporate crime was defined as "a violation of a criminal statute either by a corporate entity or by its executives, employees, or agents acting on behalf of and for the benefit of the corporation, partnership, or other form of business entity."

The first component of the study was a mail survey of 632 district attorneys with jurisdictions located in or near urban areas. Completed questionnaires were received from 419 districts, a response rate of 66 percent.

One conclusion is that local prosecution of corporate crime is becoming more widespread. More than one-quarter of the survey respondents said that corporate prosecutions have increased during their tenure in office. One-quarter reported that they expected to prosecute more corporate crime in the future. Less than 1 percent had seen or anticipated a decrease in prosecutions. . . .

In 1988 two-thirds of the survey respondents said their offices prosecuted at least one of nine types of corporate crime. Although local prosecutors handled a wider variety of corporate crimes in 1988 than in previous years, economic crimes still made up the bulk of their corporate crime caseload.

Consumer fraud was the most frequently prosecuted corporate offense, with 41 percent of the offices prosecuting at least one case of consumer fraud.

False claims and insurance fraud followed as the most frequently prosecuted economic crimes, with 31 percent of the offices prosecuting at least one offense in these categories.

Only one type of noneconomic crime—environmental offenses—was prosecuted as often as economic crime. In 1988, 31 percent of the offices handled at least one environmental offense. . . .

Source: Edited from Michael L. Benson, Francis T. Cullen, and William J. Maakestad, *Local Prosecutors and Corporate Crime*, National Institute of Justice, Research in Brief, U.S. Department of Justice, Office of Justice Programs Washington, D.C.: Government Printing Office, January 1993.

Summary & Conclusion

White-collar crime is an important and controversial subject because it involves a society's key institutions and leaders. Its consequences, as in the case of the savings and loan scandal, may be so far reaching and costly as to threaten the social and economic well-being of the nation. What makes it so insidious is that its roots lie in the nature of urban-industrial society. Innumerable individuals and groups, woven together in a highly complex division of labor, are involved in the production and distribution of basic goods and services. Because the opportunities for error and manipulation are virtually unlimited and exceedingly difficult to control, many attempt to take advantage of the situation for personal gain. Succumbing to the temptation is encouraged by a society that over emphasizes goal achievement and under emphasizes conformity to the appropriate means to attain ends. We are a society that emphasizes the value of monetary gain and minimizes the necessity of governmental interference. As Lincoln Steffens (1904, 5) once described the American commercial "spirit:

> The commercial spirit is the spirit of profit, not patriotism; of credit, not honor; of individual gain, not national prosperity; of trade and dickering, not principle. "My business is sacred," says the business

> man in his heart. "Whatever prospers my business, isgood; it must be. Whatever hinders it, is wrong; it must be. A bribe is bad, that is, it is a bad thing to take; but it is not so bad to give one, not if it is necessary to my business.

The police function is exacerbated by the fact that the American economy is based on the sanctity of private property, deep restrictions on the invasion of privacy, and the presumption of innocence until proven guilty.

The detection and control of white-collar crime may well hinge on the violation of democratic principles, in spirit if not in fact. For example, an aggressive effort to contain organizational crime, would undoubtedly entail harassment, from threats of impending legal action unless certain changes are made to raids on corporate offices and physical plants. The inevitable abuses and errors of such actions doubtlessly prohibit their use. But a noncontroversial solution to the problem is not apparent.

In any event, the free enterprise system is the generating milieu of white-collar crime in America, whether it is the crime of an individual or an organization. Organized crime has flourished in the same context. Therefore the possibility much be entertained that the cure for the one is the cure for the other. Organized crime is the subject of the next chapter.

References

Alexander, Charles P. 1985. "Crime in the Suites: A Spree of Corporate Skulduggery Raises Questions and Concerns." *Time*, June 10, 56–7.

Becker, Gary S. 1989. "Making the Punishment Fit the Corporate Crime." *Business Week*, March 13, 22.

"Boesky in Country Club Jail." 1988. *the Boston Globe*. March 25.

Boland, John C. 1985. *Wall Street's Insiders*. New York: Morrow.

Braithwaite, John. 1984. *Corporate Crime in the Pharmaceutical Industry*. London: Routledge & Kegan Paul.

Carlson, Kenneth and Jan Chaiken. 1987. *White Collar Crime*. Bureau of Justice Statistics Special Report Washington, D.C.: Government Printing Office.

Carlson, Margaret. 1991. "Then There Was One." *Time* 137 (March 11), 69.

Chernow, Ron. 1990. *The House of Morgan*. New York: Atlantic Monthly Press.

Clinard, Marshall B. and Peter C. Yeager. 1980. *Corporate Crime*. New York: the Free Press.

Clinard, Marshall B., P.C. Yeager, J.M. Brissette, D. Petrashek and E. Harries. 1979. *Illegal Corporate Behavior*. Washington, D.C.: Government Printing Office.

Coleman, James W. 1987. "Toward an Integrated Theory of White-Collar Crime." *American Journal of Sociology* 93 406–39.

Cross, Wilbur. 1988. *Investor Alert! How to Protect Your Money from Schemes, Scams, and Frauds*. New York: Andrews and McMeel.

Dalton, Don R. and Idalene F. Kesner. 1988. "On the Dynamics of Corporate Size and Illegal Activity: An Empirical Assessment." *Journal of Business Ethics* 7 861–70.

DeMuth, Jerry. 1972. "GE: Profile of a Corporation." In *The Radical Attack on Business* edited by Charles Perrow, New York: Harcourt Brace Jovanovich.

"Drexel Burnham Lambert Bankruptcy." 1991. *The Guide to American Law Supplement 1991*. New York: West, 346–50.

"E.F. Hutton to Refund $650,000." 1987. *the Boston Globe*, October 14.

Edelhertz, Herbert. 1979. *The Nature, Impact and Prosecution of White Collar Crime*. Washington, D.C. Government Printing Office.

Facts on File World News Digest. 1990. "Bush Administration." May 11, 384.

———. 1991. "Corporate Crime Guidelines Proposed." April 26, 323.

———. 1993. "Savings and Loan Crisis." July 15, 1993.

Farber, Daniel. 1988. "Corporate Punishment: How to Make Crime Stop Paying for Companies." *The New Republic* 199 16,18.

"Gall in the Family." 1991. *Forbes* 148 (July 8).

Green, Mark J., Beverly C. Moore, Jr. and Bruce Wasserstein. 1972. *The Closed Enterprise System*. New York: Bantam Books.

"Guilty Plea by Unisys Is Expected." 1991. *The New York Times* September 6.

Hearings before the Committee on the Judiciary: U.S.Senate April. *White Collar Crime (E.F. Hutton)*. 1986. Washington, D.C.: Government Printing Office. April 17 and May 8.

Hirschi, Travis, and Michael Gottfredson. 1987. "Causes of White-Collar Crime." *Criminology* 25 949–74.

———. 1989. "The Significance of White-Collar Crime for a General Theory of Crime." *Criminology* 27 359–71.

"Insider Trading." 1989. *U.S. Securities and Exchange Commission Fifty-Fifth Annual Report*, 6–8.

"Junk Bonds." 1990. *The Guide to American Law Supplement 1990*. New York: West, 161–63.

Koepp, Stephen. 1988. "Fraud, Fraud, Fraud." *Time*, August 15.

Langevoort, Donald C. 1987. *Insider Trading Handbook: 1987 Edition*. New York: Boardman.

Levine, Dennis B. 1991. *Inside Out; An Insider's Account of Wall Street*. New York: Putnam's.

Mayer, Martin. 1992. *The Greatest Ever Bank Robbery*. New York: Collier.

Myers, Gustavus. 1937. *History of the Great American Fortunes*. New York: Random House.

Pizzo, Stephen, Mark Fricker and Paul Muolo. 1989. *Inside Job: The Looting of America's Savings and Loans*. New York: McGraw-Hill.

Posner, Richard. 1970. "A Statistical Study of Antitrust Enforcement." *The Journal of Law & Economics* 13 365–420.

Shapiro, Susan P. 1984. *Wayward Capitalists*. New Haven: Yale University Press.

———. 1990. "Collaring the Crime, Not the Criminal: Reconsidering 'White-Collar'." *American Sociological Review* 55 346–65.

Smart, Tim and Michele Galen. 1990. "Soon, Corporate Crime May Really Not Pay." *Business Week*, February 12, 35.

Smith, Richard A. 1963. *Corporations in Crisis*. New York: Doubleday.

Sutherland, Edwin H. 1949. *White Collar Crime*. New York: Holt, Rinehart and Winston.

Steffens, Lincoln. 1904. *The Shame of the Cities*. New York: Hill and Wang.

Steffensmeier, Darrell. 1989. "On the Causes of 'White-Collar' Crime: An Assessment of Hirschi and Gottfredson's Claims." *Criminology* 27 345–58.

Stewart, James B. 1991. *Den of Thieves*. New York: Simon and Schuster.

"Texan Gets Five Years in Big S.& L. Collapse." 1991. *the Boston Globe*, April 3.

U.S. Code, Congressional and Administrative News. 1985 "Insider Trading Sanctions Act of 1984." St. Paul, Minn.: West.

"US Says it Won $275 Million Last Year in Contractor Fraud Damages." 1990. *the Boston Globe*, November 27.

Waldman, Michael. 1990. *Who Robbed America?* New York: Random House.

Weisburd, David, Ellen F. Chayet and Elin J. Waring. 1990. "White-Collar Crime and Criminal Careers: Some Preliminary Findings." *Crime & Delinquency* 36 342–55.

Willis, Rod. 1986. "White-Collar Crime: The Threat from Within." *Management Review* June, 22–7, 30.

Notes

[1]. Webster's *New World Dictionary* defines an arbitrageur as one who engages in arbitrage, or simultaneous buying and selling in two separate markets in order to profit from a price difference between them. A related term, risk arbitrage, is defined as involving the timely purchase of large numbers of shares in firms in anticipation of profiting from a merger or takeover. Some investment firms have abolished the position of arbitrageur as its success is seen virtually to depend on the acquisition of inside information.

[2]. "Junk bonds: a slang expression for a corporate bond that credit-rating agencies rate below investment grade. Such bonds are considered speculative in nature and pay higher yields than investment-grade bonds. Junk bonds vary considerably in quality, however, with some ranking immediately below investment-grade bonds and others being so speculative that they are not rated at all" (*The Guide to American Law, Supplement 1990* (New York: West, 1991).

Chapter 5

Organized Crime

Of the many kinds of crime, none has stirred the interest, fear, and imagination of people more than organized crime. Even so, until recently it was a poorly documented subject. In a 1971 publication, Joseph Albini could say with confidence that "there is no question that much of the material written in the area of organized crime thus far is not scholarly in nature, all too frequently falling into the medium of the journalistic and sensation-oriented style of writing where documentation of sources is either at a minimum or completely absent" (1971, 8).

Most of what was known was learned from a few informants, members opting to become prosecution witnesses or to testify before government committees in return for a reduced sentence or immunity from prosecution. To encourage more to do the same, the Federal Witness Security Program was implemented in 1970, but it was initially underutilized. The same is true of two other federal laws enacted around the same time: Title III of the Omnibus Crime Control Act of 1968, which authorizes "wiretapping" and other means of electronic surveillance under specified conditions; and the Racketeer Influenced Corrupt Organizations Act (RICO) of 1970 (a means of prosecuting organized illegality). For a number of reasons, including its newness, complexity, and conceptual ambiguity, RICO was not used against organized crime until 1980. But since the early 1980s, both it and electronic surveillance, as well as the witness protection program, have been used with considerable regularity and effectiveness. Consistent use of the three measures over the past decade has provided the best available documentation of the nature and extent of organized crime in the United States and elsewhere. To put this information in perspective, it is important to outline the available historical evidence on organized crime, what it is and when and where it arose, and how it has changed. Subsequent topics discussed include the structure and activities of organized crime and official responses to the problem. We begin by examining the historical record on organized crime in Europe and the United States. Underlying the entire discussion are questions important for causally relevant social policy: To what extent is organized crime "home grown"? Is it an alien institution brought to North American by certain immigrant groups? Is it a combination of the two?

The Rise of Organized Crime in Europe and the United States

According to the 1967 presidential commission on the subject, organized crime is defined "as a society that seeks to operate outside the control of the American people and their governments" (1967, 205). The "society" is described as involving "thousands of criminals," possessing a structure "as complex as any large corporation," whose actions are "the result of intricate conspiracies, carried on over many years and aimed at gaining control over whole fields of activity in order to amass huge profits" (1967, 205). The "society" is, of course, the *Mafia*, an entity dominated by individuals of Italian and Sicilian descent. But before discussing its present status and cultural roots, it is important to note common background factors in the rise of groups engaged in illicit activities both in Italy and the United States.

To begin with, there is a tendency to equate the rise of outlaw gangs with the rise of cities. But gangs were much in evidence in America's rural past. The James-Younger gang of Missouri and the Reno brothers of Indiana are merely two well known examples. As Richard Maxwell Brown reminds us, "Organized interstate gangs of criminals are an old story, going well back into the 18th century" (1969, 44).

Furthermore, the *Mafia* arose in rural parts of southern Italy, mainly western Sicily, primarily "the cattle-raising and fruit-growing areas around Palermo and in the sulphur-mining regions of Caltanissetta and Agrigento" (Nelli 1976, 11). Some basic social, political, and economic factors associated with its growth were also present in the United States. Highly associated with the emergence of secret societies and criminal gangs is a generally unorganized or disorganized social milieu lacking effective means of social control, such as established and respected laws and governing structures. In the United States, governmental structures traditionally follow and respond to, rather than lead, social and economic change and development. In the nation's early days, it was not disorganization but the absence of organization that was the generating milieu behind the rise of outlaw gangs. In Italy, the generating context was social disorganization produced by a feudal heritage, a country dominated by independent city-states engaged in internecine warfare, and periodic occupation by neighboring powers (Austria, France, Spain). After Italy's unification in the nineteenth century, widespread absentee ownership of landed estates was conducive to overseers' use of any means at their disposal to control and exploit the peasants. "Predictably," says Nelli, "peasants viewed themselves as subsisting in surroundings that threatened individual and family security, and saw all officialdom and all gentry as malefactors seeking to impoverish and destroy them" (1976, 7). The peasants began to turn to protectors and benefactors, kin and nonkin, to defend and aid them. "Such a man became the patron of a large number of people; he became a locally important person, a *capo mafioso*" (Nelli

1976, 7). Nelli cites a resident of Sicily and prominent Italian jurist who described the situation in the 1870s as characterized by "the laws scoffed at, corruption everywhere, favoritism the rule, justice the exception; crime enthroned where the guardian of public weal should be; criminals in the place of judges; judges become criminals, and a horde of persons interested in crime become arbiters of the liberty, honour and life of the people" (1976, 8).

The *Mafia* arose, then, in a sociocultural situation in which, because of the absence of a strong and respected political institution (the state), people turned to another social structure for protection and sustenance. The alternative institution was the extended and expanded family. As Ianni describes it,

> Each man and each family know what they owe to others and what is due to them from others. Favors become obligations and wrongs become debts which demand redress: "*Si moru mi voricu; si campu t'allampu*" ("if you kill me they will bury me; if I live, I will kill you"). The spirit of *mafia* persists because it is born of the culture. It is, in turn, the progenitor of the secret organizations, the *Mafie*. (1972, 26)

Mafie are thought to have arisen from the *compagnie d'armi*, private armies maintained by landowners to protect their families and property from bandits.[1] Private armies surfaced during the feudal period and with the collapse of feudalism in the wake of the Napoleonic victory in 1812 became the mechanism for the maintenance of social order. They served as a mediating force between the competing claims of the old aristocracy and the peasant masses.

The *Mafie*, secret organizations with private armies, sold their services to both ends of the social spectrum. Some were employed by the aristocracy; others worked for the peasantry. Eventually, they became the most powerful political force in Sicily.

> By 1900, a loose confederation of the local gangs had begun to emerge, bound together by a complex policy of infiltration into all spheres of activity. There was a dual organization. First there was the local *Mafia* family which was, and continues to be, the basic organizational unit. Modeled after the extended family which is the ideal of Sicilian social organization, the *Mafia* family at first was always made up of relatives by blood or marriage, but as it grew in size and strength, *amici*—friends—became associated with it. The rank and power of the family were determined by the fearlessness and cunning of its members, particularly the *cappo* [the chief], who was always the most authoritative member. (Ianni 1972, 29–30)

Some villages have more than one *Mafia* family, and in such cases each has its own area of influence. When two or more families agree to share certain functions, they are referred to as a *cosca* (*cosche* is the plural form). Combinations of *cosche* are *consorterie*. Ianni claims that in Sicily all the *consorterie* constitute what is thought of as "the *Mafia*." But instead of being referred to by that name, they are identified as the *Onorata Societe*, the honorable society.

A way out of the situation was, of course, emigration, a choice invoked by thousands of Italians in the later nineteenth and early twentieth centuries. The question is, to what extent did those who came to the United States simply impose the *Mafia* on the country or encounter conditions similar to those in their native land that led some to use it as a means of adaptation? Francis Ianni's position is that

> similarities between conditions in the south of Italy and in the Italian-American ghetto lead one to speculate on a possible relationship. Cultures have often preserved, almost unnoticed for long periods, some traditional pattern of response to particular kinds of stress. It is possible that southern Italian immigrants in America resurrected the *Mafia* model, under the stress of ghetto poverty and lawlessness. (1972, 11)

Some scholars emphasize a more direct connection. The rise of fascism during the 1920s and 1930s was a mortal threat to the *Onorata Societe*. Mussolini sanctioned its wholesale elimination. Although he did not accomplish his goal, he did succeed in driving the society underground, and many of its leaders were compelled to seek refuge in other countries, including the United States. That some rose to positions of prominence in Italian-Sicilian-led branches of organized crime during the Prohibition era is not surprising. As the journalist Claire Sterling indicates, Sicilians from fascist Italy who became *Mafia* family leaders include "Joe Profaci from Villabate, Carlo Gambino from Palermo, Gaetano Lucchese from Palermo, and Joe Bonanno from Castellammare del Golfo" (1990, 52).

An early student of organized crime in America, Donald Cressey, cites a former Brooklyn assistant district attorney who alleged that during the early 1930s one New York *Mafia* leader was chiefly concerned with smuggling into the country criminals driven out of Italy and Sicily. "However," Cressey observes, "it might be a mere coincidence that the Italian-Sicilian domination of American illicit syndicates began shortly after Mussolini's eradication campaign" (1969, 14). Then again, he hastens to add, the gang wars and peace settlement behind the presumed shape of organized crime did, after all, occur during the 1930s.

The problem that Cressey wrestled with was the extent to which the American sociocultural setting or elements of an alien subculture were implicated in shaping organized crime during and after the 1930s. To focus on one side of the equation, the role of outside influences, is to risk indulging in scapegoating. As Cressey reasoned,

> If the Italian and Sicilian *Mafia* is responsible for organized crime in the United States, then documenting that fact and identifying the *Mafia* as the cause of our troubles are more science than scapegoatism. On the other hand, if the American cartel and confederation is a response to conditions of American life, documenting that fact is the critical problem. In a very real sense, then, deciding whether or not the American organization is a branch of the Sicilian one is a problem of deciding whether organized crime is "owned" by American society. (1969, 16)

To put the problem in perspective, criminal gangs existed in America before Italians and Sicilians came to these shores in significant numbers. The earliest documented urban-based gangs were dominated by the Irish. Sections of New York City witnessed the activities of the Bowery B'hoys, Roach Guard, Patsy Conroys, Shirt Tails, Atlantic Guards, Daybreak Books, Hookers, Swamp Angels, and Buckoos. According to August Bequai, "New York's gangs enjoyed national notoriety throughout the nineteenth century and were imitated in many cities" (1979: 30).

In mid-nineteenth-century Chicago, Michael McDonald was the crime leader. He established a gambling casino that became known as the unofficial city hall. Bequai credits him with establishing "the city's first well-organized criminal syndicate" (1979, 30).

After the Irish came the Jews. In the 1920s they were the dominant ethnic group engaged in organized crime. Albert Fried believes that the early Prohibition era Jewish gangs were probably more aggressive than non-Jewish gangs. He bases his assertion on the premise that Jewish gangs lacked a readily available market for liquor because of the low consumption of alcohol in Jewish communities. Hence they had to establish themselves in gentile neighborhoods, and this meant "muscling in" on their Irish and Italian competitors. One of the more ruthless Jewish gangs was led by "Dutch Schultz," born Arthur Flegenheim. "His South Bronx gang beat down, or coopted one neighborhood rival after another, supplying beer and liquor to speakeasies, restaurants, and clubs as far away as Manhattan's Upper West Side and Harlem" (Fried 1980, 103).

Detroit's "Purple Gang" was led by the Fleisher brothers and the Bernstein brothers. In common with other street gangs, they engaged in gambling, prostitution, extortion, and loan-sharking.

Cleveland had the "Cleveland Four": Louis Rothkopf, Morris Kleinman, Morris Dalitz, and Samuel Tucker. Dalitz had apprenticed with the "Purple Gang." Other notorious Jewish gangs were based in Minneapolis, St. Paul, Kansas City (MO), Boston, Newark, Philadelphia, and most other major cities.

As for their impact on the future course of organized crime in America, Arnold Rothstein was probably the most important of the early Jewish gangsters. His example is said to have provided Lucky Luciano and other *Mafia* leaders with "a blueprint for growth."

Rothstein was unique in many ways. Unlike most underworld figures, he was born of relatively wealthy parents. He lived in "a fine house," but found life in New York's Lower East Side Jewish ghetto more to his liking. Gambling was his chief passion and business (he is rumored to have been behind the infamous Black Sox scandal of 1919). His first patron was "Big Tim" Sullivan, the Lower East Side's leading underworld figure. Sullivan made Rothstein manager of a gambling casino. Soon after, he established his own place. Albert Fried describes him as a master of public relations and highly adept in the subtleties of "self-advertisement," one with the ability to attract wealthy customers and take them "for astronomical amounts of money" (1980, 24).

Rothstein's air of respectability and success captured the imagination of Lucky Luciano (born Salvatore Lucania in Lercara Friddi, Sicily), the generally accredited organizer of the American *Mafia*. According to Luciano, Rothstein "taught me how to dress, how not to wear loud things but to have good taste; he taught me how to use knives and forks, and things like that at the dinner table, about holdin' a door open for a girl. If Arnold had lived a little longer [he was murdered in 1928], he could've made me pretty elegant; he was the best etiquette teacher a guy could ever have—real smooth" (Hammer 1975, 41).

By emulating Rothstein, Luciano sought to avoid the stereotype of the mobster as a crass and tactless lower-class thug. And by assuming the manners of a respectable businessman, Luciano could deceive the gullible. But apparently this was not his only motive. Fried suggests that by changing their style and appearance, these mobsters were affirming a social system that "would eventually accept, even embrace them" (1980, 109). In fact, they found considerable acceptance among the higher echelons of business, politics, and society. At the height of his powers, Luciano directed syndicate operations from the Waldorf-Astoria under the pseudonym Charles Ross.

Luciano's upwardly mobile success may suggest that organized crime is to be viewed as a response to social and economic stimuli, a means of providing goods and services for which there is widespread public demand. Seen this way, and "serving as an intermediary source between the legal normative and the social normative systems in society, the syndicated criminal dedicates his energy and skills toward erecting a structure that, although illegal, then becomes a functioning part of the social system within which it operates" (Albini, 10). In a nutshell, the syndicated criminal does not create but responds to a preexisting need. While this "functional" perspective requires careful consideration by anyone wishing to account for the emergence and persistence of organized crime, it should not obviate the effort to account for the emergence and persistence of those of Sicilian and Italian descent as organized crime leaders. The two earliest often cited indicators of *Mafia*-influenced crime are the Hennessey and Petrosino cases.

The Hennessey Case

The vast majority of Italian and Sicilian immigrants arrived after 1880; by 1975, more than 5 million had come to the United States. This is the second-largest contingent from any one nation (Germany ranks first). Many of those who came did not stay long. Thus, between 1887 and 1907, 2,231,961 came and 972,695 departed. Reasons for leaving included dissatisfaction with the American way of life, poor health, homesickness, and the attainment of enough money to live more comfortably in Italy (Saloutos 1974, 136).

Of course, most of those who came stayed. "Little Italys" sprung up in major cities throughout the country. New Orleans was one of the first to evidence the presence of a sizable population of Italian immigrants and allegedly the *Mafia*. In 1890, the city witnessed a number of brutal murders. "Shotguns, bombs, and daggers—the traditional Mafia methods were accounting for several murders a week" (Sondern 1972, 79).

The city's police chief, David Hennessey, conducted a thorough investigation of the murders. He reportedly found them to be by-products of a power struggle between two *Mafia* families (the Provenzanos and the Matrangas) for control of the docks. All ships and importers were required to pay a fixed tribute to one or the other family for protection and service. But before Hennessey was able to present his evidence to a grand jury, he was shotgunned to death.

Hennessey's slaying outraged the citizenry. A grand jury investigation concluded with the statement that "the existence of a secret organization known as the Mafia has been established beyond doubt" (Sondern 1972, 80). Soon after, nineteen Sicilian immigrants were indicted for Hennessey's murder. There were more than fifty witnesses for the prosecution. Nonetheless, defended by a team of some of the nation's finest lawyers, all but three of the defendants were found innocent. The public response to the trial was swift and brutal. To complete certain legal formalities, all the defendants were taken to the Parish Prison. Almost immediately, citizen execution squads entered the prison while deputy sheriffs quietly departed. Some of the prisoners were summarily hanged, and the others were executed by firing squads.

Some contemporary scholars are highly critical of the claim that Hennessey's death was *Mafia* inspired. They question attributing the crime to the *Mafia* because the weapon used, a shotgun, was alleged to be "a typical Mafia weapon." To Albini, for example, "There has never been a typical 'Mafia' weapon" (1979 159–60).

Moreover, Hennessey may not have been an unbiased observer in the case. Some argue that he was a close friend of the Provenzano family. When two Provenzano brothers were arrested in the wake of a conflict with their rivals, Hennessey is said to have attempted to assist them. It is suggested that he was slain because of his announced intention of testifying against the Matranga family by presenting evidence indicating their connections with the *Mafia*. Albini questions this interpretation. In his view, "The vendetta between the Matrangas and the Provenzanos was not specifically a 'Mafia' mode of behavior, but rather one common to Sicilian kinship groups" (1979, 160). Nelli puts it this way: "If the Matrangas were responsible for Hennessey's murder, the killing was merely part of a vendetta involving two feuding factions and did not represent an effort to establish *mafia* control over the city" (1976, 66).

Whatever the truth of the matter, the Hennessey case is typical of early incidents attributed to the *Mafia*. Convincing evidence of a connection between a crime or series of crimes and the *Mafia* is presented, only to be met by serious questions as to its quality or the logic of the conclusions drawn. Racism born of fear and distrust of others' cultural differences and traditions and a tendency to blame everything but the American way of life undoubtedly account for part of the problem.

The Petrosino Case

Another case often used to demonstrate the *Mafia* presence in America is the 1909 murder of Lieutenant Joseph Petrosino of the New York City Police Department. An Italian-born immigrant, Petrosino was determined to protect the good name of Italians by doing his utmost to eradicate the blot on their escutcheon that is the *Mafia*. Through his efforts, an Italian squad, a special unit within the department, was formed. Its immediate target was the Black Hand extortion racket.

The stenciled imprint of a black hand on ransom notes or threatening letters was the symbol used by extortionists to convince wealthy Italians to meet their demands. The symbol struck terror in the heart of the recipients because the violent reputation of its users was well established in both the "old" and the "new" country.

Petrosino thought solving the problem lay not only in deporting captured perpetrators but also in preventing Italian and Sicilian criminals from entering the country. Accordingly he was authorized to go to Italy and Sicily and consult with local officials in areas of known *Mafia* activity. He undertook the trip under an assumed name and obtained identification credentials from the Italian government. He began his investigations in Palermo, and it was there, on the morning of March 12, 1909, that he was shot to death in the Piazza Marina, apparently among a crowd of people.

Petrosino's death was unhesitatingly attributed to the *Mafia*. In the public mind, as Dwight Smith points out, the ramifications of the murder were as follows:

> 1. The site of Petrosino's death—Palermo—"proved" a relationship between the Sicilian Mafia and the American Black Hand as sister organizations.
> 2. The murder demonstrated that the Black Hand/Mafia would even kill a policeman to protect is criminal activities.
> 3. As the Mafia had presumably learned its lesson from the Hennessey case, so the police learned from Petrosino's murder, and the subsequent increase in Black Hand crime, that an assault by an organized crime figure on a policeman must be avenged (1975, 54).

Petrosino's murderers were never found, and so such inferences have never been validated or invalidated. Some think it highly unlikely that a Black Hand organization had anything to do with the murder. Smith thinks Petrosino's murder was most likely a case of revenge for shadowing the defendant in an important murder trial or retaliation for his having arrested one Enrico Alfino, the primary defendant in an Italian murder trial.

Again, until recently, scholars and public officials were inclined to be highly skeptical of a *Mafia* presence in the United States, especially the likelihood of a secret organized crime society affiliated with, if not led by, elements of Sicilian organized crime. In a 1990 publication the journalist Claire Sterling contended that Petrosino, too, doubted the existence of Sicilian-orchestrated organized crime in the United States until he encountered a murder that he thought implicated a known Sicilian *Mafia* leader, one Don Vito (Vito Cascio Ferro). According to Sterling,

> Petrosino came across Don Vito in 1903, when a dismembered head with genitals stuffed into its mouth was found in a barrel on New York's Eleventh Avenue. The victim was a Sicilian immigrant who had worked for Black Hand higher-ups. Petrosino was persuaded by the evidence that Don Vito was responsible. (1990, 50)

As Sterling tells it, with Petrosino after him, Don Vito was forced to leave the country for his native Sicily. He is said to have carried Petrosino's picture in his pocket, "an assassin's mark." She suggests the facts indicate that after a Black Hand meeting in New Orleans, two "emissaries" were sent to Sicily to meet with Don Vito and that "the three of them shot Petrosino twice in the back of the head and once in the face" (1990: 51). Sterling contends that Don Vito was the *Mafia's* first boss of bosses (*capo di tutti capi*), the initiator of what she contends is now a worldwide orchestrated organization engaged in a variety of illegal activities (from loan sharking to heroin distribution). But this is to get ahead of the discussion. At the time of Petrosino's assassination, the official view was to downplay, to deny the existence of, an American *mafia*, especially the notion of a secret organized crime society with close Sicilian ties. The beginning of a change of view occurred in 1940 with the testimony of an admitted *Mafia* turncoat, Abe "Kid Twist" Reles.

Witness Abe Reles

Reles's revelations were made to William O'Dwyer, Brooklyn's chief prosecutor. They came as a result of Reles's having been arrested for a murder committed in 1933. By 1940, Reles, then thirty-two, had a record of forty-two previous arrests, of which six were for murder. What prompted Reles to confess was the hope of being absolved of all charges and a chance to start a new life. After consulting with colleague Burton Turkus, O'Dwyer agreed to Reles's conditions.

According to O'Dwyer, Reles identified eighty-three murders in which he personally took part. The credibility of his story was bolstered by police records. Turkus described Reles as having

> the most amazing memory [he had] ever encountered. He could recount minutely what he ate at a particular meal years before, or where he was and with whom, and all without a single reference or reminder of any kind. And investigation proved him entirely accurate, down to the pinpoint check, on every detail he mentioned. The Kid rattled off names, places, facts, data on one manslaughter after the other, days on end, without once messing up. (Hammer 1975, 11–12)

Reles claimed that he and others were employed by a national syndicate with an interlocking directorate. His declarations on the workings of Murder, Inc. led to the conviction and execution of seven individuals. It is said that his evidence would have convicted Albert Anastasia (the alleged boss of organized crime in New York City) had not death intervened. Reles fell to his death from his apartment ("guarded" around the clock by eighteen plainclothesmen) in a Coney

Island hotel. The cause of the fall was never determined, but rumor had it that "the Organization paid handsomely for the murder of a dangerous informer" (Hammer, 33).

Reles may have committed suicide. There is some indication that he had lost confidence in the willingness of the authorities to take full advantage of his information. He was certain that his efforts would be meaningless, his life forfeit, if the syndicate's alleged leaders were not prosecuted—men such as Anastasia, Meyer Lansky, and Bugsy Siegel. But the case against them was not pressed.

O'Dwyer's handling of the matter—both Reles's testimony and his death—left much to be desired. In 1951 a U.S. Senate committee headed by Senator Estes Kefauver of Tennessee investigating organized crime learned that a thorough investigation of Reles's death had never been launched. Furthermore, shortly after Reles's death, Burton Turkus wrote a memorandum to O'Dwyer calling for "redoubled effort" in the investigation of Anastasia and his associates. But twenty-six days after Turkus's memorandum, "the 'wanted cards' that showed they were being hunted for the offense of murder were removed from the police files" (Cook 1966, 149). Apparently the files were ordered removed by James J. Moran, O'Dwyer's "Man Friday." Moran never admitted the act, but he was later imprisoned for running an extortion racket in New York City's Fire Department. O'Dwyer flatly denied ordering anyone to remove the files. "In the murky background of the case," says Cook, "was the old specter, the utter corruption of Brooklyn politics by the underworld" (1966: 147).

The Kefauver Committee

Between the disclosures of Abe Reles and a second major witness to organized crime, Joseph Valachi, the Kefauver Committee reported the results of its investigation of the nature and extent of organized crime in interstate commerce. The committee was established in 1950, and over a seventeen-month period conducted public hearings in major cities across the country.

The committee's working assumption was that the *Mafia* was well-established in America and that it was part of a worldwide criminal conspiracy whose goal was total societal domination. The *Mafia* threat was equated with another threat, the specter of world communism. The chairman of New York's Anticrime Committee expressed the fear of many when he observed that "Joe Stalin, if he had planned it that way, could not find a speedier and surer way to defeat the democracies than by subsidizing these gangsters. I wonder if the Soviet is not, at least in some measure, inciting these vermin to defile our system of law and order" (Fried, 257).

The committee listened to six hundred witnesses. Put on public display—the hearings were televised—were notables such as Tony Accardo and Jake Guzik from Chicago, Mickey Cohen from Los Angeles, and Meyer Lansky and Frank Costello (at the time, the presumed overlord of organized crime in America) from New York.

The investigation uncovered the unsurprising fact that casino gambling was organized crime's chief activity. The senators were told that syndicate leaders cooperated with one another, that they carefully documented one another's investments and meted out profits accordingly. In other words, instead of uncovering a secret and sinister conspiracy, the committee found a little-concealed and well-organized business operation.

Of course, the open and widespread nature of illegal gambling could occur only with the approval and cooperation of public officials. The discovery of nationwide collusion between local officials and criminal syndicates alarmed the senators more than the public. "While Americans made gambling illegal," says Daniel Bell, "they did not in their hearts think of it as wicked—even the churches benefitted from the bingo and lottery crazes" (1962, 136).

There was, of course, some value in putting the nation's top gangsters on public display, in revealing the extensiveness of political corruption, and in showing how little resistance grassroots democracy offered organized crime. But these accomplishments fell far short of the committee's goal of "unraveling...the Mafia plot to bring down America." Fried argues that the committee failed because of a false operating assumption: that the country was divided into two camps, the gangsters on one side and the plain folk on the other. "It never entertained the possibility that gangsters were at the bottom middlemen who took the risks, and won the rewards, of satisfying the needs of upper-world citizens" (Fried, 265). At bottom, however, the committee failed, in Fried's view, because it did not consider the possibility that "organized crime was in fact an expression of, not a departure from, conventional American morality" (1980, 265).

Interestingly enough, throughout the 1950s, *Mafia* violence was relatively infrequent. Reflecting the character of the times, its activities became more businesslike and orderly than ever. Public appeasement and acceptance were the order of the day. But this changed during the 1960s, apparently chiefly as younger members resented not being able to supplant their elders in power and the reluctance of older leaders to expand drug operations at a time of increased public demand for and consumption of drugs. Eventually, such differences came to the fore in the form of violent intrafamily power struggles and interfamily conflict over control of newly developing gambling and drug markets. Public demand for the restoration of "law and order" required an effective law-enforcement response from all levels of government, even if this entailed making concessions to mobsters such as Joseph Valachi.

Witness Joseph Valachi

Although the Kefauver Committee acquired information about prominent criminals, it did little to illuminate the "syndicate's" organizational structure. The breakthrough on this important topic was provided by Joseph Valachi. The manner in which his knowledge was made available, as well as other elements of his case are comparable to those surrounding the testimony of Abe Reles and many others since Valachi. Valachi told his story because he was marked for death by his "boss," Vito Genovese. Several attempts had been made on Valachi's life, but it was his killing of a fellow prisoner in the Atlanta Penitentiary in 1962 (he mistakenly thought the man was his appointed executioner) that led to his confessions.

Knowing that the U.S. attorney in the case was preparing to ask for the death penalty, Valachi got word of his plight to New York narcotics officers (he had been convicted of heroin smuggling), who in turn informed Atlanta officials of his potential importance as a witness on organized crime. Consequently, Valachi was allowed to plead guilty to second degree murder, the penalty for which was life imprisonment rather than death.

Valachi was the first insider to identify the group he worked for as *La Cosa Nostra*. Peter Maas, in *The Valachi Papers*, tells us how this came about in an interchange between Valachi and FBI agent James P. Flynn. As Maas tells it, the discussion went as follows:

"Joe, let's stop fooling around. I want to talk about the organization by name, rank and serial number. What's the name? Is it Mafia?"

"No," Valachi said. "It's not Mafia. That's the expression the outside uses."

"Is it of Italian origin?"

"What do you mean?" Valachi parried.

"We know a lot more than you think," Flynn said. "Now I'll give you the first part. You give me the rest. It's Cosa—"

Valachi went pale. For almost a minute he said nothing. Then he rasped back hoarsely, "Cosa Nostra! So you know about it." (1968, 29–30)

The validity of the words *Cosa Nostra* in reference to organized crime has been questioned by many. Albini claims that in Italian they are not used in reference to an organization. As a common Italian phrase, the words, he says, mean "our affair," "our concern," "our interest," "or something relating to what a group may consider its particular province of concern at any given time" (1971, 224).

Maas, recognizing the controversial nature of the *Cosa Nostra* phrase, points out that it had cropped up on wiretaps and for "at least a year before Valachi came along the FBI had reason to believe that it represented what was commonly called the Mafia" (1968, 29).

Controversy, which has since diminished considerably, also surrounded Valachi's description of the organizational structure of *La Cosa Nostra*. He described it as consisting of twenty-four families, each with total control of its agreed-upon area or areas of operation in thirteen cities: Boston, Buffalo, Chicago, Cleveland, Detroit, Kansas City, Los Angeles, Newark, New Orleans, New York City, Philadelphia, Pittsburgh, and San Francisco. Resort cities such as Miami and Las Vegas, said Valachi, were regarded as open territories, places where any family could operate.

Each family was said to be headed by a *capo* (boss). *Capos* had *consiglieres*, or counselors. Beneath the *capo* came *subcapos* (underbosses), also referred to as lieutenants. Attached to lieutenants were soldiers. In 1967, the President's Commission on Law Enforcement and Administration of Justice diagrammed the structure and functions of a *La Cosa Nostra* family as it appears in Figure 5.1.

Although disputed and challenged for years, Valachi's description of the structure of *La Cosa Nostra's* administrative structure has been upheld by recent disclosures with only slight modifications. These include the finding that *caporegima* may be referred to as either lieutenants or captains and that there has been some expansion of both legitimate (banking, cleaners and laundries, entertainment) and illegitimate (arson, truck hijacking) endeavors.

Valachi's account of the emergence of *La Cosa Nostra* confirmed prevailing theory. It was after the so-called Castellammarese War of 1930, he said, that organizational unity was achieved among the various Italian and Sicilian gangs engaged in criminal activity.

It was during Prohibition that Italians and Sicilians in significant numbers got deeply involved in racketeering. Bootlegging was the chief activity; it was something they were particularly well-suited to take advantage of because of the widespread practice of home distilling among the Italian and Sicilian population. At the end of the era, the major gangs were led by two dominant figures: Giuseppe Masseria and Salvatore Maranzano.

Affiliated with Masseria were Al Capone, Lucky Luciano, Vito Genovese, Willi Moretti, Joe Adonis, and Frank Costello. Aligned with Maranzano were men from the Sicilian town of Castellammare del Golfo: Joseph Bonanno ("Joe Bananas"), Joseph Profaci, Stefano Magadinno, and Joseph Aiello.

According to Valachi, the war erupted in response to Masseria's attempt to become the organization's supreme power. Valachi sided with Maranzano. His affiliation required an initiation ceremony, which he described in some detail.

Valachi said he was brought into a room where about forty men were sitting around a table. When he entered, all present rose. He was introduced to "Don Salvatore Maranzano," who was described as the one who was to be boss "throughout the whole trouble we are having." He was told to sit, after which a knife and a gun were put before him. Maranzano told him that they represented what he was to live by. Then Maranzano asked all those present to rise and "throw

Figure 5.1
An organized crime family.

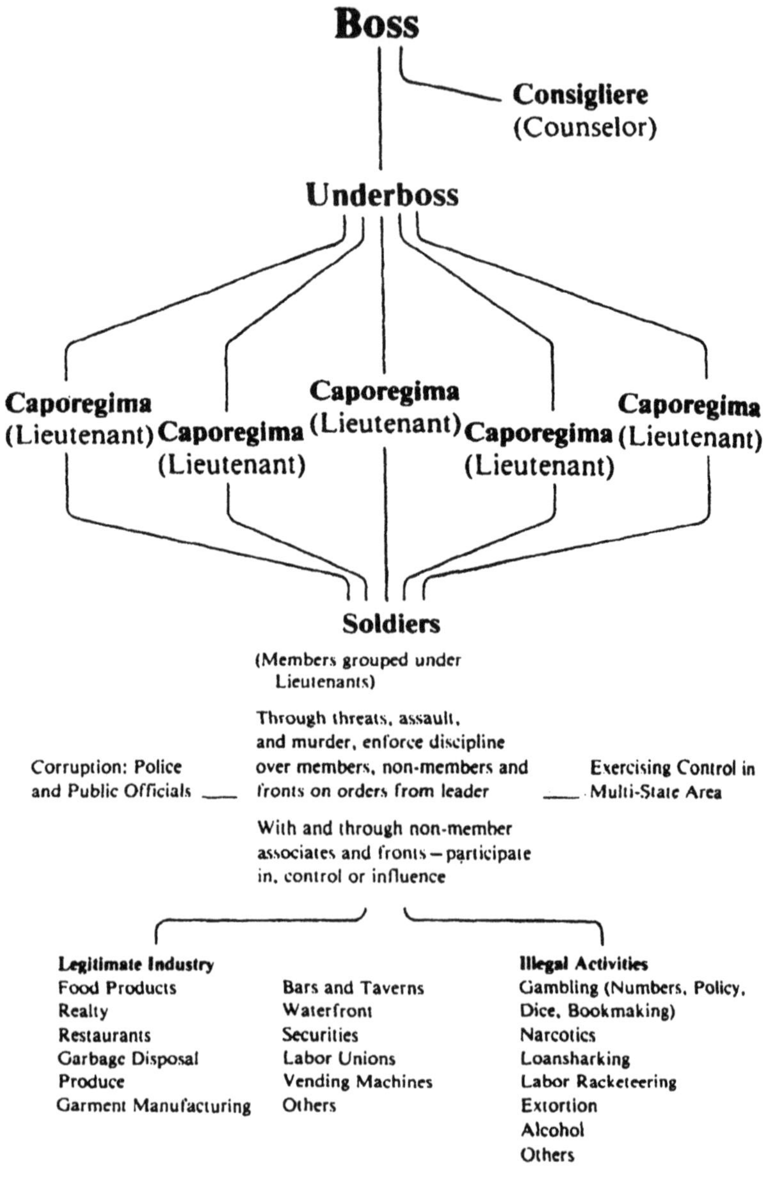

Source: Task Force on Organized Crime, *Task Force Report: Orqanized Crime,* Washington, D.C.: Government Printing Office, 1967, 9.

a finger from zero to five." This done, Maranzano proceeded to count fingers until reaching forty-eight. The significance of the number was not explained. Valachi said Maranzano laughed when he saw where the number fell, and then turned to him and said, "Well, Joe [Joe Bananas], that's your *gombah*"— "meaning he was kind of my godfather and was responsible for me."

Next, Joe Bananas asked Valachi to present his trigger finger. The finger was pricked with a pin until it began to bleed. At this point, Maranzano declared, "This blood means that we are now one family" (Maas 1968, 95–7).

The Castellammarese War ended in 1931. Sixty were killed in various parts of the country, mostly in New York City. The immediate victor was Maranzano, who declared himself *capo di tutti capo*. But his reign was brief. Within months, he, along with forty-odd others, was slain by order of Lucky Luciano. "Soldier" Valachi wound up a member of the Genovese family.

As Valachi told it, Luciano quelled interfamily disputes by establishing *consiglieri*. Each family had a counselor, and one of his jobs was to protect soldiers from arbitrary punishment at the hands of lieutenants.

Luciano, said Valachi, also eliminated the position of "boss of bosses." In addition, he resisted clannishness in favor of the development of working ties with non-Italian/Sicilian gangs. In fact, he is credited with having established a *Commissione*, a group or commission of approximately twelve top *capos* whose primary function was to coordinate gang activities around the country and regulate disputes among the membership.

In summary, Joseph Valachi's value as a witness was an insider's knowledge of the functioning structure of organized crime. His information, unlike Reles's, did not lead to a number of important convictions. Valachi is said to have provided important evidence leading to a conviction in only one instance, a 1968 hijacking trial. Also unlike Reles, Valachi did not die prematurely or "accidentally." He died of natural causes in prison. Maas's assessment of the quality of his evidence has been bolstered by subsequently acquired information. As Maas said, "It is virtually impossible to fault Valachi on even the most obscure details of his story—the name of a policeman who arrested him in the 1920s, a tabloid headline in the early 1930s, the price on a race one of his horses won in the 1940s" (1968, 50–1).

A particular event described by Valachi is worth some attention because it sheds light on the strength and unity of organized crime in America. It is the Apalachin conference of 1957.

The Apalachin Meeting

In 1936 Luciano was given a thirty- to fifty-year sentence for running a prostitution ring. At the same time, Vito Genovese, his would-be successor, left the country to avoid prosecution on a murder charge. Consequently, the reins of leadership passed to the number-three man, Frank Costello.

After World War II, Genovese returned to the United States, avoided prosecution for murder, and unseated Costello. The machinations of the two came to a head in 1957 with an unsuccessful attempt on Costello's life and the murder of his close associate, Albert Anastasia. These events prompted Genovese to call a national summit meeting to be held in Apalachin, a hamlet in upstate New York.

More than a hundred gangland leaders attended the Apalachin conference. The first item on the agenda was Genovese's request to be recognized by the *Commissione* as a family boss. This was granted, and the next matter to be considered was Genovese's violation of *Commissione* rules by the attempt on Costello's life and the murder of Anastasia. According to Valachi, Genovese argued that it was a case of kill or be killed, but after listening to his story, the *Commissione* required him not to pursue the matter further.

The facts and details of the meeting, the number and identity of those present were documented by a New York State police sergeant who sensed what was happening in his jurisdiction and established a roadblock. As Valachi reported it, there were between twenty-five and thirty *La Cosa Nostra* families in the country with a combined membership of approximately 5000. The Apalachin meeting had representatives from all the families. When those attending got word of the roadblock, there was something of a panic. Many took to the surrounding woods, but sixty were caught. Twenty-one were charged with conspiracy to obstruct justice by refusing to divulge the reason for their presence at the conference. They were tried, convicted, and in January 1960 sentenced to prison for terms varying from 3 to 5 years. The convictions were appealed and overturned that June. Nonetheless, knowledge of the meeting and its nature represented a turning point in awareness of the nature and extent of organized crime in the United States. As noted in the summary report of President Reagan's organized crime commission, "After the Apalachin incident few denied organized crime's existence, and law enforcement and government officials began to focus on combating the problem" (1986, 22). But, strangely enough, not immediately.

The Oyster Bay Conference and President Johnson's Crime Commission

The years after the Apalachin meeting and Valachi's testimony were characterized by a decreased interest in organized crime. A summit meeting, what Dwight Smith refers to as "Law Enforcement's Apalachin Conclave," to revitalize public and official interest in the problem was not called until 1965. It was held in Oyster Bay, Long Island, and was attended by thirty-three people from various parts of the country and representing different positions in government.

The stated purpose of the meeting was "to start a dialogue between persons working to control organized crime and to determine if it would be possible or useful to create a new doctrine defining the nature of organized crime and developing the most effective means of controlling it" (Smith 1975, 244). The conference led to fruitful discussions about organized crime and a general recognition of the need for further meetings.

Conferees rejected the notion of organized crime as "an invisible government of crime" in favor of its being a number of "criminal enterprises." The family structure identified by Valachi was accepted but not his name for the group. Instead of *La Cosa Nostra*, it was identified as a "confederation."

Conferees aimed to develop not only a satisfactory conceptual means of specifying and analyzing organized crime but also a way of arousing public concern. They thought that the public should be informed of the financial losses it incurs as a result of organized crime's prevalence and that they should be urged to refrain from using "confederation" services. To accomplish these aims, better relations between law enforcement and the media had to be developed. A conference on this subject was held with media personnel, but it produced more debate than agreement. If the public was to be properly educated about the problem, it had to be without the direct cooperation of the mass media. This line of thinking led to a 1966 publication, *Combating Organized Crime*. It and the Oyster Bay conference greatly influenced the principal contributors to a more widely disseminated work, *Task Force Report on Organized Crime of the President's Commission on Law Enforcement and Administration of Justice* (1967).

The report left little doubt as to the seriousness of organized crime, who and what was behind it, and what could be done about it. The actions of organized crime were said to be "the result of intricate conspiracies." The goal of organized crime was nothing short of the "nullification" of legal government by such means as monopolization, terrorism, and extortion.

At the core of organized crime were twenty-four groups described as "criminal cartels" located in the nation's largest urban centers. Cartel members were said to be "exclusively Italian" in close contact with one another, whose activities were coordinated and maintained by "a national body of overseers." Only the FBI claimed to have been able to "document fully" the range of cartel activities across the nation, and the FBI had learned that the name of the organization was *La Cosa Nostra* rather than the *Mafia*.

In 1967, the official view of organized crime was that it was an organization led by individuals imposing alien values on American society. *La Cosa Nostra's* aims were subversive. In the words of the commission,

> Organized crime is not merely a few preying upon a few. In a very real sense it is dedicated to subverting not only American institutions, but the very decency and integrity that are the most cherished attributes of a free society. As the leaders of Cosa Nostra and their racketeering allies pursue their conspiracy unmolested, in open and continuous defiance of the law, they preach a sermon that all too many Americans heed: The government is for sale; lawlessness is the road to wealth; honesty is a pitfall and morality a trap for suckers. (1967, 209)

Having defined the threat posed by organized crime as akin to a subversive plot by a foreign power, the commission proposed the development and implementation of appropriate countermeasures. It recommended that (1) grand juries be impaneled annually in areas where organized crime was known to be active; (2) grand juries be given special powers of investigation and prosecution; (3) a general immunity statute be enacted to encourage witness testimony; (4) legislation be enacted to permit wiretapping and bugging in organized crime matters; (5) legislation provide for long-term prison sentences in felony cases related to organized crime; (6) local facilities be established for witness protection during litigation; (7) state attorneys-general establish special information-gathering and prosecution units; (8) special investigation units be established in police departments; (9) a centralized computer facility be established for processing data on organized crime obtained by all federal agencies; (10) intelligence assistance be provided by the Justice Department to facilitate regional intelligence data-collection efforts; (11) a technical assistance program be established to enable local areas to obtain the help of federal prosecutors; (12) a permanent joint congressional committee on organized crime be established; (13) permanent organized crime commissions be established in all states; (14) citizen and business groups organize permanent crime commissions; (15) groups in federal and state departments of justice be established to combat the infiltration of legitimate businesses by organized crime; (16) private business associations develop strategies to detect unfair and illegal business tactics by organized crime; (17) all newspapers in major cities appoint a full-time reporter to investigate and report organized crime activity; and (18) law-enforcement officials regularly brief heads of government at all levels on the nature and extent of organized crime.

The Organized Crime Control Act of 1970 incorporated many of these recommendations; for example, the establishment of a witness protection program and the requirement that a federal grand jury on organized crime be established not less than every eighteen months in jurisdictions with at least a million inhabitants, and the Racketeer Influenced and Corrupt Organizations Act (RICO).

The RICO statute does not contain a definition of organized crime. Instead, it defines racketeering activity as "any act or threat involving murder, kidnapping, gambling, arson, robbery, bribery, extortion or dealing in narcotic or dangerous drugs and other denominated crime" (*President's Commission on Organized Crime* 1986, 24). Further, for racketeering to be a crime it must be patterned. A racketeering pattern "requires at least two acts of racketeering activity, one of which occurred after the effective date of this chapter and the last of which occurred within ten years (excluding any period of imprisonment) after the commission of a prior act of racketeering activity" (Abadinsky 1991, 423). Conviction under a RICO provision may result in a fine of not more than $25,000 or imprisonment up to twenty years. Additionally, RICO provides for the defendant's forfeiture of business and property acquired in violation of its provisions and the freezing of assets before trial (Abadinsky 1991, 423).

As noted earlier, RICO was little used to combat organized crime until the early 1980s. According to President Reagan's commission on organized crime, "Because RICO is not written in typical criminal law format, prosecutors have had difficulty interpreting the law and its use and have only recently felt comfortable using the law as it was intended" (1986, 47–8). As the commission notes, electronic surveillance in the federal prosecution of organized crime was legalized in 1969. Two developments in the early 1980s provided the necessary impetus to use these resources: placing the Drug Enforcement Administration (DEA) in the FBI, and increased cooperation between official agencies in the United States and Italy.

Prosecution of Organized Crime in the 1980s

The application of RICO and the witness protection program (through 1989, nearly 5000 witnesses had been relocated and given new identities; see Cox 1992, 11) resulted in the conviction of some 1000 *Mafia* members and associates from 1981 to mid-1988 (Cox 1992, 380). Most of the nation's twenty-four *Mafia* families (total membership is currently estimated at 4000–5000, with half belonging to New York's five families dominated by the Gambino family) suffered indictments and convictions. Family leaders have been convicted in major cities such as Boston, Chicago, Cleveland, Denver, Kansas City, MO., Milwaukee, New Jersey, New Orleans, New York, Pennsylvania, St. Louis, and Tucson. Two widely documented cases occurred in Boston and Philadelphia.

Mafia activities in Boston were led by an underboss, Gennaro ("Jerry") Angiulo (the New England Crime boss was Raymond Patriarca of Providence, R. I. who died in 1985 and was succeeded by his son Raymond Patriarca, Jr., arrested and indicted in 1990) and his three brothers, Franceso ("Frankie"), Donato ("Danny"), and Michele ("Mickey"). All told, some twenty members of the family were indicted and eighteen went to trial. Leaders convicted in 1986 were Jerry Angiulo (45 years, $120,000 fine), Francesco Angiulo (25 years, $60,000 fine), Donato Angiulo (10 years, $40,000 fine), Michele Angiulo (3 years, $5,000 fine), and Samuel Granito (a *caporegima*, 20 years, $35,000 fine). Among the family's twelve soldiers convicted, one received a sentence of 18 years (for racketeering), two received 12-year sentences (one for conspiring to murder a witness and the other for racketeering), and one a 6-year sentence (for conspiring to impede a grand jury investigation).

"The evidence for the successful prosecution of the Angiulo family was obtained by means of a "bug" installed in 1981. In one recorded interchange between three family members, Jerry Angiulo identifies the family's activities as arson, bookmaking, drug peddling, loan sharking ("Shylocking"), and prostitution. As Jerry Angiulo read the RICO statute, "If they don't prove that a legitimate business was infiltrated, we're off the hook. We can do any fuckin' thing we want. They can stick RICO" (Goode 1988, 141).

Conviction of the top leaders and soldiers of the Angiulo family did not eliminate *Mafia* influence in Boston. In 1989, FBI agents arrested five individuals alleged to be *mafia* members and the successors to the Angiulo family in Boston. Joseph Russo, Vincent Ferrara, and Robert Carrozza were charged with conspiring to extort $500,000 from Boston bookmakers and described as "capo regimes, or lieutenants."

Of all recent *Mafia* cases, the one that has received the greatest amount of journalistic coverage has been devoted to the demise of the entire Philadelphia-based Scarfo family (see Anastasia 1991; Cox 1992; Friel and Guinther 1990). More than sixty individuals were convicted through the efforts of an Organized Crime Task Force established in 1982. Boss Nicodemo Scarfo was convicted of three offenses: extortion (a 14-year sentence), racketeering (a 55-year sentence), and murder (a life sentence). Successful prosecution of the family was enhanced by testimony of five of its members, who turned state's evidence after being indicted and informed of the witness protection program. The last "turncoat" was the family's underboss, Phil ("Crazy Phil") Leonetti, Scarfo's nephew, close confidant, and once rumored successor.

Leonetti has been a particularly important prosecution witness because of his ability to withstand cross-examination and intimate knowledge not only of the activities of his own *Mafia* family but also those operating in Connecticut and the New York-New Jersey area as well. He has testified of hearing John Gotti admit having planned the murder of Paul Castellano. According to journalist Marguerite Del Giudice, "Leonetti is betting that an effective performance against Gotti will make the difference when he time comes for his own 45-year sentence for murder and racketeering to be reconsidered" (1992,32).[2]

The question is, does the recent nationwide success in prosecuting and convicting *Mafia* family members, even to the extent of eliminating whole families as in the case of Philadelphia, mean that we are witnessing the end of organized crime in the United States? Few, if any, recognized authorities on the subject would answer in the affirmative. If nothing else, the vacuum created in places such as Philadelphia is likely to be filled either gradually by individuals perhaps operating alone at first but later joining together to mitigate conflict and promote order or all at once by new groups. The latter was a chief consideration of President Reagan's commission on organized crime.

Recent Developments: From the Reagan Commission to the Present

President Ronald Reagan established a Commission on Organized Crime in 1983. Toward the end of its recommending administrative and legislative improvements to improve the ability to combat organized crime, the commission was directed to "make a full and complete national and region-by-region analysis of organized crime; define the nature of traditional organized crime as well as emerging crime groups, the sources and amounts of organized crime's income, and the uses to which organized crime puts its income; and develop in-depth information on the participants in organized crime networks" (*The Impact* 1986, 9).

The initial problem dealt with by the commission was a proper definition of organized crime. Commissioners noted that the problem was not in defining the crimes, but in the nature of the organization. As they noted, "Organized criminal activity is not necessarily organized crime" (1986, 19). Thus, instead of developing its own definition, the commission reviewed past authoritative definitions and outlined what it considered to be the delineating features of organized crime.

As noted earlier, President Johnson's Commission on Law Enforcement and the Administration of Justice defined organized crime as "a society that seeks to operate outside the control of the American people and their government [and involving] thousands of criminals, working within structures as complex as those of any corporation, subject to laws more rigidly enforced than those of legitimate governments" (1967, 205). The commissioners' basic criticism of this definition was its failure to "sufficiently emphasize the importance and roles of groups other than *La Cosa Nostra* in American organized crime" (1986: 23). Accordingly, commissioners proposed the following characteristics of the "criminal group" as a more useful, less time-restricted way of conceptualizing organized crime: (1) *continuity* (organized crime is conducted by enduring collectivities whose members subordinate personal interests to those of the larger whole); (2) *structure* (organized crime is conducted by collectivities with divisional ranks and chains of command); (3) *membership* (organized crime groups have restrictive, highly selective membership rules—membership is often determined by race, ethnicity, and blood ties—as members must prove loyalty by willingness to sacrifice everything to the interests of the group); (4) *criminality* (organized crime is based on the provision of illegal services for economic gain and law violation when necessary to enhance and maintain and expand influence and power); (5) *violence* (organized crime relies on violence as a method of control and protection); and (6) *power/profit goal* (organized crime seeks the use of all means necessary to determine its continuity, expansion, and ability to control all desired outcomes) (1986, 26–9).

Crucial to the last are *the protectors*, "a complement of corrupt public officials, attorneys and businessmen, who individually and collectively protect the criminal group through abuses of status and/or privilege and violations of the law" (*The Impact* 1986, 29). These individuals are organized crime members, and with their employers depend on *specialist support* "such as pilots, chemists, arsonists, and hijackers" (1986, 31).

In appraising the extent of organized crime as in the mid1980s, the commission spoke of "an emerging awareness" that groups other than *La Cosa Nostra* had to be taken into account. It spoke of "more than a dozen" other groups based on ethnicity and originating in prisons and outlaw motorcycle gangs. Commissioners stressed, however, that *La Costra Nostra* would continue to be the dominant group in organized crime and that it was likely to continue to expand drug operations.

Outlaw motorcycle gangs are not, of course, a recent phenomenon. But the commission noted that in recent years their members' behavior had become more "surly" and "openly criminal." The country was estimated to have between 800 and 900 outlaw motorcycle gangs, ranging from the unaffiliated and "loosely organized" to highly organized entities with chapters throughout the nation and other countries (Europe and Australia). The major gangs identified are Hell's Angels (founded in southern California about 1950), the Outlaws (founded in Chicago in 1959), the Bandidos (founded in Houston in 1960), and the Pagans (founded in Maryland in 1959). The four have ties with *La Cosa Nostra* and engage in a variety of criminal activities (murder, extortion, drug trafficking). Other important outlaw motorcycle gangs include the Sons of Silence (operating in the Midwest), the Vagos (operating in Los Angeles and Mexico), the Peacemakers (operating in the Southeast), and the Dirty Dozen (operating in Arizona and the Southwest). But the commission had it on good authority that these last four had not yet become "true organized crime groups."

According to the historian Stephen Fox, involvement in drug trafficking around 1970 began the ascent into organized crime by major outlaw motorcycle gangs. As Fox sees it, their early specialty "was synthetic drugs—methamphetamines (speed), PCP, LSD—manufactured from available materials, therefore produced locally. Explicitly taking cues from Mafia families, the bikers organized themselves with national officers and policy boards" (1989, 412). During the 1980s, the total membership of outlaw motorcycle gangs was estimated at over 3000.

Another "home-grown" organized crime element not discussed by the commission is the recent emergence of black gangs. As whites have moved out of inner cities and blacks have moved in, formerly Italian- and Sicilian-dominated illicit activities have been replaced by black leaders in several major cities. As Stephen Fox states,

> in Buffalo, blacks seized control of numbers gambling from the Magaddinos, at first paying a token tribute of 10 percent profits, then no tribute at all. In Newark, they snatched the numbers trade from Richie Boiardo, a Genovese Capo. "Everybody wants his turn at making it," said an Italian gangster pushed out of East Harlem. "We had ours and I guess it's their turn now." (1988, 413)

Black-led gangs are also known to be heavily involved in drug trafficking. Fox claims that the first black narcotics ring appeared in New York in the 1960s. Heroin and cocaine were imported from South American and distributed by a team of more than a hundred (1988, 414). As Fox notes, during the 1970s it was generally assumed that blacks would soon replace Italian and Sicilian-dominated organized crime throughout the country. But this did not and it is not likely to occur for reasons discussed below. For the moment, it is important to indicate that the Reagan commission stressed the importance of what it perceived as growing organized crime involvement by Asian groups— in particular, Chinese *Triads* and *Tongs* and the Japanese *Yakuza*.

The first *Triad* originated during the seventeenth-century Manchu dynasty. Its members were revolutionary monks who developed an elaborate set of operating rules, including a most demanding membership induction ritual (see Posner 1988, 51–3). The same basic conditions conducive to the rise and institutionalization of the *Mafia* in Sicily were present in China during the Manchu dynasty: a level of governmental corruption and incompetence conducive to the chaos and resentment that make the masses available to alternative groups for protection and maintenance of social order. "As the Manchu dynasty was increasingly riddled with corruption," says Posner, "it disenfranchised millions of people, and the role of and stature of [the *Triads*] expanded" (1988, 30). *Triads* rather quickly spread to all corners of the country.

As contemporary crime entities, *Triads* are based in Hong Kong, which is said to have at least fifty (one, the 14K *Triad*, has a membership estimated at 30,000). *Triads* and their members are principally designated numerically. As Posner explains it,

> Triad members are assigned numbers, always divisible by 3, a number the Chinese consider magical. All Triad positions have corresponding numbers, [which are] the intricate result of combining various Chinese superstitions with the numerical representations for creation, longevity, and rebirth. The numbers also hinder the police task of pinpointing Triad officers, since the gangster is always referred to by his number and never by his real identity. (1988, 29)

Triads now control heroin and cocaine production in the Golden Triangle, a mountainous area touching on three countries: Burma, Laos, and Thailand. They have worldwide operations and were estimated in 1986 to control at least half of the street-level traffic in heroin. In 1988, according to Posner (1988, 10), the Drug Enforcement Administration found Chinese syndicates responsible for 70 percent of the heroin coming into New York (the major distribution site). With mainland China scheduled to regain control of Hong Kong in 1997, *Triad* involvement in international organized crime is expected to grow exponentially. Expansion of their North American operations is abetted by the decline of *Mafia* influence in the wake of recent and continued law enforcement efforts.

Assisting *Triad* involvement in the United States are *Tongs. Tongs*, or benevolent associations, were formed by Chinese immigrants in the nineteenth century. They exist today in cities with large Chinese populations. President Reagan's organized crime commission describes many as "fronts" for Chinese crime groups "that prey mainly on Chinese immigrants and ChineseAmericans" (1986, 86). The commission notes that *Tong* members control usual organized crime activities such as extortion, gambling, narcotics trafficking, prostitution protection schemes, and pornography. Two of the more powerful *Tongs* identified are the *On Leong Tong* based in New York and the *Hop Sing* operating on the West Coast. *Tongs* are long known to have developed strong ties with *La Costra Nostra* families. According to the commission, "the LCN has provided loansharking capital and untraceable weapons to Chinese gangs, and the two groups have cooperated in illegal gambling houses" (1986, 92).

The commission did not find a connection between the presence of the *Yakuza* in American and early Japanese immigrant organizational practices. Its roots, like those of the Chinese *Triads*, trace to feudal times, to sixteenth- and seventeenth- century Japan (see Iwai 1986, 208–33). When the feudal era gave way to a centralized national government, some local samurai warriors became vagabonds and referred to as *Yakuza*, "a gambling term for numbers that are worthless or losers" (Iwai 1986, 98). In time, the expression became synonymous with outlaw. As organized crime entities, they came to the fore with Japan's rapid economic expansion after World War II.

There are seven major *Yakuza* groups. The largest, with a 1988 estimated membership of 20,000, is Yamaguchi Gumi. Its organizational structure is described as comparable to that of a *Mafia* family in the United States. The six others are described as confederations of smaller gangs possessing even more complex organizational structures. These confederations or alliances control illicit activities in delimited territories. The largest, Sumiyoshi Rengo, has a membership estimated at 8000 to 15,000.

Membership in the *Yakuza* is demanding and ritualistic. Among the more exotic practices are tattooing and finger amputation. As Abadinsky points out, by subjecting their bodies to virtually complete tattooing from neck to ankles, members demonstrate pain toleration and group commitment (1991, 247). Finger amputation, says Abadinsky, is done with a short sword in a ritual that serves as a sign of contrition for mistakes. The amputated finger tip is put in a small bottle of alcohol with the person's name written on it and is sent to the person whose forgiveness is sought (1991, 247).

The president's crime commission stated that on the international level, the *Yakuza* engage in drug trafficking (mostly amphetamine smuggling from the United States to Japan) and the sale of illegal firearms. In a speech delivered in 1990, FBI Director William Sessions described the Yakuza (as he points out, the Japanese National Policy Agency prefers to call the group the *Boryokudan*, "the violent ones") as "active in the United States" and engaged "in various activities, including murder, kidnapping, extortion, home invasions, prostitution, gambling, weapons smuggling, insurance fraud, and money laundering" (1990, 70). Sessions went on to point out that the *Boryokudan* are among the world's largest criminal organizations and in 1988 grossed nearly $10 billion (about a third was based on the sale of methamphetamines in Japan). *Boryokudan* also control 90 percent of the crystal methamphetamine (or "ice") coming into Hawaii and spreading to the West Coast. But the *Boryokudan* are involved in more than drug trafficking. According to Sessions, "They also smuggle guns from the United States into Japan; they run tourist rip-off schemes in the U.S. and Japan; they extort corporations; and they deal in prostitution, pornography, and loansharking" (1990, 70). Lastly, in an article in *Business Week*, Karen Lowry Miller states that the Yakuza "are closing ranks in Southeast Asia to smuggle weapons, recruit prostitutes for Japan, and horn in on the Golden Triangle drug trade" (1991, 29).

The Reagan organized crime commission also briefly examined reports of gangs of Vietnamese immigrants engaged in organized crime. As to how many exist and their future prospects, the commission did not say. It did indicate that Vietnamese gangs are known to cooperate with other Asian crime groups and that Chinese gangs in Los Angeles and San Francisco have Vietnamese branches.

Notwithstanding the growing role of Asian collectivities in worldwide organized crime and the numerous groups engaged in drug trafficking, it is intergroup cooperation rather than intergroup conflict that is the recurrent theme in the recent literature on organized crime. As Claire Sterling says in reference to the Sicilian *Mafia*, the Chinese *Triads*, and the Columbia drug cartels, "the three don't fight" (1990, 311). In Sterling's estimation, and that of many others as well, the worldwide leader in drug trafficking, despite its apparent weakening by law-enforcement efforts throughout the 1980s, continues to be the Sicilian *Mafia* and its *La Cosa Nostra* American counterpart. The key to this fact lies in certain developments that occurred over the past thirty or forty years.

Sterling contends that in the late 1950s, at a meeting in Palermo between American and Sicilian *Mafia* leaders, the Sicilians were given control of heroin trafficking in North America and elsewhere. But the extent of Sicilian involvement in North American drug trafficking was not uncovered until the Pizza Connection Case of the mid-1980s. Through the efforts of agents and wiretaps, the FBI discovered that pizza parlors around the country were being used to distribute drugs and launder money and that they were run by Sicilians. The initial assumption, as Sterling tells is, is that the Sicilians were being used by *La Cosa Nostra* families. Only later was it recognized that the Sicilian *Mafia* was the directing force.

To Sterling, the Sicilian *Mafia's* early entry into drug trafficking enabled it to expanded worldwide in the manner of an octopus or a creature with a seemingly infinite number of tentacles to reach out and grasp desired prey. The basic evidence on the global reach of the Sicilian *Mafia*, says Sterling, emerged in the testimony of numerous witnesses during a massive trial conducted in Italy in 1986. As she reports it, witnesses (that is, *Mafia* members) testifying for the prosecution described the Sicilian *Mafia* as "global, unitary, rigidly regimented, and vertically structured, governed from the top down by a Cupola with absolute powers over policy, money, life, and death" (1990, 282).

In the final pages of her treatise, Sterling cites an interview in March 1989 with an FBI agent who described the Sicilian *Mafia* as "still the biggest" with "routes that we've never found and know nothing about" (1990, 313–14).

Summary & Conclusion

Organized crime, enduring administratively structured criminal groups engaged in diverse illegitimate and legitimate activities, is a worldwide phenomenon. The origins of the oldest criminal groups, the Chinese *Triads* and the Japanese *Yakuza*, have been traced to feudal times. The Sicilian *Mafia*, the major Western organized crime element, arose only in the nineteenth century, but out of a feudal tradition.

Although criminal gangs in the United States antedate the *Mafia* (or as it came to be referred to in the 1960s, *La Cosa Nostra*), it has been the most enduring. Organized crime in the United States has been dominated by the Sicilian- and Italian-led *La Cosa Nostra* for more than sixty years. The durability of this leadership and organization requires some explanation, especially if the aim is to develop an effective public policy for combating and containing its spread and influence.

La Cosa Nostra has survived by its ability to recruit new members from both nuclear and extended families in the "new" and the "old" country. And recently discovered evidence indicates that the ties may be directed more from Sicily than the United States. Italian and Sicilian immigrants are not so much used by *La Costra Nostra* as *La Costra Nostra* is used by the Sicilian *Mafia* to effect its aims. Sterling's analysis suggests that efforts to destroy *La Costra Nostra* must be paralleled by an effort to destroy the Sicilian *Mafia*. But most consider the goal unlikely: evidence suggests that the Sicilian *Mafia* is too deeply embedded in the sociocultural fabric of Sicily and Italy. And even if all *La Cosa Nostra* families were eliminated, there is no shortage of others who would take their place. In particular, as 1997 approaches, and Hong Kong reverts to China, Chinese immigration, including that of *Triad* members, is likely to increase. But this is not to imply that organized crime in America is altogether "a foreign import" to be managed by new and more restrictive immigration policy. Our social and economic institutions, too, must be considered by one wishing to confront the problem. Racism, social and economic discrimination, poverty, and frustrated upward mobility are just some of the social and cultural facts that contribute to the problem. And even if these could be "solved," one must still confront general human qualities such as greed, corruption, the thrill of risk taking, and so on. In any event, there are both foreign and domestic issues to confront, and doubtlessly the best that can be realistically hoped for is the development of policies based on integration of as many elements of both as possible toward the goal of measurably reducing and containing organized crime.

References

Abadinsky, Howard. 1991.*Organized Crime*. 3rd ed. Chicago: Nelson-Hall.

Albini, Joseph L. 1971. *The American Mafia: Genesis of a Legend*. New York: Appleton-Century-Crofts.

Anastasia, George. 1991.*Blood and Honor*. New York: Morrow.

Bell, Daniel. 1962."Crime as an American Way of Life." In Bell, *The End of Ideology*. New York: Collier Books.

Bequai, August. 1979. *Organized Crime*. Lexington, Mass.: Lexington Books.

Brown, Richard Maxwell. 1969."Historical Patterns of Violence in America." In *Violence in America* edited by Hugh David Graham and Ted Robert Gurr. New York: Signet, 43–80.

Cook, Fred. 1966. *The Secret Rulers*. New York: Duell, Sloan and Pearce.

Cox, Donald. 1992. *Mafia Wipeout*. New York: S.P.I. Books.

Cressey, Donald R. 1969.*Theft of the Nation*. New York: Harper & Row.

Del Giudice, Marguerite. 1992. "The Mobster Who Could Bring Down the Mob." In *Criminal Justice 92/93*, edited by John J. Sullivan and Joseph L. Victor. Guilford, Conn.: Dushkin.

Fox, Stephen. 1989.*Blood and Power: Organized Crime in Twentieth-Century America.* New York: Penguin.

Fried, Albert. 1980. *The Rise and Fall of the Jewish Gangster in America.* New York: Holt, Rinehart and Winston.

Friel, Frank and John Guinther. 1990. *Breaking the Mob.* New York: McGraw-Hill.

Goode, James. 1988.*Wiretap: Listening in on America's Mafia.* New York: Simon and Schuster.

Hammer, Richard. 1975. *Hoodlum Empire.* Chicago: Playboy Press.

Ianni, Francis A.J. 1972. *A Family Business.* New York: Russell Sage Foundation.

Iwai, Hiroaki. 1986. "Organized Crime in Japan." In *Organized Crime: A Global Perspective* edited by Robert J. Kelly. Totowa, New Jersey: Rowman & Littlefield.

Maas, Peter. 1968. *The Valachi Papers.* New York: Putnams.

Miller, Karen Lowry. 1991. "Suddenly, The Japanese Mob Is Out of The Shadows." *Business Week,* July 8, 29.

Nelli, Humbert S. 1976. *The Business of Crime.* New York: Oxford University Press.

Posner, Gerald L. 1988.*Warlords of Crime.* New York: Penguin.

President's Commission on Law Enforcement and Administration of Justice. 1967. *The Challenge of Crime in a Free Society.*Washington, D.C.: Government Printing Office.

President's Commission on Organized Crime. 1984. *Organized Crime of Asian Origin.* Washington, D.C.: Government Printing Office.

———. 1986. *The Impact: Organized Crime Today.* Washington,D.C.: Government Printing Office.

Saloutos, Theodore. 1974. "Exodus U.S.A." In *Divided Society* edited by Colin Greer. New York: Basic Books.

Sessions, William S. 1990. "International Crime in the "90's" and the 21st Century." *Vital Speeches of the Day* 57, 69–71.

Smith, Dwight C. Jr. 1975. *The Mafia Mystique.* New York: Basic Books.

Sondern, Frederick Jr. 1972. "How the Mafia came to America." In *Mafia U.S.A.* edited by Nicholas Gage. Chicago: Playboy Press.

Sterling, Claire. 1990. *Octopus.* New York: Simon and Schuster.

Notes

[1]. A similar practice existed in rural America. In nineteenth century Wyoming, for example, cattlemen's associations hired private armies to protect and assert their interests. The infamous Johnson County War was the product of such a situation (see Brown 1969, 144–218).

[2]. As it turned out, it was the testimony of a member of his own Gambino family, Salvatore ("Sammy Bull") Gravano, and his own tape-recorded words, that led to Gotti's downfall. Gravano, who confessed to nineteen murders, testified that Gotti planned the murder of Paul Castellano, and that they sat in a car a block away when the execution took place. And on an exceptionally clear tape, Gotti is heard to say: "Every time we got a partner that don't agree with us, we kill him; you go to the boss and your boss kills him; he kills 'em; he OKs it" (*New York Times*, April 3, 1992: B2). On April 2, 1992, John Gotti and his underboss, Frank Locasio, were convicted on all counts and received life sentences.

PART II

The Field of Criminology

Chapter 6

The Rise of Criminology: From Utilitarianism to Determinism

Students of crime quickly learn that there are nearly as many definitions of criminology as there are criminologists. Among the most influential definitions is that of the late Edwin Sutherland. In his classic text on the subject, first published in 1924, Sutherland defined criminology as

> the body of knowledge regarding crime as a social phenomenon. It includes within its scope the processes of making laws, of breaking laws, and of reacting toward the breaking of laws. (1960, 3)

Sutherland's criminology has three subdivisions: the sociology of law (the scientific study of the conditions behind the development of criminal law); criminal etiology (the scientific study of the causes of crime); and penology (crime control). Criminology's objective, said Sutherland, "is the development of a body of general and verified principles and of other types of knowledge regarding law, crime, and treatment or prevention" (1960, 3).

Sutherland's conception reflects the fact that by the 1920s, criminology had become an appendage of sociology. This should not be surprising because sociology was initiated by those concerned to synthesize all scientifically acquired knowledge of human social behavior toward the goal of ameliorating the human condition. Criminology continues to be heavily influenced by sociology, and sociologists continue to study criminological phenomena along the lines described by Sutherland. But criminology now shares the study of crime with criminal justice. The field of criminal justice arose in the United States in the mid-1960s for a number of reasons, including dissatisfaction with the dominance of the sociological view of crime and a demand for different and more practical treatments of subjects such as law enforcement and the administration of correctional institutions. Crime had become a major social problem, and politicians, reflecting the concerns of their constituents, called for immediate and systematic treatment of the crime problem. Interestingly, those who initiated what is regarded as modern criminology were also motivated by practical concerns. If contemporary criminologists are particularly concerned to ferret out the causes of crime in order to minimize its occurrence, early criminologists were especially concerned to reform criminal law to eliminate inhumane punishment and enhance community protection. This chapter outlines the views and orientations of those Europeans who played key roles in the initiation and establishment of basic criminological perspectives—from the emergence of utilitarian theory in the latter half of the eighteenth century to the appearance of the sociological viewpoint in the nineteenth century.

The World of the Founders: Social Change and Crime

Although most criminologists believe that the term criminology was first used in the late nineteenth century, they trace the roots of the discipline to the eighteenth century and two writers in particular: the Italian jurist Cesare Beccaria and the English philosopher Jeremy Bentham.

Europe in the eighteenth century was marked by contrasts. On the one hand, "it was pre-eminently a century of good sense; of sobriety of thought and action; of growing toleration and humanity; of declining superstition; of rapidly extending knowledge; of great hopefulness about the future" (Tobias 1967, 34). On the other hand, the penal systems of the age were "a mass of incongruities, absurdities, contradictions, and barbarities" (Phillipson 1970, 166). Judges, or magistrates, had virtually absolute power, not only in determining the guilt or innocence of those unfortunate enough to be brought before them, but also in deciding the kind and degree of punishment to be imposed on the guilty. Due process had no meaning. Obtaining confessions by torture was a sanctioned and routine practice. The convicted were punished much less frequently by incarceration than by bodily abuse and death. England had over two hundred capital offenses. One could be executed for what today would be regarded as petty theft. Hanging was the usual means of putting someone to death. "Sometimes the death was lingering and unspeakably horrible; and the relatives and friends of a victim were known to lay hold of his legs when he was hanging in order to end his agony" (Phillipson 1970, 172).

Adherence to the biblical principle of *lex talionis*, "an eye for an eye," was an important factor behind the cruel manner in which legal codes were enforced. Of no less significance was the effort of the established classes to protect themselves by the ruthless oppression of those who would defy them and challenge their authority. As George Vold describes it, "This arbitrary and tyrannical practice of power, in which the judges took the part of one class in its struggle with the members of other classes, [occurred] in a society rapidly becoming mobile and fluid" (1958, 19). The ancient social order was ending, and a new and incompatible society was in its infancy. The disjunction was the product of industrialization, urbanization, and population increase. The interplay of these three factors is worth examination for several reasons, the most important of which for our purposes is to put the contributions of Beccaria, Bentham, and those who followed them in proper perspective.

Industrialization, Urbanization, and Population Growth

In England especially, but in Western Europe generally, the Industrial Revolution took place from the middle of the eighteenth century to the middle of the nineteenth century. A number of interrelated technical innovations (including the development of the steam engine and the factory system of production) propelled the rapid industrialization and urbanization of England. And as Tobias (1967, 35) points out, "the coming of the factory in its turn led to the growth of towns, for the workers had now to cluster round the factory so as to be within easy reach, so as to be able to start work on time."

Between 1750 and 1850, London's population increased 169 percent, from less than 900,000 to more than 2.3 million. The only European city to rival London's growth was Paris. Its population expanded by 134 percent, from less than 600,000 to more than 1.3 million. Italian cities grew moderately: Naples, the largest city, experienced a relatively modest 28 percent increase, from 324,000 to 416,000. Rome's population increase was only 13 percent, from 151,000 to 170,000 (Ferri 1967, 94).

In England, city growth was most pronounced from 1800 to 1850. Manufacturing cities generally experienced dramatic population growth. For example, Liverpool experienced a 455 percent increase (from 76,000 to 422,000), Manchester a 398 percent increase (from 81,000 to 404,000), and Birmingham a 308 percent increase (from 72,000 to 294,000) (Chandler and Fox 1974, 18–20).

In 1750, about one-fifth of the English lived in places with 5000 or more inhabitants. By 1850, the corresponding figure was three-fifths. As late as 1900, England was the only nation on earth whose population was predominantly urban.

While England's population increased nearly 4 million from 1700 to 1800, nearly 14 million were added between 1750 and 1850 (a 233 percent increase). In France, the population increased 54 percent between 1750 and 1850. In Italy, the best available information dates from 1770. From that year until 1850, the country experienced a 60 percent population increase. By 1850, France had a population of 34 million, Italy 24 million, and England 20 million (Rusche and Kirchheimer 1968, 86).

Population growth in Europe during the Industrial Revolution correlated with a lowering of the death rate. The death rate declined for many reasons, but chiefly because of improvements in the production and distribution of foodstuffs. In England, for example, "The price of corn was low. Meat in London was cheap and plentiful, the markets and stalls were being increasingly well supplied with fruit and vegetables. Trade was growing and the country was financially prosperous" (George 1965, 27).

Nonetheless, prosperity all too quickly generated an extreme division of wealth and considerable divisiveness between the "haves" and the "have nots."

By the end of the eighteenth century, Europe was in the grip of widespread social unrest. By the beginning of the nineteenth century, crime was on the rise.

Social Disorder & Crime during the Industrial Revolution

Social unrest in Europe in the late eighteenth and early nineteenth centuries was greatly influenced by population increase, the mechanization of work, and high rates of population concentration or urbanization. Most urban migrants were young and were ill-prepared for life in their new surroundings. And burgeoning towns and cities lacked the facilities to respond properly to the problems created by a rapid influx of newcomers. The eventual result was a labor surplus and high unemployment. While some were able to increase their wealth, many others were forced into poverty. In the 1780s the French philosopher Mirabeau described living conditions as generally precarious. "Those who have the means," he said, "devour them by the pursuit of a fortune, but the men obliged to live by the work of their hands, who expect nothing from the government, business, or inheritance, lean upon the idea of public charity" (Cited in Rusch and Kirchheimer 1968, 92). A decade later, London was said to contain at least 20,000 individuals who "rose every morning without knowing how they were to be supported through the day or where they were to lodge on the succeeding night, and cases of death from starvation appeared in the coroner's list daily" (Rusch and Kirchheimer 1968, 93). At least 50,000 women supported themselves either partially or wholly by prostitution.

By all accounts, conditions in France were even worse. In the late eighteenth century, 30,000 people in Lyons existed on public charity, two-thirds of the population of Reims lived in poverty, and Paris contained some 100,000 indigent families. Riots against the high cost of living erupted in major cities throughout the period; for example, Reims in 1770, Poitiers in 1772, Paris in 1775, 1788, and 1789, and Aix-en-Provence in 1785 (Durant and Durant 1967, 934).

In most countries, property crime rather than violent crime was on the increase (Phillipson 1970, 164). This pattern continued well into the nineteenth century. From 1821 to 1827, for example, convictions for larceny in London increased by 48 percent, from 6629 to 9803. In France, larceny convictions between 1825 and 1842 increased 181 percent, from 7132 to 20,022 (Rusche and Kirchheimer 1968, 96–97).

In Italy, violent crime rather than property crime was on the rise. For example, from 1758 to 1769, Rome, with a population of approximately 160,000, reportedly had 4000 murders. Similarly high rates were reported elsewhere, along with high rates of execution (see Crow 1965, 327–28). Lawlessness and violence were exacerbated by the fact that Italy was not a unified country. Throughout the eighteenth century it was under the dominion of

Austria. Before Austria, Spain had been the ruling power. In consequence, Italy had a plethora of legal codes and a highly arbitrary system of law enforcement. According to John Crow, Naples had "at least ten different legal codes: Roman, Norman, Spanish, French, Austrian, and several others." The result was that "people got into a state of mind where they lacked confidence in all laws, trusted no one, and believed the only right they had was to fend for themselves as best they might" (Crow 1965, 327–28).

As is usually the case, as crime increased, so did the demand for harsh penalties. Thus, as Rusche and Kirchheimer note,

> People declared that the penal system had become humbug, and that punishment should once again become something that the wrong-doer felt to the very marrow of his bones, something that tortured and destroyed him. The ax, the whip, and starvation ought to be reintroduced to root out the criminals. (1968, 97).

This was the milieu that nurtured *On Crimes and Punishments,* published in 1764 by Cesare Beccaria.

The Classical Utilitarian Perspective

The Marchese Cesare Beccaria Bonesana was born in 1738 in Milan. Of an aristocratic family, he studied law at the University of Pavia and received a doctorate in 1758. On returning to Milan, he became a member of an avant garde society, the "academy of fists." According to one of Beccaria'a biographers, "academies of this type, which flourished in Italy in the seventeenth and eighteenth centuries, had witty or ludicrous names, such as the Lunatics, the Extravagant, the Drowsy, the Apathetic, the Anxious, the Confused, the Fanatic, the Ethereal" (Maestro 1973, 6). The "academy of fists" was led by Pietro Verri, an engaging and charismatic intellectual. Verri stimulated Beccaria's interest in legal and penal reform and encouraged him to read works on these subjects by French and English authors, particularly Hume, Helvetius, Locke, Montesquieu, and Rousseau.[1]

Although Beccaria's treatise was essentially a passionate appeal for penal reform, it was structured in a manner consistent with Hume's rationalist philosophy. At the outset, "Beccaria warns those who would criticize him that he means to proceed in the 'geometric spirit,' establishing what ought to be in the sphere of law by systematic deduction from a set of self-evident principles which his reader must be intelligent enough not to expect him to prove" (1963, xviii).

On Crimes and Punishments was greatly influenced by Montesquieu's *Spirit of The Laws*, published in 1748. Montesquieu advocated codification of the law, elimination of the use of torture to extract confessions, making punishment proportionate to the severity of the crime, and many other ideas and proposals elaborated on by Beccaria. In reference to Montesquieu, Beccaria wrote that "I shall count myself fortunate if I, as did he, can earn the secret gratitude of the little-known and peace-loving followers of reason and if I can inspire that sweet thrill with which sensitive souls respond to whoever upholds the interests of humanity" (Young 1986, 4).

Social contract theory, Rousseau's interpretation in particular, also deeply impressed Beccaria. Echoing Rousseau, Beccaria held that laws are the means by which essentially autonomous individuals, "tired of living in a constant state of war and of enjoying a freedom made useless by the uncertainty of preserving it, unite in society" (Young 1986, 7).

Certain consequences follow the establishment of a social contract, above all, the principle of the "primacy of the law," or the idea that no one has the right to interfere in the affairs of another unless a valid law empowers one to do so. Laws become the means to social order and freedom when they come to be regarded as ends in themselves. This is the only way to prevent them from becoming the tools by which some enslave others. Observing the historical record, Beccaria notes that laws have generally been the product of "the passions of a few persons" rather than "agreements among free men." "Sometimes," he says, "laws arise from a fortuitous and transient necessity, but they have never been dictated by an impartial observer of human nature who can grasp the actions of a multitude of men and consider them from this point of view: *the greatest happiness shared among the greatest number*" (Young 1986, 3).

In this utilitarian frame, laws were to be devised and implemented to maximize the protection of, and minimize the inconvenience to, the greatest number. Laws were to protect people by preventing and deterring crimes rather than punishing criminals. To prevent crimes, (1) laws must be understood and enforced by everyone; (2) people must be made to fear the law, not one another; (3) virtuous behavior must be rewarded; (4) judges must be compelled to serve and not corrupt the law; and (5) people must be educated to understand that respect for law is a precondition of their freedom (Young 1986, 74–9). Beccaria concluded his treatise by stating that his work leads to the following "very useful theorem": "*In order that any punishment should not be an act of violence committed by one person or many against a private citizen, it is essential that it should be public, prompt, necessary, the minimum possible under the given circumstances, proportionate to the crimes, and established by Law*" (Young 1986, 81).

In France utilitarian ideas and principles were espoused by those whose efforts spurred a revolution; in England, as in Italy, they were disseminated by those whose works fostered social and penal reform. The Englishman most influenced by Beccaria's utilitarian perspective was Jeremy Bentham (1748–1832).

After Reading Beccaria, Bentham wrote" "Oh, my master, first evangelist of Reason, you who have made so many useful excursions into the path of utility, what is there left for us to do?" (Phillipson 1970, 180). While Bentham did not introduce the utilitarian concept, he is credited with developing it into a widely applicable philosophical viewpoint. As Phillipson points out, "Bentham's originality lay in emphasizing and extending [utilitarian thinking], in insisting throughout that the promotion of general happiness must necessarily be the invariable aim of the legislator and the moralist" (1970, 180).

In Bentham's England as in Becarria's Italy, the criminal code was inconsistent and law enforcement was capricious and arbitrary. The nature and form of the punishment imposed on the offender was largely in the hands of essentially autonomous judges; hence there was extraordinary variation in the penalties imposed from one circuit to another. As was true of Beccaria, so Bentham was above all concerned with systematically reforming the criminal code and punishment on the basis of the utilitarian principle of ***the greatest happiness to the greatest number.***

Because he accepted Beccaria's premise that legislation should promote the greatest happiness and least unhappiness in a community, Bentham presumed that punishment is "useful" only insofar as its application prevents more unhappiness than it creates. Again, following in Beccaria's steps, Bentham held that laws protect communities when they deter the commission of crime and minimize the severity of crimes committed. As he posited the driving force behind human behavior to be the search for pleasure and the avoidance of pain, Bentham assumed that individuals contemplating a criminal act could be deterred if they believed its commission would produce greater pain than pleasure. From the individual's vantage point, the degree of pleasure or pain derived from an act is influenced by seven "circumstances": its intensity, duration, certainty or uncertainty, celerity or swiftness, chances of producing further feelings of the same kind, and the chances of its not producing the opposite effect ("that is, pains if it be a pleasure: pleasures, if it be a pain") (Phillipson 1970, 39).

The punishment, of course, must fit the crime. To attain this end, Bentham proposed the following paraphrased rules: (1) the pain of possible punishment must exceed the potential pleasure of committing an offense; (2) the less certain the punishment for a given offense, the more severe it should be; conversely, the more certain the punishment, the less severe it should be; (3) when an offender may choose which of two offenses to commit, the punishment for the more serious of the two should be such as to induce him to commit the lesser offense; (4) as any given offense may have more than one component, punishment should be adjusted to deter the commission of any and all of its parts; (5) avoid the evils of over- and under-punishing offenses; and (6) since the same crime may be committed for different reasons, punishment should vary in accordance with individual circumstances.

Bentham and Beccaria took the view that the criminal offender acted on the basis of the same general utilitarian motivational principle as the nonoffender. People generally, they believed, were motivated to pursue self-gratification, logically and otherwise. Concomitantly, they rejected the premise that criminal acts were primarily expressions of ignorance, irrationality and emotional depravity. In their view, criminal acts were no less the product of free will, or calculation and decision making, than noncriminal acts. As Bentham responded to those critical of his philosophical position and rules of punishment,

> When matters of such importance as pain and pleasure are at stake, who is there that does not calculate? Men calculate, some with less exactness, indeed, some with more: but all men calculate. I would not say, that even a madman does not calculate. Passion calculates, more or less, in every man: in different men, according to the warmth or coolness of their dispositions: according to the firmness or irritability of their minds; according to the nature of the motives by which they are acted upon. (Bentham 1961, 177).

In accordance with the assumption that crimes are utilitarian acts of calculating individuals, Beccaria and Bentham proposed the control and prevention of crime by indirection or the reform of the criminal justice system (penal codes, law enforcement, the courts) toward the end of deterring crime rather than punishing offenders. Punishment, in their view, should not be an emotional act of revenge motivated by the principle of "an eye for an eye," but the reasoned act of those concerned to impose penalties that deter wrongdoers and others tempted to follow in their path. For this to occur, punishment must be proportional to the harm committed, and it must be certain and swift.

Not surprisingly, neither Beccaria nor Bentham advocated the death penalty. It did not play an essential role in their philosophical outlook. Both rather grudgingly acknowledged its imposition in extraordinary circumstances (during times of serious threat to social order such as civil wars and revolutions), but they hastened to express their objections to its imposition under normal conditions. To Beccaria, for example, "under the calm rule of law, and under a regime that has the full support of the nation, that is well armed against external and internal enemies with force and public opinion, where only the true sovereign holds the power to command, and where riches buy pleasure and not authority, I see no necessity whatever for destroying a citizen" (1986, 48). Bentham regarded capital punishment as "in an eminent degree *unfrugal* [an act producing excessive pain having little general deterrent value]; which forms one among the many objections there are against the use of it, in any but very extraordinary cases" (Bentham 1961, 185).

The ideas and philosophical outlook of Beccaria and Bentham have had considerable and enduring impact. Beccaria has been described as "the first systematic modern criminal law reformer in point of time; and if we take as a criterion the far-reaching results brought about by his work, we must also account him the greatest" (Phillipson 1970, 128). His work is acknowledged to have stimulated the abolition of the gallows and the wheel in Russia (1767), the abolition of the use of torture in Denmark (1771) and Austria (1776), the prohibition of torturing the unconvicted in Spain (1775), the mitigation of punishment and the institution of proportionate punishment in France (1790), and reduction of the number of capital offenses from twenty to one in the United States (1794).

Bentham's influence was no less significant. Reform measures in England attributable to Bentham include (1) the abolition of the pillory in (1816), hanging in chains (1834), and the public execution of murderers in (1868); (2) the reduction of the number of capital offenses after 1821; (3) acts protecting the rights of children in 1840 and 1864; and (4) acts preventing the confinement of the sane in mental institutions in 1828.

Utilitarian philosophy is very much alive. Advocates of harsher criminal sentences, including the imposition of the death penalty, rely fundamentally on the theory of deterrence developed by Beccaria and Bentham. But it has a rival, the positivist school of Italian criminology, which developed in the latter decades of the nineteenth century.

Positivist Criminology: The Early Italian School

The philosophy of positivism was introduced by a Frenchman, Auguste Comte, in the aftermath of the French Revolution. Comte thought the route to an improved social order lay through the development of a science of society (sociology) rather than politically motivated, ideologically rationalized, violent revolution. The purpose of the science of society was to discover the social and behavioral laws presumed to be prerequisite to informed and effectively guided social reform. The means to the end was the scientific study of human society by the methods of the so-called positive sciences, physics, chemistry, and so on.

In positive science, events are not random but are determined by verifiable causes, or antecedent factors. As applied to the social realm, the search for causes was presumed to entail the identification of factors that determine human actions independently of individual will. Individual and social acts are assumed to be determined by unknown but empirically identifiable phenomena. The early Italian school of criminology adopted the positivist viewpoint with the aim of uncovering facts presumed necessary to understand and treat the underlying causes of crime effectively. The acknowledged initiator of the school was a physician, Cesare Lombroso (1835–1909).

Lombroso's perspective on the crime problem was the dialectical opposite of the so-called classical school, or utilitarian thinking, as developed by Beccaria and Bentham. Fundamentally, Lombroso rejected the classical school's emphasis on free will in favor of a deterministic viewpoint, and he advocated reorienting the analytic gaze from crimes to criminals. To Lombroso, the criminal is different from, not essentially similar to, the noncriminal. According to Lombroso's daughter, whose interpretation of his work he approved, Lombroso stressed that the difference between his and Beccaria's view, the essential difference between the positive and classical schools, was that the classical school was concerned with "the application of the law, not of offenders themselves" (Lombroso-Ferrero 1972, 4). Furthermore,

> The Classical School based its doctrines on the assumption that all criminals, except in a few extreme cases, are endowed with intelligence and feelings like normal individuals. The Modern, or Positive, School, on the contrary, maintains that the antisocial tendencies of criminals are the result of their physical and psychic organizations, which differ essentially from those of normal individuals. (Lombroso-Ferrero 1972, 4–5)

Lombroso's interest in criminology grew out of his experience as an army physician. He thought he could detect certain physical differences between reliable and unreliable soldiers. The latter, he noticed, tended to tattoo their bodies with obscene figures and slogans, whereas the former tended to be much less inclined toward tattooing or tattooed with less coarse subjects. But the idea, he says, "bore no fruit" (Lombroso-Ferrero 1972, xxii).

Another military assignment enabled Lombroso to study hospitalized mental patients. The experience led him to suspect an organic basis not only to mental illness generally but also criminal insanity in particular.

After military service, Lombroso became a prison physician. In this capacity he had an opportunity to observe and examine hundreds of inmates. But one prisoner played a decisive role in the development of his thought. Lombroso became acquainted with the notorious criminal Vilella and after his death was able to perform an autopsy on him. He was certain that Vilella's brain gave clear evidence of atavism, or characteristics long absent in humans but present, presumably, in humankind's primitive ancestors. "At the sight of that skull," he says, "I seemed to see all of a sudden, lighted up as a vast plain under a flaming sky, the problem of the nature of the criminal—an atavistic being who reproduces in his person the ferocious instincts of primitive humanity and the inferior animals" (Lombroso-Ferrero 1972, xxv). "Thus explained," he says, "were"

> the enormous jaws, high cheek-bones, prominent superciliary arches, solitary lines in the palms, extreme size of the orbits, handle-shaped or sessile ears found in criminals, savages, and apes, insensibility to pain, extremely acute sight, tattooing, excessive idleness, love of orgies, and the irresistible craving for evil for its own sake, the desire not only to extinguish life in the victim, but to mutilate the corpse, tear its flesh, and drink its blood (Lombroso-Ferrero 1972, xxv).

Physical indicators of atavistic degeneracy included abnormal jaw and cheek bones; large ears; fleshy lips; a cleft palate; a receding chin; chest defects; extra nipples, fingers, and toes; long arms; and cranial asymmetry. This, then, was the born criminal.

Later, and in no small part because of criticism of his atavistic theory, Lombroso searched for an additional organic source of criminality. He thought epilepsy was the trait he was looking for. He believed that epilepsy contributed to the degeneration of body organs and the nervous system.

All told, Lombroso eventually identified five kinds of criminals: the born criminal, the epileptic criminal, the insane criminal, the criminal by passion, and the occasional criminal. There were three types of occasional criminals: (1) pseudocriminals, those who commit a crime by accident; (2) criminaloids, those who commit a crime due to physical proximity or opportunity such as bank teller embezzlement, and (3) habitual criminals, those born in social circumstances where crime is a way of life. Lombroso was convinced that organic factors played a role in all criminality.

Over the years, Lombroso's work has been subject to a great amount of critical scrutiny. Most credit Charles Goring, author of *The English Convict* (1913), with the most cogent critical dissection. Goring took issue with Lombroso's research methods, his sampling and control-group techniques most of all. But as Marvin Wolfgang reminds us, although Lombroso's "ill defined measurements, unwarranted deductions and inadequate control groups constitute serious deficiencies of his research," he "also manifested imaginative insight, good intuitive judgment, intellectual honesty, awareness of some of his limitations, attempts to use control groups and a desire to have his theories tested impartially" (Wolfgang 1972, 271).

Current interest in the biomedical bases of criminality and the so-called psychopathic or sociopathic personality (those presumed to be serial killers) have led to greater attention to Lombrosian theorizing. In a work on the serial killer, the psychologist Joel Norris states that "on the basis of substantive interviews with more than a dozen serial killers and their immediate families and extensive casework interviews with neurologists, surgeons, psychiatrists, social workers, medical examiners, and research chemists, we have developed biological and social profiles of the potential serial killer" (1988: 210). Some of the indicators of the genetic disorders serial killers are alleged to manifest include bulbous fingertips; hair whorls; head circumference outside a normal range; malformed ears; high-steepled palate; and larger than normal gap between first and second toes (1988, 240).

An important member of the early Italian positive school of thought, and one who influenced as much as he was influenced by Lombroso, was Enrico Ferri (1856–1929). He is among the first to advocate broadening the search for the causes of criminality by including the social realm. Ferri was a trial lawyer, a highly popular law professor, a successful politician (he was elected to the Italian parliament as a socialist), and a journalist (he founded and edited the socialist newspaper *Avanti*). The range of his intellect impresses all who delve into his writings. One gets the impression of him as someone who was bold without being dogmatic and tolerant without being inane. His writing style appeals by its apparent honesty and vitality.

Ferri's major work in criminology was *Criminal Sociology* (1884). In the introduction to the first American edition of the book, published in 1917, Charles Ellwood, an outstanding early American sociologist, refers to Ferri as "the first of living criminologists" (1917, xxvii). Ferri begins the book by differentiating his views from the classical school introduced by Beccaria and what he and his colleagues referred to as the "anthropological" school of thought pioneered by Lombroso.

To Ferri, the classical school was primarily interested in diminishing and suppressing punishment and in moral and juridical reforms. In Ferri's terms the classical school sought in practice "the diminution of punishments" and in theory "the abstract study of crime considered as a juridical entity" (1967, 18). Instead of focusing on crime and punishment, the positive school of criminal law focuses on the criminal and the causes of his behavior. Or, again in Ferri's language, in practice the positive school seeks to reduce crimes via the study of crime "as a human act, as a natural and social fact: consequently it undertakes to study not only crime in itself as a juridical relation, but also, and in the first place, to study him who commits the crime, that is, the delinquent" (1967, 18).

Ferri advocated a sociological and positivist approach to the study of crime and its amelioration. Out of experimental developments in biology and psychology since 1850 "was born the positive school of criminal law, with the essential object of studying the natural genesis of crime, whether in the delinquent or in the surroundings in which he lives, in order the more appropriately to apply different remedies to different causes" (1967, 2). Ferri regarded the positive school of criminal law as a branch of general sociology; thus he felt its proper title to be *criminal sociology*.

Ferri credited Lombroso, under whom he studied at the University of Turin, with initiating application of the positive approach to the study of crime and criminality. He accepted Lombroso's theory of the born criminal—indeed, some believe that Ferri coined the term—but not his mentor's tendency toward biological determinism. Ferri believed that criminality was caused by three sets of factors: individual or "anthropological," environmental or "physical," and social. Individual factors include the offender's age, sex, civil status, occupation, residence, social class, education and training, organic and mental constitution. The environmental or physical factors include climate, temperature, soil fertility, the daily cycle, the seasons, meteorological variables, and the annual temperature. Social factors include population increase and decrease, migration, public opinion, customs, religion, the family, politics, economics, the police and their administration, the structure of education and social welfare, and penal and civil legislation.

"In a word," notes Charles Ellwood, "Ferri finds that crime is a product practically of all the forces in the universe, though these forces manifest themselves in varying proportions in different crimes and criminals" (1967, xxxi). Be that as it may, Ferri's aim was to expand rather than prematurely restrict the focus of criminal science, a fault that underlay his criticism of both the classical and anthropological schools. He was also concerned to draw attention to means other than punishment for the treatment of the crime problem. These "equivalents for punishment" or "penal substitutes" include both the deregulation of some practices and greater regulation of others. They are the establishment of free trade, freedom of emigration, a progressive income tax, public works projects, restrictions on the manufacture and sale of alcohol, the substitution of metallic coinage for paper money to reduce counterfeiting, laws prohibiting economic monopolies, more effective banking regulations to reduce fraud and forgery, better roads and railways, better street illumination, the elimination of ghettoes and slums, cheap housing for working people, cooperative and mutual assistance societies, the erection of foundling homes, and the suppression of gambling houses.

The third member of the positive school of criminal science, Rafaelle Garofalo (1852–1934), found much to criticize in Ferri's list of "penal substitutes." His major objection was that the list represented an attempt to alleviate crime commission by increasing more than decreasing legislation and governmental involvement. Garofalo took the view that Ferri's proposed new legislation, even though it would likely lessen the commission of some crimes, would provoke new crimes. As he put it, "every new restriction will have its transgressors, and consequently result in the creation of offenses which before had no existence" (1968, 184). Garofalo thought, for example, that the best way to deal with alcohol abuse was to create legislation that would lessen rather than prohibit its use. He was convinced—and his opinion on the subject was published in

1885—that absolute prohibition would create more crime than it would prevent. Doubtless the failure of the Volstead Act (1919) in the United States contributed to the interest later taken in his work by American jurists and criminologists.

Behind Garofalo's critical reaction to Ferri's legislative proposals lay an aversion to socialist thinking. Garofalo authored a work entitled *Socialist Superstitions*, which prompted Ferri to pen a pamphlet in which he states: "R. Garofalo was born in Naples, in 1852, of an old patrician family, hence perhaps by atavism he is debarred from being a socialist" (cited by Allen 1972, 339n).

Garofalo was a lawyer who served as a prosecutor and a magistrate. He was also a professor of criminal law at the University of Naples. The reform of the criminal law and the criminal justice system were abiding interests of his, and his ideas on these subjects were published in *Criminology* (1885).

Garofalo begins his book by declaring the reformist's need for a working definition of crime. He notes that the study of the criminal from a natural science perspective dates from the end of the 1800s. The problem is that "although the naturalists speak of the criminal, they have omitted to tell us what they understand by the word crime" (1968, 3). The concept he sought was not a legal notion but "a word which expresses an idea accessible to every one, irrespective of his knowledge of the law. In a word, we must arrive at the notion of the *natural crime*" (1968, 4). By "natural" he means "that which exists in a human society independently of the circumstances and exigencies of a given epoch or the particular views of the law makers (1968, 4). "Natural crime," then, is not the result of factors intrinsic to society or unique in history, but the expression of something within the individual that he imposes on society at certain times. The "true criminal" is one who commits crime in any social setting in which he may be, regardless of nationality, quality of socialization and all other "external" factors.

Even though he believed that the true criminal was not a "sociologic" product, Garofalo regarded crime as sociologic, that is, a violation of the moral sentiments of a given group. The moral sentiments of major importance to him were *the sentiment of pity* (revulsion to the imposition of pain and suffering on others) and *the sentiment of probity* (revulsion to the violation of property rights). True criminals, he believed, are incapable of adhering to either sentiment. In his view, there was no such thing as the casual offender. As he explains,

> Without doubt, external causes such as tradition, prejudices, bad examples, climate, alcoholic liquors, and the like are not without an important influence. But in our opinion, there is always present in the instincts of the true criminal, a specific element which is congenital or inherited. There is no such thing as the casual offender—if by the use of this term we grant the possibility of a

> morally well organized man committing a crime solely by the force of external circumstances. (Garofalo 1968, 95–6)

True criminals, then, are driven to their acts by their inherent psycho-organic constitutions. The trouble is that endemic qualities are not capable of scientifically precise measurement. Nonetheless, Garofalo was convinced that

> one fact alone seems to have been definitely established, namely, that among criminals certain characteristics are found oftener in one class than another. The murderer, for example, as Lombroso says, almost always "has a cold and glassy look, sometimes bloodshot eyes, always a large nose which is frequently aquiline or hooked, long ears, heavy jaws. Thieves on the other hand, appear very often to be characterized by cranial anomalies [such as] submicrocephaly, oxycephaly, scaphocephaly, and trococephaly. (1968, 70–1)

Garofalo identifies four classes of offenders: typical criminals or murderers, violent criminals, criminals deficient in probity, and lascivious criminals. The task of the criminologist is to develop the scientific means necessary to identify the physical qualities that differentiate each from the other and all from the normal population.

Garofalo advocates three kinds of punishment: absolute elimination (death), relative elimination (imprisonment and transportation), and enforced reparation. The first is to be imposed on murderers, those proven to have intended their act and who acted without victim provocation. Life internment is prescribed for habitual or professional thieves. Indeterminate sentencing (variable terms depending on individual circumstances and rate of reformation) is prescribed for nonprofessional thieves who are recidivists and dangerous criminals of the violent or lascivious type. Reparation is required of all nondangerous criminals not lacking means of support.

In summary, and despite their differences, Lombroso, Ferri, and Garofalo agreed on the possibility and necessity of the scientific study of crime and criminals. Each was convinced that criminal behavior was not to be viewed as the product of free will; rather, it was to be viewed fundamentally as the product of organic qualities peculiar to certain individuals.

Lombroso held the least-qualified position in regard to the organic basic of criminality; he was essentially a biological determinist. Of the three, Ferri paid the most attention to the influence of external factors in the commission and control of crime. Garofalo, although minimizing the causal impact and correctional import of social facts, was unique in tracing the fact or existence of crime to an overriding social fact: group morality. None was willing to accept the sociological premise that criminal behavior is primarily determined by factors external to the individual and endemic to society.

Crime in Sociological Perspective

Among the earliest, most influential, and uniquely sociological theory of criminal behavior was developed by Gabriel Tarde (1843–1904). Tarde's perspective grew out of his experience as a lawyer and a magistrate; it was articulated in two works published in 1890, *Penal Philosophy* and *The Laws of Imitation.*

Tarde completely rejected the notion of the born criminal. He did not believe that criminals are unique either physically or psychologically. One may be born vicious, but, he insisted, "one becomes a criminal."

Becoming a criminal is a learning process. Learning is a social phenomenon, and Tarde views all social phenomena as a product of imitation.

> All the important acts of social life are carried out under the domination of example. One procreates or one does not procreate, because of imitation; the statistics of the birth rate have shown us this. One kills or one does not kill, because of imitation; would we today conceive of the idea of fighting a duel or of declaring a war, if we did not know that these things had always been done in the country which we inhabit? One kills oneself or one does not kill oneself, because of imitation; it is a recognized fact that suicide is an imitative phenomenon to the very highest degree. After this how can we doubt but that one steals or does not steal, one assassinates or does not assassinate, because of imitation? (1968, 322)

The question is, why might one imitate the example of the minority who are criminal rather than the majority who are not? Tarde's answer is based on one of his laws of imitation, namely, *the greater the physical proximity, the greater the tendency to imitate*. "Thus it would be permissible for the child who was the most normally constituted to be more influenced by half a score of perverse friends by whom he is surrounded than by millions of unknown fellow-citizens" (1962, 252–53).

Since physical proximity is influenced by population density, the greater the population density, the greater the amount of imitation. "Great modern cities are characterized by the intensity of their imitation of internal things; it is proportionate to the density of their population and to the multiform multiplicity of the relations of their inhabitants" (1962, 239). Once introduced, then, criminal behavior tends to increase more rapidly in the city than the country.

Tarde believed that criminal behavior is much more likely to originate in the compact physical and social milieu of larger cities than elsewhere. He accounts for this by another law: *imitation of the superior by the inferior.*

Historically, Tarde observes, it has been the practice of nonelites to ape the mannerisms and values of elites. This is not because elites have been especially inventive, but because they have the power of initiative. "Invention can start from the lowest ranks of the people, but its extension depends upon the existence of some lofty social elevation" (Tarde 1962, 221). And as he states, aristocracies have been historically adept at perceiving, importing and imitating foreign novelties. Tarde identifies a number of vices and crimes that now prevail among the "lower" social orders but that were transmitted to them from "above," from alcoholism to forcible rape.

To Tarde, modern cities function in the manner of the traditional nobility in that they breed and attract the trend setters—the brightest, youngest, and most diverse segments of society. "While crime formerly spread from the nobility to the people, and while the nobility, in those remote times, drew to itself the audacious and criminal elements of the people, today we can see crime spreading from the great cities to the country, from the capitals to the provinces, a new kind of ennobling" (1968, 338).

To lessen the commission of crime, according to Tarde, it is not sufficient to offer what Ferri refers to as "penal substitutes." Tarde did not believe that the path to a solution to the crime problem lay through social institutions and their reform. Laws and social institutions are for Tarde only "the outer skin of society." The "inner kernel" is human inventiveness. Invention precedes imitation, and imitation fosters fashion, custom, and institutionalization. Inventions are the combined product of human individuality and interaction. As crime is an invention, argues Tarde, it cannot be eliminated without preventing inventiveness.

Thus, from Tarde's vantage point, alleviation of the crime problem requires an effort to determine the moral sensitivity of the offender. Toward this end, he thought it necessary to determine whether or not offenders are aware of basic societal moral precepts, and whether or not they were aware of the criminal nature of their acts at the time of the commission and adjudication (at either point, a judgment of insanity would be a mitigating factor). He proposed assigning responsibility for determining these conditions to a panel of experts (doctors, psychologists). Once the degree of moral responsibility is ascertained, sentencing by judge or jury is to be individualized.

Fundamentally, Tarde sought a middle ground between the poles of free will and determinism, between those who believed that criminal behavior was a matter of individual choice and those who believed it to be something that happened to or was imposed on the individual, for example, by irresistible impulse or social repression. To Tarde, moral responsibility is an important and complex issue, something requiring continuous study as opposed to abrupt resolution by means of one dogmatic principle or another. To Tarde, as Terry Clark put it, "no point of view respecting responsibility can lightly brush aside every difficulty" (1968, 513).

Many of Tarde's ideas have had an enduring impact on criminology. His emphasis on crime as something learned by normal people in the course of adapting to the people and conditions of their social milieu anticipated the theory of differential association and the ecological school of crime, both of which are discussed later.

In his own day, Tarde was greatly esteemed. He was not, however, without his critics. Among the most important of them was Emile Durkheim (1858–1917). Durkheim's contributions were not systematically developed in a treatise on the subject. They were contained in works devoted to the establishment of sociology as a theoretically distinct and positivistically scientific discipline.

To Durkheim, the phenomena of sociology are social facts. Social facts are all ways of acting, feeling, and thinking (customs, laws, norms, roles, sentiments, values) that societies impose on their members to make them orderly, predictable, and trustworthy. Social facts are "external" to individuals and "coercive" of their behavior. The best example is language, something that antedates our birth and is imposed on us without our consent.

Social facts are observed only indirectly. Their presence is indicated by the application of observable sanctions (rewards and punishments) to different kinds of behavior. Interestingly, Durkheim was much more concerned with behavior that provokes punishment than reward. The sanctions applied in a given situation emanate from what Durkheim calls "the collective conscience," or the beliefs and sentiments common to societal members.

As he aimed to make sociology a quantifiable science, Durkheim wished social facts to be regarded as "things," distinct quantities capable of exact measurement. Moreover, he insisted that the causes of social facts are not to be sought in individuals (as either biological or psychological entities) but in other social facts. "The determining cause of a social fact should be sought among the social facts preceding it and not among the states of the individual consciousness" (Durkheim 1938, 110). Social facts also are to be viewed as having a determining influence on human thought and behavior. "We conceive of them as deterministic rather than arbitrary" (1938, xxxix).

Tarde, and many others as well, reacted to Durkheim's work by accusing him of metaphysical thinking, of attributing reality to a mystical concept. Durkheim answered his critics by saying that he had no intention of conveying the notion that social facts were material things but that sociologists should, for objective and scientific purposes, "assume a certain mental attitude toward them on the principle that when approaching their study we are absolutely ignorant of their nature, and that their characteristic properties, like the unknown causes on which they depend, cannot be discovered by even the most careful introspection" (1938, xliii). Of major concern to Durkheim was that "while the scientist who studies physical nature is very keenly aware of the resistance it offers him, and which he has so much difficulty overcoming, the sociologist seems to move in a sphere perfectly transparent to his view, so great is the ease with which the most obscure questions are resolved" (1938, xlvi).

To illustrate his point, Durkheim analyzed Garofalo's concept of natural crime. Garofalo, he says, is interested only in certain crimes, those that offend "the most general and universal of the moral feelings." Moral sentiments and crimes punished for their commission that have not endured are deemed unworthy of the criminologist's attention. This elimination, according to Durkheim, can be made only "by an entirely personal conception of morality." To Durkheim, "the variable aspects of the moral sense are not less grounded in the nature of things than are the immutable" (1938, 40). Thus, Garofalo's concept includes only a portion of all the crimes it should. Garofalo, in other words, does not rely on objectively defensible criteria in excluding certain crimes from his definition.

Durkheim believed that objective concepts must be based on observable characteristics of the object in question. "The subject matter of every sociological study should comprise a group of phenomena defined in advanced by certain common external characteristics, and all phenomena so defined should be included with the group" (Durkheim 1938, 35). He points out that certain acts in a given society have the common characteristic of evoking formal public punishment for their violation. All such acts share a common label, crimes, and crimes are the subject of criminology, a scientific discipline.

Durkheim noted the absence of objectivity not only in the way in which criminologists defined their phenomena but also in their uncritical acceptance of the common view of crime as something totally inimical to social well-being. As people generally do, he found criminologists predisposed to judge crime as entirely pathological rather than in some ways "normal." As he reasoned, if crime is an essential feature of all known societies, might it not have certain positive functions, that is, in some way contribute to social health?

Durkheim thought of a healthy society as one capable of making continuous adjustments to changing conditions. Social change is unlikely in the absence of a degree of toleration for innovation and social deviation. Without social deviance, we would lack many of the essential freedoms that promote social harmony. Freedom entails the expression of individuality and originality, and the expression of individuality and originality entails the possibility, if not the inevitability, of crime. "In order that the originality of the idealist whose dreams transcend his century may find expression, it is necessary that the originality of the criminal, who is below the level of his time, shall also be possible" (Durkheim 1938, 71).

However harsh our regard for criminals, their transgressions may have certain positive social consequences. Crime commission enables people to observe the limits of social toleration, to gain a sense of just "how far they can go" without "getting into trouble." And, of course, when members of a group agree on the punishment for wrongdoing and actively participate in its implementation, they reinforce common ties and mutual obligations.

Durkheim's willingness to examine the positive social functions of crime and deviance should not be construed to suggest that he harbored anarchistic sympathies. Hardly, his great fear or concern was not too much, but too little, social constraint. Those who lacked social bonds, he determined, were unusually susceptible to suicide and other unhealthy forms of behavior. He was particularly interested in the absence of social bonding due to *anomie*. Anomie denotes the condition of a society whose normative structure is so attenuated that people lack sufficient information and motivation to know and even care about what their mutual obligations are or should be. Instances where people have abruptly lost important social anchoring (e.g., the sudden loss of a child, friend, mate, job) were the focus of his attention. Abrupt tears in the social fabric create "normlessness," and those lacking the guidance of social norms are, Durkheim thought, susceptible to all manner of aberrant thoughts and acts, including crime.

It is important to note here that Durkheim's concept of anomie is a social fact; it is "something" originating in society, or outside of, rather than within, people. Its causes are to be traced to other social facts, for example, economic recession, not to states of individual consciousness.

Karl Marx's social theory also seeks the source of major social problems in social rather than individual social facts. The first systematically to apply the Marxist perspective to the study of crime was Willem Bonger (1876–1940).

Bonger was both a sociologist and a criminologist. He was trained in the law, and his doctoral dissertation, *Criminality and Economic Conditions*, published in 1905 but not translated and published in English until 1916, is, along with his *Race and Crime* (first published in 1943), the major source of the ideas to be discussed.

As a sociologist, Bonger views criminal behavior as a function of social organization: Societies with different organizational structures are likely to generate different attitudes and motives toward crime commission on the one hand and probably different amounts and types of crime on the other. He did not test this viewpoint by comparing different social structures (e.g., socialist and capitalist societies) by means of specified empirically verifiable hypotheses. Instead, he sought to account for the prevalence and nature of crime in capitalistic societies by means of the insights of Marxist theory.

To Bonger, as to Durkheim, a crime is behavior that violates the moral sentiments of a group. In contrast to Durkheim, however, who regarded violations of group morality to be equally offensive to all (a threat to the integrity of "the collective conscience"), Bonger maintained that they are equally threatening only when all have an equal interest in maintaining the status quo. In complex societies, those with social classes possessing different amounts of power and influence, some have a greater interest than others in the preservation of "law and order." It is not by accident that "in every society which is divided into a ruling class and a class ruled, penal law has been principally constituted according to the will of the former" (Bonger 1916, 379–80). Crime, to Bonger, following Marxist premises, threatens and, therefore, provokes the power of the state: "Crime is a serious antisocial action to which the State reacts purposely through the application of penance (punishment or other measure)" (1940, 27).

But it is criminal motivation, not crime as a power struggle, that chiefly fascinates Bonger. "Why," he asks, "does an individual do acts injurious to the interests of those with whom he forms a social unit?" (1916, 381). Or, what causes someone to act egoistically?

Answers to the question, Bonger feels, fall into two categories. One, that preferred by biological determinists such as Lombroso, attributes criminality to humankind's innate egoism. The second, that preferred by sociologists and those who believe that criminality is something learned, attributes criminality to sociocultural and other "environmental" factors. Bonger rejects the first on a number of grounds, including the great variability of crime from one society to the next. Echoing Tarde's essential premise, Bonger feels that "no person comes into the world a criminal" (1940, 105). He favors instead the Rousseauian notion that humankind's nature is essentially altruistic, and therefore that egoism and criminality are to be traced to the influence of certain forms of group living. This is the tack that leads him to examine the criminogenic elements of life in capitalist societies. "We shall show," Bonger says, "that, as a consequence of the present environment [read capitalism], man has become very egoistic and hence more *capable of crime* [emphasis in the original], than if the environment had developed the germs of altruism" (1916, 402).

Bonger, then, believes the link between capitalism and crime to be egoism, the priority given in capitalist societies to self-centered striving for fame, fortune, power, and influence. He hastens to add, however, that egoism per se is not a sufficient cause of criminality. Something additional is needed, something that makes the commission of crime a natural extension of the egoistically motivated personality. Bonger thinks the catalytic agent to be at the very heart of capitalism, namely, exchange.

To make profits, the capitalist—and he means not merely "the captains of industry" but all members of capitalist societies—must engage in exchange. The aim is to get as much as possible from others by commodity trading, and, one hopes, acquire more than it is necessary to give. Capitalists, says Bonger, must "make war" in two directions. Their self-interest is pitted against those from whom they buy and those to whom they sell. Here is the way Bonger connects capitalistic exchange and criminality:

> The interests of the capitalists are opposed not only to those from whom they buy or to whom they sell, but also to those of their fellow producers. It is indeed claimed that competition has the effect simply of making the product better and cheaper, but this is looking at the question from only one point of view. The fact which alone affects criminality is that competition forces the participants, under penalty of succumbing, to be as egoistic as possible. Even the producers who have the means of applying all the technical improvements to perfect their product and make it cheaper, are obliged to have recourse to gross deceits in advertising, etc., in order to injure their competitors. Rejoicing at the evil which befalls another, envy at his good fortune, these forms of egoism are the inevitable consequence of competition. (1916, 405)

Bonger identifies four kinds of crime according to the self-serving motives of their perpetrators: (1) economic crimes (theft, robbery, bribery, embezzlement, procuration, counterfeiting, and anything else, including murder and arson, with an "economic aim"; (2) sexual crimes (adultery, child molesting); (3) crimes of vengeance (from insults and malicious mischief to assault and homicide); and (4) political crimes. The influence of "the present form of society" on each is analyzed, and all, to one degree or another, are attributed to the cupidity aroused by capitalism, the demand for insatiable consumption and the attainment of self-gratification by whatever means.

As negative as they appear, the results of his analysis, insists Bonger, are a cause for optimism concerning the human future. If crime and other major social problems are the product of society rather than the expression of the human organism, they can be corrected. Thus he closes his dissertation with the following words:

> It is society that prepares the crime," says the true adage of Quetelet. For all those who have reached this conclusion, and are not insensible to the sufferings of humanity, this statement is sad, but contains a ground of hope. It is sad, because society punishes severely those who commit the crime which she has herself prepared. It contains a ground of hope, since it promises to humanity the possibility of some day delivering itself from one of its most terrible scourges. (1916, 672)

Summary and Conclusion

This chapter has identified key founders of criminology and outlined their contributions. The point, as Jeffery has stated, is that "twentieth century criminology is a product of the theories of the eighteenth and nineteenth centuries," and that "if we understand the pioneers, then we can better understand the current issues in criminology" (1972, 458).

Subjects of central concern to eighteenth- and nineteenth-century criminologists were penal and legal reforms, the criminal and criminal behavior, and crime, what it is, its frequency and variety.

The perspectives used to analyze subjects of concern were *legalistic* (the meaning of the law and the logic of punishment), *utilitarian* (law and punishment based on the principle of "the greatest happiness to the greatest number"), *biological* (criminal behavior as the consequence of innate human qualities), *individualistic* (criminal behavior as the product of "free will"), *positivist* (criminal behavior as a phenomenon determined by scientifically identifiable forces beyond the control of the offender), and *sociologistic* (crime as learned behavior and as a phenomenon determined by "social facts").

The legalistic viewpoint reflected the founding of the discipline by many with formal training in the law (Beccaria, Benthan, Bonger, Ferri, Garofalo, and Tarde). Lawyers Beccaria and Bentham championed both the utilitarian and individualist perspectives. The biological orientation was developed by Lombroso, a physician, and was supported and elaborated on by Ferri and Garofalo. These three were also responsible for introducing the positivist perspective in criminology. The sociologistic perspective was introduced by Tarde, a lawyer and a magistrate, by Bonger, whose doctorate was in criminal law, and by Durkheim, a philosopher and sociologist.

As an academic discipline, criminology has been heavily influenced and, until recently, taught primarily by sociologists. This is not entirely by accident. Those who initiated sociology saw it as a synthetic discipline. It was to synthesize the knowledge of all the other sciences (physical, biological, behavioral, social, and cultural) preliminary to the development and implementation of plans to improve the human condition. Although its lofty goals have diminished with the passage of time, sociology remains an eclectic discipline, a natural haven for subjects as complex and as broadly studied as crime and criminality. Early American sociological perspectives on the crime problem are the subject of the next chapter.

References

Allen, Francis. 1972. "Raffaele Garofalo." In *Pioneers in Criminology* 2nd edition edited by Herman Mannhein. Montclair, New Jersey: Patterson Smith, 318–40.

Bentham, Jeremy. 1961. *An Introduction to The Principles of Morals and Legislation*. New York: Dover.

Bentham, Jeremy. 1970. In *An Introduction to the Principles of Morals and Legislation* edited by J.H. Burns and H.L.A. Hart. London: University of London, The Athlone Press.

Beccaria, Cesare. 1963. *On Crimes and Punishments*. Translated by Henry Paolucci. Indianapolis: Bobbs-Merrill.

———. Cesare. 1986. *On Crimes and Punishments*. Translated by David Young. Indianapolis: Hackett.

Bonger, Willem Adriaan. 1916. *Criminality and Economic Conditions*. Boston:Little, Brown.

———. Willem Adriaan. 1969. *Race and Crime*. Montclair, New Jersey: Patterson Smith.

Chandler, Tertius and Gerald Fox. 1974. *3000 Years of Urban Growth*. New York: Academic Press.

Clark, Terry N. 1968. "Tarde, Gabriel." In *The International Encyclopedia of the Social Sciences* edited by David L. Sills. New York: Macmillan and Free Press, 509-14.

Crow, John A. 1965. *Italy*. New York: Harper & Row.

Durant, Will and Ariel Durant. 1967. *Rousseau and Revolution*. New York: Simon and Schuster.

Durkheim, David Emile. 1938. *The Rules of Sociological Method*. New York: Free Press.

Ellwood, Charles. 1967. "Introduction" to Enrico Ferri, *Criminal Sociology*. New York: Agathon Press.

Ferri, Enrico. 1967. *Criminal Sociology*. New York: Agathon Press.

Garofalo, Raffaele. 1968. *Criminology*. Montclair, N.J.: PattersonSmith.

George, M. Dorothy. 1965. *London Life in the 18th Century*. New York: Capricorn.

Goring, Charles. 1913. *The English Convict*. London: H.M. Stationery Office.

Jeffery, C. Ray. 1972. "The Historical Development of Criminology." In *Pioneers in Criminology*, 2nd Edition edited by Herman Mannheim. Montclair, N.J.: Patterson Smith, 458–98.

Lombroso-Ferrero, Gina. 1972. *Criminal Man: According to the Classification of Cesare Lombroso*. Montclair, N.J.: Patterson Smith.

Maestro, Marcello. 1973. *Cesare Beccaria and the Origins of Penal Reform*. Philadelphia: Temple University Press.

Norris, Joel. 1988. *Serial Killers: The Growing Menace*. New York: Doubleday.

Phillipson, Coleman. 1970. *Three Criminal Law Reformers*. Montclair, N.J.: Patterson Smith.

Rusche, Georg and Otto Kirchheimer. 1968. *Punishment and Social Structure*. New York: Russell & Russell.

Sutherland, Edwin H. and Donald R. Cressey. 1960. *Criminology*. New York: J.B. Lippincott Company.

Tarde, Gabriel. 1962. *The Laws of Imitation*. Gloucester, Mass.: Peter Smith.

———. Gabriel. 1968. *Penal Philosophy*. Montclair, N.J.: Patterson Smith.

Tobias, J.J. 1967. *Urban Crime in Victorian England*. New York: Schocken.

Vold, George B. 1958. *Theoretical Criminology*. New York: Oxford University Press.

Wolfgang, Marvin. 1972. "Cesare Lombroso." In *Pioneers in Criminology*, 2nd Edition edited by Herman Mannheim. Montclair, N.J.: Patterson Smith, 232–91.

Young, David, trans. 1986. Cesare Beccaria, *On Crimes and Punishments*. Indianapolis: Hackett.

Note

[1]. Verri is also known to have read and heavily edited Beccaria's *On Crimes and Punishments*. For a discussion of Verri's and others' influence on the writing of *On Crimes and Punishments*, see David Young's "Note on the Text" in his recent translation of the work (Indianapolis: Hackett 1986), xix–xx.

Chapter 7

Criminological Theory in American Sociology

The forces instrumental in the rise of the field of criminology—industrialization, urbanization, and population increase—generally had their greatest social impact in western Europe before 1850 and in the United States after that date. Concern with the socially disruptive consequences of rapid industrialization and urbanization led to the establishment of the first department of sociology in America at the University of Chicago in 1893. Chicago, a city whose population grew from 29,963 to 1,698,575 between 1850 and 1900, became the first American city to be closely examined for its criminal patterns by sociologists.

The theoretical orientations of Chicago School sociologists occupy the initial pages of this chapter. Particular attention is given to differential association theory, a social learning interpretation of the origins of criminality introduced by Edwin Sutherland, a Chicago School-trained sociologist. Middle and latter sections examine other early and more recent major sociological perspectives on crime, such as Merton's anomie or "strain" theory, Becker's labeling theory, and the Marxist-based social conflict theories of Chambliss, Quinney, and Turk.

The Chicago School and Its Ecological Perspective

In studying crime and delinquency, sociologists at the University of Chicago employed an ecological approach. They looked at human behavior in the same way that plant and animal ecologists looked at their subjects—as an adaptive response to environmental conditions and pressures.

Human ecology was introduced by Robert Park and Ernest W. Burgess in 1921. They conceived of the human habitat as a number of interrelated niches, or "natural areas." These functional areas and neighborhoods were presumed to be the product of "the struggle for existence."

The first task of those who studied crime under the tutelage of Park and Burgess was to plot its geographical location. Once located, it would then be possible to analyze the source of the problem, that is, the culturally influenced social and economic conditions of particular population segments. As Clifford Shaw put it,

> The sociological approach, then, is an attempt to relate behavior to the social and cultural setting in which it arises. Persons live and act in families, clubs, schools, playgroups, gangs. These groups reflect community life, and the community in turn itself reflects larger cultural and social processes. (1929, 9–10)

Shaw and his coworkers were guided in their efforts to locate the "natural areas" of crime and delinquency in Chicago by Burgess's concentric zone hypothesis. Burgess identified the spatial structure of a city as a series of zones arrayed in concentric circles: (1) The inner zone was the central business district; (2) surrounding the central business district was a zone in transition, an area of slums, ghettoes, and factories where vice and crime flourished; (3) a zone containing the homes of working people, primarily immigrants who earlier inhabited the zone in transition; (4) a zone containing more expensive housing; and (5) an outer zone inhabited by the suburban commuter.

Shaw's initial study, published in 1929, confirmed Burgess's expectations. Over the twenty-seven-year period studied, the zone in transition surrounding the Loop, Chicago's central business district, contained the highest rates of truancy, juvenile delinquency, and adult crime. In general, the areas containing the highest rates of the three measures of deviance were physically deteriorated and were losing population. Another major finding was the discovery of an inverse relationship between the rates of the three factors and the distance from city center; that is, as the distance from the city center increased, the incidence of truancy, juvenile delinquency, and adult crime decreased.

Shaw's findings were upheld by a considerable amount of subsequent research. Eventually, however, contradictory evidence began to appear. First, not all migrants to deteriorated innercity neighborhoods were adversely influenced by their environment. The Japanese residents of such areas, for example, maintained their law-abiding traditions. Second, high-crime areas in other places did not conform to the concentric zone hypothesis. They were variously distributed in different cities (Korn and McCorkle 1959, 288).

The upshot of such findings was that urban ecologists began to place less emphasis on the physical milieu and more on the social and psychological antecedents of criminality. Two possible levels of analysis were available. First, as they were particularly interested in basic human adaptation to environmental constraints, physical and social, human ecologists could have chosen to study national social organization, especially the American institutions of business and government and how their structure and interaction influence criminal behavior. Second, the ecologists could study local community organization and the way it structured criminality. With the notable exception of Edwin Sutherland, those trained in the Chicago tradition concentrated on local-level analyses.

The strategy was to identify high-crime areas and then, by analyzing life history materials, to reconstruct the social context that produced the criminal behavior in question. In *The Jackroller*, for example, Shaw presented a case study of a young male delinquent, one of two hundred studies of paroled male recidivists under age seventeen. Shaw believed that the case study should include family history; the findings of medical, psychiatric, and psychological examinations; the individual's complete criminal record; a description of his "play group" companions and relationships; and anything else that might help specify the offender's character and background. Not to be neglected, of course, was the offender's own story. As Shaw saw it, and in conformity with the "situational" perspective developed by the Chicago-trained sociologist W.I. Thomas and his co-author, Florian Znaniecki (1918), the offender's story supplied three useful kinds of information: the meaning the offender attached to his or her behavior, a sense of the offender's attitudes and values, and the sequence of events and experiences that culminated in deviance.

In essence, criminality was defined as learned behavior, an adaptive response by an individual to social and cultural conditions. As Burgess assessed Shaw's work: "It shows how the cultural patterns, of his home, of his associates in the neighborhood, of the delinquent and criminal groups outside and especially inside correctional and penal institutions, define his wishes and attitudes and so control, almost in a deterministic fashion, his behavior" (1929, 388).

Differential Association Theory

A University of Chicago-trained sociologist whose thinking was greatly influenced by Clifford Shaw's social-psychological approach to the study of crime and its origins was Edwin H. Sutherland. His work, developed in the 1920s and 1930s, has had a deep and enduring impact on criminology.

Sutherland believed that criminal behavior was the product of "differential association." This meant:

1. Criminal behavior is learned rather than biologically transmitted.

2. Criminal behavior is learned in interaction with other persons in a process of communication.

3. The principle part of the learning of criminal behavior occurs within intimate personal groups.

4. When criminal behavior is learned, the learning includes *(a)* techniques of committing the crime, which are sometimes very complicated, sometimes very simple; and *(b)* the specific direction of motives, drives, rationalizations, and attitudes.

5. The specific direction of motives and drives is learned from definitions of the legal codes as favorable or unfavorable.

6. A person becomes delinquent because of an excess of definitions favorable to violation of law over definitions unfavorable to violation of law.

7. Differential associations may vary in frequency, duration, priority, and intensity.

8. The process of learning criminal behavior by association with criminal and anticriminal patterns involves all of the mechanisms that are involved in any other learning.

9. While criminal behavior is an expression of general needs and values, it is not explained by those general needs and values since noncriminal behavior is an expression of the same needs and values (Sutherland and Cressey 1960, 77–9).

Unfortunately, Sutherland did not explain in detail the precise meaning of his nine statements. They were presented on two pages in a textbook, and as Daniel Glaser has noted, "Illustration, elaboration, and interpretation [of the statements] were not systematic in the rest of that volume" (1962, 427).

Nevertheless, Sutherland left little doubt as to his reason for identifying the nine statements. He aimed to develop a general theory of crime capable of empirical interpretation. The problem is that his statements, regardless of their intuitive plausibility, are not a series of deductively linked propositions containing precisely defined variables. Sutherland added further confusion to the situation by identifying statement 6 as "the principle of differential-association theory" without saying how this qualified or influenced the status of the other statements. Thus, says Glaser, "It is not clear whether 'differential-association theory' refers only to the sixth proposition, to all nine propositions taken collectively, or to the entire chapter in which they appear" (1962, 429).

Without doubt, none of the nine statements has attracted more critical scrutiny than statement 6. In 1965, Sheldon Glueck, among the most ardent of Sutherland's critics, wrote: "Has anybody actually counted the number of definitions favourable to violation of law and definitions unfavourable to violation of law, and demonstrated that in the pre-delinquency experience of the vast majority of delinquents and criminals, the former exceed the latter?" (1965, 96) From his vantage point, the most likely answer is that offenders and nonoffenders are overwhelmingly bombarded with definitions unfavorable to law violation by influential sources from the family of orientation to the general community.

To date, the available evidence is not sufficient to validate or invalidate "the principle of differential association." Most likely, as Victor Matthews observes, it may not be "directly testable" (1968, 377).

Among the other statements, tests have been made of the variables identified in statement seven with mixed results. On the one hand, James Short's study of the bearing of "frequency, duration, priority, and intensity of interaction" on delinquency have generally confirmed expectations (Matthews 1968, 378). On the other hand, after examining delinquency among friendship triads, Reiss and Rhodes concluded that "the association of boys with the same kind of delinquent behavior in close friendship triads while somewhat greater than chance is well below what one would expect from the learning hypothesis in differential-association theory" (1964, 223).

Whatever its empirical limitations, differential-association theory is a major point of departure for criminological investigation. Writing in 1962, Glaser saw it as "the most satisfactory theory for interpreting the great bulk of major crimes, particularly larceny, burglary, and robbery, which comprise 90 percent of felonies tabulated in the FBI's *Uniform Crime Reports*" (1962, 440). Nonetheless, he sought clarification of conceptual ambiguity and developed an alternative slant.

Differential Identification

Glaser takes the view that the vulnerability of differential-association theory to criticism is largely the result of Sutherland's failure to convey a clear and penetrating image of the genesis and spread of criminal behavior. Glaser argues that any compelling theory specifies a frame of reference within which to observe relevant phenomena. One cannot look at something as complex as criminal behavior from all possible angles at once. Attention must be focused on a spot and from a vantage point that provides the greatest likelihood of observing something important. What Sutherland did was to advocate looking at the entire range of criminal behavior from an unclearly identified viewpoint. For example, is it quantity of contacts or quality of contact between criminal and noncriminal elements that is crucially differentiating?

To resolve the fundamental problem of an imprecise theoretical perspective, Glaser advocates the reconceptualization of differential-association theory in terms of what he calls "differential identification." Says Glaser, "What we have called 'differential identification' reconceptualizes Sutherland's theory in role-taking imagery" (1956, 440). Seen this way, "a person pursues criminal behavior to the extent that he identifies himself with real or imaginary persons from whose perspective his criminal behavior seems acceptable" (1956, 440).

Differential identification, according to Glaser, is based on a conception of crime as voluntary behavior. As he does not elaborate on this important point, one may infer that within his frame, criminal behavior is the conscious act of an individual free and able to choose among both criminal and noncriminal role possibilities. Glaser does not discuss the factors that may lead certain individuals to be more predisposed to criminal than noncriminal role choices, and one criminal role rather than others.

Like Sutherland's theory, Glaser's has not generated a great deal of empirical research. In a study intended to examine Glaser's theory as well as Sutherland's, Victor Matthews found support for the hypothesis that an individual's involvement in delinquency is directly related to the delinquency involvement of his best friends (1968, 383). But no effort was made to determine how it was that an individual came to identify more with those playing delinquent than nondelinquent roles.

Another study concerned with testing Glaser's theory focused on identifying the reference groups from which incarcerated youthful offenders derived criminal attitudes, rather than the individuals whose criminal roles were emulated. Three indices of criminal reference-group orientation were employed: (1) *criminal identification*, the degree to which "respondents perceive themselves as similar to 'general criminal others'"; (2) *associational preference*, "the degree to which the respondents prefer to associate with law breakers"; and (3) *inmate loyalty*, the degree to which respondents trust, share, and sacrifice for one another. The independent variable in the study was "attitudes toward law violation." The hypothesis tested was that "attitudes favoring violation of the law will be positively associated with criminal reference group orientation." All three criminal reference-group measures were found to be positively associated with "attitudes favoring law violation," but "not large enough to be more than suggestive." Still, the author concluded that his findings supported Glaser's expectations (Stratton 1967, 256–62).

Another effort to specify Sutherland's formulation more clearly was developed by Robert Burgess and Ronald Akers. They refer to their viewpoint as differential-association reinforcement theory.

Differential-Association Reinforcement Theory

Burgess and Akers sought to revise differential-association theory in keeping with the theoretical orientation and experimental technique of behavioral psychology. They were led in this direction by Sutherland's insistence that his theory was basically a learning theory. As behavioral psychologists had shown that learning-theory concepts could be successfully operationalized (i.e., interpreted so as to be capable of measurement), they believed that "applying an integrated set of learning principles to differential-association theory should adequately provide the revision needed for empirical testing" (1966, 131). Accordingly, Sutherland's nine statements were reduced to seven and rephrased in language consistent with the principles of operant conditioning. For example, statement 2 now reads as follows: "Criminal behavior is learned both in nonsocial situations that are reinforcing or discriminative, and through that social interaction in which the behavior of other persons is reinforcing or discriminative for criminal behavior" (Burgess and Akers 1966, 137).

More than a decade later, and with, among others, Burgess's and Aker's work in mind, Keith Halbasch questioned the usefulness of behavioristic interpretations of Sutherland's work. He argued that attempts to operationalize Sutherland's ideas must be based on a highly sophisticated theory of behavior, and that "behavioristic principles are not adequate for predicting sophisticated behavior" (1979, 228).

Whatever the truth of the matter, empirical testing of differential-association theory remains a difficult and infrequent undertaking. But no other criminological theory has attracted more sustained or more serious attention. A sociological theory that has attracted considerable attention was put forth by Robert Merton in the late 1930s.

Merton's Strain Theory

The difficulties encountered by those wishing to assess the validity of differential-association theory stem from the general nature of its subject matter (all criminal behavior) and its theoretical orientation (one is to look at crime as a result of the interaction of psychological and sociocultural factors). Although it too is couched at a high level of abstraction, Merton's criminological theory has a more restricted substantive range and analytical focus than does Sutherland's.

Merton, following Durkheim, restricts his analytical gaze to the external realm, or to the impact of social and cultural conditions on the behavior of individuals. Merton's "primary aim is to discover how some social structures exert a definite pressure upon certain persons in the society to engage in nonconforming rather than conforming conduct" (1957, 135).

The subjects of particular importance to Merton are culturally defined goals and institutionally prescribed means. The context of study is a particular kind of society, one in which more emphasis is placed on goals than on the proper means for their attainment. "In this context," says Merton, "the sole significant question becomes: Which of the available procedures is most efficient in netting the culturally approved value? The technically most effective procedure, whether culturally legitimate or not, becomes typically preferred to institutionally prescribed conduct" (1957, 135).

In such a society, five kinds of "adaptation" are possible: conformity, innovation, ritualism, retreatism, and rebellion. The *conformist* adheres to both the culturally prescribed goals and the means for their realization. The *innovator* accepts the goals, but reserves the right freely to select the means for their attainment. The *ritualist* has learned to scale down aspirations, but continues to abide by established norms "almost compulsively." The *retreatist* is the social "dropout," the one who avoids adhering to either the culturally defined goals or the norms of society. The *rebel* rejects both established goals and means but, unlike the retreatist, the rebel's reaction is active rather than passive. Such people aim not to modify or reform existing institutions but to create a new structure for need gratification.

Of the five "modes of adaptation," Merton is most interested in innovation. It captures the American situation and relates the behavior of different segments of the population; for example, robber barons on the one hand and *Mafia* leaders on the other. In regard to the former, Merton writes: "The history of the great American fortune is threaded with strains toward institutionally dubious innovation as is attested by many tributes to the robber barons" (1957, 141). On the other side of the social ledger was Al Capone, who "represents the triumph of amoral intelligence over morally prescribed 'failure,' when the channels of vertical mobility are closed or narrowed in a society which places a high premium on economic affluence and social ascent for all its members" (1957, 146).

Despite the fact that his theory is capable of illuminating the criminal propensities of people variously situated in society, Merton feels that it is most suitable for analyzing the crimes of the lower rather than the higher social strata. As he reasons, "Whatever the differential rates of deviant behavior in the several social strata, and we know from many sources that the official crime statistics uniformly showing higher rates in the lower strata are far from complete or reliable, it appears from our analysis that the greatest pressures toward deviation are exerted upon the lower strata" (1957, 6).

If Merton was less concerned than Sutherland with analyzing the criminality of the social strata, he was more interested than Sutherland in specifying the social facts that make it more likely that some rather than others will engage in certain kinds of deviance. To be sure, Sutherland tells us that crime is socially learned behavior, but he does not identify a causal agent, mechanism, or condition in the learning process that channels behavior more in the direction of certain kinds of criminal behavior than others. It is here that Merton's theory has an edge on Sutherland's.

Basically, Merton's theory is a frustration-aggression theory. All Americans are encouraged to pursue certain general and ideal goals—for example, the attainment of esteemed occupational status; but many, if not most, do not have access to legitimate means such as funding for quality schooling for their realization. Frustrated in this sense, a certain number of people, according to Merton, can be expected to invent or adopt illegitimate means to accomplish their purposes. He then asks which individuals are most susceptible to using proscribed means and decides that the best answer is persons of low rather than high social status. With minimal reservations and until recent years, most students of crime and deviance were predisposed to accept Merton's position on this important point. The turning point emerged in the 1960s and in the wake of the perceived failures of the War on Poverty programs, the Vietnam war, and the revelations and consequences of the Watergate case. Such events contributed to a loss of confidence in prevailing sociological theory generally and in the ability of the American social system to solve important problems such as crime and delinquency. A variety of perspectives arose to challenge the tenets and relevance of "conventional" criminological theory. Among the first was labeling theory.

Labeling Theory

The most detailed and influential labeling perspective was advanced by Howard S. Becker. He began with a brief critique of what he and others saw as the "functional" model of deviance. Functionalists such as Merton, according to Becker, study social phenomena as physicians analyze bodily activities, that is, as either contributing to or detracting from health and continuity. Factors that promote continuity are functional, and factors that interfere with it are dysfunctional. The problem is that a judgment one way or the other is subject to debate and conflict. What is functional or dysfunctional for a group of any size and complexity is invariably a political question. "If this is true," writes Becker, "then it is likewise true that the question of what rules are to be enforced, what behavior regarded as deviant, and which people labeled as outsiders must also be regarded as political" (1963, 7). By ignoring the political element, then, functional theory is seen as promoting a limited understanding of events and social processes.

Becker goes on to acknowledge the basic sociological conception of deviance as norm-violating or rule-breaking behavior. While admitting that this position is close to his own, he points out that it suffers from the same drawback as the functionalist position. It assumes normative homogeneity rather than heterogeneity—that America, for example, is a single group rather than congeries of groups with compatible and incompatible norms and values, similar and dissimilar concepts of conformity and deviance.

As one might expect, advocates of the mainstream view disagree. They believe that enough basic norms are held in common to minimize the fact and possibility of confusion. While regarding the issue as subject to empirical resolution, Becker believes it best to begin with a definition of deviance applicable to both unambiguous and ambiguous normative circumstances.

Consistent with the conventional sociological view, Becker claims that deviance is created by society. Contrary to convention, he does not view deviance as caused by situational stimuli or compelling social facts. As he sees it,

> Social groups create deviance by making the rules whose infraction constitutes the deviance, and by applying those rules to particular people and labeling them as outsiders. From this point of view, deviance is not a quality of the act the person commits, but rather a consequence of the application by others of rules and sanctions to an "offender." The deviant is one to whom that label has successfully been applied; deviant behavior is behavior that people so label. (1963, 9)

What Becker's conception does, then, is reverse the established frame for the study of deviant behavior. As he would have it, deviance is to be accounted for in the reactions of "insiders," or those with the power to assess and punish what they define as deviance rather than in the character of "outsiders," or those who commit deviant acts. In this frame, one studies deviancy not to isolate the unique character and motives of so-called deviants, but to gain an understanding of the agents of social control and what motivates them.

What motivates some to uphold established norms is the threat of change posed by perceived deviance. Here the alleged deviant may not be so much a wrongdoer or sinner as an innovator, rebel, or revolutionary. In other words, deviance may be a kind of social conflict. As John Lofland puts it, "deviance is the name of the conflict game in which individuals or loosely organized small groups with little power are strongly feared by a well-organized, sizable minority or majority who have a large amount of power" (1978, 31).

Such an interpretation of crime and deviance is not as radical as it may appear. Writing in the 1890s, Durkheim pointed to connections between crime and progressive social change. "Crime implies," he says, "not only that the way remains open to necessary changes but that in certain cases it directly prepares these changes" (1938, 71). Thus, in prerevolutionary and revolutionary times, a revolutionary may be defined by the defenders of the status quo as a criminal. But if he wins, he may become a "founding father."

From looking at crime and deviance as a category of socially innovative behavior, it is a short step to casting the criminal or "outsider" in the role of the "underdog," someone whose position is worth defending and advocating. The rebellious atmosphere os the 1960s was conducive to this way of thinking. Becker discussed his position in the matter in a presidential address at the annual meetings of the Society for the Study of Social Problems in 1966.

Becker's presentation focused on the problem of bias in social research. He argued that as we must study a subject from one point of view rather than another, "we can never avoid taking sides." As sociologists tend to be liberal, Becker observed, they generally take the side of subordinates or underdogs. When they do this, they are accused of bias as they challenge the existing "hierarchy of credibility"—the view that the opinions and judgments of "responsible professionals" such as policemen take precedence over those "with whom they deal" (1970, 208). To Becker, "We take sides as our personal and political commitments dictate, use our theoretical and technical resources to avoid the distortions that we might introduce into our work, limit our conclusions carefully, recognize the hierarchy of credibility for what it is, and field as best we can the accusations and doubts that will surely be our fate" (1970, 216).

In reacting to Becker's presidential address and labeling theory, Alvin Gouldner detected a concept of the underdog as helpless victim. "Becker's school of deviance views the underdog as someone who is being mismanaged, not as someone who suffers or fights back. It is not man-fighting-back that wins Becker's sympathy, but rather, man-on-his-back that piques his curiosity" (1970, 229).

Many of those who came to articulate conflict and radical criminological theory, although sympathetic to Becker's labeling perspective, found it wanting for reasons such as Gouldner's. But before examining their ideas, some summary remarks in regard to labeling theory are in order.

Labeling theory is fundamentally a frame-of-reference. The labeling theorist, reversing the conventional view, looks at crime as caused by authoritative reactions to behavior, rather than as deviant behavior caused by a variety of factors that provoke authoritative response. Few would argue with the claim that authoritative reactions to perceived norm violation (on the part of parents, policemen, judges, teachers, and so on) can exacerbate and even promote criminality. The problem is that labeling theorists have emphasized that societal reactions to behavior are *the* cause of crime.

Among the first to stress the importance of the reactive element in the study of deviance was Edwin Lemert. He distinguished between primary and secondary deviance. The former is caused by any number of possibilities (biological, psychological, sociological, culturological); the latter stems from societal reactions, particularly incarceration. As Nanette Davis has noted, "It was this 'secondary deviation' thesis that generated the largest outpouring of research, in spite of Lemert's warning that such processes did not 'cause' deviance, but were only one of the mechanisms that acted to stabilize the deviant identity" (1972, 452). Thus, critics have said that labeling theorists in fact study only one type of labeling: successful stigmatization. This is because they tend to attribute the "system" or "establishment" with omnipotence. In fact, interaction between alleged offenders and authorities entails considerable ambiguity. In Lemert's words,

> Often the concomitant interaction is confusion, uncertainty, and inconsistency instead of the unanimity and consensus implied in "successful labeling." Total rejection and relegation as an "outsider" does not well describe the handling of the deviant in modern

> society, for often he or she is subjected alternately to penalty and aid, assistance and rejection. For some types of deviance, notably alcoholism, stuttering, and shoplifting, ambivalence, duality, and intermittency seem to be the most significant aspects of the societal reaction. (1972, 20)

A related criticism is that labeling theorists ignore or underestimate the influence of the alleged deviant in the labeling process. Ronald Akers put it this way: "One sometimes gets the impression from reading this literature that people go about minding their own business, and then—'wham'—bad society comes along and slaps them with a stigmatized label" (1968, 462). As Joseph Scimecca makes the point: "The premise that an individual may simply reject or fight back against the labeling process is as likely an outcome as one which posits complete acceptance" (1977, 656). Considering the disparity between detected and undetected deviance, one might well infer that acceptance of the deviant label is probably the exception and avoidance the rule. But the question is, of those known to have been subjected to the same degree of authoritative exposure, who accepts or succumbs to, and who rejects or resists, the deviant label? A satisfactory empirically determined answer remains to be determined.

When subjected to empirical scrutiny, the basic assumptions of labeling theory have generally not been upheld. Of particular note is Charles Wellford's examination of the evidence for basic labeling-theory assumptions such as the following identified by Clarence Schrag:

1. No act is intrinsically criminal.
2. Criminal definitions are enforced in the interest of the powerful.
3. A person does not become a criminal by violation of the law but only by the designation of criminality by authorities.
4. Due to the fact that everyone conforms and deviates, people should not be dichotomized into criminal and noncriminal categories.
5. The act of "getting caught" begins the labeling process.
6. "Getting caught" and the decision making in the criminal justice system are a function of offender as opposed to offense characteristics.
7. Age, socioeconomic class, and race are the major offender characteristics that establish patterns of differential criminal justice decision making.
8. The criminal justice system is established on a free-will perspective that allows for the condemnation and rejection of the identified offender.
9. Labeling is a process that produces, eventually, identification with a deviant image and subculture, and a resulting "rejection of the rejectors" (Wellford, 1975, 333).

As Wellford finds that criminological research has not supported such assumptions, "One should conclude that to the degree that these assumptions can be taken to be basic to the labeling perspective, the perspective must be seriously questioned; and criminologists should be encouraged to explore other ways to conceptualize the causal process of the creation, perpetuation, and intensification of criminal and delinquent behavior" (1975, 343).

As Paternoster and Iovanni point out, "After a series of influential critiques the validity of [labeling] theory had fallen into question by 1980 and was pronounced dead by 1985" (1989, 359). In their view, however, there are grounds for a restatement and revitalization of the theory. They base their argument largely on the claim of misinterpreted hypotheses and inappropriate empirical testing. "For the most part," they say, "empirical tests of labeling propositions have been conducted with grossly misrepresented hypotheses that are more caricature than characteristic of the theory" (1989, 360).

However it may have been incorrectly empirically interpreted, labeling theory, by shifting the analytical focus from the offender to the agents of social control, provided a compelling rationale for an overdue critical analysis of the criminal justice system. While some believe that labeling theorists pushed their thesis too far, others believe they did not push it far enough. Some of those in the latter camp have advocated a more ideologically committed approach, one that stresses the connection between capitalist political and economic institutions and major social problems. Tony Platt, for example, found "the analytical categories of labeling theory totally inadequate for understanding the major crimes of American society: imperialism, racism, sexism, unequal wealth, etc." (cited in Currie 1973, 22). Platt advocated the development and implementation of conflict-oriented Marxist criminological theory. But this is not to say that there is not considerable difference among advocates of conflict criminological theory. Some advocate ideologically commitment and adherence to revolutionary Marxist theory. Such individuals have variously referred to themselves as devotees of the "new" criminology, radical criminology, and more recently, "critical criminology." Others advocate maintenance of a strictly scholarly approach and the practice of scientific objectivity.

Conflict Criminological Theory

Among the foremost advocates of conflict criminological theory are William Chambliss, Austin Turk, and Richard Quinney. Discussion of their ideas reveals how much variation is possible among those concerned with illuminating the elements and basic importance of an important social process.

Chambliss begins by relating the emergence of conflict theory in criminology to a "paradigm" shift in sociology that prompted Alvin Gouldner's 1970 treatise, *The Coming Crisis in Western Sociology.*

The paradigm concept Chambliss has in mind was developed by Thomas Kuhn (1962). To Kuhn, a paradigm is essentially a scientific achievement that for a time provides model theory, problems, and methods to a group of scientists. Although Kuhn questions the applicability of the concept in social science, it has nonetheless crept into the everyday vocabulary of the sociologist. Kuhn's thesis is that at some point, an existing paradigm becomes unable to answer important questions; a crisis state is reached. It is eventually resolved via "a revolution." A revolution is deemed necessary as the defenders of the old, established paradigm resist its replacement to the bitter end. Thus, to Kuhn a scientific revolution is an event in which an old paradigm is replaced partly or wholly by a new and incompatible alternative. The old paradigm in sociology is functionalism, and the new one is conflict theory. As Chambliss wrote: "There is, at the very least, a gigantic struggle between the previously dominant, functional paradigm and the emergent conflict paradigm" (1976, 1).

Chambliss traces the core elements of functional theory to the works of Durkheim and the core elements of conflict theory to the works of Marx. Chambliss argued that since sociologists of crime have either ignored or distorted Marxian theory, it was time to consider a "more balanced" Marxist approach.

According to Chambliss, the chief law-related postulates of functionalism are as follows:

1. The law represents the value consensus of the society.
2. The law represents those values and perspectives that are fundamental to social order.
3. The law represents those values and perspectives that it is in the public interest to protect.
4. The state as represented in the legal system is value neutral.
5. In pluralistic societies the law represents the interests of the society at large by mediating between competing interest groups (1976, 4).

Chambliss believes the heart of Durkheimian functionalism to be the assumption of value consensus among societal members. This interpretation is based on Durkheim's conception of social solidarity as an attribute or expression of a "collective conscience," the totality of beliefs and customs common to the members of a society. Chambliss finds that research evidence on the origins of Anglo-American law does not support the thesis that laws codified customs based on value consensus. "In short," he says, "Durkheim and those who pursue this theory are simply wrong" (1988, 112).

It must be pointed out, however, that Durkheim distinguished between two kinds of solidarity: mechanical and organic. Mechanical solidarity characterizes the small, noncomplex society, one that has a minimal division of labor. What holds people together is value consensus that results from the dominance of custom and tradition. Organic solidarity characterizes urban industrial societies, those with advanced divisions of labor. What binds people together here is not their similarities but their dissimilarities, not primarily value consensus but a high degree of social and economic interdependence. The question of major concern to Durkheim was the tenuous nature of social solidarity in contemporary urban-industrial societies and its attendant negative possibilities, such as crime, due to the weakening, if not the elimination, of value consensus produced by an ever developing complex division of labor. As Chambliss's interpretation of the postulates of functionalism in regard to law stems from Durkheim's concept of mechanical rather than organic solidarity, he appears less concerned with explicating the range of Durkheim's solidarity theory than in emphasizing some of Durkheim's ideas in order to clarify an opposing viewpoint. The postulates of Chambliss's conflict paradigm are as follows:

1. The law is an expression of class conflict, that is, the clash between the rulers and the ruled.

2. The law represents those values and perspectives that are fundamental to the preservation of the power and authority of the ruling class.

3. The law represents those values and perspectives that it is in the interests of the ruling class to protect.

4. The state, "which is the organized reflection of the interests of the ruling class, passes laws which serve the ruling-class interests."

5. In capitalist societies the "laws are then enforced primarily against those classes who are struggling to overthrow the ruling class" (1976, 5).

"From the perspective of the conflict paradigm," says Chambliss, "customs explain little and are only a reflection of economic realities" (1976, 5). If unqualified, such a statement is tantamount to "vulgar Marxism," that is, the notion that individual thoughts and values as well as social institutions are economically determined consequences. While Marx emphasized the overriding influence of economic reality in everyday life and customs, he acknowledged the independent causal influence of individual ideas and customs. As Marxist theorist Maurice Cornforth states:

> While in general, ideas and institutions are products of economic conditions, the exact form which they take in a particular country at a particular time cannot be explained exclusively from the economic conditions of that country at that time. On the contrary, while the influence of economic development always asserts itself, current ideas and institutions must always depend on a variety of factors in a country's life, including the character and traditions of its people. (1962, 91)

The importance placed on alleged ruling-class domination in capitalist society suggests that Chambliss holds a decidedly deterministic, if not ideologically one-sided viewpoint. Recent statements, however, indicate a more qualified viewpoint than one might infer from the above-stated conflict paradigm postulates. In a 1988 publication Chambliss says

> That there is ruling-class interest and influence in vast areas of law cannot be denied. That it is the only force responsible for law creation or law implementation, however, is erroneous. What is called for is not a theory that argues for either total control by the ruling class or no control at all, but one that recognizes both the strengths and limitations of ruling-class influence on the legal order. (1988, 119)

Nonetheless, while Chambliss is highly critical of Durkheimian-based functional theory, he is relatively uncritical of Marxist conflict theory. How much this is the consequence of ideological predisposition as opposed to other considerations is, of course, unknowable. Unlike Chambliss, Turk confronts the problem of ideological predisposition in criminological theorizing.

Turk begins a 1979 publication by observing that ideologically loaded debates about proper theoretical procedure in criminology have generated more confusion than clarity "about the nature of scientific inquiry and the difficult conceptual and methodological problems confronting criminologists" (1979, 459). Those who believe that conflict theory should be partisan critique, he notes, base their view on the assumption that "any theory is nothing more than an ideology." Turk believes that ideological considerations inevitably influence theoretical and methodological orientations but that they are the result of subjective disposition rather than logical necessity. It may be necessary to analyze a subject from a certain ideological vantage point, but this does not logically entail commitment to one ideological position above all others. He suggests that if criminology is a science, criminologists, whatever their ideological persuasions, must objectify their work; they must state their premises and specify their logical interconnection and empirical bases.

Turk regards criminology as that branch of social deviance devoted to the analysis of official deviance. He defines his theoretical perspective as an evolving blend of "substantive conflict sociology" and "conflict systems analysis."

Turk predicates his orientation on working premises such as individual divergence in "understanding and commitments" and that divergence, may, "under specifiable conditions," lead to conflict. He feels that his premises have certain implications for the development of a general theory of social deviance. First, all human interaction manifests "deviating and correcting behavior." He posits the idea that any human encounter involves an element of risk—the possibility that it may increase or decrease life chances. Further, encounters encourage people to correct one another's perceived deviations from expectations on the basis of the primary fact of self-preservation. Deviation, then, is behavior felt to be threatening. Second, absolute standards of "rightness or wrongness" are not empirically discernible. Hence, deviance is always relative to the norms held by the subjects of concern. Third, conflicts underlie all human relationships, but especially those of a hierarchical type (those involving different amounts of power and authority such as occur in formal bureaucracies with "chains of command" and "spans of control").

After proclaiming the omnipresence of conflict, deviance, and authoritative differences in human society, Turk goes on to identify the questions he believes are the chief concern of conflict criminology. These include the following, and it is to be noted that they are a blend of the tenets of labeling theory and conflict theory:

1. Has the behavior attribute in question been treated as deviance (labeled) by the relevant others (e.g., the legal authorities), or is it either unknown or ignored (denied)?

2. Is the labeler personally concerned about the deviance in question (i.e., morally indignant, acting authentically), or impersonally performing an institutional role?

3. Is the actual or potential labelee deliberately resisting the labeler's normative expectations or demands, or resistant only because of ignorance, indifference, or incapacity?

4. Is the primary objective of labeling the control of actually or potentially deviant individuals (person control), or the maintenance of a generalized structure of authority relationships (population control) (1979, 467–68)?

Turk advocates seeking to answer such questions by means of formal theory construction, the development of empirically measurable propositions. Toward this end, for example, he assumes that ethnically complex societies such as the United States are high in potential conflict because of the high probability of a disjunction between generally prescribed legal norms and the particular social norms of different ethnic or cultural enclaves. On this assumption, propositions such as the following are developed:

1. The probability that a cultural difference between authorities and subjects will result in conflict will depend upon the extent to which this difference corresponds to a difference in social norms. In general, the greater the cultural difference, the greater the probability of conflict.

2. When the normative conflict has been interpreted by authorities in legal terms, the probability that members of the opposition will be officially dealt with as criminals will depend upon (a) the status of the legal norm in the culture of the authorities, (b) the status of the opposing norm or illegal attribute in the culture of the opposition, (c) the congruence of the legal norm with the cultural and social norms of those specifically charged with enforcement, (d) the relative power of enforcers and resisters, and (e) the realism of moves made by the conflict parties.

The greater the behavioral significance of the legal norm for authorities, the greater the probability that violators will be assigned criminal status. (1966, 347 48)

In summary, Turk eschews taking sides in an ideological debate on proper theoretical procedure in social science. Thus he rejects the claim that conflict theory in criminology should be applied as a partisan critique of a despised social order and its criminal justice system. Instead, he seeks to expand knowledge of deviance and crime by means of a conflict orientation with specified premises capable of empirical scrutiny and eventual confirmation or rejection. He does not attribute conflict with a decisive role in human history; he does not expressly regard conflict as either inherently progressive or a necessary prerequisite to meaningful social change. To Turk, conflict is and always will be an omnipresent fact of life; it may be subject to regulation but not complete eradication. Consequently, he urges his colleagues to seek the "truth" about conflict and to check their political and moral biases. In his words, "While the analyst as a person may prefer, and even join, one side instead of another, as analyst she/he must value demonstrable truth above any political or other moral commitment" (1979, 464).

Turk embodies much of what radical criminologists chiefly object to about the "old" or so-called conventional criminology: a perceived unexamined penchant of its members for working within or on behalf of the established structure of criminal justice. As Barry Krisberg put it: "Critics of the 'Old' Criminology have commented on how that field has prostituted itself in serving law enforcement and criminal justice agencies" (1975, 15–16). "Prostitution" is alleged to manifest itself in the conduct of empirical studies that enhance the ability of the "ruling class" to keep the masses in their place and the construction of criminological theory on the basis of ruling class concepts and premises. The widespread acceptance of multiple causation in the old criminology is similarly interpreted. To Krisberg,

> Since there are so many causes of a problem, no one solution is feasible; rather, a group of possible solutions must be evaluated. Piecemeal reform efforts, when applied to social issues such as crime...support the myth that progress and improvement can occur without major restructuring of the social order. A solution in terms of the redistribution of societal resources or in terms of self-determination is not permissible by liberal standards and is often rejected as impractical. The standards of practicality are always taken from those who rule and who wish to preserve their status quo. (1975, 18)

On the construction of a new and radical criminology, Tony Platt sees the first order of business as a critical analysis of prevailing criminological theory, especially the role it has played "in helping to manufacture and legitimize a repressive criminal justice system." This calls for a new and socialist definition of crime. "A socialist human rights definition of crime frees us to examine imperialism, racism, capitalism, sexism and other systems of exploitation which contribute to human misery and deprive people of their human potentiality" (1974: 6). Further, theoretical and substantive specialization should be avoided and focused effort emphasized. As Gramsci said, "all the essential questions of sociology are nothing other than questions of political science, that is who controls and benefits from the established order, how is power and wealth distributed, how can change occur, etc." (Platt 1974, 6). Although Platt was among the first to outline the elements of the new, radical, critically oriented criminology, Richard Quinney stands out for having done more than anyone else to make it into a systematic criminological theory.

Quinney's views are anchored in the tenets of Marxian historical materialism. In this frame, norms, values, ideas, philosophies, and so-called nonmaterial facts are defined as part of a superstructure whose infrastructure or source is a particular mode of production (in this case, capitalism). He postulates that all modes of production are subject to constant change as a result of certain inherent contradictions.

Modes of production have two basic components: the forces of production and the relations of production. The forces of production are people (workers) and instruments (tools, machinery). The relations of production denote the manner in which the division of labor is organized. In capitalism, the owners of the means of production (land, factories, resources, and so on) decide worker placement in the division of labor. The owners constitute the ruling class and their employees the working class.

In the Marxist frame of reference, crime, and all other forms of behavior, conforming and nonconforming, is regarded as a reflection of the overriding influence of a given mode of production. To Quinney, therefore, crime in America must be studied in relation to developments within capitalism. "All social life in capitalist society, including everything associated with crime, must be understood in terms of the economic conditions of production and the struggle between classes produced by these conditions" (1977, 36–7). In his view, the major problem with conventional criminology is that its practitioners have not traced the causes of crime to the mode of production, the material conditions of social life. Further, Quinney claims that conventional criminologists have not unwittingly but deliberately avoided tracing the causes of crime to the material facts of life in capitalist society. "The failure of conventional criminology," he says, "is to ignore by design, the material conditions of capitalism" (Quinney 1977, 35).

Quinney identifies two major categories of crime: crimes of domination and crimes of subjection. Crimes of domination arise from an inherent contradiction: Some of the laws of capitalism must be broken in order to maintain its existence. Four kinds of crimes of domination are identified: (1) *crimes of control*, those that occur in the course of law enforcement, such as police brutality, civil liberties and due process violations, and the use of provocateurs; (2) *crimes of government*, those committed by elected and appointed public officials, such as the Watergate burglary and political assassinations; (3) *crimes of economic domination*, particularly corporate offenses such as price fixing, bid rigging, and pollution; and (4) *socially injurious crimes*, offenses not usually specified in legal codes, such as acts by capitalists and the capitalist state that are racist, sexist, and economically exploitative.

Crimes of subjection, those offenses committed by the working classes, are viewed as adaptive responses to ruling-class domination and exploitation. They are (1) the *predatory crimes* of the so-called *lumpenproletariat*, or unproductive workers, such as burglary, robbery, drug dealing, hustling; (2) the *personal crimes* of the *lumpenproletariat*, such as murder, assault, rape; and (3) *working-class resistance crimes* such as assembly-line sabotage. As Quinney sees it,

> Crimes of accommodation and resistance thus range from conscious reaction to exploitation, to conscious acts of survival within the capitalist system, to politically conscious acts of rebellion. These criminal actions, moreover, not only cover the range of meaning but actually evolve or progress from *unconscious reaction* to *political rebellion*. Finally, the crimes may eventually reach the ultimate stage of conscious political action—*revolt*. In revolt, criminal actions are not only against the system but are also an attempt to overthrow it. (1977, 59)

Quinney, following orthodox Marxian thinking, views the state as having arisen to protect ruling-class interests. It is seen as a tool to control the subordinate classes. Hence, prisons in capitalist society are mostly for those who commit certain crimes—"street" crimes such as robbery, larceny, and assault. Criminals of the capitalist class ("suite," or corporate white-collar offenders) are, Quinney claims, excluded. "This means that prisons are institutions of control for the working class, especially the surplus population of the working class" (1977, 138).

Indicative of biased ideological predisposition, Quinney has not similarly critically analyzed either Marxist theory or Marxist societies. This is somewhat surprising as he has accepted the basic tenets of "critical theory" (Quinney 1974, 11–16), a perspective developed by members of the so-called Frankfurt School—deceased notables such as Theodor Adorno, Max Horkheimer, and Herbert

Marcuse and their highly influential living heir, Jurgen Habermas—to "emancipate" the individual via the practice of critical analysis of all prevailing theories and philosophies toward the end of independent decision making or the practice of free will. Witnesses to Stalinist repression legitimized by Marxist theory and refugees from Nazi Germany, Adorno, Horkheimer, and Marcuse came to view uncritically adopted social theory as inimical to freedom from oppression because of their inevitable tendency to become accepted as dogma or not-to- be-questioned revealed truth. Quinney's one-sided implementation of critical theory is a reflection of a leftist ideological movement in social science that emerged in the 1960s.

In 1980, at the beginning of the Reagan era and its emphasis on returning the American economy to a more pure, less legally constrained capitalistic condition, Quinney renounced Marxist materialism in favor of wedding theology and socialism. In Quinney's view, "The socialist struggle of our age is a search for God at the same time that it is a struggle for justice in human society" (1980, 204). Decisive in his change of view was his perception of the essential emptiness and aimlessness of the materialistic way of life. As Quinney put it,

> Among the vacuous characteristics of present civilization are a mode of production that enslaves workers, an analytic rationalism that saps the vital forces of life and transforms all things into objects of calculation and control, a loss of feeling for the translucence of nature and the sense of history, a demotion of our world to a mere environment, a secularized humanism that cuts us off from our creative sources, a demonic quality to our political state, and a hopelessness about the future (1980, 30–1).

As Lilly, Cullen, and Ball point out, Quinney argued that what was needed "was a 'prophetic understanding' of reality" (1989: 173).

Predictably, critical reactions to more radical versions of conflict theory such as Quinney's were not long in coming. Carl Klockers's critique ranks among the most vigorous and provocative. His analysis centers on the following themes: (1) evidence for the causal connection between social class and crime, (2) evidence for ruling-class domination and the absence of value consensus on crime and punishment, (3) the dogmatic application of Marxist premises in historical analysis, (4) the tendency of Marxist theorists to be critical of everything but their own assumptions, and (5) unfounded faith in socialism as the solution to the crime problem.

To Klockars, Marxist conflict theory is predicated on the dogma of social class. Societies with social classes are postulated to be inherently divisive, exploitative, and criminogenic. Class divisions are held to be incompatible with value consensus and compatible with the imposition of the values of the superordinate class on the subordinate classes. Therefore, conceptions of crime and punishment are taken to reflect the power of a minority rather than the will of the majority. But, says Klockars, the bulk of the available evidence contradicts the theory. After reviewing the conclusions of studies conducted from 1964 to 1976, Klockars concludes that "there has been strong evidence to show that the American bourgeoisie and proletariat (no matter how you slice it) share an overwhelming consensus on the relative seriousness of most common crimes" (1979, 490–91). Further, cross-cultural research involving respondents from India, Indonesia, Iran, Sardinia, Yugoslavia, and the United States found considerable consensus both on the "wrongness" and severity of punishment for certain offenses.

To Klockars, Marxist criminologists, unlike conventional criminologists, are predisposed to impose rather than test theoretical assumptions. As Klockars puts it,

> For the Marxist theorist, the object of theory is to change history. For the conventional criminologist, history—past, present, and future—is a test of theory. For the Marxist, the theory is sacred; for the conventional criminologist, history and theory both must be. (1979, 501)

As Klockars emphasizes, scholars are most adept at demythicizing thought and questioning the claims of dogma. In his words, "Grounded by history and trained in the skills of evaluating what is and what has been done and testing in small and controlled increments what might be, conventional criminologists are best suited to saying what has not worked, what ought not be done" (1979, 507).

But neither Klockars's viewpoint nor the positivist orientation he invokes is above criticism. Shortly after the publication of his article, Herman and Julia Schwendinger characterized it as "a demagogic description of Marxist ideas." As far as they are concerned, "His claim that Marxist theory is irreconcilable with all heretofore acceptable standards of academic scholarship is, to quote the Bard, 'a tale told by an idiot, full of sound and fury, signifying nothing'" (1979, 3).

Doubtless, the emergence of Marxist criminology is related to the limitations of conventional positivistically inclined criminology. As Piers Beirne pointed out,

> Positive criminology had for twenty years "virtually ignored the implications of Sutherland's work on white-collar crime" and "was not only unable to explain the crimes routinely committed by government and large corporations, [but] also had no competent explanation of the violence coextensive with civil rights, minority and anti-war movements." (1979, 376)

Marxist criminologists were able to illuminate these events because they aimed to "demystify" and expose the biases of conventional criminology. As Robert Meier indicated, the tasks of the new criminology have been: (1) to 'demystify' criminal law, both in its origins and applications, since to do so will uncover the interests of the powerful; (2) to conduct studies of social control agencies, bureaucracies, and mass media to expose their complicity with an elitist ideology (3) to propose new criminal definitions which, correcting the imbalance created by the elite's influence on legislation, will include violations of certain inherent rights; and (4) to put the new criminology's theory into practice (termed 'praxis') by attempting to alter the existing economic and political arrangements of capitalism, which are believed to give rise to the present situation (1976, 463).

More recently, Lilly, Cullen, and Ball credit Marxist conflict theories with broadening the criminological perspective to include the offender's viewpoint and sensitizing conventional criminological thought to previously neglected moral questions. By accepting the law as given, Lilly and colleagues point out, conventional criminologists were accused of accepting the status quo without question and actively supporting the prevailing view that solving the crime problem requires searching for its causes in behavioral factors peculiar to individual offenders. Marxist theorists "maintained that this very search tended to exaggerate the notion that the criminal was in some important way 'different from the rest of us' when in fact the problem lay in the creation and enforcement of the laws that produced the criminals" (Lilly et al. 1989, 179). Furthermore, in advocating the practice of value-free social science and "by refusing to take a moral stand, the critics of positivism charged, conventional criminology was implicitly accepting the moral ideology provided and forced on the powerless" (1989, 179–80).

Lilly and colleagues point out that critical reactions have also led to important changes in Marxist conflict criminological theory. It is said to have become more a perspective for analyzing the structural bases of social conflict and change than a strident activist ideology. They feel it differs from Turk's brand of conflict theory "by taking a more historically relative position, maintaining that the key to understanding [the dynamics of social systems] lies not in formal logic, which deals with social systems in the abstract, but in a 'dialetical logic,' which is rooted in an understanding of the structural features of capitalism in particular" (Lilly et al. 1989, 179).

Summary & Conclusion

The development of criminology in the United States has witnessed the ascendancy of those who stress the extrasomatic (the physical environment, social organization, culture) roots of criminal behavior. From the vantage point of members of the Chicago School of human ecology, devotees of Sutherland's differential-association theory, and proponents of Merton's stroin theory, criminal behavior is something acquired and learned, especially a form of adaptation to the social and economic status of one's family of origin. Thus the analyst seeks the antecedents of crime in the offender's social and cultural background, presumably toward the end of developing the social policies and programs to cure the problem.

In the generally radical mood of the 1960s, however, the offender began to viewed as less the source of the crime problem than a victim of inherently criminogenic capitalist society. Labeling theorists such as Howard Becker urged the view that crime was something defined by lawmakers rather than something committed by law violators. To understand crime, its cause and presumed cure, one had to study and determine why certain people have the ability to label others as wrongdoers and punish them accordingly. Pushing the implications of labeling theory to a logical conclusion, Marxist theorists advocated social system change (the revolutionary replacement of capitalism with socialism) as the way to solve the crime problem.

The two brands of criminology continue to exist. Although conventional viewpoints dominate, the Marxist position has made significant inroads in mainstream criminology. As Jack Gibbs sees it,

> Controversy in criminology appears to be winding down. The protagonists have been talking past each other for years, and the issues are becoming murkier. So, it may appear that criminology's long ferment has had no outcome, let alone a constructive one. To the contrary, the ferment points to a new direction in criminological theory, one suggested by this generalization: any criminological theory that ignores the problematical character of reactions to acts is empirically indefensible. The generalization is stated not to pass judgment on its validity; rather, the statement serves to identify what has become a major issue in criminology. (1987, 821–22)

One can no longer, Gibbs suggests, build criminological theory without considering the entire range of crimes and offenders ("suite" crimes as well as "street" crimes and "upper class" as well as "lower class" criminals). The sources of crime are now to be sought as much in the habits and conditions of the law-abiding as the non-law-abiding, the two now seem intimately correlated.

But this is the mainstream situation. In the larger world, the conservative reactionary public mood has generated a concerted challenge to structural social theory in favor of more individualistic views, a position favoring increasing punishment of offenders as the proper way to respond to the crime problem. There is renewed interest in psychological and biological explanations of crime.

Within sociology, control-oriented theories have received renewed interest. These and related topics are the subject of the next chapter.

References

Akers, Ronald L. 1968. "Problems in the Sociology of Deviance: Social Definitions and Behavior." *Social Forces* 46 455–65.

Becker, Howard. 1963. *Outsiders*. New York: Free Press.

Becker, Howard. 1970. "Whose Side are We on?" In *The Sociology of Sociology* edited by Larry T. and Janice M. Reynolds. New York: McKay, 204–217.

Beirne, Piers. 1979. "Empiricism and the Critique of Marxism on Law and Crime." *Social Problems* 26 373–85.

Burgess, Ernest W. 1929. In his Postscript to *Delinquency Areas* by Clifford R. Shaw et al. Chicago: University of Chicago Press.

Burgess, Robert L. and Ronald L. Akers. 1966. "A Differential Association-Reinforcement Theory of Criminal Behavior."*Social Problems* 14 128–47.

Chambliss, William J. 1976. "Functional and Conflict Theories of Crime." In *Whose Law What Order?* edited by William J. Chambliss and Milton Mankoff. New York: Wiley, 1–28.

———. William J. 1988. *Exploring Criminology*. New York: Macmillan.

———. William J. 1989. "On Trashing Marxist Criminology." *Criminology* 27 231–38.

Cornforth, Maurice. 1962. *Historical Materialism*. New York: International Publishers.

Currie, Elliott. 1973. "Dialogue with Anthony M. Platt." *Issues in Criminology* 8 1933.

Davis, Nanette J. 1972. "Labeling Theory in Deviance Research: A Critique and Reconsideration." *Sociological Quarterly* 13 447–74.

Gibbs, Jack P. 1987. "The State of Criminological Theory." *Criminology* 25 821–40.

Glaser, Daniel. 1956. "Criminality Theories and Behavioral Images." *American Journal of Sociology* 61 433–44.

Glaser, Daniel. 1962. "The Differential Association Theory of Crime." In *Human Behavior and Social Processes* edited by Arnold Rose. Boston: Houghton Mifflin, 425–42.

Glueck, Sheldon. 1965. "Theory and Fact in Criminology." *British Journal of Delinquency*. 7 92–109.

Gouldner, Alvin W. 1970. "The Sociologist as Partisan: Sociology and The Welfare State." In *The Sociology of Sociology* edited by Larry T. and Janice M. Reynolds. New York: McKay, 218–55.

Gouldner, Alvin W. 1970. *The Coming Crisis of Western Sociology*. New York: Basic Books, Inc.

Halbasch, Keith. 1979. "Differential Reinforcement Theory Examined." *Criminology* 17 217–29.

Klockars, Carl. 1979. "The Contemporary Crises of Marxist Criminology." *Criminology* 16 477–515.

Korn, Richard R. and Lloyd W. McCorkle. 1959. *Criminology and Penology*. New York: Holt.

Krisberg, Barry. 1975. *Crime and Privilege: Toward New Criminology*. Englewood Cliffs, N.J.: Prentice-Hall, Inc.

Kuhn, Thomas S. 1962. *The Structure of Scientific Revolutions*. Chicago: The University of Chicago Press.

Lemert, Edwin M. 1972. *Human Deviance, Social Problems, and Social Control*. Englewood Cliffs, N.J.: Prentice-Hall.

Lilly, J. Robert, Francis T. Cullen, and Richard A. Ball. 1989.*Criminological Theory: Context and Consequences*. Newbury Park: Sage.

Lofland, John. 1978. "Deviance as Social Conflict." In *Deviance: The Interactionist Perspective*, 3rd edition edited by Earl Rubington and Martin S. Weinberg. New York: Macmillan, 30–3.

Matthews, Victor. 1968. "Differential Identification: An Empirical Note." *Social Problems* 15 376–83.
Meier, Robert F. 1976. "The New Criminology: Continuity in Criminological Theory." *Journal of Criminal Law and Criminology* 67 461–69.
Merton, Robert K. 1957. "Social Structure and Anomie." In *Social Theory and Social Structure*. New York: Free Press.
Paternoster, Raymond and LeeAnn Iovanni. 1989. "The Labeling Perspective and Delinquency: An Elaboration of the Theory and Assessment of The Evidence." *Justice Quarterly* 6 359–94.
Platt, Tony. 1974. "Prospects for a Radical Criminology in the United States." *Crime and Criminal Justice* I, 2–10.
Quinney, Richard. 1974. *Critique of Legal Order: Crime Control in Capitalist Society*. Boston: Little, Brown and Company.
———. 1977.*Class State and Crime*. New York: McKay.
———. 1979."The Production of Criminology." *Criminology* 16445–57.
———. 1980. *Class State and Crime, Second Edition*. New York: McKay.
Reiss, Albert J. Jr. and A. Lewis Rhodes. 1964. "An Empirical Test of Differential Association Theory." *Journal of Research in Crime and Delinquency* 1 5–18.
Schwendinger, Herman and Julia. 1979. "A Letter." *Crime and Social Justice* 6 3.
Scimecca, Joseph A. 1977. "Labeling Theory and Personal Construct Theory: Toward the Measurement of Individual Variation." *Journal of Criminal Law and Criminology* 681 652–59.
Shaw, Clifford R., Frederick M. Zorbaugh, Henry D. McKay and Leonard S. Cottrell. 1929. *Delinquency Areas*. Chicago: University of Chicago Press.
Short, James F. Jr. 1960. "Differential Association as a Hypothesis: Problems of Empirical Testing." *Social Problems* 8 14–25.
Stratton, John R. 1967. "Differential Identification and Attitudes Toward the Law." *Social Forces* 46 256–62.
Sutherland, Edwin and Donald R. Cressey. 1969. *Principles of Criminology*. New York: Lippincott.
Thomas, William I. and Florian Znaniecki. 1918. *The Polish Peasant in Europe and America*. Boston: Badger.
Turk, Austin T. 1966. "Conflict and Criminality." *Criminology* 31 338–52.
———. 1979. "Analyzing Official Deviance: For Nonpartisan Conflict Analyses in Criminology." *Criminology* 16 459–76.
Wellford, Charles. 1975. "Labeling Theory and Criminology: An Assessment." *Social Problems* 22 332–45.

Chapter 8

Major Themes in Contemporary Criminological Theory

As suggested in Chapter 7, criminological theorizing is often heavily influenced by political currents and trends. In the liberal and leftist political climate of the 1960s, advocates of the "new" criminology proposed a radical shift in analytical focus, one emphasizing the offender as societal victim rather than victimizer. Criminologists were urged to seek the causes of crime and criminality not in the unique behavioral antecedents of those adjudged to be criminal but in the people and social institutions that define what and who is criminal. To the more radically inclined adherents of this perspective, nothing short of a revolution, the replacement of capitalism with socialism, was required to solve the crime problem.

Associated with the reassertion and ascendancy of political conservatism has been the resurrection of basic tenets of the "classical" or "utilitarian" school of criminology, as well as other viewpoints emphasizing intraindividual rather than extraindividual sources of criminality. Structural perspectives, those focusing on societal institutions and cultural traditions as the generating source of criminality and necessary target of the change prerequisite to effective treatment of the crime problem, have been repudiated by politically influential intellectuals[1] who advocate the view that criminality is a an expression of individual choice and as such best responded to by the imposition swift and certain punishment to protect society and promote self-discipline and control. Nationwide interest in more punitive law-and-order measures such as "determinate," or flat, sentencing and the reinstitution of the death penalty are indicative of the popularity and effectiveness of their viewpoint.

Associated with the effort to depress the value and importance of structural perspectives has been an attempt to reduce and counter the influence of sociological views by an effort to reemphasize and modernize alternative perspectives on crime and its treatment. To date, biological and psychological slants have been given the greatest attention. Recent biological theories and one psychological theory of crime in particular (H.J. Eysenck's viewpoint on the bearing of personality and criminality) are the subject of the initial pages of this chapter.

Within sociology, the generally conservative political climate of the day has encouraged renewed interest in social- control theory. The social-control theory that has attracted the greatest interest in criminology was devised by Travis

Hirschi. His viewpoint and research, as well as the work of those who have sought to build on his lead, are the subject of the latter portions of the chapter.

Biological Factors and Crime

Research on the relationship between biological factors and criminality was negligible until roughly 1980. The mostly justified critical reception accorded Lombroso's pioneering efforts in the field undoubtedly discouraged many from pursuing the subject. The greater deterrent, however, has been the long history of the use of biological assumptions by racists and political demagogues such as Hitler to justify the abuse, neglect, and elimination of groups on the basis of their alleged biological inferiority. "Given this history," state Mednick et al.,

> it is not surprising that men and women interested in social justice have a tendency to view with suspicion any new speculations or empirical investigations linking biological factors with human social conduct, especially crime among the underprivileged. Nor is it cause for wonder that they prefer to seek causes of crime among economic, social, and political factors. (1981, ix)

One should not be surprised, then, by the tendency of modern investigators not only carefully to explain the nature of their theoretical assumptions and methodological procedures but also to explain any possible interpretive ambiguity in regard to their motives and qualify their conclusions.

Mednick et al. (1981, 22) define biological factors as "nonsocial, nonbehavioral measures of [humankind's] constitution and functioning." Two subjects in particular have been the source of biological measures of particular interest to criminologists: biochemistry and genetics.

Biochemistry and Crime

In a 1978 publication Leonard Hippchen contends that criminological theory has yet to benefit "from the extensive research that has been conducted in biochemistry in recent years" (1978, 10). In his view, biochemistry can be of inestimable help in treating institutionalized offenders, the early detection of criminal propensities, the diversion of offenders from the criminal justice system, and the prevention of crime. He claims that biochemical research has led to a new field, orthomolecular medicine.

In the orthomolecular perspective, the causes of crime and delinquency are traced to "chemical deficiencies or imbalances in the body" and brain toxicity

(Hippchen 1978, 13). Orthomolecular theorists emphasize two biochemically induced irregularities that may lead to criminal behavior: (1) distorted perception as a consequence of either nutritional deficiency or brain allergy, and (2) hyperactivity as a consequence of either nutritional deficiency or hypoglycemia (low blood sugar). Indicators of these "irregularities" include vitamin dependencies and saccharine diseases.

Vitamin dependency occurs in those who require more than the normal amount of certain vitamins. Alcoholics, for example, require excessive amounts of thiamine because of poor dietary practices. Vitamin deficiency and dependency diseases may lead to severe sensory distortion and violence. Higher than normal rates of vitamin B3–B6 dependency have been found among incarcerated adult offenders (Hippchen 1978, 14).

Saccharine diseases result from diets high in refined carbohydrates (sugar, starch, and syrup) and low in fiber. It is hypothesized that those who have saccharine disease experience a level of "thought disorder" conducive to antisocial behavior.

Among the most studied of the dietary diseases is hypoglycemia. Its symptoms include irritability, suspiciousness, hallucinations, and anxiety. It is thought to be associated with stealing, rape, arson, assault, and homicide.

In the orthomolecular approach, crime and delinquency are as much as anything else medical problems requiring early and accurate detection and treatment. Hippchen believes that orthomolecular approaches could greatly improve the effectiveness of treating types of criminal behavior, particularly those entailing violence. The evidence suggests to him that orthomolecular treatment could reduce recidivism rates among prison populations from 25 to 50 percent. Most investigators would not go this far. After reviewing the assessment of Sechrest, White, and Brown (1979), for example, David Farrington (1987, 42) finds Hippchen's claim "amazing."

Farrington expresses the prevailing view that a one-to-one relationship between criminality and biological factors is "comparatively rare." In his (1987, 48) view, a theory aimed at causally explaining criminal behavior must include all the relevant variables, from those intrapersonal (biological and psychological facts) to those extrapersonal (social and cultural facts) in nature. With such a theory "it would be possible to establish whether biological variables add to nonbiological ones in predicting criminal events or tendencies (Farrington 1987, 49).

Specification of the dependent variable (the criminal act, crime rates, a juvenile delinquent, and so on) is a major stumbling block for anyone wishing to differentiate biological from nonbiological crime-causing factors precisely. To do so would require identification of an exclusively biological conception of crime (a definition free of the contaminating influence of personal, social, and cultural influences), identification of equally uncontaminated potential biological causes, and controlled experimentally accurate measurement of the precise connection among the variables selected for study. Having yet to solve this problem, all investigators rely on some convenient conception of the dependent variable such as formal court adjudication—a criminal offender is one convicted of a crime or crimes. This conception is, of course, a "social," not a biological, fact. A common way of responding to this problem is to admit that crime is too complex to be anything but an interdisciplinary subject. Interestingly, often those who take this view tend to call not for the development of a new general theoretical approach, one that synthesizes all the relevant variables, but one that calls for independent disciplinary analyses. To Gordon Trasler (1987, 7), for example, "There are social, psychological, and physiological correlates of persistent criminality, and these demand explanation within the framework of the relevant discipline."

Biochemical causation studies have focused heavily on a general dependent variable: "antisocial behavior." The term is used in reference to the least (petty theft) and the most (murder) serious offenses. To the psychologist, antisocial behavior may be the product of antisocial personality disorder. To be diagnosed an antisocial personality, "The individual must be at least 18 years old and have a history, before the age of 15, of three or more symptoms that include truancy, expulsion or suspension from school, delinquency, running away, lying, substance abuse, thefts, vandalism, fights, and so on" (Rubin, 239). After age eighteen, the individual must exhibit at least four or more symptoms ranging from "inconsistent work patterns" to "unlawful activities." Regardless of age, however, there must be a consistent pattern of antisocial acts not interpretable as the consequence of "severe mental retardation. schizophrenia, or manic episodes" (Rubin 1987, 240).

As Rubin points out, semantic difficulties interfere with studies of the causes of antisocial behavior. The problem again is the difficulty of accurate conceptualization of the dependent variable. When crime is the subject, for example, the focus has been on rape, assault, and homicide, that is, crimes of interpersonal violence. Unfortunately, students of the subject have been susceptible to the charge of overgeneralization as they invariably fail to distinguish between key terms such as violence and aggression. Thus, Rubin (1987, 240) interprets *aggression* to mean "an active encounter with one's environment for the purpose of coping with environmental stressors." But here, too, complexity is created by the fact that aggression so defined requires sub-type specification. Moyer, for example, identifies the following subtypes: "predatory, intermale, fear-induced, irritable, territorial, maternal, and instrumental" (Rubin, 240). Significantly, the biochemical correlates of each are different. In animal studies, for example, testosterone has been found to influence intermale aggression but not predatory aggression.

According to Rubin (1987, 241), violence is "destructive behavior directed against members of the same species (one's fellow humans) in situations and circumstances in which alternative forms or adaptive behavior are possible." And as in the case of aggression, violence too may be variously sub-typed. Lief (1963), for example, distinguishes between violence driven by rage or emotion, as in the case of "crimes of passion," and two types expressed in an emotionally detached manner: (1) that which stresses the act of violence per se (juvenile gang attacks), and (2) that which stresses violent object destruction (warfare) (Rubin 1987, 241). According to Rubin, the particular neuroendocrine and neurochemical causes of each appear particularly difficult to differentiate, "particularly with reference to rageful violence and detached violence in which the significant aspect is the violent act" (1987, 241). In his view, the causal antecedents of identified forms of violent behavior are undoubtedly a complex combination of biological, psychological, and sociocultural factors. Even so, specification of these factors seems "an almost insurmountable task" (Rubin, 241). Rubin supports his view in an analysis of studies concerned with measurement of the bearing of neuroendocrine and neurochemical factors on antisocial human behavior.

In the studies analyzed, subjects' (quite often, incarcerated offenders) responses to a violence scale is far and away the most frequent measure of level of violence or aggression. Occasionally, violence or aggression is determined by direct observation.

Because crime, particularly offenses involving violence and aggression, is a predominantly male activity, much research has focused on the influence of circulating levels of the male-determining hormone testosterone. Could it be, for example, that more violent and aggressive males have higher levels of circulating testosterone than their more docile counterparts? In studies of normal subjects (e.g., college students), Rubin finds no "consistent correlation" between study findings. Higher levels of circulating testosterone have not been found to be consistently related to either violence or aggression as measured by rating scale responses. But a correlation has been found in studies involving incarcerated violent offenders. Rubin (1987, 246) cites Kreuz and Rose (1972), who he says account for the finding by hypothesizing that "in a population predisposed by social factors to develop antisocial behavior, testosterone may be an important additional factor placing some individuals at risk for committing more violent crimes during adolescence, when testosterone levels are increasing."

There is some evidence that hormones other than testosterone are implicated in the observed relationship between hypoglycemia and violent offending. Hypoglycemia in violent offenders is invariably the product of poor dietary practices and excessive alcohol consumption. In noting the evidence indicating faster recovery rates from hypoglycemia with insulin treatment among habitually violent offenders than those who express their violence intermittently,

Virkkunen observes that the difference "might depend on the hormones released as counterregulatory response to hypoglycemia: epinephrine, norepinephrine, cortisol, growth hormone, and glucagon" (1987, 306). At least one other investigator (Marks 1978), notes Virkkunen, has "speculated that abnormalities in these hormonal responses would not only predispose to the development of hypoglycemia but also delay recovery from it" (1987, 306).

The path leading to this inference began with Virkkunen's interest in exploring partial evidence indicating a relationship between cholesterol level and criminal behavior. He hypothesized that low cholesterol level may be the consequence of alcohol- induced violent behavior. To test the notion, Virkkunen studied three groups of homicidal offenders and a group of nonhomicidal controls. The first group was composed of those with antipersonality disorder, the second those with intermittent explosive disorder. To qualify for the second group, individuals were required "to have displayed several discrete episodes of loss of control of aggressive impulses (grossly out of proportion to any precipitating psychosocial stressor) resulting in serious assault or destruction of property" (1987, 294–95). The third group was composed of those who had not demonstrated habitually violent offending under the influence of alcohol. The controls were individuals with antisocial personality who had not demonstrated a tendency to become violent under the influence of alcohol. Virkkunen found

> both Group 1 and Group 2 subjects at two age levels (under 20 and 21–30 years) had lower cholesterol levels than Group 3 homicidal offenders and controls. In Group 2 (intermittent explosive disorder) the cholesterol level differences were significant when compared with Group 3 in the three older age groups as well. These results suggest that there may be two subgroups in the diagnostic category of antisocial personality disorder, persons with a habitually violent response to alcohol consumption and persons without such a pattern. These subgroups can be discriminated by their differing serum cholesterol levels as well as by the clinical histories of their antisocial acts. (1987, 295)

The precise causal connection between alcohol intake, cholesterol level, hypoglycemia and violent offending remains to be determined. The prevailing assumption is that a variety of biochemical factors (some whose origins are endogenous and others exogenous) may directly or indirectly provoke antisocial impulses or violent behavior. Whatever their origin, biochemically induced antisocial behavior is presumed to be the product of central nervous system abuse. Hypoglycemic-related violent offending, for example, is assumed to be the expression of brain malfunction. As is it is known that the brain is "completely dependent on the blood stream for its glucose supply" (Newman 1985,

131), a decrease in blood sugar level can cause the brain to malfunction and promote aggression. But factors other than low blood-sugar level may induce brain malfunction and aggression. Any number of hormones, neurotransmitters, and allergens may be involved.

Serotonin, a biochemical that functions both as a hormone and neurotransmitter, has been the subject of much recent research as it is known that it plays an important role in regulating aggression. In an extensive review of recent studies, Fishbein reports consistent finding of lower than normal levels of serotonin in "individuals characterized as violent or impulsive in comparison with those who are not" (1990, 47). A recent study by Virkkunen et al. (1989) found lower levels of serotonin among violent offenders and arsonists most likely to recidivate. The authors contend that such offenders are treatable with serotoninergic drugs, and that the treatment could not only "ameliorate a serotonergic deficit," but also "it has been reported to reduce alcohol consumption in humans and improve abnormal glucose metabolism in experimental animals" (1989, 603).

Of course, the relationship between serotonin level and other aggression or violence influencing biochemicals in humans remains undetermined. Also to be determined is the impact on serotonin level of genetic factors and dietary practices. The same caution must be kept in mind when examining evidence of violence-producing allergens in humans.

An allergy is an unusual reaction to factors in one's environment (dust, pollen) or substances in one's body (foods, microorganisms). A common source of neuroallergies (those that influence the brain and other parts of the nervous system) is a diet lacking variety and nutritional value. Those whose diets are high in "junk foods," items rich in chemical additives, are particularly susceptible. The symptoms may include hyperemotionality, hyperaggressiveness, hyperactivity, and violent behavior. Newman (1985, 131) reports the case of a boy found repeatedly to develop violent temper tantrums within twenty minutes of eating bananas. "Although," he says, "there are few documented cases as serious as that of the banana boy, there are certainly many clinical reports of reactions of irritability, combativeness, anger, violent temper, paranoia, peevishness, and many others occurring in response to particular allergens" (1985, 131). But as Newman warns, the bulk of the available evidence is based on case studies, not controlled experiments demonstrating the causal connection between allergens and aggression.

Allergic-like symptoms may be produced by exposure to trace elements such as lead. Lead poisoning is associated with brain impairment as indicated by lowered intellectual ability and behavioral irregularities, including irritability, hyperactivity, and impulsivity. Fishbein (1990, 49) reports a study by Pihl et al. (1982) that found high concentrations of lead in violent but not in nonviolent offenders. But here, too, carefully controlled experimental studies are not the rule.

A frequently employed means of measuring central nervous system impairment has been the electroencephalogram (EEG), a tool used to study offenders since the 1940s (Volavka 1987). As H.J. Eysenck explains it, "This instrument records brain waves from the external surface of the cortex, and among these we are particularly concerned with the so-called alpha waves, i.e., regular waves occurring with a frequency of between 8 and 13 or so per second" (1977, 85). Those found to have abnormal alpha wave measurements include juvenile thieves (Mednick et al. 1981), psychopaths (Nassi and Abramowitz 1987), and murderers (Hill and Pond 1952). What is unknown is the extent to which the measured brain wave abnormality is a consequence of dietary, social-psychological factors including substance abuse, and genetics. As all may be involved, future controlled multi-variate experiments are clearly in order.

Genetics and Crime

Genetics is that branch of biology whose subject is heredity. A standard dictionary definition of heredity is "the transmission of characteristics from parent to offspring by means of genes in the chromosomes." For the criminologist, the question is, to what extent is criminality inherited, that is, passed on biologically from parent to child? Interestingly, one is hard pressed to find a reputable contemporary student of the subject who will go so far as to say that there is a crime gene or a set of genes that inexorably determines criminality or human behavior of any kind. As Wilson and Herrnstein put it, "There is no 'crime gene' and so there is no such thing as a 'born criminal'" (1985, 69). And in the words of the behavioral geneticist Robert Plomin,

> There are no genes for behavior just as there are no genes for beauty or athletic ability. Genes are chemical structures that can only code for amino acid sequences. These amino acid sequences interact with all of what we are and can thus *indirectly* [emphasis added] affect endpoints as complex as behavior, but there is no gene for a particular behavior. (1990, 20)

As prevailing theory has it, hereditary endowment is assumed to "influence," not determine, neurochemical transmitters, which in turn stimulate the central nervous system. But the exact behavioral reaction is thought to be a complex product of unique intra- and extrasomatic factors. "Behavioral genetics," says Plomin, "is the study of genetic and environmental factors that create behavioral differences among individuals" (1990, 4).

In effect, Plomin's statement is basically an acknowledgment of the fact that behavioral genetics is an inexact science in the manner of any behavioral or social science. Thus, if there is no precise means for determining the exact relationship between an inherited variable and a given item of human behavior, what can be said about the bearing of heredity on criminality? According to Wilson and Herrnstein, for example,

> If having a criminal natural brother is more predictive of crime for a person than having a criminal foster brother, then with certain reservations and qualifications, genes probably play some role in criminal behavior. We could not yet say what the genetic role is, for it would remain to be shown what inherited psychological characteristics are predisposing the individual to break the law, but, given enough data like this, we could estimate the size of the genetic contribution. (1985, 90)

In the early 1960s, some behavioral geneticists thought they had discovered a direct link between violent crime and genetics in what is now commonly referred to as the "XYY chromosome affair." It was discovered that some males have an extra Y chromosome (Y is the male sex chromosome). Subsequent small-sample studies indicated an unusually high percentage of XYY men among incarcerated violent offenders. The proportion of men with the XYY chromosome in the general population is estimated to be about 1 per 1000 (Wilson and Herrnstein 1985, 101). Among the criminally incarcerated their proportion has been found to be "ten to twenty times larger, about 1 to 2 percent of the institutionalized population" (Wilson and Herrnstein 1985, 101). However, later studies based on large samples did not uphold the image of the XYY male as all that violent or criminally dangerous. The most important of these was based on analysis of 4139 men in Denmark (Witkin et al. 1977). The twelve XYY men found in the sample turned out to be "mildly criminal but not at all violent" (Mednick 1987, 2). Minor property crimes represented most of the offenses committed by the twelve. As Wilson and Herrnstein summarize the findings: "Though they were more often criminal, XYY men did not appear to be more violent or aggressive than the XY men with criminal records, contradicting the occasional reports in the press of the special cruelty of XYY crimes" (1985, 102).

Interestingly, the XYY chromosome is not presumed to be inherited directly but something that develops in certain individuals. It is of special interest to the behavioral geneticist because its presence can be precisely identified, and it is something whose origins are incontestably biological. This does not mean that its behavioral effects are direct or uninfluenced by environmental circumstances, that is, social and cultural variables. In the Danish study, XYY men of comparable socioeconomic status to XY men were found to be lower in tested intelligence and educational achievement. The precise role played by social and cultural factors in such findings remains to be determined. Thus, for the present, the best that may be said about the XYY chromosome is that it does appear to have some predisposing behavioral consequences that makes the individual somewhat more susceptible than XY men to criminality, depending on the sociocultural circumstances. The best evidence for a connection between genetics and crime is generally regarded to stem from the evidence of twin and adoption studies.

Several studies of criminality in twins have been conducted. The first was published in 1931 (Lange) and the most recent major study in 1977 (Christiansen et al.). Twins are of two types. Identical twins are the product of a single egg (monozygotic, abbreviated MZ) and fraternal twins of two eggs (dyzogotic, abbreviated DZ). Identical twins are the same sex, and fraternal twins may or may not be the same sex. The gene comparability of identical twins is 100 percent and fraternal twins 50 percent.

The first studies of adult criminality among twins involved small samples and invariably reported extremely high rates of concordance for identical twins and much higher concordance rates for identical than fraternal twins. In the Lange study, for example, the concordance rate for thirteen sets of identical twins was 77 percent and 12 percent for thirteen sets of fraternal twins. The most recent study by Christiansen entailed both a much more rigorous sampling process and careful manner of measuring criminality. Christiansen reported a 34 percent concordance rate for 73 pairs of male and 20 percent for 15 pairs of female identical twins. A concordance rate of 18 percent was found for 146 sets of male and 7 percent for 28 sets of female fraternal twins. Although the concordance proportion varies by study, all show higher comparability among identical than fraternal twins. The finding may be variously interpreted. To some, it indicates the causal importance of the genetic factor. To others, it suggests the need for a tempered inference. After reviewing twin-study research, for example, Eysenck and Gudjonsson observe that "Altogether, these studies powerfully support the view that genetic factors play a large part in the causation of criminal behavior, although the failure of the MZ concordance to be complete suggests a strong environmental influence as well" (1989, 98).

The question is, then, how much of the criminal concordance among identical twins is due to genetics and how much to comparable environmental circumstances? As Plomin states the problem, "If identical twins are treated more similarly for nongenetic reasons than are fraternal twins, greater behavioral resemblance of identical twins could be due to environment rather than heredity" (1990, 49). Thus, for example, the greater overlap in criminality among identical than fraternal twins could be due to the fact that they are more similarly socialized and treated. People treated the same should be expected to share the same basic attitudes and values and behave comparably. Unfortunately, studies designed to control for environmental influences of this sort are few and their results are inconclusive. A study of criminality in twins (Dalgaard and Kringlen 1976) found that concordant criminality was not influenced by whether or not subjects were similarly or dissimilarly treated (as indicated by measures such as grooming and dressing expectations). But the study's methodological limitations led investigators such as Ellis (1985, 72) to suspend judgment on the question.

Unfortunately, because of methodological factors such as sampling complexity, studies of criminality among identical twins raised apart are also, as Wilson and Herrnstein state, "too few to permit a decisive conclusion" (1985, 95). Adoption studies provide the best available evidence on the relative contributions of heredity and environment to criminality.

Among the most important adoption studies to date was one conducted by Mednick et al. The study sample was composed of all nonfamilial adoptions (some 14,427) in Denmark between 1924 and 1947. The criminality measure was court conviction. Conviction data were collected on male and female adoptees, adoptive fathers and mothers, and biological fathers and mothers. Not surprisingly, male adoptees had much higher conviction rates than female adoptees. Conviction rates for male adoptees and their biological fathers were "considerably higher" than rates for adoptive fathers. And compared to adoptive fathers, the recidivism rates for male adoptees and their biological fathers was much higher. While evidencing a much lower rate of recidivism than males, the same basic pattern held for females. That is, female adoptees and their biological mothers had higher conviction rates than adoptive mothers.

Consistent with the assumption that heredity carries greater weight than environmental influences were the following findings: (1) 20 percent of the adopted sons had convictions when adoptive parents did not but biological parents did; (2) 24.5 percent of the adopted sons had convictions when both adoptive and biological parents had convictions; (3) 14.7 percent of the adopted sons had convictions when biological parents did not and adoptive parents did have convictions; and (4) 13.5 percent of the adopted sons had convictions when neither set of parents had convictions. No statistical relationship was found between type of biological parent conviction and type of adoptee conviction. The authors (Mednick et al. 1987, 90) cautiously conclude that "some factor is transmitted by convicted parents that increases the likelihood that their children will be convicted for criminal law offenses."

An earlier study by Mednick et al. based on the same data examined the influence of urban and rural residence on incidence of criminality among adoptees. Of a total of 2592 nonfamilial male adoptees, nearly a third (32 percent) resided in a large metropolitan area (Copenhagen), a little more than a third (34 percent) lived in intermediate-size cities and towns, and a little more than a third (34 percent) were rural residents. As the goal was "to examine the influence of the type of environment in mediating a genetic high risk for criminality, only adoptees of families in which neither adoptive parent has ever been convicted of a criminal law offense were studied" (1984, 648–49).

As expected, regardless of place of residence, adoptees were more likely to be convicted when their biological parents had also been convicted. Further, urban-residing adoptees (both metropolitan and smaller-city residents) had higher rates of conviction than rural residents. Hence, study results indicated that "both genetic factors and environmental factors contribute independently to criminality" (1984, 650).

To summarize this section briefly, it may be said that recent studies indicate to their authors that inherited factors play a role in criminality. However, social scientists contend that any conclusion on the subject would be premature, primarily because of certain perceived methodological limitations and weaknesses. After reviewing recent research, Walters and White, for example, take the following position:

> Genetic factors are undoubtedly correlated with various measures of criminality, but the large number of methodological flaws and limitations in the research should make one cautious in drawing any causal inferences at this point in time. Our review leads us to the inevitable conclusion that current genetic research on crime has been poorly designed, ambiguously reported, and exceedingly inadequate in addressing the relevant issues. (1989, 478)

Walters and White score recent research on a number of particulars, but especially the lack of a consistent and meaningful crime measure to permit replicability, failure to control adequately for the influence of a variety of intervening variables (social class, intelligence, time spent with biological parents before adoption), absence of a longitudinal design, and poor theoretical organization. "Until methodological improvements are made and a coherent theoretical framework found," contend Walters and White, "little progress is anticipated in the effort to determine whether genes play a meaningful role in the evolution of criminal behavior" (1989, 479).

In a rejoinder to Walters and White, Brennan and Mednick in turn scored Walters and White for failure to be specific. In their words,

> The major flaw of many of Walters and White's critical comments is their lack of specificity. They repeatedly present vague or global criticisms of the research, without specific supporting arguments. Unfortunately, the nonspecific nature of a criticism such as this is little more than name-calling. (1990, 657)

Glenn Walters' responded by saying that

> The problem is not with Walters and White's review, but with genetic research on crime. Efforts to discount the message and discredit the messenger conceal the fact that research on the heritability of criminal conduct has failed to move us toward a meaningful resolution of the gene-crime question. Until researchers in this area of investigative endeavor elevate the conceptual rigor, methodological sophistication, and theoretical relevance of their studies, research on the genetic bases of crime will continue to promise more than it can deliver. (1990, 666).

Whatever one's position in the matter, Walters's concluding sentence is as applicable to the social sciences as it is to behavioral genetics. There is nothing to indicate that measurement in the former is any more sophisticated and accurate than the latter. Ideological predisposition and sociocultural bias are concomitants in social and genetic science. Value-free, completely objective science is an ideal whose proximation is always questionable. It is with this and other factors in mind that many advocate a unified, multidisciplinary approach to the study of crime. In this view, interdisciplinary research offers the best opportunity for objective analysis by comparing the results of different perspectives on the same subjects. Presumably, the higher the comparability of findings in such research, the higher the confidence in their validity. An important component in an interdisciplinary approach is the psychological perspective. Psychologists have long studied the problem of crime, and their interest in the subject appears to have risen as the challenge to the preeminence of sociology in the crime field has increased. Among the most noteworthy contemporary psychological perspectives is one that has attracted widespread and international attention: H.J. Eysenck's personality theory of criminality.

Criminality and Personality: The Eysenck Perspective

In the recent edition of his text, the psychologist Curt Bartol points out that "authors continue to regard 'psychology' from a classical Freudian viewpoint, often combined with a vague biological—genetic 'trait' or dispositional focus" (1991, xi). Psychologists are increasingly emphasizing a cognitive social-learning approach to crime and focusing on subjects such as the offender's "perceptions, beliefs, reasoning, and attitudes and the processes that contribute to their versions of the world." Nevertheless, Freudian and neo-Freudian psychoanalytic approaches continue to hold sway in forensic psychiatry, that is, in the psychiatric approach to the origin and treatment of criminality. In psychoanalytic theory, criminality is the expression of individual personality. And individual personality is thought to be heavily influenced, if not determined, by an inherent instinctual element referred to in Freudian terminology as the *id*. Early childhood socialization is thought to produce two other elements, a *superego*, or conscience, representing the imposition and learning of societal norms and values, and an *ego*, an individual's self concept. Individual's are assumed to be largely unaware of their essential motives because behavior is assumed to be driven or compelled by unconscious "primitive" biopsychological drives whose intricate manifestations require ferreting out in psychoanalysis. According to Bartol, the contemporary psychological approach to crime does not rely on this perspective. As Bartol tells it,

> The vagaries of the id, the ego, the superego, unconscious urges and impulses, behavioral symbolism, and psychosocial development as explanations of crime are well known to most criminologists, and they hold a dominant place in forensic psychiatry. However, they are not accepted by most contemporary psychologists. In fact, most Freudian and neo-Freudian concepts have never found a secure place in mainstream psychology, especially within the academic realm. (1991, 18)

However generally valid Bartol's observations, neo-Freudian concepts and assumptions are an integral part of a major contemporary psychological theory of criminality, namely, H.J. Eysenck's work on personality and crime. As will become evident, Eysenck's approach leans heavily on biological assumptions. As he states, "Heredity plays an important, and possibly a vital part, in predisposing a given individual to crime" (1964. 5). For this reason, psychologists have been inclined to categorize Eysenck's approach as a theory of social control, a viewpoint based more on the premise that criminality is something certain individuals must learn to avoid rather than to do.

Eysenck assumes that criminality reflects the interaction of individual psychobiological traits and environmental stimuli. However much it might seem to follow that he would therefore opt for a multidimensional viewpoint aimed at specifying the causal role of a variety of variables, he nonetheless makes it clear that he seeks the causes of criminal behavior within the individual rather than both within the individual and society. In a recent coauthored work, Eysenck and Gudjonsson offer the following explanation for their perspective: "We have concentrated on psychological causes of crime, not only because as psychologists we are more competent to deal with these factors, but also because we believe that they have been relatively neglected in recent years and require explicit statement and justification" (1989, 1).

They begin with a critical assessment of sociological theories of criminality that came to prominence after World War II and that they believe "are fundamentally erroneous and counter to fact" (1989, 1). The sociological theories they have in mind are those in the economic (crime as a consequence of poverty, unemployment, and so on) and Marxist (crime as a consequence of inherent contradictions within capitalist societies) traditions. Varieties of the two are identified and critically assessed by means of selected supporting evidence. As Eysenck and Gudjonsson emphasize,

> Whatever is done by situational management—that is, by changing laws, by introducing penalties not involving incarceration, or by changing our whole system from capitalism to communism, or vice versa—all these activities *can only influence conduct along psychological pathways and are hence subject to psychological analysis.* Whatever we do, we are dealing with people whose reactions to social changes are difficult to predict and are usually different from person to person depending on personality, temperament, mood, and the like. *No system of criminology has any meaning that disregards this central feature of all criminology: the individual person whom we are trying to influence* [emphasis in the original]. (1989, 8)

Eysenck seeks the causal origins of crime in human personality. But he and his collaborators do not offer a precise definition of the term. Instead, personality is described as something based on "ability" and "temperament." Ability is an expression of intelligence and temperament by three factors: extraversion-introversion (the E factor), neuroticism-stability (the N factor), and psychoticism (the P factor). Particular combinations of the four factors are thought to account for different personality types. In their turn, the four factors are assumed to be indicated by certain clusterings of "traits." For example, traits indicative of (1) extraversion include assertiveness and sociability, (2) neuroticism include depression and low self-esteem, and (3) psychoticism include impersonality and impulsiveness. What, then, according to Eysenck, differentiates the criminal from the noncriminal personality?

A review of the research literature indicates to Eysenck and Gudjonsson a consistent correlation between low IQ and criminality. Their theoretical interpretation of this finding runs as follows:

> The lower the IQ, the lower the learning ability; the lower the learning ability, the lower the ability to achieve academically; thus, the lower the IQ, the lower the ability to achieve academically.
>
> The lower the ability to achieve academically, the fewer the satisfying employment opportunities.
>
> The fewer the satisfying employment opportunities, the higher the susceptibility to higher rewarding illegal alternatives.

> Thus, the lower the ability to achieve academically, the higher the susceptibility to higher rewarding illegal alternatives.

Nonetheless, Eysenck and Gudjonsson conclude by saying that although intelligence is causally related to criminality, "its contribution is probably smaller than one might have thought at first" (1989, 50). This is explained by the finding of a correlation between intelligence and temperament, and a much stronger correlation between temperamental factors and criminality than intelligence and criminality. As indicated above, the indicators of temperament are the E factor (extraversion-introversion), the N factor (neuroticism-stability), and the P factor (psychoticism). Eysenck has constructed a personality inventory scale to measure the three factors and his and his collaborators' research indicate that criminals are more inclined to be extra- than introverted, more neurotic than emotionally stable, and more inclined to manifest symptoms indicative of severe mental problems.

The premises underlying the theory are clearly specified. On the E factor, or extraversion, Eysenck finds the evidence to indicate that extraverted personalities (those high in sociability, self-confidence, and so on) are inclined to be difficult to condition, to influence in ways that contradict their predispositions. Thus, the lower the ability to be conditioned, the less effective the socialization process. And the less effective the socialization process, the lower the ability to contain antisocial impulses, that is, to effect social control. Again, it should be remembered that behind Eysenck's thinking is the notion that antisocial behavior and criminality are inherent urges that will be expressed unless they are prevented by the available means of social control.

The theoretical premise behind the N factor (neuroticism) and criminality is that the emotionally, anxiety-ridden neurotic is more susceptible to deviant, including antisocial, behavioral adaptations than the emotionally stable, more rationally self-contained nonneurotic personality. As R.E. Passingham summarizes Eysenck's thinking:

> Neurotics are high on anxiety or emotionality. Anxiety acts as a drive which multiplies with habit. Therefore neurotics with habitual antisocial responses will tend to engage in these responses more strongly than non-neurotics. (1972, 344)

The P factor (psychoticism) is not meant to be taken as a synonym for diagnosed severe mental illness. Eysenck has in mind something short of the extreme, someone more like the psychopath who is able to give the appearance of normality while harboring life-threatening attitudes, an amoral world-view, and indifference toward the pain and suffering of others. Thus, Eysenck's P-scale measures are designed to identify not one who is psychiatrically ill but one inclined to be solitary, troublesome, cruel, unempathic, sensation-seeking, hostile, and foolhardy. As Eysenck sees it, then, the greater the number of personality traits indicative of psychoticism, the higher the susceptibility of the individual to antisocial behavior and criminality.

Eysenck is well-aware of the fact that the dependent variable, criminality, is complex and that his theory may have greater relevance for an understanding of some types of offenders than others. Accordingly, five groups of prisoners were studied: "confidence tricksters," property offenders, violent offenders, "inadequate criminals" (those who "drift into crime" because "they simply cannot cope with the complexities of modern life" (Eysenck 1977, 59), and a residual category composed of those whose offenses were too diverse to classify among the other four. The Eysenck personality inventory was administered to the prisoners, and it was found that con men had particularly high P scores, "inadequates and residuals" had particularly high N scores and property and violent offenders particularly low N scores, and violent offenders and "residuals" had relatively high E scores and "inadequates" and property offenders relatively low E scores. "We may perhaps conclude provisionally," said Eysenck, "that there is some evidence that personality is connected with criminality, and that within a criminal group personality is connected with the particular type of crime most frequently practiced" (1977, 61).

Over the several years of its development, Eysenck's theory has been subjected to considerable critical scrutiny and empirical assessment. Taylor, Walton, and Young cite the following observation made by Richard Christie of Eysenck's research techniques:

> Errors of computation, uniquely biased samples which forbid any generalizations, scales with built-in biases which do not measure what they purport to measure, unexplained inconsistencies within the data, misinterpretations and contradictions of the relevant research of others, and unjustifiable manipulation of the data. Any one of Eysenck's many errors is sufficient to raise serious questions about the validity of his conclusions. *In toto*, absurdity is compounded upon absurdity, so that where the truth lies is impossible to determine. (Taylor, Walton, and Young 1973, 58)

Taylor, Walton, and Young's essential criticism is that Eysenck's search for the biological causes of criminality is "misguided." It is misguided, they think, because it treats biology as a predetermining entity rather than a potential influence that is itself influenced. In their view, humans are more appropriately to be viewed as engaged in a continuing process of self-realization than behaving according to a script determined by their biological endowment. In their words, a person's "definitions of [himself or herself] evolve not as a determinate result of the addition of social factors onto a biological substratum but rather as *praxis*, as the meaningful attempt by the actor to construct and develop his own self-construction" (1973, 56).

Not surprisingly, Taylor, Walton, and Young's Marxist-oriented work is singled out for special criticism by Eysenck in his recent collaborative effort with Gudjonsson. It is described (1989, 1) as an example of "modern sociological writing" stressing crime as something rather arbitrarily defined by the prevailing ruling class in a given society in accordance with their particular economic and social interests. Eysenck and Gudjonsson contest this viewpoint by arguing that "the same types of antisocial activities (e.g., theft, burglary, physical attacks, murder, rape) have from the beginning of time been outlawed in practically all those societies of which we have knowledge" (1989, 2). They go on to claim that "many—if not most—sociological theories boil down to what might be called *economic* theories, i.e., crime as the result of poverty, whether relative or absolute, deprivation, and similar economic causes" (1989, 4). As psychologist Curt Bartol points out in a review essay of the Eysenck and Gudjonsson work,

> I suspect few criminologists will be able to read beyond the first six pages without resenting the dogmatism and naivete about sociological theory on crime. *The New Criminology* is hardly the only modern representative of sociological theory in criminology. Hirschi's social control theory, Sutherland's differential association, and Merton's stain theory all have received considerable attention and commentary since World War II, the era which Eysenck and Gudjonsson choose to herald as modern. (1990, 468)

Elsewhere, Bartol finds some research evidence that supports Eysenck's theory but more that does not. To date, the bearing of "psychoticism" on criminality has not received as much attention as "extraversion" and "neuroticism." Work done by Lane (1987) and others, however, tends to support Eysenck's prediction of high measured levels of P in habitual offenders and psychopaths. The influence of "extraversion" and "neuroticism" in criminality appears to be more complicated than anticipated by Eysenck. In his recent study of samples of children, for example, Lane reports that extraversion "does discriminate for general behaviour in school and type of conduct disorder, but plays little role in delinquency or therapy outcome" (1987, 805). He judged the impact of neuroticism to lie "more consistently" in the direction of low rather than high measures of N.

Bartol's assessment of the evidence is consistent with Lane's. The expectation of higher extraversion scale measures by criminals and other antisocial populations, Bartol says, "has not been consistently supported" (1991, 54). On neuroticism, Bartol finds the evidence to be unequivocal. "The research results examining the relationship between neuroticism and criminal or antisocial behavior are clear: It is not supported" (1991, 55). Bartol finds the evidence on psychoticism to be less consistent with Eysenck's expectations than does Lane. While he finds that some study results indicate that psychoticism-scale scores are higher for criminal and antisocial personality types, other studies indicate no significant correlation.

However accurate and whatever the shortcomings of the Eysenck theory, it will undoubtedly continue to receive considerable attention because as Bartol indicates, it is among the few general psychological theories of criminality that is empirically interpretable. The sociological counterpart to Eysenck's theory is Travis Hirschi's social-control theory.

Hirschi's Social-Control Theory

Hirschi's theoretical perspective is built on the same basic premise as Eysenck's, that humans are animals requiring taming and nurturing if they are to become civil and trustworthy. Thus, to Hirschi, the proper subject of criminological investigation is not what causes criminality but what prevents it.

Hirschi indicates that his perspective is based on a different response than is customary to the Hobbesian question, "Why do men obey the rules of society?" Prevailing theoretical slants, such as Merton's "strain theory," says Hirschi, "assume that the Hobbesian question has been answered, that the important question is, 'Why do men *not* obey the rules of society'" (1969, 10). From this vantage point, deviance is the problem, not conformity. But to the control theorist the Hobbesian question is not assumed to have been adequately answered. To the control theorist, says Hirschi, the question is: "Why do men obey the rules of society" (1969, 10)? In other words, the subject of concern is not deviancy but conformity.

Following Durkheim, Hirschi views conformity as a product of social bonding. As his subject is delinquency, he tells us that control theorists take the view "that delinquent acts result when an individual's bond to society is weak or broken" (1969, 16). Hirschi identifies the following as the basic elements of the social bond: *attachment*, *commitment*, *involvement*, and *belief*.

By *attachment*, Hirschi means the extent to which basic norms and values are internalized in the socialization process to yield a conscience or a superego. Crucial here is the influence of, or in Hirschi's view, attachment to, parents, teachers, and other "significant others."

Commitment refers to devotion to conventional expectations and behavior. Hirschi assumes that the more one invests time and energy in conventional activities such as academic achievement and occupational mobility, the less the likelihood of involvement in unconventional activities such as crime and delinquency. "To the person committed to conventional lines of action," he says, "risking one to ten years in prison for a ten-dollar holdup is stupidity, because to the committed person the costs and risks obviously exceed ten dollars in value" (1969, 20).

Involvement denotes the behavioral counterpart to commitment. That is, the more occupied one is in conventional activities (e.g., school and church attendance and participation), the less time available for participating in unconventional activities. As Hirschi reasons, "The person involved in conventional activities is tied to appointments, deadlines, working hours, plans, and the like, so the opportunity to commit deviant acts rarely arises" (1969, 22).

Belief refers to acceptance of "the moral validity" of conventional norms and values. The greater one's belief in group rules and values, the less the tendency to deviate.

It is important to point out that Hirschi takes the view that there is considerable possible variation in the extent to which individuals manifest attachment, commitment, involvement, and belief. He presumes neither that all members of a certain society manifest a certain degree of each nor that all conformists and nonconformists can be expected to evidence a certain degree of each. He does assume certain relationships among the four. Thus, while some assume a tendency for attachment and commitment to be inversely related, Hirschi assumes that they "tend to vary together." The more attached one is to conventional norms and values, the greater the involvement in conventional activities. Similarly, commitment is presumed to promote involvement, and attachment is presumed to foster belief. "In the end, then," Hirschi says by way of summary,

> Control theory remains what it has always been: a theory in which deviation is not problematic. The question "Why do they do it?" is simply not the question the theory is designed to answer. The question is, "Why don't we do it?" There is much evidence that we would if we dared. (1969, 34)

As noted above, Hirschi's theory was developed to explain delinquency. He defines delinquency as "acts, the detection of which is thought to result in punishment of the person committing them by agents of the larger society" (1969, 47). He acknowledges the fact that his definition "is not widely used," primarily because it treats delinquency as a general and homogeneous phenomenon. In turn, he argues that prevailing conceptions, such as "role" and "syndrome" definitions, have major limitations that justify his choice.

Hirschi points out, for example, that those who study delinquency as role behavior stress the need to differentiate a random act from a sustained pattern of deviancy. In this view, it is persistent rather than non-repetitive or infrequent deviancy that should be the subject of concern. As Hirschi (1969: 52–53) sees it, in addition to excluding the acts of those regarded as nondelinquents,

> Role definitions of delinquency propose an analogy between delinquency and other social roles that confuses more than it clarifies; they prematurely and unnecessarily restrict the study of delinquency to small segments of the population while acknowledging that delinquency is prevalent throughout the social structure and without giving any good reason for believing that the causes of delinquent acts are different from one class to another. (1969, 52–3)

As with role definitions, syndrome definitions, too, says Hirschi, seek to identify the factors that differentiate committed from casual delinquency. "In this view," he says, "it is not the first act, or the third, that defines a boy as 'delinquent,' but it is some, often ineffable combination of acts that distinguishes the 'true' delinquent from the 'pseudo'-delinquent and the 'true' nondelinquent" (1969, 49). Because of "their ultimate ambiguity," Hirschi regards the frequent use of syndrome definitions in empirical studies as "particularly unfortunate." "The not-very-far-beneath-the-surface assumption that delinquency is a disease of which delinquent acts are a symptom allows users of these definitions to diagnose boys committing few delinquent acts as 'delinquent' and other boys committing many delinquent acts 'nondelinquent'" (1969, 53).

Notwithstanding these limitations, Hirschi acknowledges the fact that it is not possible to cite a theory capable of providing an "irrefutable answer" to those who contend "that delinquency cannot or should not be treated as a homogeneous phenomenon" (1969: 53). Thus, he defends his position by arguing that social-control theories are as successful in explaining crime in general as special theories are in explaining specific types of deviance. Additionally, he claims that available empirical evidence suggests that correlations between antecedent variables and specific delinquent acts have not been as significant as those obtained when delinquency is defined more generally.

Hirschi tested his theory on a sample of Richmond, California, junior and senior high school students in 1964. Self-administered questionnaires were completed by 4077 students, and additional data were obtained from school and other public records.

Hirschi's findings supported his theory. He found that the higher the attachment to parents, the lower the involvement in delinquency. Also upheld was the predicted inverse relationship between attachment to school and delinquency. As he states, the evidence consistently supported the assumed "causal chain," which "runs from academic incompetence to poor school performance to disliking of school to rejection of the school's authority to the commission of delinquent acts" (1969, 132). The effect of attachment of peers on delinquency was also as predicted. But here Hirschi was particularly concerned to determine a possible reciprocal relationship between the variables. For example, does joining a delinquent gang precede becoming a delinquent, or is it that joining a delinquent gang comes after becoming a delinquent? Hirschi found that the delinquent gang "only rarely recruits 'good' boys" and that "the evidence strongly supports the view that the boy's stake in conformity affects his choice of friends rather than the other way around" (1969, 159).

Commitment was indicated by responses to questions relative to respondents' "passage to adult status" and educational and occupational aspirations. As to the first of the three factors, Hirschi examined the connection between involvement in adult activities such as smoking, driving, drinking, and dating and delinquency. He found that involvement in such activities had a cumulative effect, namely, "the more the boy is involved in adult activities, the greater his involvement in delinquency" (1969, 168–9). He also found that the higher individuals' educational and occupational aspirations, the lower their delinquency rate.

Hirschi could not find straightforward support for the predicted inverse relationship between involvement in conventional activities and delinquency. The data suggested to him that the type of activity engaged in is more important than amount of time devoted to an activity. "We must consider, then," he says, "*what* the child is doing, and assiduously avoid the idea that doing 'something'—anything—is better than, that is, inhibitive of, the commission of delinquent acts" (1969, 190–91). His evidence suggests to him, for example, that involvement in leisure activities such as "time spent on homework," "time talking to friends," and "time riding in car" may have an overriding influence on delinquency. As he states, "Boys who smoke, drink, date, ride around in cars, find adolescence "boring" and so on, are more likely to commit delinquent acts than boys who do not have these attitudes and do not engage in these activities, *regardless* of commitment to education and involvement in school-related activities" (1969, 196).

The last element in Hirschi's theory, *belief*, concerns an assumed negative correlation between internalization of conventional beliefs and delinquency. Put another way, delinquency may be regarded as the result of an individual's failure or inability to learn and accept prevailing group norms. As Hirschi notes, delinquency theorists have emphasized the bearing of three sets of beliefs on values: middle class, lower class, and criminal. Hirschi found no essential difference in the beliefs of middle-class and lower-class youth. Both groups appeared equally to accept prevailing cultural norms and values. Further, delinquents were not found to have internalized norms favorable to law violation either before or after the fact. In regard to one set of findings, for example, Hirschi notes that "attitudes toward persons may be favorable to the violation of law without being transformed into beliefs more or less consistent with those attitudes" (1969, 204).

In his concluding chapter, Hirschi critically appraises the validity of strain, cultural deviance, and control theory in the light of his findings. Strain theory is found to have the least support. It is based, he says, on a presumed causal connection between social class-status and delinquency. It may be assumed, for example, that the lower-class boy who wishes to attain culturally valued goals but lacks access to prescribed means for their attainment is more likely than his middle-class counterpart to experience the strain of frustration conducive to aggression and law violation. The problem, in Hirschi's view, is that delinquency and social class are not "importantly related" (1969, 226).

In cultural deviancy theory, notes Hirschi, it is assumed that delinquency is the result of adherence to subcultural norms that violate the dominant larger cultural norms. Thus, as in the case of one version of this theory, a lower-class culture is presumed to exist whose norms conflict with those of general society. Hirschi examined the subject in a variety of ways but most of all by comparing the level of attachment in lower-class and other youth. To Hirschi, the evidence indicates that the effects of attachment are not social class specific. That is, regardless of social class, "the stronger the attachment, the less likely the child is to be delinquent" (1969, 229).

Control theory was also found to have its weaknesses, the most important of which was that it underestimated the role of delinquent friends in delinquency involvement and overestimated the role of involvement in conventional activities in delinquency prevention. Both "miscalculations" are traced to a common assumption: That delinquency is the result of "natural motivation." But, says Hirschi, if "natural motivation" was of overriding importance, having delinquent friends and participating in conventional activities would have no bearing on the relative frequency or infrequency of delinquency (1969, 230). Hirschi's theory and findings have spawned and continue to spawn a considerable amount of research, not all of which is supportive. Studies tending to uphold the validity of the theory have been of the cross-sectional variety and those tending in the opposite direction of the longitudinal variety. Cross-sectional studies are based on data collected at a particular time, while longitudinal studies are based on data collected on subjects over time. A review of some of the major research efforts in each category reveals the current status of Hirschi's social-control theory.

A study often cited that basically supports Hirschi's theory and findings was conducted by Wiatrowski et al. (1981). Their data were obtained from a 1966 survey of tenth-grade boys. They thought Hirschi had neither sufficiently clarified the extent to which the four factors were mutually exclusive nor controlled for the influence of variables such as students' ability and grade in school. When they controlled for these variables in examining the simultaneous influence of all four elements on reported delinquency, the findings yielded the strongest support for Hirschi's theory. They found strong correlations in the predicted negative direction between parental and school attachment and delinquency but only moderate negative correlations between the other three factors and delinquency.

Another study yields evidence supportive of Hirschi's control theory was conducted by Thornberry et al. (1985). They found that control theory, rather than strain theory, more satisfactorily accounted for the measured effect of dropping out of high school on criminal behavior. As they indicate, strain theory predicts a negative and control theory a positive correlation between dropping out of school and later criminal behavior. While the authors claim that their findings should not be construed as indicating general support for one theory versus the other, their conclusion is that "with respect to dropping out of school, where the theories do offer contradictory predictions, the evidence from this study is quite clear: dropping out is significantly and positively related to subsequent criminal involvement as predicted by social control theory" (Thornberry et al. 1985, 17).

In an earlier publication, Thornberry and Christenson introduced a theme that appears to have become increasingly evident, that is, the likely reciprocal nature of the relationship between delinquency and Hirschi's four elements. They tested this idea in examining the relationship between unemployment and crime.

Thornberry and Christenson point out that as unemployment is the major conventional adult male activity, "the hypothesis that unemployment should increase criminal behavior is explicitly developed within a control model" (1984, 400). On the other hand, they find the reciprocal hypothesis, "that crime influences unemployment, is only implicit in these models" (1984, 400). They found unemployment to have an "immediate effect on criminal involvement" and criminal involvement "a more long-range effect on unemployment" (1984, 400). Hence they call for the replacement of traditional criminological theories based on the assumption of unidirectional causation with theories based on the assumption of reciprocal causation.

A study published a year later, by Liska and Reed, made the same essential point. They examined the relationship between ties to conventional institutions (as indicated by attachment to parents and school) and delinquency. They found the relationship to be reciprocal. That is, their findings indicated that "parental attachment affects delinquency, that delinquency affects school attachment, and that school attachment affects parental attachment" (1985, 556–57). Paralleling Thornberry and Christenson, Liska and Reed conclude by calling for the development of criminological theory based on a more complex causal orientation "than implied in most social control theories and research" (1985, 558).

Also in 1985, studies began to appear calling for the need of social-control theory to take into account the dynamic nature of human development. LaGrange and White, for example, examined the ability of a modified version of Hirschi's theory (they included the variable of companion influence) to account for delinquency in three different adolescent age groups (twelve, fifteen, and eighteen year olds). They found Hirschi's theory most applicable to the middle group of fifteen- year-olds. To explain this result they suggest that those in this age group may have reached a critical developmental period, a period when the individual is leaving childhood behind but only beginning to become an adult. LaGrange and White felt that a major implication of the finding is the need of delinquency theory to incorporate a more dynamic conception of age than has been the case. As they reason, "If adolescence is a stage in life of tremendous change, growth, and development, it is likely that the most salient etiological processes of delinquency may also change as youths age through adolescence" (1985, 36). In effect, they call for studies employing longitudinal designs, the approach taken by Robert Agnew in the succeeding article in the same journal edition.

Agnew's approach incorporated the notion that over time, one must consider the fact that delinquency itself may exert a causal impact on social bonds (a point previously emphasized by Thornberry and Christenson, 1984). As Agnew indicates, delinquency may cause family and school problems that result in weakened attachment. He tested this notion in surveys of 1866 boys conducted in 1966 and 1968. The findings indicated to Agnew that "the importance of Hirschi's social control theory has been exaggerated" (1985, 58). The longitudinal statistics employed accounted for only 1 to 2 percent of the measured amount of delinquency. Agnew attributes this finding "to such things as the causal impact of delinquency on social control, the high stability of delinquency among the adolescents in the sample, and the declining importance of Hirschi's social control variables among older adolescents" (1985, 58).

In a more recent study, Agnew points out that prevailing longitudinal research on social-control theory suffers from at least one of the following problems: invalid measures of social control, the use of causal models that do not include important variables, and a variety of methodological limitations. Agnew seeks to overcome these problems and employs a causal orientation that *(a)* include(s) measures of prior delinquency and delinquent associates, *(b)* examine(s) indirect as well as direct effects, *(c)* examine(s) reciprocal effects, and *(d)* examine(s) the contemporaneous rather than the lagged effect of social control on delinquency. (1991, 133) Agnew's data "suggest that the elements of the bond as described by Hirschi are unimportant in predicting general delinquency among adolescents" (1991, 152).

Interestingly enough, Hirschi and his colleague Michael Gottfredson have written an article entitled "The Methodological Adequacy of Longitudinal Research on Crime" (Gottfredson and Hirschi 1987). The gist of their position is that the growing popularity of longitudinally designed studies in criminology is not methodologically justified. Its use, they say, has led criminologically theory in "unproductive directions, has produced illusory substantive findings, and has promoted policy conclusions of doubtful utility" (1987, 581). They contend further that the longitudinal design is too expensive and that properly designed cross-sectional studies can yield "many of the same benefits" at a lower cost (1987, 501). They neither mention the 1985-published Agnew study nor examine the implications of longitudinally based research for Hirschi's social-control theory.

Summary and Conclusion

In the politically left-leaning 1960s and 1970s, structural theories of crime advocated by sociologists gained the ascendancy. In structural perspectives, the causes of offending are sought not within individual offenders but in the sociocultural context of their life situations. In theories of this type, the necessary prerequisite to solving the crime problem is social change. In the 1960s and 1970s, some, particularly devotees of a Marxist-based "new" criminology, advocated radical transformation of the entire social order.

In the late 1970s and early 1980s, and in the wake of the conservative reaction to the perceived radicalism of the 1960s and early 1970s, renewed interest was expressed in traditional assumptions regarding the causes of crime and the proper response to the crime problem. The causes of crime were not to be sought in the social sphere but within the individual offender. Alleged failures in recent efforts at social change were invariably invoked to justify reversing the frame of reference.

The programs of the War on Poverty were said to have failed not because of administrative error and limited commitment of resources, but because of mistaken premises concerning the malleability of human nature. Social behavior such as criminality could not to be eradicated by correcting economic inequality and racism but by acknowledging the fact that the root causes of crime are intraindividual and not susceptible to easily apparent remedy. The best that can be done is to improve the efficiency by which offenders are captured and punished. As James Q. Wilson phrased it, "Wicked people exist," and "nothing avails except to set them apart from innocent people" (1983, 260). In short, human nature is the culprit, and its facets and dimensions remain to be specified.

Wilson and Herrnstein (1985) examined the bearing of human nature on criminality from a behavioral science perspective. Arguing against the idea of a crime-causing gene, they nonetheless conclude by suggesting that there is evidence (e.g., from twin and adoption studies) to indicate that some individuals appear to inherit a greater "predisposition" than others to engage in crime.

Others have sought to specify antisocial and criminally predisposing factors by analysis of the biochemical bases of behavior. Subjects frequently studied for their bearing on criminality include dietary and vitamin deficiencies, saccharine-related diseases, alcohol dependency and hypoglycemia, hormones and aggression, and allergies and antisocial behavior. Studies indicate some connection between each and crime, but exactly how much remains an open question.

In addition to studies of the biochemical antecedents of criminality, recent biologically oriented research has focused on the genetic factor. Mednick (1987) and others have conducted large-scale examinations of criminality among twins and adoptees. Despite acknowledged limitations, methodological and otherwise, Mednick, Gabrielli, and Hutchins (1987) conclude by stating that their study results indicate, particularly with chronic offenders, that parents who are convicted offenders transmit "some factor" that increases the likelihood that their children will become offenders. But, of course, the "factor" is yet to be specified.

Relying on the evidence of such studies, Hans Eysenck has developed an influential theory based on a presumed connection between psychological predisposition and antisocial conduct. He believes that there is a connection between low intelligence and criminality and that intelligence is something largely inherited. But more important he stresses the connection between criminal and other antisocial conduct and three intraindividual variables: *neuroticism*, *psychotocism*, and *extraversion*. He has constructed a scale to measure these factors and contends the evidence to indicate a correlation between criminality and those high in each of the three. Research by others has yielded both supportive and contradictory results. Thus, here, too, the validity of the theory remains to be determined.

Eysenck's is a control theory in that it is rooted in the premise that humans must learn not to commit, rather than to commit, crime. That is, Eysenck, following a basic inclination in those who seek the intraindividual causes of antisocial behavior, suggests that the way to prevent or at least mitigate criminality is to develop effective ways of socializing those identified as innately predisposed to offend. This is the essential premise of a major sociological theory, Travis Hirschi's social-control theory.

To Hirschi, social bonding that promotes conformity to prevailing customs, laws, norms, and rules is prerequisite to crime control. He identifies four measurable elements of the social bond, *attachment* (ties to significant others such as parents and teachers), *commitment* (adherence to conventional norms), *involvement* (participation in conventional activities such as schooling), and *belief* (acceptance of conventional moral and ethical prescriptions). In a survey of high-school-aged students, Hirschi found considerable support for this theory and the relevance of his four elements.

Studies by others have more often than not supported Hirschi's theory. Nevertheless, recent longitudinal studies indicate to some that the validity of the theory may have been overstated. As the theory continues to generate considerable thought and research, future work will most likely clarify the nature of the theory's strengths and weaknesses.

The point to emphasize here is that a major trend in recent criminological analysis is a switch from a perspective emphasizing the causal impact of factors external to the individual (social and cultural constrains such as economic inequality) to one stressing the causal import of factors internal to the individual (biochemical variables, inherited genetic traits). That both sides of the subject are involved is undoubtedly the case. How the intraindividual factors can be examined free of racist and victim-blaming intrusions is highly debatable. Notwithstanding this issue, there is growing awareness of the need to develop an integrated, multidisciplinary empirically interpretable theory of criminality. How this might be accomplished has yet to be given the close attention required.

References

Agnew, Robert. 1985. "Social Control Theory and Delinquency: A Testof Theory." *Criminology* 23 47–61.

———. 1991. "A Longitudinal Test of Social Control Theory and Delinquency." *Journal of Research in Crime and Delinquency* 28 126–56.

Bartol, Curt R. 1990. "Staking Out Territory in Criminology: Crime from a Psychological Perspective." *Criminal Justice and Behavior* 17 467–73.

———. 1991. *Criminal Behavior: A Psychosocial Approach.* 3rd edition. Englewood Cliffs, New Jersey: Prentice-Hall.

Brennan, Patricia A. and Sarnoff A. Mednick. 1990. "A Reply to Walters and White." *Criminology* 28 657–61.

Christiansen, Karl O. 1977. "A Preliminary Study of Criminality Among Twins." In *Biosocial Bases of Criminal Behavior* edited by Sarnoff A. Mednick and Karl O. Christiansen. New York: Gardner Press, 89–108.

Dalgaard, O.S. and E. Kringlen. 1976. "A Norwegian Twin Study of Criminality." *British Journal of Criminology* 16 213–32.

Ellis, Lee. 1985. "Genetics and Criminal Behavior: Evidence Through the End of the 1970's." In *Biology, Crime and Ethics* edited by Frank H. Marsh and Janet Katz. Cincinnati: Anderson, 65–92.

Eysenck, H.J. 1964. *Crime and Personality.* London: Routledge Kegan Paul.

———. 1977. *Crime and Personality.* London: Routledge & Kegan Paul.

———. and Gisli H. Gudjonsson. 1989. *The Causes and Cures of Criminality.* New York: Plenum.

Farrington, David P. 1987. "Implications of Biological Findings for Criminological Research." In *The Causes and Cures of Crime: New Biological Approaches* edited by Sarnoff A. Mednick, Terrie E. Moffitt, and Susan A. Stacks. New York: Cambridge University Press, 42–64.

Fishbein, Diana H. 1990. "Biological Perspectives in Criminology." *Criminology* 28 27–72.

Gottfredson, Michael, and Travis Hirschi. 1991. "The Methodological Adequacy of Longitudinal Research on Crime." *Criminology* 25 581–614.

Hill, D., and D.A. Pond. 1952. "Reflections on 100 Capital Cases Submitted to Electroencephalography." *Journal of Mental Science* 98 23–43.

Hippchen, Leonard J. 1978. "The Need for a New Approach to the Delinquent-Criminal Problem." In *Biochemical Approaches to Treatment of Delinquents and Criminals* edited by Leonard J. Hippchen. New York: Van Nostrand, 3–19.

Hirschi, Travis. 1969. *Causes of Delinquency.* Berkeley: University of California Press.

Kreuz, L.E. and R.M. Rose. 1972. "Assessment of Aggressive Behavior and PlasmaTestosterone in a Young Criminal Population." *Psychosomatic Medicine* 34 321-32.

LaGrange, Randy L. and Helene Raskin White.1985. "Age Differences in Delinquency: A Test of Theory." *Criminology* 23 19–42.

Lane, David A. 1987. "Personality and Antisocial Behaviour: A Long-Term Study." *British Journal of Criminology* 8 799–806. Lange, J.1931. *Crime as Destiny*. London: Allen & Unwin.

Lange, J. 1929. *Crime as Destiny*. Leipzig: Thieme.

Lief, H.I. 1963. "Contemporary Forms of Violence." In *Violence and War: With Clinical Studies, Science and Psychoanalysis VI* edited by J.H.Masserman. New York: Grune & Stratton, 55–68.

Liska, Allen E., and Mark D. Reed. 1985. "Institutions and Delinquency." *American Sociological Review* 50 547–60.

Mednick, Sarnoff A., Jan Volavka, William F. Gabrielli, Jr., and Turan M. Itil. 1981."EEG as a Predictor of Antisocial Behavior." *Criminology* 19 219–29.

Mednick, Sarnoff A. and William F. Gabrielli, Jr. 1984."Urban Environment, Genetics, and Crime." *Criminology* 22645–52.

Mednick, Sarnoff A., William F. Gabrielli, Jr., and Barry Hutchings. 1987. "Genetic Factors in the Etiology of CriminalBehavior." In *The Causes of Crime: New Biological Approaches* edited by Sarnoff A. Mednick, Terrie E.Moffitt, and Susan A. Stack. New York: Cambridge University Press, 74–91.

Mednick, Sarnoff A. 1987. "Introduction: Biological Factors in Crime Causation: The Reactions of Social Scientists." In *The Causes of Crime: New Biological Approaches* edited by Sarnoff A. Mednick, Terrie E. Moffitt, and Susan A. Stack. New York: Cambridge University Press, 1–6.

Marks, V.1978. "Alcohol and Carbohydrate Metabolism." *Clinics in Endocrinology and Metabolism* 7 333–48.

Nassi, A.J. and S.I. Abramowitz. 1976. "From Phrenology to Psychosurgery and Back Again: Biological Studies of Criminality." *American Journal of Orthopsychiatry* 46 591–607.

Newman, Graeme. 1985. "Born to Kill." In *Biology, Crime & Ethics* edited by Frank M. Marsh and Janet Katz. Cincinnati: Anderson.

Passingham, R.E. 1972. "Crime and Personality: A Review of Eysenck'sTheory." In *Biological Bases of Individual Behavior* edited by V.D. Nebylitsyn and J.A. Gray. New York: Academic Press, 342–71.

Pihl, R.O., F. Ervin, G. Pelletier, W. Diekel, and W. Strain. 1982. "Hair Element Content of Violent Criminals." *Canadian Journal of Psychiatry* 27 533.

Plomin, Robert. 1990. *Nature and Nurture: An Introduction*. Pacific Grove, Calif.: Brooks/Cole.

Rubin, Robert T. 1987. "The Neuroendocrinology and Neurochemistry of Antisocial Behavior." In *The Causes of Crime: New Biological Approaches* edited by Sarnoff A. Mednick, Terrie E. Moffitt, and Susan A. Stack. New York: Cambridge University Press, 239-62.

Sechrest, L., S.O. White, and E.D. Brown. 1979. *The Rehabilitation of Criminal Offenders*. Washington, D.C.: National Academy of Sciences.

Taylor, Ian, Paul Walton, and Jock Young. 1973. *The New Criminology: For a Social Theory of Deviance*. London: Routledge & Kegan Paul.

Thornberry, Terrence P., and R.L. Christenson. 1984."Unemployment and Criminal Involvement." *American Sociological Review* 49 398–411.

Thornberry, Terrence P., Melanie Moore, and R.L. Christenson. 1985. "The Effect of Dropping Out of High School on Subsequent Criminal Behavior." *Criminology* 23 3-18.

Trasler, Gordon. 1987. "Some Cautions for the Biological Approach to Crime Causation." In *The Causes of Crime: New Biological Approaches edited by* Sarnoff A. Mednick, Terrie E. Moffitt, and Susan A. Stack. New York: Cambridge University Press, 7–24.

Virkkunen, Matti. 1987. "Metabolic Dysfunctions Among Habitually Violent Offenders: Reactive Hypoglycemia and Cholesterol Levels." In *The Causes of Crime: New Biological Approaches* edited by Sarnoff A. Mednick, Terrie E. Moffitt, and Susan A. Stack. New York: Cambridge University Press, 292–311.

Virkkunen, Matti, Judith De Jong, John Bartko, Frederick K. Goodwin, and Markkun Linnoila. 1989. "Relationship of Psychobiological Variables to Recidivism in Violent Offenders and Impulsive Fire Setters." *Archives of General Psychiatry* 46 600–3.

Volavka, Jan. 1987."Electroencephalogram Among Criminals." In *The Causes of Crime: New Biological Approaches* edited by Sarnoff A. Mednick, Terrie E. Moffitt, and SusanA. Stack. New York: Cambridge University Press, 137–45.

Walters, Glenn D., and Thomas W. White. 1989. "Heredity and Crime: Bad Genes or Bad Research?" *Criminology* 27, 455–85.

———. Glenn D. 1990. "Heredity, Crime, and The Killing-the Bearer-of-Bad-News Syndrome: A Reply to Brennan and Mednick." *Criminology* 28 663–67.

Wiatrowski, Michael D., David B. Griswold, and Mary K. Roberts. 1981. "Social Control Theory and Delinquency." *American Sociological Review* 46 525–41.

Wilson, James Q. 1983. *Thinking About Crime*, Revised Edition. New York: Basic Books.

Wilson James Q., and Richard J. Herrnstein. 1985. *Crime & Human Nature*. New York: Simon and Schuster.

Witkin, H.A., S.A. Mednick, F. Schulsinger, E. Bakkestron, K.O. Christiansen, D.R. Goodenough, K. Hirschhorn, C. Lundsteen, D.R. Owen, J. Philip, D.B. Rubin, and M. Stocking. 1976. "XYY and XXY Men: Criminality and Aggression." *Science* 193 547–55.

Witkin, H.A., S.A. Mednick, F. Schulsinger, E. Bakkestron, K.O. Christiansen, D.R. Goodenough, K. Hirschhorn, C. Lundsteen, D.R. Owen, J. Philip, D.B. Rubin, and M. Stocking. 1977. "Criminality, Aggression and Intelligence Among XYY and XXY Men." In *Biosocial Bases of Human Behavior* edited by Sarnoff A. Mednick and Karl O. Christiansen. New York: Gardner Press, 165–88.

Notes

[1]. Especially worthy of note are George Gilder, *Wealth and Poverty* (New York: Basic Books, 1981); and Charles Murray, *Losing Ground: American Social Policy, 1950–1980* (New York: Basic Books, 1984).

Part III: Justice and Corrections

CHAPTER 9

Policing in America

Despite the seemingly nonstop action portrayed in police stories featured in Hollywood films and on American television, in reality policing America is not nearly as exciting as we are led to believe! As two veteran officers from Seattle's police force put it: "Some nights it's domestic disputes; other nights it's fights in a tavern or two winos goin' at it on the street or maybe it's chasing off a pack of hookers. Ordinary, sometimes boring.... And we hear every excuse under the sun: 'But, officers, there's been a big a misunderstanding here. We just had a little family disagreement, that's all.' Or, 'He started in, he messed with me.' This is 80 percent of our average day, that is, when we're not busy doing paperwork!"

Even though everyday policing may be mundane, functioning more like a human service than a criminal justice organization, probably no agency in the justice system is more important than the police. In fact, because they are entrusted with keeping the peace and with maintaining order, the police come into contact with virtually all segments of the population and in the most diverse circumstances imaginable. Moreover, because they are also responsible for making the initial determination that a crime has been committed and for apprehending the perpetrator, they activate the entire system.

To enforce the law and maintain order, the police are granted broad discretionary powers and provided with exceptional means to enforce decisions and protect themselves. They are expected to act judiciously and make vitally important decisions quickly. And as the opportunity for error and the abuse of power is great, they have an ambiguous status. Thus, to some the police are guardians. To others, they are at best inept blunderers and at worst capricious tyrants.

The capacity to effect great good or harm puts the police in a delicate position, one that is subject to constant critical scrutiny. The problem is not one that Americans have only recently recognized. Concern with the disadvantages of extensive police powers has occupied the thoughts of Americans from the beginning of the republic. Thus, to assess the current status of the police and criminal justice system properly, it is important to have some familiarity with the origins of the police in America and the controversy that has always surrounded the police function. In addition to a historical perspective, this chapter also considers the police role; police discretion in decisionmaking; police abuse of power; current trends in policing; and the police subculture.

The Origins of Police

Some assume the police function to be an inevitable by-product of the human need to congregate and form communities in order to survive. To the historian Charles Reith (1956, 14), for example, "There comes, always and inevitable, discovery or recognition of the facts that some members of the community will not keep some or all of the rules; that by their behaviour in this respect they weaken and endanger the welfare and lives of other members and the existence of the community as a whole; and that to ensure its continuing welfare and survival, means must be found for compelling observance of rules" (Reith 1956, 14).

Effective means of law enforcement, says Reith, always entail the use of force. Force, he argues, is wielded from two basic positions: from the people upward or authoritative leadership downward. The origin of the term *police* and a policing system is traced to the application of force from a leader downward.

A French king, Charles V, is said to have invented a police force ostensibly to promote "the happiness and security" of his people. But according to Griffiths in the 1910 edition of the *Encyclopaedia Britannica*: "It developed into an engine of horrible oppression, and as such was repugnant to the feelings of a free people." The term police, says Griffiths, was not used widely in England until the nineteenth century. It symbolized a method of foreign oppression.

Reith and many other historians claim that the early police structures common to England and America evolved from kinship units that later became sanctioned by rulers. The more important of these institutions include the Frankpledge System and the parish constable.

The word *frankpledge* is a Norman translation of the Anglo-Saxon *frithborh*. Frithborhs were institutions based on "the custom whereby the inhabitants of a district [or shire] were responsible for any crime or injury committed by one of their number" (*Encyclopaedia Britannica* 1910, 34). The custom required all free men to give a pledge; and a pledge, ordered William the Conqueror, "must hold and bring him to justice if he commits any offence." A pledge was made in an association consisting of ten men at least twelve years of age. Such an association was called a tything, a decima, or a tenmanne tale. Under the Normans, the associations contained twelve men.

According to Reith, the roots of the Frankpledge System lay in kinship units; it was a method of maintaining law and order that emanated from the people upward. During the second half of the twelfth century, it was efficiently operated by a centralized Norman administration. But "central government efficiency soon gave way to central government tyranny, on account of which the Frankpledge System broke down. . . . The shire court . . . became, often, merely an instrument for collecting unjust and oppressive fines and taxes" (Reith 1956, 28).

One of the survivors was the institution of the tithing-man. By tradition, ten parish tithing groups composed a leading group of a hundred men. The leader of the hundred was the tithing-man. or chief pledge. Between the twelfth and fourteenth centuries, he became the parish constable, the local man most responsible for maintaining law and order.

Parish constables were either elected or appointed. Typically they served for a year and were unpaid. They could, however, exact fees for certain services, and all able-bodied men were expected to aid them as needed. Constable-led groups were also referred to as the The Watch. Often, Watches functioned only at night.

The informal method of policing by parish constables became totally ineffective during the Industrial Revolution. The complete breakdown of the parish constable system occurred very early in the eighteenth century, and the consequences were widespread. Throughout England, there was a rise in "uncontrollable crime" and frequent outbreaks of "uncontrollable riot-disorder."

Industrialization uprooted and redistributed population on a massive scale. London and other cities soon contained many more people than could be adequately housed and legitimately employed. Tensions and crime grew in the most crowded areas, and the unemployed, underfed (but greatly plied with cheap and even free gin) masses were susceptible to rioting (Reith 1956).

Riots often erupted for the slightest reason. "During the first half of the century riots were mostly the outcome of personal or group quarrels and pursuit of revenge. . . . Frequently, the objectives sought were the sacking and burning of the house of a private citizen, the murder of its inhabitants, or the destruction and looting of the shops or premises of a group of shopkeepers or small tradesmen who had made enemies" (Reith 1956, 45).

In the latter half of the eighteenth century, mob riots were instigated by the politically ambitious and economically powerful. Most were apparently directed by wealthy merchants using mob violence to intimidate legislators or challenge legislation perceived as a threat to their interests. "The numerous weavers' riots which historians...have usually attributed to the economic sufferings and grievance of the Spitalfields weavers were mostly due to the direct instigation of merchants whose aim was not the relief of genuine economic distress, but financial profit for themselves" (Reith 1956, 50).

Limited in number and authority, parish constables could do little to contain the crime and rioting. Indeed, many constables were businessmen more interested in exploiting conditions for selfish gain than enforcing rules and regulations for the common good.

The impotence and corruption of established police structures resulted in the application of military force to quell disturbances. More often than not, this spawned even greater violence. The situation reached a point where even the most reluctant were compelled to recognize the need for a new and formal police system. Under the leadership of Sir Robert Peel, the first modern police department was established in metropolitan London in 1829. Before the identification of their proposed numbers and tasks, the new police were denounced as "the instruments of a new despotism, the enlisted members of a new standing army, under the centralized authority, riding roughshod over peaceable citizens" (*Encyclopaedia Britannica* 1910, 978). Simply put, there was no historical precedent in which people could have faith that more good than harm would stem from the establishment of a widely based and potent police force. Much too often, history had shown police forces to be a means of enforcing despotism. That they could be constructed and applied to promote the greatest good to the greatest number could be only a hope. Within two years of its implementation, London's first police system managed to dispel the people's worst fears.

All the basic elements that led to the inauguration of England's first police department were present in America. Rioting was widespread in the country's major cities in the early decades of the nineteenth century. In the 1830s, Boston had three major riots. One Sunday in 1837, the residents of the city's Irish tenements were attacked and beaten by a mob of some 15,000 (Lundman 1980). Too, the failures and limitations of informal policing, whether sponsored by private or public means, led to the use of militias to contain threatening situations. And, as in England, urban mobs were often manipulated for special interests. In New York City, for example, poor whites were encouraged by local merchants with ties to southern planters to attack blacks and abolitionists. "Over two thousand uniformed militia, together with a large body of citizens organized as constables, did nothing for three days in 1844 while a White mob rioted against Blacks, badly damaging the Episcopal African church, and pulling down and looting the homes of many Blacks and abolitionists" (Center for Research on Criminal Justice 1975, 23).

Reith argues that law enforcement in England has always been more effective than in America because the police in England were allowed to become instruments of law rather than policy. "The weakness of law-enforcement machinery in the United States is due to the fact that...the police were allowed to become, corruptly, the instruments and servants, not of law, but of policy, and of local and corrupt controllers of policy" (Reith 1956, 83). Americans, he says, have always valued the individual's right to accumulate wealth much more than his/her observance of the law.

Reith's position is compatible with that of many radical criminologists. Moreover, concern with the political and economic corruption of the police in America is of longstanding interest. Turn-of-the-century muckrakers such as Lincoln Steffens did their utmost to document and dramatize the extent of the problem. But such work, although of unquestioned importance, may obscure as much as it clarifies. As is brought out later in the chapter, most police work has little or nothing to do with the fact or the likelihood of corruption.

Efforts to Modernize Police Organizations

Although America's first police departments, in Boston in 1838 and New York City in 1845, tended to model their philosophies and operation after London's police system, they were also significantly shaped by local and municipal governments, where elected officials such as city councilmen, aldermen, or selectmen exercised considerable political patronage. And since police officers were chosen by leaders in wards or precincts, the police became a natural extension of the patronage system (Monkkonen 1981; Lane 1967).

It is hardly surprising, therefore, that policing in American cities during the nineteenth century became closely tied to local standards and expectations of enforcing laws, rather than to institutional or legal authority. While this encouraged officers to establish their own style of informal law enforcement, it also resulted in significant differences between how laws were enforced from one precinct or neighborhood to another. Thus the nineteenth-century police were more of a political than a professional force, with allegiance to the local politicians who gave them their jobs (Monkkonen 1981).

Nor were police officers particularly skilled in how to exercise their law-enforcement functions. Arrest procedures, proper apprehension techniques, and especially knowledge of the laws of arrest were more often than not matters of intuition rather than police training. Patrolmen, who walked daily beats for up to six hours, relied on their personal styles and knowledge of the community to keep the peace (Monkkonen 1981; Lane 1967).

During the nineteenth century and well into the twentieth, police corruption and abuse of power, such as brutal arrest tactics or accepting payoffs for police favors, were recurring themes in the evolution of police. Important critical investigations of police practices were conducted by the Lexow Commission in 1894 (which focused on the New York City police), the Wickersham Commission in 1930 (a nationwide investigation instigated by the Hoover administration), and the Knapp Commission in 1972 (another examination of the New York City police).

These and other less-publicized studies over the years (including those of small cities) have documented a consistent pattern of extensive corruption at all departmental levels. Earlier investigations uncovered much more brutality than those of more recent vintage. The Wickersham Commission of the 1930s, for example, found substantial evidence of "street brutality by policemen, loose kidnapping or false arrests, unlawful imprisonment and 'incommunicado' confessions, and perjury indulged in by policemen to gain convictions" (Platt and Cooper 1974). In contrast, the Knapp Commission of the 1970s reported that 'by far the most widespread form of misconduct . . . found in the Police Department was the acceptance by police officers of gratuities in the form of free meals, free goods, and cash payments" (Knapp Commission 1978, 145). This is not to suggest that "active" power abuse is no longer prevalent. On the contrary, studies in Boston, Chicago, and Washington, D.C., have found evidence of police brutality in at least half the encounters between the police and the public.

Professionalization of the Police

By the end of the nineteenth century, broad efforts, such as those by a group known as the Progressives, were underway to reform the police from instruments of political machines and local politicians to organizations with leadership, qualified personnel and discipline. Mostly through legislation, modest progress was accomplished from the 1890s to the 1920s, such as establishing police commissions to investigate corruption and establishing civil service examinations to upgrade the quality of police personnel.

Yet the impetus that led to reforms that were to professionalize the police came from police chiefs themselves. August Vollmer (Berkeley, California), O.W. Wilson (Chicago), William H. Parker (Los Angeles), and Richard Sylvester, (Washington, D.C.), are outstanding examples. Their vision was to adopt a professional model of police departments, emphasizing the police as the trained experts in performing policing functions, as efficient in delivering policing services through modern technology and innovative professional practices, and especially as autonomous and independent of political influence.

August Vollmer

Unquestionably the most innovative of the avant-garde chiefs of police from the early 1900s into the 1950s was August Vollmer (1876–1955). Vollmer first attracted national attention by innovations in police administration and patrol tactics he introduced while serving as the first police chief of the Berkeley, California, force, a position he held from 1909 to 1932. His ideas were promulgated in the university classroom; he taught police administration at the University of Chicago and the University of California at Berkeley, where he led a drive to establish a school of criminology. Vollmer authored a number of books, the most influential of which was *The Police and Modern Society,* first published in 1936.

Vollmer, unlike most of his colleagues, did not believe that police corruption, for example, could be controlled by stricter internal supervisory measures. What needed to be done was to stop imposing on the police responsibility for regulating vice. Toward this end, he urged the decriminalization of the major illegal vices (prostitution, gambling, drug abuse). As he reasoned, ". . . Repression by legislation against [the above human vices] has failed miserably. . . . As long as the immoral qualities remain unaltered, just so long will the possessor of the qualities behave in a manner adverse to the moral code, and it is absurd, and stupid as well, to think that fines and jail sentences can change the character of an individual" (Vollmer 1971, 175). As it was,

> . . .The effect of attempted repression of vice upon police personality is unfortunate, resulting as it almost invariably does, in the corruption of some members of the force. Powerful vice leaders will take the trouble to corrupt individual members of the force, from the police chief to the lowliest recruit. Friction is thus caused between men and between groups of men in the department; cliques are formed which endeavor to frustrate one another's efforts, and the unity of action necessary to efficient police service is made quite impossible (Vollmer 1971, 85).

Vollmer's ideas on the proper qualifications of a police officer were based on a careful attempt to balance idealistic and realistic expectations. He did not believe that the police officers could possibly live up to all that was expected of them.

> The citizen expects police officers to have the wisdom of Solomon, the courage of David, the strength of Samson, the patience of Job, the leadership of Moses, the kindness of the Good Samaritan, the strategical training of Alexander, the faith of Daniel, the diplomacy of Lincoln, the tolerance of the Carpenter of Nazareth, and, finally, an intimate knowledge of every branch of the natural, biological, and social sciences. If he had all these, he might be a policeman (Vollmer 1971, 228).

While the ideal may be unattainable, nonetheless it was clear to Vollmer that society should have exceptional people do its policing. He believed that police officers should be superior in intelligence, physically sound, and emotionally secure. Also, they should have character traits that ensure integrity, honesty, and efficiency. Lastly, they should have the kind of personality that enables them to get along well with one another and the general public.

What Vollmer sought was nothing less than the professionalization of police work. As he saw it, the failure to adopt professional criteria for personnel selection, evaluation, and management made the typical American police department an anachronism. "Health, public works, park, recreational, and school departments have moved forward rapidly in the past quarter-century, but the police, although they have progressed slightly, continue to lag far behind the rest of the public services in the march toward better government" (Vollmer 1971, 223–24).

Above all, better government rested on better personnel selection. The best people for given jobs were to be selected not on the basis of subjective (political) but objective (scientific) criteria and methods. Vollmer believed above-average intelligence to be the chief prerequisite to improved and quality policing. He thought that the civil service examinations of his day raised intellectual standards "but little." Vollmer found that cities with civil service boards using intelligence test scores as an employment criterion did not select officers of noticeably higher intelligence than cities that selected policemen from lists supplied by ward bosses whose sole criterion was party loyalty.

The problem was traced to the administration of civil service examinations by independent commissions. By nature, suggested Vollmer, commission members tend to be jealous of their prerogatives and inclined to reject recommendations for needed improvement by outside sources. But instead of outlining an alternative system, Vollmer chose to emphasize the failure of civil service procedures to improve the quality of police personnel effectively.

Although existing intelligence and aptitude tests had their drawbacks and limitations, Vollmer believed them capable of being administered and interpreted (but he did not specify how or by whom) to improve personnel quality greatly. In addition to being tested by such instruments, Vollmer also believed that police candidates should be given thorough medical, agility, and neurological examinations—and that all the information obtained should be given to a psychiatrist to aid the discovery of character traits and mental problems that might militate against effective police work.

After being carefully selected, police recruits were to be properly trained. "If the legal, engineering, or medical profession recruited its members at random, with no requirements of preliminary training, from among all the persons who might desire to hang out a professional 'shingle,' disaster would be the inevitable consequence. . . . If a skyscraper or a large bridge is to be constructed, we certainly do not go to the medical professional, legal profession, or the trades for designs for the structure; we go to the experienced bridge engineers. . . . It has not yet been recognized that the work of the modern policeman requires professional training comparable to that required for the most skilled profession" (Vollmer 1971, 230–31).

What Vollmer hoped for was the establishment of state police institutes. All local police officers would be required to attend a training institute for not less than two years. Vollmer also thought it desirable for recruits to take college-level courses in the social, biological, and physical sciences. As he summarized his position:

> A condition for entrance into police departments should be certification from an accredited police institute in the same way that men in other professions must demonstrate that they have been trained in their fields, and no person should be permitted to perform the duties of a policeman until he has been so certified and has had at least one year's "interne" experience in a police department without pay. Through the establishment of such standards the quality of police service can be greatly improved and at the same time greatly reduced in cost to the taxpayers; police work can attain the full dignity of a profession and the acknowledgment of its value that the possibilities of its service to humanity should command (Vollmer 1971, 234).

Vollmer has been described as one "as comfortable and as confident exploring the role of the police in our society as he was in setting out the most detailed police operating procedure; as interested and conversant in the theories of criminality as he was in investigating the activities of an alleged pickpocket; and as desirous of discussing the value of the criminal sanction as a control over victimless crime as he was in contributing toward the development of an improved system for counting crimes" (Goldstein 1977, 229). In sum, Vollmer had enormous impact on the movement to professionalize police departments. In the words of Richard Lundman , Vollmer was "the leading spokesperson for police professionalism and his ideas continue to form the core of the professional movement" (1980, 175).

Vollmer also influenced a number of college administrators to initiate college degree programs. The first to do so was the University of California at Berkeley in 1923. A Berkeley police officer was awarded a bachelor of arts in economics with a minor in criminology; the course of study was designed by Vollmer. The second degree program was at the University of Southern California; in 1928 a full academic curriculum in police science was developed and located in the Department of Public Administration. The third program was initiated at San Jose State in 1930; students in the law-enforcement program, for example, received associate of arts degrees upon completion of a two-year course of study.

The 1930s and 1940s witnessed the emergence of several important police training institutes and academies. The FBI's National Academy began in 1935. Located in northern Virginia, the main training program lasts sixteen weeks. In addition, the academy offers hundreds of training sessions; they range from three days to four weeks. The FBI also has a Field Training Program, which provides instruction to more than 300,000 police officers per year.

Still other programs followed. Northwestern University (Illinois) introduced its Traffic Institute in 1936, awarding academic credit to police who completed its nine-month program. In 1946 the Delinquency Control Institute, which offers academic courses and awards a certificate to those completing its curriculum, was inaugurated at the University of Southern California. And, in 1951 the University of Louisville established the Southern Police Institute to train police administrators.

O.W. Wilson

In the 1950s, administrative reform became the preoccupation of those involved in the professionalization movement. A Vollmer protégé, O.W. Wilson (1900–1972), became the leading authority on the subject. Wilson began his law-enforcement career as a patrolman in the Berkeley Police Department in 1921. He later became chief of police in Fullerton, California (1925–26), Wichita, Kansas (1928–39), and Chicago (1960–67). Between the last two posts, he was a professor of public administration and dean of the School of Criminology at the University of California at Berkeley.

Wilson, like Vollmer, sought to professionalize all aspects of police work. He too stressed the need for superior personnel and higher education, especially at the leadership level. "The best hope for long-term improvement of police service lies in the development of superior personnel to carry out future planning and direction. ... The best way to achieve this objective is through college-level education" (Wilson and McLaren 1963, 310).

Talented and educated people were needed to execute the complicated administrative reforms Wilson had in mind. He had studied different bureaucracies and believed that the implementation of principles such as the following would greatly improve the effectiveness of any police department:

1. Tasks, similar or related in purpose, process, method, or clientele, should be grouped together in one or more units under the control of one person.

2. Specialized units should be created only when overall departmental capability is significantly increased, and should not be created at the expense of reduced control and decreased general interest.

3. Lines of demarcation between the responsibilities of units should be clearly drawn by a precise definition of the duties of each, which should be made known to all members so that responsibility may be placed exactly.

4. Each individual, unit, and situation should be under the immediate control of one, and only one, person, thus achieving the principle of unity of command and avoiding friction that results from duplication of direction and supervision.

5. The span of control of a supervisor should be large enough to provide economical supervision, but no more units or persons should be placed under the direct control of one person than he is able to manage.

6. Each task should be made the unmistakable duty of someone; responsibility for planning, execution, and control should be definitely placed on designated persons.

7. Persons to whom authority is delegated should be held accountable for the use made of it and for the failure to use it (Wilson and McLaren 1963, 59–60).

William H. Parker

The monocratic or militaristic, bureaucratic model favored by Wilson gained widespread acceptance in the 1950s. One who applied it in a manner much admired by Wilson was William H. Parker. In a book he edited on Parker, Wilson observed:

> My acquaintance with William H. Parker has extended over a great many years. . . . Since his appointment as Chief of Police of Los Angeles [in 1950], I have watched his operations with an interest stimulated by the discovery that he was making the most of his rare opportunity to modernize and professionalize police service. He immediately reorganized his department to simplify and assure his control over its operations and to facilitate the attainment of police objectives (Wilson 1957, vii).

In the 1950s Parker became one of the most celebrated law-enforcement officials in the nation's history. He was praised for the maintenance of exceptionally high personnel standards, for the design of special units to handle difficult assignments (e.g., the control of organized crime), but above all, for his control over all phases of departmental affairs and operations. He became the model police administrator.

By the late 1960s, however, Parker's authoritarian style became the target of severe criticism from many quarters. On college campuses the police came to be regarded by many as agents of fascism. The repressive police reaction to the civil rights movement, the ghetto riots, and various student protests created deep-seated resentment and hostility among those who might otherwise have been attracted to police work.

Notwithstanding the rebellious mood of the times, Parker and his emulators, in professionalizing police work as they did, failed to create the kind of image of the police officer that would appeal to college students. In Bittner's terse language: ". . . to gain the upper hand over sloth, indolence, brutality, and corruption, officials like the late Chief William Parker of Los Angeles militarized the departments under their command. . . . The new image of the policeman as a snappy, low-level soldier-bureaucrat created no inducement for people who thought they could do better to elect police work as their vocation" (1980, 141). Moreover, and as Bittner points out, the reformers had failed to prevent, or sufficiently contain, the efforts of police veterans to resist the upgrading of recruitment educational requirements. As Bittner says: "It seems quite understandable that the chiefs, captains, and even veteran patrolmen would not be happy with the prospect of having to work with recruits who outrank them educationally" (Bittner 1980, 141; see also Box 9.1).

Box 9.1 Policing "Fear City, USA"

Nothing shatters the professional image of police departments and officers faster than a good, old-fashioned dispute between administrators and rank-and-file police officers, especially when union contracts and job benefits are at stake.

In December 1993 at Boston, patrolmen had worked for four years without a signed contract between their union and the city. On the eve of their opening negotiation session, the Boston Police Patrolmen's Association began distributing leaflets in the city mostly in busy downtown locations, shopping centers, Logan International Airport, commuter bus and train terminals, and the hotel districts. Featuring the "Grim Reaper" on its front cover, the leaflet warned the public not to venture out after 6 p.m., to avoid the "high risk" subway system, and to stay away from "known trouble spots," ironically picking fashionable locations that have almost no reputations as crime centers.

Although many pedestrians seemed to appreciate the "tips" on how to avoid criminal victimization, many were also puzzled by the leaflets. City officials were not. Outgoing Police Commissioner William Bratton called it "a disgrace they should hang their heads in shame" (Hutchinson 1993, 1). "Despicable," said newly elected Mayor Thomas Menino. The *Boston Globe* (1993b, 22) devoted its lead editorial to the leaflet, proclaiming it "a ludicrous attempt to pressure the city into concessions on the next contract." And in a letter written on behalf of the Greater Boston Chamber of Commerce, its president pointed out that "Boston is a safe city."

Although Boston may not be a "safe" city by suburban and rural standards, it is far from a leader in crime statistics. Comparing crimes rates on homicide, rape, robbery, and aggravated assault from January to September 1993, Boston had a crime rate of 1421 crimes per 100,000 people, compared to Chicago (2129), Baltimore (2220), and Los Angeles (1845), making it comparable or only slightly ahead of Dallas, Memphis, Houston, and Seattle. And Boston has experienced slight decreases in the crime rates (*Boston Globe* 1993a, 1).

Not surprisingly, the "Grim Reaper" leaflet failed to point out these statistics. "City go-ers," proclaimed the *Boston Globe* "know better than to be taken in by a propaganda barrage. They have their own internal danger/safety index and are hardly likely to be swayed by an alarmist flier. They know that downtown Boston, from Massachusetts Avenue to the waterfront, is among the safest, most vibrant places in urban America" (1993b, 22).

Source: Adapted from Hutchinson 1993; *Boston Globe* 1993a, 1993b.

Structure of Modern Law-Enforcement Agencies

Unlike many countries in Europe and elsewhere, the United States does not have a national police force. Instead, law enforcement entails a relatively complex stratification of police systems. In fact, there are currently about 25,000 police organizations in the public sector alone—a figure that does not include numerous private police and security organizations. While public police agencies share in common similar bureaucratic structures, they vary in size and in their jurisdiction of responsibility. It is important, therefore, to become familiar with the most important police agencies.

Federal Law-Enforcement Agencies

Federal law-enforcements agencies fall within the executive branch of government. Due principally to an aversion to a national policing system after the American Revolution, no provisions were made for a federal police. Instead, Congress established in 1789 the first federal law-enforcement agency, the ***U.S. Marshal's Office***. There is currently one marshal for each federal judicial district, each containing deputy marshals. Operated as a separate bureau within the U.S. Department of Justice, which is headed by the U.S. Attorney General, marshals provide security to federal courts and their personnel, including jurors, and have responsibilities for transporting federal prisoners, serving summonses, and overseeing property and money seized under federal authority.

Although not often seen as a law-enforcement agency by most people, the ***U.S. Custom Service*** has law-enforcement powers in the form of customs agents charged with examining baggage and cargo entering U.S. borders. In fact, Customs inspectors function as an important defense for policing illegal importation of contraband, such as narcotics. Established by Congress in 1891, the ***Immigration and Naturalization Service*** (INS) administers laws concerning naturalization and immigration. Their border patrols police international land and coastal boundaries of the United States and are entrusted with apprehending and deporting illegal aliens. Similarly, the ***Bureau of Alcohol, Tobacco, and Firearms*** (ATF), originally established in 1791 to enforce taxes on spirits, has important law-enforcement powers, much of their work today focusing on criminal use of explosives, arson, and illegal firearms. In addition, both the ***Internal Revenue Service*** (IRS) and the ***Postal Inspection Service*** possess police powers. The IRS is charged with enforcing revenue and tax laws, and the Postal Inspection Service, the second-oldest continually active federal agency with law-enforcement power, investigates crimes against the Postal Service. The ***Secret Service,*** established in 1865 as a bureau of the U.S. Department of the Treasury, investigates crimes involving counterfeiting of currency and forgery of government checks, securities, and bonds. Since President William McKinley's assassination in 1901, the Secret Service has been entrusted with guarding the president.

Unquestionably the most visible agencies with federal policing authority are the ***Federal Bureau of Investigation*** (FBI) and the ***Drug Enforcement Administration*** (DEA). The FBI, which had its origins in the Department of Justice in 1870, has expanded its law-enforcement powers to encompass more than two hundred crimes, in addition to assisting state and local agencies in apprehending offenders who have committed crimes in local jurisdictions. Under the leadership of J. Edgar Hoover, who headed the FBI from 1925 until 1972, its policing powers widened considerably. Viewed by its critics as controversial because of its investigations into suspected radical and "subversive" movements during war and peace, the FBI continues to have powerful policing authority in cases of espionage.

Like the FBI, the DEA is an agency of the Department of Justice. Its authority, however, is confined to enforcing and apprehending violators of federal narcotics and drug legislation. Because drug trafficking typically involves international routes, many DEA agents work outside U.S. boundaries in cooperation with foreign governments. (Chapter 2 provides further information about the role of the DEA in policing drug trafficking laws. Chapter 5 also briefly details another Department of Justice agency, the ***Organized Crime and Racketeering Section.***)

In addition to these organizations, many other divisions of the federal government contain agencies or bureaus with law-enforcement powers in very specific areas. Among these are the ***Federal Trade Commission*** (FTC) and ***The Securities and Exchange Commission*** (SEC), as well as others in the ***Department of Defense*** **and** ***Department of Interior.***

State Law-Enforcement Agencies

In addition to agencies at the federal level, each state also operates police systems. These vary in size and complexity by state. Across the fifty states more than 800,000 personnel are employed in state and local law enforcement agencies (Maguire/BJS 1993).

State Police Agencies. The beginning of a state police authority can be traced to Texas in the early part of the nineteenth century, when it established the now famous Texas Rangers. Massachusetts and Connecticut, however, were the first to establish a state police. In modern times, state police forces (sometimes called highway patrols) have jurisdiction statewide. State officers patrol the state highways and have authority to apprehend and arrest offenders who have committed or are suspected of committing crimes.

Entrance requirements for state police service are rigorous, as is the training they receive in police academies and in some states at colleges and universities. Most states entrust the state police with operating a crime laboratory and criminalistics division.

County Sheriff Departments. The sheriff's department within states also may enforce criminal laws, usually in rural and unincorporated areas. Their policing powers vary widely by state, depending on their relationship to municipal or city police departments. Headed by a sheriff and employing a force of deputies, county sheriff departments operate county jails (and in some states houses of correction), where they confine detainees awaiting trial and transport prisoners to and from court.

Municipal Police Departments. By far the largest number of law-enforcement officers are members of municipal or city police departments. The complexity of a department and its size vary widely, ranging from the nation's largest department in New York City (nearly 30,000 officers) to a force of only one or two officers in small towns. Larger cities operate their own police academies, where training in compliance with state requirements is provided all new recruits or cadets. Cadet training and the retraining of experienced officers in smaller towns are usually provided by academies operated by the state, typically under the authority of a criminal justice training authority or the state police.

The administrative structure of municipal police departments, typically organized along the lines of a paramilitary organization, also varies widely. Large cities are headed by a police commissioner, together with a police chief. Others are headed by only a chief, with deputy chiefs in charge of patrol, detective, and support services (e.g., communications, records) divisions. Many large city police departments also contain specialized units or divisions, such as vice, fiscal affairs, public information, community services, and internal affairs. Whatever their size, all departments have access to state resources and to modern technologies to support police needs in crime detection and apprehension, identification, criminalistics, and communications. In addition, many police departments enjoy capable leadership, enabling them to work cooperatively with other city and state agencies (see Box 9.2).

Box 9.2 Police Responses to Homelessness

"I feel badly about the problems homeless people face," a male officer in Los Angeles explained, "but they make for a 'lot of law enforcement' in the downtown precinct and take up a hell of a lot of our time." In Phoenix, according to a female officer: "They are in a bad situation, but they can be a major nuisance for us to deal with." In Seattle homeless panhandlers have become so aggressive that police have to enforce "open container" laws to "move the homeless" out of

Pioneer Square, ironically the district from which Skid Row derives its name. In Detroit, Denver, and Atlanta police enforce city ordinances to curb aggressive begging and open-air sleeping.

All of this "law enforcement" comes at enormous expense to taxpayers, in that it consumes inordinate amounts of police time. This is especially true of problems created by homeless derelicts, drug abusers, and the mentally ill, who collectively may account for as many as 75 percent of the nation's 3 to 5 million homeless people.

Many police departments are seeking creative solutions to their law-enforcement problem. One response is to develop cooperative relationships with human service organizations, such as detoxification centers, city or county emergency medical assistance units, and public and private shelters.

The first step in this process involves personnel from all organizations, including police officers, meeting with one another so that each understands the role of the other. The goal of the meetings is to create a team approach. For the police, the problem may be how to divert homeless derelicts from the criminal justice system; for the detox center, the problem is how to funnel public inebriates into their facilities.

A Los Angeles task force included personnel from the district attorney's office, police department, the superior court, and the fire department, each having the authority to commit their organizations to implementing the coalition agreement. In Washtenaw County (Michigan), the sheriff's department was assisted in preparing instructions for deputies on to how to deal with persons requiring psychiatric services. Police academy classes in Oregon now make visits to the Hooper Detox Center in Portland to observe how detoxification services operate, and in Madison, Wisconsin, social workers and police train one another on how to handle homeless public inebriates.

At Montgomery County, Pennsylvania, where an agreement led to a mental health emergency ambulance, results of an evaluation study showed that the network saved police 218 hours in just one month. San Diego Police are required to take all public inebriates, most of whom are homeless, to the privately contracted Inebriate Reception Center, which averages seven minutes of police time.

In Boston, police are instructed to bring the homeless who might otherwise be locked up as public nuisances to the Pine Street Inn, sparing the city police booking, court, and lock-up costs. As one Boston officer explains it, "Everybody wins—the police and court system, Pine Street, and most of all, the homeless."

Source: Adapted from Garrett 1993; Schutt and Garrett 1992; Finn 1985; and Finn and Sullivan 1988.

The ability of a police department to deliver effective law enforcement depends almost entirely on the quality of its personnel. Thus, modern approaches to policing emphasize recruiting men and women who have college degrees, who meet physical requirements necessary for strenuous police duty, and who show promise of becoming effective police officers. Far more than in past decades, police departments today understand that these qualities can be found in every social group, including women; racial, ethnic and linguistic minorities; gays and lesbians; the physically challenged; and others.

What follows is a personal statement written by an officer working in the gang unit in a large West Coast city. Competent and dedicated to his work, he shares personal details about his life, how he became involved in police work, and how he feels about his policing duties.

> In my senior year in college I had to decide on what I really wanted to do. When the job fair came to school, I interviewed with all the big companies, since I was getting a business degree. As I was walking away from the last interview, I noticed the booth for the local police. At first I didn't give it too much thought, so I went to our campus "watering hole" and had a beer with a frat brother. Later I went back to the booth and talked with the police recruiter for almost two hours. Three weeks later I took the abilities test, which I passed, then the physical abilities, which I also passed. After graduation I got a phone call from the police department, asking me to come in for a few tests. After I passed them, they offered me a place in the next academy six months later.
>
> After academy training, I was assigned to one of the toughest parts of town, with the best FTO [Field Training Officer] any LEO [Law Enforcement Officer] could have. While working the streets, I learned a lot about myself and the ways of the street. Like every police officer I need to get the respect of fellow officers, which wasn't too hard. When things got tough I was right there in the middle of things! So I quickly gained a reputation of being there when things get heavy, and I earned their trust.
>
> After five years on the streets, I transferred to our Gang Unit (Detective Unit), where I have worked for almost four years. I handle everything that deals with gangs, so I guess you can say I'm a gang expert. I've learned how to read gang graffiti, which I call "the underground newspaper," and I can tell what is going on just by what is written.
>
> I work in plain clothes and use an unmarked police car. Almost every day I deal with gang members on a one-to-one basis, talking with them, getting to know them, and letting them get to know me.

> Whenever a gang is involved with anything—drive-by shooting, car jacking, stabbing, drug dealing, gang violence—I'm right there!
>
> Besides being a cop I am also a "social worker," which is where I see police work heading in the future—toward community service. In this role I deal with gang members on a ongoing basis, trying to get them to calm down and finding out what is going on with the gang. Most of them know me to a point that they somewhat trust me. I've come to know when they are giving me bullshit and when they are not.
>
> Being in the Gang Unit isn't for everybody. It's a tough job and probably ranks right there with undercover and homicide. But for me, after eight years on the force, I couldn't see myself doing anything else. I enjoy and love this job!
>
> —Anthony Ferdaise

Private Police and Security Agencies. In the past few decades especially, private police or security organizations have undergone vast expansion. This primarily reflects the growing importance of security and employee safety at businesses, industrial complexes, and large office parks. Private security forces can be traced to the "Pinkertons" in Chicago, a private security and detective agency founded by Allan Pinkerton in 1850. Soon afterward, the Wells Fargo Company was founded, specializing in guarding railroad yards, train baggage cars, and especially protecting trains from robberies. Since then, these private agencies have proliferated; some states now grant certain private security officers the authority to make arrests for felony offenses. Cities such as New York City use private police to patrol specified areas or facilities. Industry trends suggest that needs for private law enforcement and personnel will continue to grow.

The Police Role

Generally speaking, the role of the police is to enforce laws and keep the peace. But these role expectations do not adequately distinguish the police role from the general citizen role. All citizens are expected to obey the law, report crime, and help maintain social order. In a number of important articles, Egon Bittner emphasized that the unique quality of the police role is that it entails the capacity to use force nonnegotiably. Whatever task the police are called on to undertake, "police intervention means above all making use of the capacity and authority to overpower resistance to an attempted solution in the native habitat of the problem. . . .Accordingly, the question, 'What are policemen supposed to do?' is almost completely identical with the question, 'What kind of situations require remedies that are nonnegotiably coercible?'" (Bittner 1980, 40–41). The words "nonnegotiably coercible" mean that "when a deputized police officer decides that force is necessary, then within the boundaries of this situation, he is not accountable to anyone, nor is he required to brook the arguments or opposition of anyone who might object to it" (Bittner 1980,-41). This, he says, is not a legal but a practical rule. As he notes, the right of a citizen legally to resist the police is highly complicated. As Bittner observes, it is not legitimate to resist police coercion in emergency situations.

Dangerous versus Routine Law Enforcement

The police capacity to apply force "nonnegotiably" may be what leads us to "call the cops," but in fact the police seldom get involved in situations requiring forceful response, especially in rural areas or small and medium-size cities. The areas of police involvement most conducive to the application of physical coercion are law enforcement and crime control. Nevertheless, the best estimate is that, on the average, only about a third of a department's officers is at any given time likely to be employed in matters involving crimes and criminals. To be sure, no other area attracts greater police attention, but much more police time is devoted to investigating complaints, writing reports, providing emergency services of all kinds, and maintaining peace and order by efforts to resolve domestic quarrels and other interpersonal disputes. Thus, much of their duty time can be seen as fulfilling protective and preventive functions, in that their intervention—even their mere presence—reduces the risk of crimes being committed.

"Noncrime" duties are nothing new to police work, as evidenced by studies conducted in major cities in past decades. In 1973, for example, Franklin Ashburn (1976, 174) reported the results of his analysis of more than 700,000 telephone calls made to the Baltimore Police Department in 1970. Six major kinds of calls were identified by percentage of call totals received:

Crime Index offenses	10.7%
Other crimes	8.4
Other calls (e.g, sick persons, dog bites, sanitation complaints, etc.)	63.0
Accidents (involving vehicles and pedestrians)	5.0
Duplicate calls (more than one person calling to report same incident)	6.8
Unfounded calls (e.g., false alarms of fire, requiring officer response)	6.1

Thus Ashburn found that more than eight of every ten calls received by the police were noncrime-related. These results closely match statistics from the Boston Police Department, which receives more than one million emergency calls each year. For example, in 1994 approximately eight of every ten calls were noncrime-related, such as traffic problems (18 percent), family troubles (5 percent), noise (3 percent), injuries (3 percent), and other, miscellaneous problems (25 percent) (Garcia 1995, 2).

In a similar study, James Q. Wilson (1968, 18) analyzed police-car radio calls in the Syracuse Police Department during a single week in June 1966. He tabulated calls in four categories: information gathering (22.1 percent), service calls (37.5 percent), order maintenance (30.1 percent), and active law enforcement, such as crime in progress, make an arrest (10.3-percent). Thus, as with Asburn's results, less than 20 percent of the radio calls involved active law enforcement.

But it is also instructive to examine data that reveal the kinds of arrests made by police, many of which do not involve dangerous law enforcement. Table 9.1, which reports the estimated arrests made by police, shows that most of the arrests made during the year—approximately four out of five—did not involve serious or index crimes, and about one of three was for crimes that are typically neither dangerous nor dramatic, such as vagrancy, liquor laws, or curfew violations.

Despite the apparent facts that the routine work of the police officer is not physically threatening and that most arrests made in the course of a year are not for index crimes, police officers do face inherent risks. Apart from the public circumstances of their work, where unpredictable events and accidents can and do happen, there is no sure-fire way of knowing whether or not even a routine task can pose danger. From 1978 to 1991, for example, 1137 law-enforcement officers were killed in the line of duty, of which 71 occurred in 1991. Of the total number of these homicides, 155 occurred in traffic pursuits or stops made by the police. Thirty-two officers were killed by mentally deranged persons, and 189 deaths came as a result of investigations of disturbance calls, such as bar fights or family quarrels. Eleven deaths were "ambush situations," such as premeditated murder, entrapment of an officer, or unprovoked attacks.

Their risk for assault is even greater. In 1991, for example, police officers suffered 62,852 assaults with dangerous weapons, such as knives or firearms, nearly four of every ten of these resulting in personal injury (Maguire/BJS 1993, 408-09).

Obviously, then, an important part of the police role entails learning to live with the fact that one is at any time subject to physical attack, from the seen to the unseen and from the most apparently dangerous to the most seemingly innocuous situations. As Bittner might see it, the strength of the police role, that is, the capacity to apply force nonnegotiably, is also its greatest weakness. If officers have the power to kill, then they must run the risk of being killed by those they threaten. The severity of the threat they pose to any given individual is influenced by a variety of factors, including the officer's handling of the discretion that his role allows.

Table 9.1
Estimated Number of Arrests, By Offense Charged, U.S., 1991

Offense Charged	Number of Arrests
Total	14,211,900
Murder and nonnegligent manslaughter	24,050
Forcible rape	40,120
Robbery	173,820
Aggravated assault	480,900
Burglary	436,500
Larceny-theft	1,588,300
Motor vehicle theft	207,700
Arson	20,000
Total Index crimes	2,252,500
Other assaults	1,041,200
Forgery and counterfeiting	103,700
Fraud	427,800
Embezzlement	14,000
Stolen property: buying, receiving	170,000
Vandalism	335,000
Weapons: carrying, possessing	232,000
Prostitution and commercialized vice	98,900
Other sex offenses	108,000
Drug-abuse violations	1,010,000
Gambling	16,000
Offenses against family/children	99,400
Driving under the influence	1,771,400
Liquor laws	624,100
Drunkenness	881,000
Disorderly conduct	757,700
Vagrancy	38,500
All other offenses (except traffic)	3,240,000
Suspicion (not included in total)	18,400
Curfew and loitering law violations	93,400
Runaways	177,300

Source: Federal Bureau of Investigation (1992, 213)

Police Discretion

Virtually all police officers exercise discretion in executing their police roles and in making judgments about how to apply the law and conduct police business. Especially during crimes in progress and during police-citizen encounters, officers are called on to make on-the-spot decisions based on situational factors and occasionally under life-and-death circumstances. Because discretion involves freedom to choose from a number of alternatives, different outcomes can occur from very similar crime situations. For example, an officer can decide to arrest a seventeen-year-old boy for shoplifting candy bars at a corner vendor after he "sassed him back" when confronted, yet let a similar offender get off with a stern lecture if he shows remorse.

Police discretion is directly influenced by the level of law enforcement expected by the community and by the degree of flexibility that police departments give their officers in fulfilling their daily duties. If rules are lax or vague, officers feel at greater liberty to use discretion and make their own decisions, rather than go "strictly by the book" in applying the law (Brooks 1989). Other factors, such as personal background and attitudes and level of police training, can influence how officers perceive and respond to citizen encounters. Thus, even though police are charged with enforcing criminal statutes, presumably in a fair and consistent manner, at the individual level, officers enjoy varying degrees of autonomy in how they actually apply the law.

Sociologists, in particular, have been interested in examining the factors affecting police discretionary power. Considerable effort has been devoted to studying specific characteristics of police-citizen encounters (e.g., Piliavin and Briar 1964; Reiss 1971; Black 1971; Smith 1981; Smith and Visher 1981), such as the dress or demeanor of the suspect or offender, the social context of the arrest, or the age and race of both the offender and the officer. Still other studies have examined the characteristics of neighborhoods where police operate (e.g., Sherman 1980; Chatterton 1983) or the personal attitudes of police officers themselves (e.g., Brooks 1989). Because these studies shed light on factors that affect police discretion, it is worthwhile to review some of the findings.

One of the first important studies to examine police discretion was conducted by Piliavin and Briar (1964), who examined police juvenile encounters. Their findings showed that except for offenders who had committed serious crimes, police exercised considerable discretion on whether or not they arrested juveniles. A juvenile whose demeanor or interaction with the officer demonstrated respect and deference was less likely to be arrested. Race, dress, and appearance of the juvenile also influenced the decision whether to arrest or not.

Still other studies suggest that race and age of suspects or victims have an important impact on police discretion. Bogomolny (1976), for example, reports that African American males are more likely to be stopped or detained for interrogation than white males, and that African Americans are much more likely to be arrested, even after the seriousness of the offense is taken into consideration (Black 1971). Age, too, is evidently an important factor. Friedrich (1977), for example, found that persons under twenty-five and over sixty-five were more likely to receive harsh consequences, such as a stern lecture, interrogation, or a greater likelihood of arrest, compared to those in middle-aged categories. Presumably this relationship is connected to demeanor, such as rebelliousness or a "know it all" attitude. Even the age of victims appears to influence decision-making by officers. As Brooks (1989) reports, if victims of crimes are older, such as the elderly, suspected offenders were more likely to be arrested and to have force applied to them, compared to circumstances involving younger victims. Conversely, if offenders were older, they were less likely to be arrested or to have force applied in their apprehension than offenders in younger age groups.

Racial and socioeconomic composition of neighborhoods also appears to influence police discretionary conduct. Thus, Rossi et al. (1974) find that "ghettos" or inner-city neighborhoods experience high rates of abusive practices by police, such as the use of force in making arrests or police brutality, compared to other residential districts. Similarly Smith (1981) reports that police are considerably more likely to use force to make arrests in predominantly black neighborhoods. On the other hand, the socioeconomic class of neighborhoods evidently brings different expectations of arrest. Smith (1981), for example, notes that the socioeconomic class of the neighborhood is a primary determinant of the decision to arrest. Residents living in high-socioeconomic-class neighborhoods usually have higher expectations that police will make arrests for criminal violations, compared to residents in inner-city or working-class neighborhoods. Thus, expectations for arrest by community residents evidently influence police discretion in making an arrest.

Others studies have pointed out that the management style of departments can take different forms, creating an administrative climate that shapes how much discretion is exercised by police officers. Wilson (1968), for example, identifies at least three management styles in police work. In the first, the ***watchman style***, primary emphasis is given to maintaining order. This style of management encourages police officers to exercise wide discretion in order to maintain order in the community. Thus, an officer's perception of criminal behavior is influenced not only by its inherent violation of criminal statutes but also by the degree to which an officer perceives this behavior as threatening public order. Formal arrests are avoided whenever possible in favor of informal problem resolution.

In contrast, Wilson's ***legalistic*** style stresses a "by the book" approach, enforcing criminal statutes "to the letter of the law." This style of police work is more likely to invoke formal processing of offenders, instead of using informal methods of law enforcement, such as issuing warnings or giving offenders a stern lecture. Thus the legalistic style restricts the degree to which officers can exercise discretion in citizen encounters.

In the ***service style***, police emphasize service to the community. Unlike the legalistic approach, officer discretion is influenced by the department's service orientation to the community, using warnings, counseling, and referrals to appropriate human service agencies or other community resources whenever possible, rather than arresting. This is especially true of violations of minor criminal laws.

Regardless of what factors influence police conduct, discretionary power poses serious problems for both officers and those concerned with containing the police function. For officers, the judicious application of power is generally more problematic in matters concerned with order maintenance than law enforcement. As James Q. Wilson states:

> Chasing a speeding motorist, the officer is running risks of his own choosing. Chasing a fleeing robber, he anticipates violence . . . and the issues are clear. But when he walks into a room where a fight is under way or stops to question a "suspicious" person, the possibility of danger makes the patrolman suspicious and apprehensive. To those fighting or to the person stopped, the patrolman seems "hostile" or "edgy," and if, as is often the case, the citizen has no intention of attacking the officer, he sees the patrolman as "unjustifiably" suspicious, hostile, or edgy. If the citizen then shows his resentment, the officer is likely to interpret it as animosity and thus to be even more on his guard. Both sides may be caught in an ascending spiral of antagonisms (1968, 20).

Whatever one's personal views on this issue, it is generally acknowledged that police discretion in a democratic society must be tempered and constrained by public will and local norms and values. Nevertheless, police organizations have vigorously resisted attempts to implement citizen control. Civilian review boards have been successfully opposed in major cities, among them Baltimore, Cincinnati, Denver, Detroit, Newark, New York City, Philadelphia, San Francisco, and Seattle. Common reasons given for police opposition to civilian control measures include the claim that secrecy is a necessary prerequisite to effective policing and the opinion that civilians, that is, those without substantial police experience, are not in a proper position to evaluate police work. As Lundman explains, "This argument is based on the belief that unless a person has been in a police uniform and been cursed; spit at; assaulted; . . . or forced to decide, quickly, whether the hand coming out of a pocket contains a pack of cigarettes or a gun, then he or she cannot possibly evaluate, much less attempt to control, police and policing" (1980, 173).

The Police Subculture

However exaggerated television or Hollywood portrayals of police stories may be, one thing seems clear: The men and women who work in law enforcement constitute a very special occupational community. Its paramilitary structure, the legitimate authority vested in police officers, their significant role in protecting citizens and in safeguarding the quality of life in the community at large, and the ever-present risks to their lives that they share in common suggest that police work fosters unique social bonding. In addition to the official bureaucratic structures and rules that operate to shape their behavior, police officers are also subject to an informal subculture that has values and norms that mold the police roles and influence daily interaction with themselves and the public. In many respects, the police subculture is not different from other subcultures, containing argot or a specialized language that develops in the course of conducting police business. Argot can convey an attitude wherein positive or negative labels are attached to events or people, and it also helps to maintain a strong sense of who "we" are (insiders) and who "they" are (outsiders).

Skolnick (1966), Niederhoffer (1967), Broderick (1977), Muir (1977), and others have offered insightful descriptions of various attributes of the "police personality" and the police subculture, and how these interrelated factors can function to isolate police from the larger community. As Harlow (1976, 86) points out, "The policemen's sense of alienation from society results in the development of a distinctive 'subculture' or 'code' among police officers by which they can live, thus providing a basis for self-respect independent to some degree of civilian attitudes".

The nature of police work and the police subculture are also known to foster a generally cynical and suspicious outlook. While such an outlook may have practical utility on the job, these attributes can also create difficulties in an officer's personal life, such as problems in family life or interpersonal relationships. When they occur, interpersonal problems contribute to the overall stress inherent in police work, which in turn promotes alienation and isolation. As the spouse of a veteran police officer puts it: "[He] can be impossible to live with at times...down on everything and everybody. . . . It worries me at times and I just leave him alone when he gets into one of those 'moods'" (Caldero et al. 1980, 247).

Kenneth Fortier (1977, 138), a police administrator, has identified the following basic characteristics of the police subculture: (1) cynicism due to extensive and daily contact with the seamy side of life; (2) personal isolationism due to public distrust; (3) solidarity because of the need for mutual support; (4) defensiveness due to doubt about the ability of nonpolice persons adequately to understand and appreciate police work; and, (5) a narrow intellectual outlook. Police officers tend to restrict their reading to the more conservative weekly magazines; and when they read the morning paper, "the only things that catch their eyes are the words 'police,' 'criminal,' 'court,'... and other key words to policemen."

As useful for its members as it may be, the police subculture can be a roadblock to change and reform. It tends to resist any change that might lessen the strength of the bond of mutual protection. The Knapp Commission encountered this principle in attempting to reform the New York City Police Department. The commission was impressed by two factors: (1) intense police suspicion of and hostility toward any outside intervention in departmental affairs; and (2) extreme esprit de corps. The commission contended that the two combined to create "the most serious roadblock to a rational attack upon police corruption: a stubborn refusal at all levels of the Department to acknowledge that a serious problem exists" (Dempsey 1977, 361). Thus, in contrast to the image of police as professionals, the police subculture operates as a powerful force to resist organizational changes, including changes that could strengthen police performance, as well as serve the goals of a modern police department.

The Community Policing Model

The 1960s and early 1970s were turbulent years in America. This was an era of intensive activity revolving around the civil rights movements, a resurgence of political activism, unrest on college campuses and the birth of student political movements, widespread protests and demonstrations against American involvement in Southeast Asia and Vietnam, and civil disobedience and urban riots, as well as rapid increases in crime rates throughout the country. While many of these events are now seen as infamous moments in American history, they also convinced many people that conventional police tactics and methods of crime control are not truly adequate for meeting the law-enforcement needs of many communities, particularly those of large cities. As interest in police reforms intensified throughout the 1970s, new concepts in policing took shape that formed the basis for what is now known as "community policing." According to Trojanowicz and Bucqueroux (1990, 3), it is the first major reform in policing in more than a half century.

Although community policing is not easily defined, it should be understood not as a program but as a philosophy or conceptual approach to policing, which contains many components and programs aimed at delivering effective law enforcement to the community. Thus it should not be confused with "police community relations units" or "team policing" or even "foot patrol," although each of these could be a part of the overall approach to community policing. Instead, it is an approach to crime control and prevention that seeks to utilize the community as a partner with the police in achieving effective police service.

Rather than merely react to crimes after their occurrence, community policing encourages proactive policing strategies that will discourage the commission of crime. In theory, the belief is that partnerships with community groups will enhance not only the effectiveness of conventional law-enforcement tactics but also the ability of the police to anticipate or more efficiently solve crime problems (Manning 1989; Glensor and Peak 1993; Langworthy and Travis 1994). As Trojanowicz and Bucqueroux (1990, 5) explain, the community policing philosophy is "based on the concept that police officers and private citizens working together in creative ways can help solve contemporary community problems related to crime, fear of crime, social and physical disorder, and neighborhood decay" (see Box 9.3).

Box 9.3 How Community Policing Works in Seattle

Southeast of downtown Seattle and the city's racially mixed Central Area lies Rainier Valley. It once resembled the rest of Seattle: prosperous, progressive, demographically two-thirds white with fair-sized African American and Asian minorities and smaller groups of Hispanics and Native Americans. After World War II, two large new public housing projects and an influx of African Americans from the Central Area increased the proportion of low-income minorities. However, Southeast Seattle failed to keep pace with the post-war economic boom. New construction in the district declined, and the crime rate rose.

Confident of their longstanding political clout, community activists met in the 1970s with city and county officials to express their concern over what they perceived to be a crime wave. Their Court Watch program helped defeat judges perceived as lax on offenders. Furthermore, a precinct commander promoted team policing and community involvement, a proposal that won enthusiastic support by Rainier residents.

In 1979, the mayor established the Economic Renewal Task Force of Rainier Valley. This was preceded by a Block Watch program to cut the rate of residential burglary; the nation's first Business Watch program to tackle commercial burglaries; and the Crime Prevention Lead to serve as the southeast Seattle business community's private crime-fighting agency.

And then crack cocaine came to Rainier Valley! Cocaine use spread in minority areas, especially in the housing developments. The city's narcotics violations rose from 582 in 1983 to 5850 in 1989. Police discovered fortified homes dealing cocaine, and street gangs infested parks, parking lots, and other public places.

Community organizations and police tried tough new tactics. A black activist became a security officer for the housing projects and gave police information they needed to get search warrants. The Rainier Chamber of Commerce launched a cleanup and anti-graffiti drive. The Seattle Police Department set up a precinct Anticrime Team, known as ACT, not to make arrests, but to disrupt or destroy drug operations. Despite widespread community support, police review of its tactics led to restructuring of the ACT operation, which emphasized strict adherence to established departmental procedures and more emphasis on making arrests.

Even though the new ACT operation netted 422 arrests in just two months, community residents continued to voice their strong support for the original ACT squad and procedures. Furthermore, the commercial burglary rate continued to rise.

After a series of community meetings with police representatives, Rainier residents decided the community itself would have to supply the "vision and imagination" to solve its problems. As the police discovered, the Rainier Valley was not a group of mere complainers looking for a quick fix, but people looking for long-term, broad-based solutions to their crime problems.

Community advisory groups felt that their partnership with police allowed them a voice in selecting police targets and goals. Despite tensions, a pattern of police-community cooperation evolved. In January 1988 the chamber of commerce resurrected the defunct Crime Prevention League, renaming it the South Seattle Crime Prevention Council (SSCPC). The SSCPC "advised" police in choosing targets for intensive policing effort—"hot spots" for crime and drug trafficking, removing abandoned cars that functioned as havens for drug sales, and surveillance of "crack houses."

Police action consisted of aggressive patrol of the Rainier Valley, with special attention to the targets. Officers were expected to visit these at least twice each shift, fully documenting the visits in special log entries. In addition, police reviewed crack house reports from the community hotline. By the end of the first year, police were working on 39 targets, successfully "completing" nearly half. By the end of the following year, the other half had been closed down, though many opened up elsewhere.

SSCPC meetings often exemplified community policing concepts. Police reported on criminal conduct at target sites. Citizen representatives reported on how citizens, no longer afraid of being accosted by drug dealers at bus stops, began to use public transportation again and how graffiti and prostitution declined in their neighborhoods. Each side learned from the other.

A number of concrete programs evolved out of the community-police partnership:

—Narcotic activity reports (NAR). Resident complaints of drug activity were received by telephone or in person, then passed along to the Narcotics Division and ACT for follow-up. In one year the police followed up on 1219 such reports.

—Criminal trespass program. Property owners gave police permission to enter private property such as parking lots or exterior stairs to investigate and arrest loiterers. More than 100 businesses signed up and 1044 persons received citations.

—Pay telephone program. Standard pay phones were put on a "call out only" status so that drug dealers could no longer use them to receive messages and instructions.

—Owner notification (drug trafficking civil abatement program) gave property owners quick notice that their tenants faced legal action for using their property for drug-involved purposes.

—Anti-graffiti program. "Paintouts" became a popular activity for anticrime volunteers, supported by both the police and SSCPC.

—Telephone hotline. This was basically an anonymous "tipline" to the police about crime activities. Callers were also encouraged to use it for crime-rated public-service problems that were not "911 emergencies."

—Garden police car program. A two-officer police car worked in two housing projects. Though not required to respond to calls other than emergencies, the officers checked on drug activities and made arrests when warranted. Since the officers became more or less permanently assigned to this beat, community residences grew to feel they "owned" the garden car.

Ultimately the SSCPC broadened its base of members, applied pressures to other agencies of the criminal justice system that assisted police in their efforts, and was successful in increasing the number of uniformed police officers and in involving other city agencies in the overall effort to fight crime.

Source: Adapted and reprinted from NIJ 1992a.

Advocates of community policing argue that it can be an effective for a number of different reasons (NIJ:1992b, 3–4):

1. Moving the police officer from a position of anonymity in the patrol car to *direct* engagement with a community gives the officer more immediate *information* about problems unique to a neighborhood and insights into its solutions.

2. Freeing the officer from the emergency response system permits him or her to engage more directly in *proactive crime prevention.*

3. Making operations more visible to the public *increases police accountability to the public.*

4. Decentralizing operations allows officers to develop a greater familiarity with the specific workings and needs of various neighborhoods and constituencies in the community and adapt procedures to accommodate those needs.

5. Encouraging officers to view *citizens as partners* improves relations between police and the public.

6. Moving decisionmaking and discretion downward to the patrol officer places more authority in the hands of the person who best knows the community's problems and expectations.

7. Developing a relationship between police and the public encourages citizens *to take more initiative in preventing and solving crimes.*

Although community policing involves an organizational strategy that shifts officers from the isolation of their patrol cars to more direct, face-to-face contact with residents, there is no precise formula as to how community police officers discharge their duties. In fact, community policing can take many different forms, depending on law-enforcement needs in the community, available police resources, the nature of the crime problem within a community, and even the political power of citizen groups with whom the police form partnerships. For example, in Wisconsin the Madison Police Department initiated an experiment at decentralizing the police command by creating substations, or "storefront police stations," in lower-income housing projects with high crime rates. Neighborhood foot patrols maintain face-to-face interaction with residents. When possible, officers assigned to these commands try to respond personally to emergency calls (NIJ 1992). In New York City, it takes a somewhat different form. In NYPD's 72d precinct, containing many deserted docks that are havens for drug-driven prostitution and robbery, personnel were added to the precinct staff and foot patrols with radio links to patrol cars, allowing police to provide rapid response to 911 emergency calls. Officers enjoy close interaction and cooperation with residents of this racially and ethnically diverse area, which provides them with valuable information useful in crime control and prevention.

According to an officer in Boston, where community policing is being implemented: "Every day is different . . . because you always meet someone new and you can usually make connections with these people. This is what makes the community policing more interesting than conventional police work."

Certainly one of the features of community policing is that it is filled with many different activities. In addition to traditional law enforcement activities, such as responding to service and emergency calls, an "average" day might involve

—Operating neighborhood substations.
—Meeting with community groups.
—Analyzing and solving neighborhood problems.
—Working with citizens on crime prevention programs.
—Conducting door-to-door surveys of residents.
—Talking with students in school.
—Meeting with local merchants.
—Making security checks of businesses.
—Dealing with disorderly people.

And, of course, in much of this work there is foot patrol (Mastrofsky/NIJ 1992).

To date, community policing has been adopted by hundreds of police departments nationwide. Among them are Los Angeles, Philadelphia, Boston, and Baltimore. Medium- and small-size cities, too, such as Reno, Nevada; Newport News, Virginia; Evanston, Illinois; Flint, Michigan; and McAllen, Texas, have embraced this approach. In 1990, the nation's largest police department, the NYPD, adopted community policing as the bedrock of its foundation.

Although there is solid evidence that community policing is effective in reducing crime problems and protecting the quality of community life, adopting the community approach has not come easy. One of the reasons is that community policing involves radical changes in the status quo. It requires proactive policing, substantial changes in the organizational structure of a department, and a redefinition of a patrol officer's mission. Predictably, police administrators and officers, like most people, tend to resist change, especially because community policing is a radical departure from conventional policing tactics. Results from evaluation studies will be instructive in determining both the effectiveness and the future of community policing in America (see Box 9.4).

Box 9.4 Learning More About Community Policing

Community policing constitutes a radical change from conventional policing concepts and policies, involving changes in the organizational structure and in the day-to-day deployment of police personnel. Because community policing can take many forms, readers interested in law enforcement or in police work as a career may want to explore other sources of information. A variety of books and articles are available.

- Dunham, Roger G., and Geoffrey P. Alpert. 1989. *Critical Issues in Policing: Contemporary Readings*. Prospect Heights, Ill.: Waveland Press. See especially James Q. Wilson and George L. Kelling, "Broken Windows"; Peter K. Manning, "Community Policing"; and Geoffrey P. Alpert and Roger G. Dunham, "Community Policing."
- Greene, Jack R., and, Stephen D. Mastrofski. 1993. *Community Policing*. New York: Praeger.

Kratcoski, Peter C., and Duane Dukes, eds. *Community Policing*. 1994. Cincinnati: Anderson.

- Langworthy, Robert, and Lawrence Travis, eds. *Policing in America*. 1994. New York: Macmillan.
- Moore, M.H., R.C. Trojanowicz, and G.L. Kelling. 1988. "Crime and Policing" in *Perspectives on Policing Series*, National Institute of Justice/John F. Kennedy School of Government, Harvard University.
- National Institute of Justice. 1992. *Community Policing* (thematic issue). *NIJ Journal*, August.

• Radelet, Louis A., and David L. Carter. 1994. *The Police and the Community* 5th ed. New York: Macmillan.
• Skolnick, Jerome, and David H. Bayley. 1988. "Theme and Variation in Community Policing." In *Crime and Justice: A Review of Research*, edited by Michael Tonry and Norval Morris. Chicago: University of Chicago Press.
• Trojanowicz, Robert, and Bonnie Bucqueroux. 1990. *Community Policing: A Contemporary Perspective*. Cincinnati: Anderson.
• Trojanowicz, Robert, and Bonnie Bucqueroux. 1994. *Community Policing: How to Get Started*. Cincinnati: Anderson.

Summary and Conclusion

Police work in America has its origins in local politics of cities and towns. Efforts by Vollmer and others to professionalize police work and operation have led to major reforms in police organizations, which include rigorous standards of eligibility, extensive training, modern concepts in management and deployment of police personnel, and the use of sophisticated technologies for crime control, prevention, and apprehension. Evidence in this chapter, however, suggests that professionalization of the police has two sides—one good, the other not. On the one side, the police training and high standards for police recruits have led to more effective law-enforcement capabilities. Modern management approaches have greatly increased police efficiency. On the other side, a police subculture that is loathe to civilian review of police work is also resistant to professionalization. At times evidence of corruption, illegal use of force, and other violations speaks to personal and professional difficulties that police often face.

Certainly the most significant reform to occur in police work over the past century is the development of community policing. Though often misunderstood and not easily implemented, evidence to date suggests that community policing can make significant progress toward achieving police objectives in crime control and prevention. Overall success, however, depends on effective implementation of community policing concepts, which cannot be achieved without strong and committed leadership by police administrators in cooperation with citizen groups.

References

Ashburn, Franklin G. 1976. "Changing the Rhetoric of 'Professionalism.'" In *Police Community Relations: Images, Roles, Realities*, edited by Alvin W. Cohn and Emilio C. Viano. New York: Lippincott.

Bittner, Egon. 1980. *The Functions of the Police in Modern Society*. Cambridge, Mass.: Oelgeschlager, Gunn and Hain.

Black, Donald. 1971. "The Social Organization of Arrest," *Stanford Law Review* 23:1087–1111.

Bogomolny, R. 1976. "Street Patrol: The Decision to Stop a Citizen." *Criminal Law Bulletin* 12:544–82.

Boston Globe. 1993a. "Fear City Leafleting Plans Decried." December 1, 1.

———. 1993b. Editorial: "Fear Strikes Out" December 2, 22.

Broderick, John J. 1977. *Police in a Time of Change*. Morristown, N.J.: General Learning Press.

Brooks, Laure Weber. 1989. "Police Discretionary Behavior: A Study of Style." In *Critical Issues in Policing*, edited by Roger G. Dunham and Geoffrey P. Alpert. Prospect Heights, Ill.: Waveland Press.

Caldero, M., G.R. Garrett, and B. Menke. 1980. "The Life and Times of a Police Officer." Unpublished manuscript, Washington State University, 1980.

Center for Research on Criminal Justice. 1975. *The Iron Fist and the Velvet Glove: An Analysis of the U.S. Police*. Berkeley, Calif.: Center for Research on Criminal Justice.

Chatterton, M. 1983. "Police Work and Assault Charges." In *The Police Organization*, edited by M. Punch. Cambridge: MIT Press.

Dempsey, Lawrence J. 1977. "Alleged Police Corruption." In *Critical Issues in Law Enforcement*, edited by Harry W. More. Cincinnati: Anderson.

Encyclopaedia Britannica, llth ed. 1910. New York: Encyclopaedia Britannica

Federal Bureau of Investigation. 1992. *Crime in the United States, 1991*. Washington, D.C.: Government Printing Office.

Finn, Peter E. 1985. "The Health Care System's Response to the Decriminalization of Public Drunkenness." *Journal of Studies on Alcohol* 46:7–23.

Finn, Peter E., and Monique Sullivan. 1988. *Police Response to Special Populations: Handling the Mentally Ill, Public Inebriate, and the Homeless*. Washington, D.C.: National Institute of Justice.

Fortier, Kenneth N. 1977. "The Police Culture." In *Critical Issues in Law Enforcement*, edited by Harry W. More. Cincinnati: Anderson Publishing Co.

Friedrich, R.J. 1977. "The Impact of Organization, Individual, and Situational Factors of Police Behavior." Ph.D. dissertation, Department of Political Science, University of Michigan, Ann Arbor (Dissertation Abstracts).

Garcia, Luis. 1995. 9-1-1 Calls for Service. Boston: Office of Planning and Research, Boston Police Department.

Garrett, Gerald R. 1993. "Homelessness, Alcohol, and Other Drug Abuse: Research Traditions and Policy Responses." In *Homelessness: New England and Beyond*, edited by Padraig O'Malley. Amherst: University of Massachusetts Press.

Glensor, R., and Ken Peak. 1993. "Improving Perceptions of the Police with Community Policing: The Reno Experience." Paper presented at the annual meetings of the Academy of Criminal Justice Sciences, Kansas City.

Goldstein, Herman. 1977. *Policing a Free Society*. Cambridge, Mass.: Ballinger.

Harlow, Eleanor. 1976. "Issues in Police-Community Relations." In *Police Community Relations: Images, Roles, Realities*, edited by Alvin W. Cohn and Emilio C. Viano. New York: Lippincott.

Hutchinson, Bill. 1993. "Officers' Cries of 'fear' Draw Criticism." *Boston Herald*, December 2, 1.

Knapp Commission. 1978. "The Knapp Commission Report on Police Corruption." In *Justice and Corrections*, edited by Norman Johnston and Leonard Savitz. New York: Wiley.

Lane, Roger. 1967. *Policing the City: Boston, 1822–1885*. Cambridge, Mass.: Harvard University Press.

Langworthy, Robert, and Lawrence Travis. 1994. *Policing in America*. New York: Macmillan.

Lundman, Richard J. 1980. *Police and Policing: An Introduction*. New York: Holt, Rinehart and Winston.

Maguire, K., et al., eds. 1993. *Sourcebook of Criminal Justice Statistics, 1992*. Washington, D.C.: U.S. Department of Justice, Bureau of Justice Statistics.

Manning, Peter K. 1989. "Community Policing." In *Critical Issues in Policing*, edited by Roger G. Dunham and Geoffrey P. Alpert. Prospect Heights, Ill.: Waveland Press.

Mastrofski, Stephen D. 1992. "What Does Community Policing Mean for Daily Police Work?" *National Institute Journal*, August, 23-27.

Monkkonen, Eric H. 1981. *Police in Urban America, 1860–1920*. Cambridge, England: Cambridge University Press.

Moore, M., R. Trojanowicz, and G. Kelling. 1988. "Crime and Policing," *NIJ Perspectives in Policing Series*, No. 2.

Muir, W.K. 1977. *Police: Streetcorner Politicians*. Chicago: University of Chicago Press.

National Institute of Justice. 1992a. *Research in Brief: Community Policing in Seattle*. Washington, D.C.: U.S. Department of Justice.

———. 1992b. "Community Policing in the 1990's," *National Institute of Justice Journal*, August, 2–8.

Niederhoffer, Arthur. 1967. *Behind the Shield*. Garden City, N.Y.: Doubleday.

Piliavin, I., and Scott Briar. 1964. "Police Encounters with Juveniles." *American Journal of Sociology* 70:206–14.

Platt, Anthony, and Lynn Cooper, eds. 1974. *Policing America*. Englewood Cliffs, N.J.: Prentice Hall.

Reiss, Albert. 1971. *The Police and the Public*. New Haven: Yale University Press.

Reith, Charles. 1956. *A New Study of Police History*. Edinburgh, Scotland: Oliver and Boyd.

Rossi, P., R. Berk, and B. Eidson. 1974. *The Roots of Urban Discontent: Public Police, Municipal Institutions, and the Ghetto*. New York: Wiley.

Schutt, Russell K., and Gerald R. Garrett. 1992. *Responding to the Homeless*. New York: Plenum.

Sherman, L.W. 1980. "Causes of Police Behavior: The Current State of Quantitative Research." *Journal of Research in Crime and Delinquency* 12:69–100.

Skolnick, Jerome. 1966. *Justice without Trial: Law Enforcement in Democratic Society*. New York: Wiley.

———, and David H. Bayley. 1988. "Theme and Variation in Community Policing." In *Crime and Justice Review: A Review of Research*, edited by Michael Tonry and Norval Morris. Chicago: University of Chicago Press.

Smith, Alexander B., and Harriet Pollack. 1980. *Criminal Justice: An Overview*, 2nd ed. New York: Holt, Rinehart and Winston.

Smith, D.A. 1981. "Street Level Justice: Situational Determinants of Police Arrest Decisions." *Social Problems* 29:167–78.

———, and Christi Visher. 1981. "Street Level Justice: Situation Determinants of Police Arrest Decisions." *Social Problems* 29:167–78.

Trojanowicz, Robert, and Bonnie Bucqueroux. 1990. *Community Policing: A Contemporary Perspective*. Cincinnati: Anderson.

Vollmer, August. 1971. *The Police and Modern Society*. Montclair, N.H.: Patterson Smith.

Wilson, James Q. 1968. *Varieties of Police Behavior: The Management of Law and Order in Eight Communities*. Cambridge: Harvard University Press.

Wilson, O.W., ed. 1957. *Parker on Police*. Springfield, Ill.: Charles C Thomas.

———, and Roy Clinton McLaren. 1963. *Police Administration*. 4th ed. New York: McGraw-Hill.

Chapter 10

Processing the Accused: From Arrest through Sentencing

The criminal justice system contains three basic parts: law-enforcement agencies, courts, and correctional institutions. In systems terminology, the three are akin to what Adams, Buck, and Hallstrom (1974, 1) refer to as "the input, process, and output components." Chapter 9 dealt with the first; Chapter 11 examines the third. This chapter deals with the second; it focuses on what is known about the number of people arrested, convicted, and sentenced in the United States. Are the police becoming more successful in identifying and apprehending offenders? Are the courts trying more criminal cases? Are more felons being convicted and sentenced to prison? What is the evidence and what are the trends?

Offenses and Arrests

To make an arrest an officer is required to have probable cause, an objectifiable reason for apprehending and detaining a citizen. The words "probable cause" appear in the Fourth Amendment to the Constitution, which reads as follows: "The right of the people to be secure in their persons, houses, papers, and effects, against unreasonable searches and seizures, shall not be violated, and no warrants shall issue, but upon probable cause, supported by oath or affirmation, and particularly describing the place to be searched, and the persons or things to be seized." This does not mean that an officer cannot stop and detain someone on the basis of suspicion. The criterion of probable cause may be satisfied by something less than physical evidence because of the need to allow for discretion in acting to prevent crime as well as to apprehend offenders.

It is important to point out, however, that the vast majority of arrests are not made for violations of the law committed in the presence of or initially detected by law-enforcement personnel. Most arrests (well over 90 percent) are made on the basis of crimes reported to law-enforcement agents and the evidence supplied by victims and witnesses. Entry into the criminal justice system via arrest initiates a process whose various stages are outlined in Figure 10.1.

After deciding to arrest a suspect, an officer is required to inform him or her of certain legal rights. These rights are contained in the Fifth and Sixth Amendments to the constitution. The relevant phrase in the Fifth Amendment

Figure 10.1 The sequence of events in the criminal justice system

From *Report to the Nation on Crime and Justice* 2nd ed. U.S. Department of Justice, Bureau of Justice Statistics, Washington D.C.: Government Printing Office, March 1988, 56–7.

What is the sequence of events in the criminal justice system?

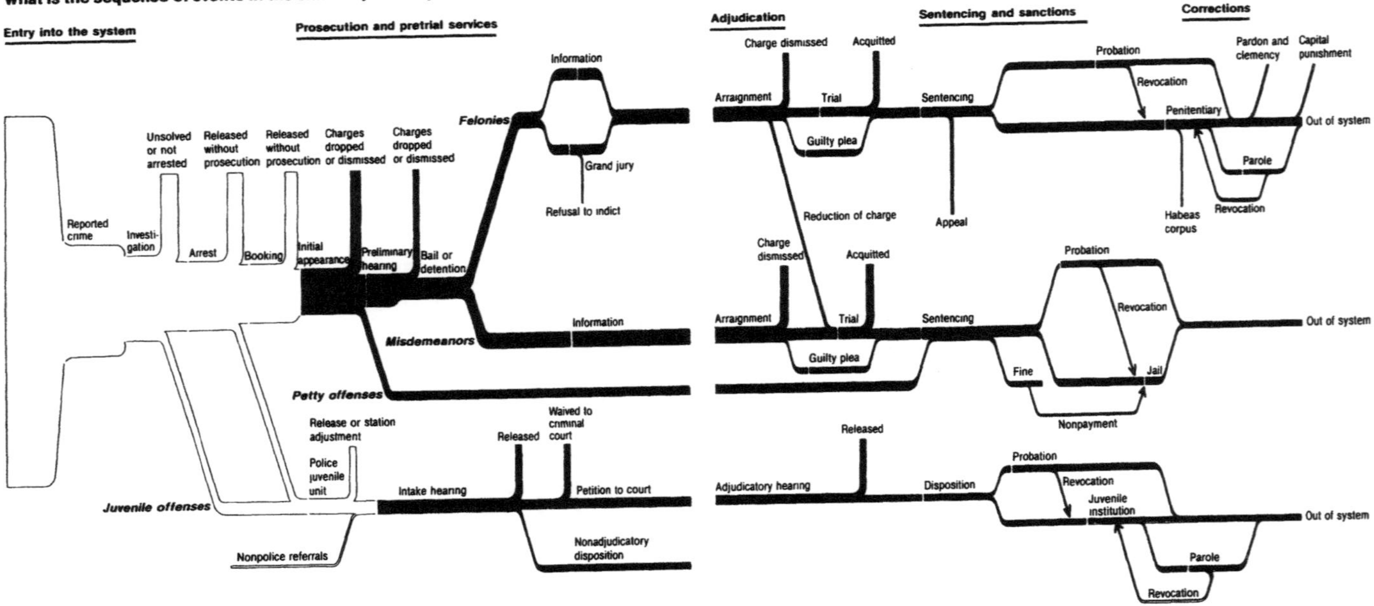

Note: This chart gives a simplified view of caseflow through the criminal justice system. Procedures vary among jurisdictions. The weights of the lines are not intended to show the actual size of caseloads.

says that no person "shall be compelled in any criminal case to be a witness against himself, nor be deprived of life, liberty, or property, without due process of law." The Sixth Amendment guarantees the accused the right "to have the assistance of counsel for his defense." Before decisions in cases rendered by the U.S. Supreme Court in 1964 and 1966, arresting officers were not required to inform suspects of these rights in the precise and timely manner they were afterward.

In the 1964 *Escobedo* case, the Court ruled that anything an accused person said orally or in writing before trial but after being taken into custody and accused of a crime could not be used against him or her at a trial if he or she either had not been informed in advance of the right to remain silent or denied access to counsel. "In another words," notes Edwin Powers, "a confession obtained from a suspect in custody voluntarily given, with no duress, force or threats of force or promises would, under these decisions, no longer be admissible unless these constitutional safeguards were observed, thus upsetting a time-honored practice" (1973, 34). In the 1966 *Miranda* case the Court bolstered its decision in Escobedo by requiring arresting officers to precisely inform those they have arrested or "otherwise deprived of freedom of action in any significant way" of their constitutional rights before questioning them to obtain evidence useful in a trial. The so-called *Miranda* rules require the arresting officer to tell a suspect:

1. He [or she] may remain silent (and of course cannot be forced to answer any question).

2. If he [or she] decides to talk, his (or her) statements can and will be used against him or her (if, and when, he (or she) later appears in court).

3. He [or she] has a right to consult with counsel (prior to or at any time during questioning).

4. If he [or she] wishes counsel but has none and cannot afford one, the state will appoint counsel for him [or her] (Powers, 35).

Given these and other constraints, how effective are the police in apprehending offenders?

The basic measure of the effectiveness of law-enforcement agencies is the extent to which they are able to "clear by arrest" known criminal offenses. According to the Federal Bureau of Investigation (FBI), "law enforcement agencies clear or solve an offense when at least one person is arrested, charged with the commission of the offense, and turned over to the court for prosecution" (*Uniform Crime Reports* 1992, 202). An offense reported as cleared in one year may have been committed in a previous year. Furthermore, more than one person may be arrested for the commission of a single crime, and multiple crimes may be cleared by the arrest of a single offender. For several years, about 20 to 21 percent of all FBI Crime Index offenses have been cleared by arrest.

Violent crimes, particularly those involving murder and aggravated assault, are more likely to lead to arrest than property crimes. Although property crimes are much more prevalent than violent crimes, they are much less likely (about three times) to be cleared by arrest. As the FBI explains it: "Clearances for crimes against persons (murder, forcible rape, and aggravated assault) are generally higher as more intense investigative efforts are often given these offenses and witnesses are frequently available to identify the perpetrators" (*Uniform Crime Reports* 1992, 202).

Interestingly, the proportion of Crime Index offenses cleared by arrest does not vary a great deal by residential area. The 1991 clearance rate for the largest cities was 21 percent. For suburban counties it was 20 percent, and for rural areas it was 23 percent. The highest total Crime Index clearance rate, 26 percent, was recorded in cities with populations in the range of 10,000 to 24,999.

Considering total Crime Index clearance rates by region, the highest total (22 percent) was shared by the West and South. Both the Midwest and the Northeast had 20 percent clearance rates.

Overall, the evidence suggests that the chances of getting caught for the commission of serious crimes are lower today than the past. Table 10.1 shows that clearance rates in 1971 were generally higher than in 1991 for the Crime Index offenses with one exception, larceny-theft, where the difference was barely negligible.

Table 10.1
Clearance Rates, 1971 and 1991

Crime	1971	1991	Difference
Murder	84%	67%	–17%
Forcible rape	55	52	– 3
Aggravated assault	66	57	– 9
Robbery	27	24	– 3
Burglary	19	13	– 6
Larceny-theft	19	20	+ 1
Motor vehicle theft	16	14	– 2

Source: *Uniform Crime Reports* (Washington D.C.: Government Printing Office, 1972 and 1992).

In the face of such evidence, it is not surprising that public opinion polls should reveal doubt about the effectiveness of police protection. Interestingly, and as can be seen in Table 10.2, the response pattern was remarkably stable between 1981 and 1989. In both years, 50 percent answered either "not very much" or "none." In 1989, there was a 1 percent decline (from 49 percent in 1981 to 48 percent in 1989) in the number who said they had either "a great deal" or "quite a bit" of confidence in the ability of the police to protect them from violent crime.

Table 10.2
"How much confidence do you have in the ability of the police to protect you from violent crime?"

Level of Confidence	1981	1989
A great deal	15%	14%
Quite a bit	34	34
Not very much	42	42
None	8	8
No opinion	1	2

Sources: For 1981; *Sourcebook of Criminal Justice Statistics—1983*. (Washington, D.C.: Government Printing Office), 245; for 1989: *Sourcebook Of Criminal Justice Statistics—1990*. (Washington, D.C.: Government Printing Office), 159.

If people are evenly split on the subject of the effectiveness of police protection, they are unequivocal in their views on the subject of the effectiveness of the courts to protect them. In a 1989 Gallup poll (Maguire and Flanagan 1991, 191), a national sample was asked the following question: "How much confidence to you have in the ability of the courts to convict and properly sentence criminals?" Fully 73 percent said they had either "not very much" (59 percent) or "none" (14 percent). Only 25 percent said they had either "a great deal" (5 percent) or "quite a lot" (20 percent) of confidence. Analysis of the best available evidence on the detection of crime and prosecution of offenders shows that public opinion has a basis in fact.

The Funneling Effect

In a 1967 report, a task force of the President's crime commission illustrated "the funneling effect from reported crimes through prison sentence," as shown in Figure 10.1. What the figure suggested (it was presented without interpretation, as if the meaning of the statistics was self-evident) was that the police were inefficient (only 26.2 percent of the reported Crime Index offenses in 1965 led to an arrest) and the judicial system lenient (only 35.5 percent of the 177,000 felony complaints resulted in a prison sentence).

Figure 10.2 The Funneling Effect
From the President's Commission on Law Enforcement and the Administration of Justice, *Task Force Report: Science and Technology* (Washington, D.C.: Government Printing Office, 1977), 61.

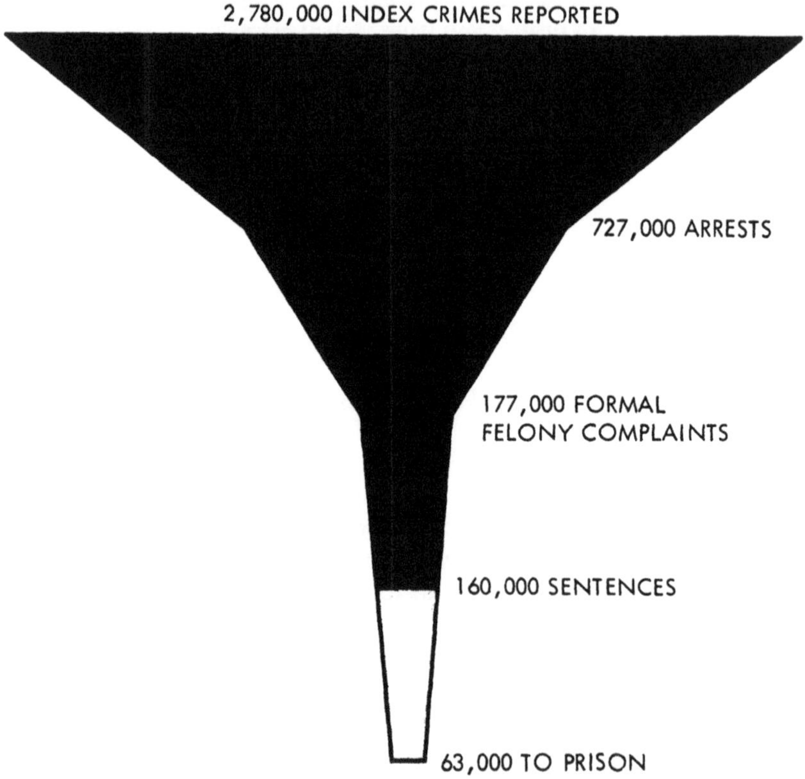

With the addition of victimization data, and considering only comparable offenses included in both National Criminal Victimization Surveys and *Uniform Crime Reports*, an even more devastating "funneling effect" of the criminal justice system can be conveyed. In 1988, for example, there were an estimated 32.8 million criminal victimizations (for Crime Index offenses). The *Uniform Crime Reports* identified (1) approximately 13.9 million (42 percent) Crime Index offenses as known to law enforcement agencies, and (2) that law enforcement agencies had made some 2.9 million arrests (21 percent of the crimes known figure) for Crime Index offenses. Furthermore, in 1988, 266,259 individuals were convicted (9.1 percent of the figure for those arrested) and 23,727 individuals (8.9 percent of the figure for those convicted) incarcerated (sent to prison and jailed) for Crime Index offenses.

While there is no denying that this manner of presenting and assessing evidence has some validity, it is neither an entirely accurate nor fair way of evaluating the effectiveness of law enforcement and the judicial process. To begin with, the categories are inconsistent. That is, with the exception of self-reported victimizations and crimes known to have been committed in a given year, those arrested, convicted, and sentenced include those whose offenses were committed in a previous year or years.

To appraise the effectiveness of law enforcement fairly, one must consider the extent of victim and general public cooperation with its efforts. Thus, national victimization data show that the percentage of victimizations reported to the police has ranged from a low of 32 percent in 1973 to a high of 39 percent in 1992. Frequent reasons given for not reporting victimization to the police include claims that the offense was a personal or family matter, fear of offender retaliation, fear of possible notoriety, a general reluctance to become involved because of inconvenience, and any number of other personal and situational motives. And once a crime is reported to the police, the likelihood of arrest, prosecution, and conviction depends critically not only on victim but also on witness cooperation.

To assess the charge of judicial leniency, one must consider recent conviction and sentencing trends. Are those arrested today more or less likely to be convicted and sentenced to prison? Are those sentenced to prison serving longer or shorter sentences?

Answers to these questions require distinguishing between state and federal data. The federal government has adopted a determinate sentencing scheme based on sentencing guidelines and the abolition of parole. For reasons such as prison overcrowding and the difficulty of acquiring public funds to expand old and build new prisons, most states maintain indeterminate sentencing and parole. Of the two sentencing systems, then, one would expect those that are indeterminate to be the most likely to manifest judicial leniency. If anything, one should expect determinate sentencing to be more strict than lenient on measures of sentencing severity.

The best data available are for federal offenders. Table 10.3 shows the evidence for three years in regard to the percentage of defendants convicted in U.S. district courts, the average length of sentence imposed, and the average time served prior to first release for current sentence. As expected, the three sets of data reveal trends indicative of increasing judicial stringency rather than leniency.

Unfortunately, comparable state-level information is not available for the same years. Table 10.4 shows that the percentage of prosecuted offenders convicted declined 2 percent between 1984 and 1988. But the average length of sentence imposed on those convicted increased by eleven months. On the other hand, the average amount of time served by state prisoners prior to first release on current offense declined by four months between 1981 and 1988. Behind this trend lies not a more charitable attitude toward prisoners but a need to alleviate the widespread prison overcrowding. As of mid-year 1990, 179 (19 percent) of the nation's state prisons were under court order to limit their populations because of crowding. The 1990 figure represents a 1 percent increase over 1984, when 123 state prisons were under a court order because of crowding (Greenfeld 1992, 9).

Table 10.3
Federal Offenders: Recent Trends in Convictions, Sentence Length, and Time Served

	1980	1985	1990
Percentage of prosecuted offenders convicted[a]	76.4	79.9	80.9
Average (mean) length (months) of sentence imposed[b]	44.3	50.7	57.2
Average (median) time (months) served prior to first release for current offense[c]	15.9	15.9	19.2

[a]. *Source: Federal Criminal Case Processing, 1980–90* (Washington, D.C.: U.S. Department of Justice, Bureau of Justice Statistics, 1992), 10.

[b]. *Source: Federal Criminal Case Processing, 1980–90*, 17.

[c]. *Source*: For 1980 and 1985. U.S. Bureau of the Census, *Statistical Abstract of the United States: 1990* (110 ed. Washington, D.C., 1990), 190; for 1990, *Federal Criminal Case Processing, 1980–90*, 18.

Behind these differences in state and federal statistical trends lie two constitutionally differentiated court systems. The various courts that handle criminal cases at each level and their interrelation are the next subject of discussion.

The Courts

After being taken into custody and "booked" (being fingerprinted, photographed, and so on), the accused is required to be taken before a magistrate without undue delay. This first court appearance is, appropriately enough, referred to as "the initial appearance." On this occasion the individual is informed of the charges against him or her, his or her constitutional rights, including the right to release pending further court action. The right to release before trial by means of bail is granted in the Eighth Amendment to the Constitution. It reads as follows: "Excessive bail shall not be required, nor excessive fines imposed, nor cruel and unusual punishments inflicted." The major varieties of bail and nonfinancially related prerelease pending further court action are contained in Box 10.1.

Table 10.4
State Offenders: Recent Trends in Convictions, Sentence Length, and Time Served

	1981	1984	1990
Percentage of prosecuted offenders convicted[a]	NA	74	NA
Average (mean) length (months) of sentence imposed[b]	NA	65	75
Average (median) time (months) served prior to first release for current prison offense[c]	17	13	13

[a]. *Sources*: For 1984: *Sourcebook of Criminal Justice Statistics—1987*, "Dispositions of Defendants in 11 States" (Washington, D.C.: Government Printing Office, 412. For 1988: *Sourcebook Of Criminal Justice Statistics—1991*, "Disposition of cases prosecuted in 14 States" (Washington, D.C.: Government Printing Office, 547.

[b]. *Sources*: For 1984: *Sourcebook Of Criminal Justice Statistics—1987*, "Average sentence length and time served for state prison releases" (Washington, D.C.: Government Printing Office, 512. For 1990: *Sourcebook Of Criminal Justice Statistics—1992*, "Average length of felony sentences imposed by State Courts" (Washington, D.C.: Government Printing Office, 1993), 529.

[c]. *Sources*: For 1981: Lawrence A, Greenfield, *Prisons and Prisoners in the United States* (Washington, D.C.: Government Printing Office, 1992), 19. For 1984: Stephanie Minor-Harper and Christopher A. Innes, "Time Served in Prison and on Parole, 1984" (Washington, D.C.: Government Printing Office, 1987), 3., For 1990: *Sourcebook Of Criminal Justice Statistics—1992*, "First releases from prisons in 34 States" (Washington, D.C.: Government Printing Office, 1993), 655.

It should be noted that all courts have limited jurisdiction; that is, the right of a court to deal with certain cases and at certain times is legally restricted. Courts that have the right to try cases are said to have original jurisdiction. Those that have appellate jurisdiction can hear requests to overturn a conviction. Some courts, for example, the U.S. Supreme Court, have both jurisdictions.

Some courts have special original jurisdiction. A magistrate's court, for example, may have the right to try cases when the matter in dispute, alleged wrongdoing or fine, does not exceed a specified dollar amount.

The concept of jurisdiction is sometimes interpreted to mean a geographical area. This is not technically correct, for it is the type of crime that determines jurisdiction, or which court has the right to hear a case, not where it was committed. The term *venue* applies to the principle of trying a case in the general area (municipality, county, state, region) where it occurred.

Box 10.1 Financial Bonds and Alternative Release Options

Financial Bonds

Fully secured bail—The defendant posts the full amount of bail with the court.

Privately secured bail—A bondsman signs a promisory note to the court for the bail amount and charges the defendant a fee for the service (usually 10% of the bail amount). If the defendant fails to appear, the bondsman must pay the court the full amount. Frequently, the bondsman requires the defendant to post collateral in addition to the fee.

Percentage bail—The courts allow the defendant to deposit a percentage (usually 10%) of the full bail with the court. The full amount of the bail is required if the defendant fails to appear. The percentage bail is returned after disposition of the case although the court often retains 1% for administrative costs.

Unsecured bail—The defendant pays no money to the court but is liable for the full amount of bail should he fail to appear.

Alternative Release Options

Release on recognizance (ROR)—The court releases the defendant on his promise that he will appear in court as required.

Conditional Release—The court releases the defendant subject to his or her following of specific conditions set by the court such as attendance at drug treatment therapy or staying away from the complaining witness.

Third party custody—The defendant is released into the custody of an individual or agency that promises to assure his appearance in court. No monetary transactions are involved in this type of release.

Citation release Arrestees are released pending their first court appearance on a written order issued by law enforcement personnel.

Source: *Report to the Nation on Crime and Justice*, 2nd ed. (Washington, D.C.: U.S. Department of Justice, Bureau of Justice Statistics 1988), 76.

Federal Courts

Article III, Section 1 of the Constitution defines the judicial branch of government as follows: "The judicial Power of the United States, shall be vested in one supreme Court, and in such inferior Courts as the Congress may from time to time ordain and establish." The U.S. Supreme Court has nine members; all are appointed by the president of the United States and are subject to confirmation by the Senate. The Court's jurisdiction is specified in Article III, Section 2 as follows:

> The judicial power of shall extend to all cases, in law and Equity, arising under this Constitution, the laws of the United States and treaties made, or which shall be made under their authority; to all cases affecting ambassadors, other public ministers and consuls.
>
> In all cases affecting ambassadors, other public ministers and consuls, and those in which a state shall be party, the supreme court shall have original jurisdiction. In all the other cases before mentioned, the supreme court shall have appellate jurisdiction, both as to law and fact, with such exceptions, and under such regulations as the Congress shall make.

The Court exercises its appellate jurisdiction much more than its original jurisdiction; indeed, according to one estimate, cases of original jurisdiction account for less than 1 percent of those heard during an average term (Waldron et al. 1980, 233). By law, a term begins the first Monday in October and lasts as long as work demands, but not usually beyond mid-June.

Beneath the Supreme Court are the federal courts of appeal, the district courts, and some specific courts. Procedures governing the activities of each and their interrelationship have been specified by the Supreme Court.

The federal courts of appeal hear cases that emanate from the district courts. Unless the Supreme Court decides to review them, all decisions made by federal appellate courts are final.

Until 1948, the federal appellate courts were called circuit courts of appeal. The nation has eleven judicial circuits; each has one federal appellate court. Depending on the workload, each has from three to nine permanent judgeships. The first ten circuits encompass the fifty states. The eleventh circuit includes only the District of Columbia.

The federal courts with original trial jurisdiction are the district courts. Each state has at least one. Again, depending on the workload, each court has from one-to-twenty-four judges. As Waldron et al. (1980, 235) point out, district courts possess original jurisdiction not only in regard to the prosecution of all cases involving federal criminal law violation but also certain civil disputes between residents of different states when the amount in question exceeds $10,000.

Crimes that demand a good deal of the attention of federal district courts involve violations of the bankruptcy, civil rights, copyright, national revenue, patent, postal, and trademark laws. Major crimes within their jurisdiction include the crossing of a state line in a stolen vehicle, kidnapping, and the killing of a president. Lastly, all crimes committed on federal property are tried in the district courts.

State Courts

As Smith and Pollack (1980, 13) tell us, there is an absence of "uniform terminology" applicable to both the state and federal courts. The terminological problem is twofold. States often use the same name for courts that try different types of cases and different names for courts that try the same types of cases. In good measure this situation reflects the fact that what is a felony in one state may be a misdemeanor in another, and vice versa. In 1973, for example, Texas regarded the possession of any quantity of marijuana as a felony punishable by a 2- to 5-year prison sentence. At the same time, marijuana smoking in Ann Arbor, Michigan, was a misdemeanor punishable by a $5 fine. Generally, however, only two types of courts handle criminal cases: those that try misdemeanors and those that try felonies. Typically, offenses such as the following are regarded as misdemeanors: drunkenness, traffic violations, simple assaults, petty theft, disorderly conduct, prostitution, and vagrancy. Major felonies include the eight Crime Index offenses: arson, murder, forcible rape, robbery, aggravated assault, burglary, larceny-theft, and motor vehicle theft.

A useful way of resolving the terminological problem has been devised by Waldron et al. (1980, 242). They classify the state courts in a four-tiered hierarchy: (1) courts of limited jurisdiction (the "minor" or "lower" or "inferior" courts); (2) trial courts of original and general jurisdiction (usually called district, circuit, or superior courts); (3) intermediate appellate courts (less than half the states); and (4) courts of last resort (usually called the Supreme Court). The first two are often referred to as "lower" courts. But the first three may be called "higher" courts. In rural areas, "courts of limited jurisdiction" usually include county courts and justices of the peace; in urban areas they would include, most often, municipal, county, and police magistrate courts.

Additionally, all states have juvenile courts. Although they handle individuals who commit crimes, they are not regarded as criminal courts.

The scene of the first juvenile court in the United States was Cook County, Illinois, in 1899. It took another quarter of a century before the founding of the second juvenile court. Traditionally, the aim of juvenile courts has been to rehabilitate rather than punish. Instead of convicting offenders, juvenile courts make individuals "wards," or dependents of their authority under the doctrine of *parens patriae* (i.e., parental substitutes).

Originally, juvenile courts dealt with young people between the ages of seven and sixteen. Today, the age range is variable. The lower limit may begin at birth. Seven is still common. At the upper limit, the general range is sixteen through nineteen.

The age at which a juvenile case may be transferred to an adult court is also variable. In fifteen states and federal districts there is no specified age. In Vermont, the age is ten; in Montana it is twelve. Georgia, Illinois, and Mississippi the age is thirteen. In fourteen state, the age is fourteen. Seven states and the District of Columbia the age is fifteen. In seven other states, age sixteen is specified. There are three ways a juvenile case may be referred to a criminal court:

1. *Concurrent jurisdiction*: The prosecutor has the discretion of filing charges for certain offenses in either juvenile or criminal courts.
2. *Excluded offenses*: The legislature excludes from juvenile court jurisdiction certain offenses usually either very minor, such as traffic or fishing violations, or very serious, such as murder or rape.
3. *Judicial waiver*: The juvenile court waives its jurisdiction and transfers the case to criminal court (the procedure is also known as "binding over" or "certifying" juvenile cases to criminal courts) (*Report to the Nation on Crime and Justice* 1988, 79).

Some cities (e.g., Chicago, Philadelphia, and New York) have both juvenile and "youth" courts. The latter have been described as adult courts guided by juvenile court principals. "They exist for youths from sixteen to nineteen or misdemeanors. Because youth courts lack exclusive jurisdiction, older boys and girls are frequently tried in the regular criminal courts" (Waldron et al. 1980, 242).

The jurisdiction of the juvenile court has long been a controversial subject. Many wish it to have jurisdiction over both those who do not commit offenses (e.g., abandoned and abused children) and those who do. Others advocate separating the two. Typically, a family court is prescribed for the one and a juvenile or youth court for the other.

Underlying the jurisdictional controversy is the difficulty of reconciling the protective and punitive functions of the juvenile court. The problem is reflected in the various ways states delegate responsibility for authoritative decision making in juvenile affairs. States that emphasize the punitive aspect grant more responsibility to the courts and the police. Those that stress protection are inclined to grant more influence to probation and welfare departments.

Regardless of the stress that may be placed on one or the other function, the juvenile courts have unusual power. They have been less constrained by due process requirements than the adult courts. Whatever the historical, logical or legal justification for this situation, it is a matter of some controversy. The 1964 *Gault* case in Arizona illustrates the point.

Fifteen-year-old Gerald Gault and a friend were taken into custody for allegedly making lewd telephone calls to a Mrs. Cook. At the first hearing, Mrs. Cook was not asked to testify, and no written record was made of the proceedings. At the second hearing, the judge denied Mrs. Gault's request for the appearance of Mrs. Cook. Subsequently, the court decided to commit Gerald Gault to the State Industrial School. As Sue Titus Reid points out,

> For this offense a fifteen-year-old boy was committed to a state institution until his majority. But the maximum legal penalty for an adult was a fine of $5 to $50 or imprisonment for a maximum of two months. An adult would be afforded due process in his trial, but a juvenile was not entitled because the state is taken to be acting in his best interests. (1976, 460)

As Reid points out, because juvenile cases could not be appealed in Arizona, a writ of **habeas corpus** was filed. The writ was denied by the superior court, and this decision was upheld by the state's supreme court. But the case was appealed to and reversed by the U.S. Supreme Court on the bases of procedural violations involving the constitutional principles of "notice of charges," "right to counsel," "right to confrontation and crossexamination," and "privilege against self-incrimination."

Gault has generated numerous reform proposals but not radical revision of the basic structure of juvenile courts. But there has been increased awareness of the need to guard against procedural violations involving the rights of alleged offenders. As is brought out in the discussion that follows, this concern, for different reasons, is as evident in the adult as the juvenile court.

Conviction

One might assume that if there has been a conviction, there has been a trial. According to the Sixth Amendment of the U.S. Constitution: "In all criminal prosecutions, the accused shall enjoy the right to a speedy and public trial, by an impartial jury of the state and district wherein the crime shall have been committed, which district shall have been previously ascertained by law, and to be informed of the nature and cause of the accusation; to be confronted with the witnesses against him; to have compulsory process for obtaining witnesses in his favor." It is generally estimated that 90 percent or more of all criminal cases are disposed of by negotiated pleas instead of trial.

If at the initial appearance or a preliminary hearing a magistrate believes there is "probable cause" that the individual(s) charged have indeed committed a crime, he or she orders the preparation of a formal charge (i.e., the preparation of a report justifying indictment) against the defendant(s). At the state level, felony indictments may be returned by prosecutors or grand juries. A grand jury indictment is compulsory at the federal level.

Indictment by grand jury is provided by the Fifth Amendment to the Constitution: "No person shall be held to answer for a capital, or otherwise infamous crime, unless on a presentment or indictment of a grand jury, except in cases arising in the land or naval forces, or in the militia, when in actual service in time of war or public danger; nor shall any person be subject for the same offense to be twice put in jeopardy of life or limb, nor shall be compelled in any criminal case to be a witness against himself, nor deprived of life, liberty, or property, without due process of law; nor shall property be taken for public use, without just compensation."

A grand jury consists of twenty-three citizens. A quorum is sixteen, but twelve votes are required for indictment.

After indictment, the accused must decide whether to plead guilty or not guilty. If guilty, he or she may choose to have the case decided by a bench or a jury trial. In the former, a judge alone determines the verdict; in the latter, the verdict is determined by a jury (the standard jury size is twelve). The number twelve is not specified in the Constitution. It is apparently based on scriptural precedent. *Duncombs Trials* (1655) provides the following account of the special meaning of the number twelve:

> If the Twelve Apostles on their twelve thrones must try us for our eternal state, good reason hath the law to appoint the number twelve to try our temporal. The tribes of Israel were twelve; the Patriarchs were twelve, and Solomon's officers were twelve. In the Exchequer Chambers there were twelve counselors of state for matters of state and he that appealed to the law must have eleven others with him who believe he says true and the law is so precise in their number of twelve that if the trial be by more less than twelve it is a mistrial. (Barnes and Teeters, 270)

However precious the right to a jury trial and the principle that one is innocent until proven guilty, the vast majority of accused felons plead guilty. Guilty pleas are prevalent for a number of reasons, but primarily because they are encouraged by the courts and their officers. The most frequently cited reason is the claim of a backlog of cases due to an increasing number of indictments, on the one hand,

and lack of public support (financial most of all) for increasing the number of judges and court personnel, on the other.

Guilty pleas generally entail a bargain. The bargain may include allowing a defendant to select which among several judges before whom to plead guilty. As Weinreb states, "since the judge who receives the plea or tries the case also imposes sentence, the defendant can hope for a lighter sentence if he pleads guilty before a judge who has a reputation for leniency; he can at least be sure of avoiding a judge who he believes would sentence him severely" (1977, 74).

Plea bargaining is routinely initiated by the lawyers involved in a case, particularly the prosecutor. According to one observer, "many prosecutors will approach a defense attorney, sometimes half in jest, and ask, "What deal are you going to be looking for?" (Jones 1979, 99). One attorney contends that bargaining generally occurs by means of "a more or less standard formula" and without "a detailed examination of the particular facts of the case" (cited in Weinreb 1977, 76–7). Another says that "most defense counsels will not enter into serious plea discussions until all of the material facts surrounding the defendant's involvement in the crimes in question have been learned, documented, and, when possible, corroborated by more than one source" (cited in Weinreb 1977, 99).

Whatever the truth, perhaps more often than many would like to admit, plea bargaining occurs for reasons other than the best interests of society or defendant. The National Advisory Commission on Criminal Justice Standards and Goals reported that a survey of some 3400 "criminal justice practitioners" (judges, probation officers, parole officers, and correctional officers) in California, Michigan, New Jersey, and Texas found that 61 percent of those responding believed it "probable or somewhat probable that most defense attorneys engage in plea bargaining primarily to expedite the movement of cases," and that 38 percent believed "it was probable or somewhat probable that most defense attorneys in plea bargaining negotiations pressure clients into entering as plea that [the] client feels is unsatisfactory" (1975, 367–68).

Some believe that the careers of many defense lawyers hinge on trying as few cases as possible. John Klein holds that negotiated pleas provide a steady income for lawyers of questionable competency, "although they are unable to give an adequate defense in an adversarial situation, they are capable of convincing a client to plead guilty and can rise to the demand of entering such a plea in the behalf of the client" (1978, 334).

Whatever the motives of those who engage in plea bargaining, its prevalence conveys the impression that one is likely to be penalized less by pleading guilty than by pleading not guilty and going to trial. The danger is that an innocent person may be encouraged to plead guilty rather than plead innocent and proceed to a trial to determine the facts in the case.

Contemporary critics of plea bargaining emphasize its possible deleterious consequences for society. Because prosecutors must give something to get someone to plead guilty, the penalty for a crime may be so reduced as to abet rather than deter its future commission. Primarily because of this and other public concerns, some jurisdictions have sought to restrict the prevalence of plea bargaining. Anti-plea-bargaining policies have been adopted in Alaska; New Orleans, Louisiana; El Paso, Texas; Blackhawk County, Iowa; Maricopa County, Arizona; Oakland County, Michigan; and Multnomah County, Oregon (*Report to the Nation on Crime and Justice* 1988, 83).

Nevertheless, with at least one notable exception, President Nixon's *National Advisory Commission on Criminal Justice Standards and Goals* (1975), which recommended abolition of negotiated pleas, most authoritative bodies (including the U.S. Supreme Court and the American Bar Association) have gone on record as accepting the practice with certain modifications. Some of the more basic changes that have been proposed include: (1) changing laws so as to "narrow the range of conduct that is declared criminal" (Weinreb 1977, 72–3); (2) better screening of cases by all investigative agencies (the police, the district attorney, the probation department); (3) earlier initiation of negotiations between prosecutors and defense counsels; (4) the entering of all guilty pleas in open court with all terms of the agreement fully stated; and (5) greater diversion of cases to appropriate treatment facilities (detoxification centers, drug abuse programs, mental treatment centers, and so on).

Each of the five proposed changes has limitations. Changing the law, for example, is easy to advocate, but difficult to accomplish. While strong arguments have been made to decriminalize offenses such as gambling and prostitution, the public mood is decidedly against liberalization of penal codes. To the contrary, the prevailing climate of opinion indicates greater support for expanding rather than reducing behavior defined as criminal.

The remaining four proposals are equally vulnerable to attack. Each may be read as providing authorities with greater power to dissuade a defendant from pleading not guilty and going to trial.

The relatively few who plead not guilty and go to trial are much more likely to be convicted than not, and are given a harsher sentence than those who plead guilty. A recent study involving twenty-six jurisdictions found their overall average (median) rate of conviction in jury trials to be 73 percent (*Report to the Nation on Crime and Justice* 1988, 84). And while sentencing patterns on this study are not reported, investigators have generally found that judges are inclined to impose more severe penalties on those convicted by trial than those who plead guilty. A prominent Brooklyn judge, for example, has stated that in his court "a defendant who pleads guilty receives mercy; a defendant who is convicted after trial receives justice" (cited in Jones 1979, 42). A colleague of the judge's reported that he imposes the minimum sentence under the law upon defendants who plead guilty, and the maximum on those convicted after trial.

Sentencing

Writing in 1972, Judge Marvin Frankel observed that although law students are taught about the criminal law, the trial process, and the rights of the accused, "they are taught by people and exposed to curricula barren of even food for thought about sentencing" (pp. 12–13). Frankel claimed that most judges are selected after twenty or thirty years of practicing law from among those who have not studied sentencing. "The most notable thing about this group," he said, "is that its members have mostly remained unencumbered by any exposure to, or learning about, the problems of sentencing" (p. 13). What chiefly concerned him at the time was the enormous powers entrusted to such individuals.

The powers Judge Frankel referred to stem largely from the institution of *indeterminate* sentencing. From the introduction of incarceration as a means of punishment in the 1790s until around 1900, offenders received fixed sentences for specified crimes. Sentencing focused on the crime committed (the offense to law, morality, and society) rather than the character of the offending individual (how best to correct or rehabilitate the offender as a unique person). In time, largely as a result of the humanitarian zeal of the reform movement, the emphasis was reversed. The reformers argued that the primary purpose of incarceration was correction and preparation for release; hence, sentencing should be flexible, something adaptable to the variable timing of individual rates of rehabilitation. What was required, then, was the replacement of determinate with indeterminate sentencing.

The first indeterminate sentencing legislation in the nation was enacted in Michigan in 1867. But by 1900, only four other states had followed suit. Fifteen years later, the majority of states had indeterminate sentencing laws. By 1960, indeterminate sentencing was a well-established practice.

Indeterminate sentencing in the United States took, and continues to take, various forms, but some combination of a minimum and/or a maximum sentence. Prominent variations include the following:

> (1) a system of both maximum (MA) and minimum (MI) terms fixed by the court (each has its own upper and lower limits set by law); (2) both MA and MI (within legal limits) fixed by court with MI not to exceed a portion of the MA; (3) MA (within limits set by law) fixed by court and MI fixed by law; (4) MA fixed by law and MI by court; (5) MA and MI fixed by law for each offense; (6) MA fixed by law but no MI in law, rather the MI is fixed by the parole board; (7) MA fixed by court, no MI; and (8) MI fixed by law and MA by the parole board. (Fogel 1975, 193)

In the 1960s, individualized punishment by means of indeterminate sentencing came under increasing criticism. Where nineteenth-century critics were deeply troubled by the harshness of determinate sentencing, 1960s reformers and radicals were disturbed by the perceived inequities produced by indeterminate sentencing.

The inequities of major concern involve disparities by area (region, state, city), court, crime, and offender characteristics, especially race and socioeconomic status. It should be mentioned that these subjects were of concern to some criminologists for several decades. In 1935, for example, Thorsten Sellin (1935, cited by Hogarth 1971, 7) called attention to the variable sentencing of native-born whites, foreign-born whites, and blacks. In 1940, McGuire and Hotzoff reported nationwide differences in sentences imposed on liquor and narcotics law violators. And in 1949, Gaudet identified inconsistent sentencing practices among judges in a single New Jersey county court. But it was in the socially volatile 1960s that the most widespread and persistent interest in detecting and correcting sentencing inequities was expressed.

During the Vietnam war, Selective Service violations, federal crimes presumably dealt with on the basis of national standards, were punished differently in different states. In Oregon, convicted offenders were generally put on probation. In Texas and Mississippi, they invariably received the maximum prison term of 5 years. Also during the 1960s, narcotics offenders were differently punished by the federal district courts. In one district, prison sentences averaged 33 months; in another the average was 74 months (Schrag 1971, 178).

By far, sentence disparities by race attracted the greatest amount of attention. Schrag (1971, 179) pointed to federal statistics showing that blacks accounted for 89 percent of those executed for rape in the United States between 1930 and 1964. Howard (1975) contended that federal and state data indicated that the death penalty was used primarily to deter the rape of white women by black men. Howard's study of rape cases in Maryland between 1960 and 1967 showed that when a prison term was involved, blacks were typically given longer sentences than whites, especially when blacks raped whites.

The latest data[1] are for 1989 and pertain to federal prisoners. The average sentence length imposed on white offenders was 51.9 months and black offenders 65.4 months. For nonfraud-related property offenses (e.g., larceny-theft and burglary), the average sentence imposed on whites was 27.4 months and blacks 24.1 months. For violent offenses, the average sentence imposed on whites was 88 months and blacks 98.4 months. For particular violent offenses such as forcible rape, the available data pertain to time served in prison for first releases for current offense in 1990. The median number of months served by whites convicted of forcible rape was 40 and for blacks 49.

A number of studies have been conducted to determine the precise connection between race of offender and sentencing (for a review of the research evidence, see Wilbanks 1987), and the results remain largely inconclusive. On the one hand, there are studies indicating that when controlling for key variables (e.g., age, income, type of offense, and offense history), the relation between race and sentencing disparities vanishes (Clarke and Koch 1976; Eisenstein and Jacobs 1972). On the other, there are those that find a relationship even after controlling for the possible effects of intervening factors (e.g., Bowers 1984; Clayton 1983).

Ideological predisposition often influences the slant taken on the subject. Consider, for example, the views of Marxist-oriented criminologist Richard Quinney, who estimated "that 1 out of every 20 black men between the ages of 25 to 34 is either in jail or prison on any given day, compared to 1 out of every 163 white men in the same age group" (1977, 138). Such evidence indicated to Quinney and other "conflict" oriented criminologists that American jails and prisons are primarily populated by the lower socioeconomic classes. In Quinney's outline of the American class structure, the lowest class is referred to as the "pauperized poor"—basically, the unemployed, a disproportionate number of whom are black. Using admissions to federal prisons for two-year periods between 1960 and 1972, Quinney found that "the number of prison admissions varies directly with the rate of unemployment" (1977, 136).

To William Chambliss, "the lower-class person is more likely to come to trial more likely to be found guilty, and if found guilty, more likely to receive harsh punishment than his middle or upper-class counterpart" (1969, 86).

Actually, few studies had been conducted to determine the bearing of class on sentencing, and as Chiricos and Waldo (1975, 755) stated at the time, "the results of these studies must be regarded as inconclusive." They measured the relationship between socioeconomic status (inmates' income, education, and occupation) and years sentenced in a study of 10,488 adult prisoners in North Carolina, South Carolina, and Florida. While Chiricos and Waldo found variation in the status positions of prisoners, they hastened to indicate that nearly 97 percent "had scores assigned which were less than 70 on a 100 point scale" (1975, 758). In other words, the 10,488 inmates did not, as they had expected, duplicate the status range one would expect to find in a general population. Simply put, the sample was skewed toward the lower end of the status continuum. Nonetheless, what their data suggested to them,

> rather conclusively is that the socioeconomic status of convicted criminal offenders is unrelated to the severity of the state's official sanction, as reflected in the length of prison terms. Such a conclusion strongly contradicts common folklore [and] the general expectations of conflict criminology." (Chiricos and Waldo 1975, 766)

Nevertheless, the sampling limitations of the study (the acknowledged fact that the inmate population represented a compressed range of the status spectrum) limit the significance of the findings. While sufficient evidence is presented to suggest that the connection between socioeconomic status and prison sentencing may not be as precise as conflict criminologists such as Quinney and Chambliss would have it, it cannot be said to have invalidated the claim that the courts punish the lower classes more severely than the upper classes. Perhaps the fairest statement to be made is that social class plays a role in sentencing, but exactly how much of a role and under what circumstances remains an open empirical question.

Some contend that the status differential between judges and offenders contributes to sentencing disparity. The evidence is that judges are drawn primarily from the middle to uppermiddle classes and offenders (primarily those charged with serious "street" crimes such as robbery) from the lower social classes. Some have hypothesized that middle-class judges should be expected to protect their class interests and impose their values on lower-class offenders by giving them relatively harsh sentences. In a study of sentencing in England, Hood (1962, cited by Hogarth 1971, 9) found that "middle-class magistrates dealing with working-class offenders in relatively small and stable communities, are likely to be relatively severe [in the sentences they impose]." But Hogarth's detailed study of Canadian magistrates produced evidence of a different sort. He found magistrates from upper-middle-class backgrounds to be more reformative than punitive oriented. "In contrast," he said, "magistrates from working class backgrounds appear to be rather more 'punitive' in their attitudes and beliefs" (1971, 212). This too is a subject requiring much more empirical scrutiny before conclusions are drawn one way or the other.

Of all the factors that may influence sentencing disparities, the one easiest to document has been outmoded and internally inconsistent penal codes. For example, the 1967 report of the *President's Commission on Law Enforcement and the Administration of Justice* refers to "a recent study of the Colorado statutes [which] disclosed that a person convicted of first degree murder must serve 10 years before becoming eligible for parole, while a person convicted of a lesser degree of the same offense must serve 15 or more years; stealing a dog is punishable by 10 years imprisonment, while killing a dog carries a maximum of 6 months" (p.142).

In 1970, Low identified inconsistencies in the Federal Criminal Code such as the following:

> Armed bank robbery is punishable by fine, probation, or any term of imprisonment up to twenty-five years. Armed robbery of a post office poses the single choice of probation or twenty-five years imprisonment. (1970, 328–29)

To Low, such inconsistencies are invariably "the product of ad hoc response to particular situations" (1977, 327). Judge Frankel put it this way: "Written at the random, accidental times when particular evils come to be perceived, the statutes are not harmonized or coordinated with each other" (1972, 9).

The 1967 presidential crime commission identified other penal code defects, most of which emanated from indeterminate sentencing. The commission referred to problems created when codes specify mandatory minimum and high maximum sentences. Mandatory minimums were alleged to compromise justice by encouraging judges who find such sentences inappropriate to dismiss cases and acquit offenders. High maximums were found wanting because they led to the granting of excessive decision making authority to parole boards. "When there is a gap between the earliest possible date for granting parole and the maximum sentence, the dangers of unfairness to individual prisoners are evident" (President's Commission 1967, 142).

An important theme that underlies the commission's critique of penal code deficiencies is that more emphasis should be given to making the punishment fit the crime. The commission's recommended penal code revisions include clearly and concisely grading crimes by seriousness so that appropriate degrees of punishment may be applied, increasing the sentencing powers of judges and decreasing those of parole boards, and specifying criteria to help judges make sentencing decisions on the basis of specified standards.

By the late 1960s, then, indeterminate sentencing was increasingly under fire for its emphasis on sentencing offenders rather than offenses. Where late-nineteenth-century reformers thought it immoral and unjust to impose flat sentences, to disregard the individuality behind a given offense and different rates of rehabilitation, late-twentieth-century reformers thought it illogical and inequitable to impose different sentences for the same crime on different individuals. Individual sentencing had become perceived as a means of discriminating against the poor and/or minorities. The perceived way to solve the problem was to replace indeterminate with determinate sentencing, to emphasize "fair and just" sentencing of offenses rather than offenders. The new "justice" model rejected the validity of rehabilitation-oriented sentencing in favor of sentencing based on the imposition of "just deserts," of making the punishment fit the crime.

Justice and Determinate Sentencing

The principle of making the punishment fit the crime is, of course, the backbone of the eighteenth-century utilitarian penal theory espoused by Beccaria and Bentham. Its twentieth-century American advocates were much in evidence by the mid–1970s. Their starting point was and continues to be the alleged failure of established means—indeterminate sentencing and parole—to accomplish their intended goal of rehabilitation. Although not necessarily inclined to reject rehabilitation efforts completely, they tend to stress societal protection as the goal of what they consider to be a realistically oriented penal code. In the words of James Q. Wilson,

> Now suppose we abandon entirely the rehabilitation theory of sentencing and corrections—not the effort to rehabilitate, just the theory that the governing purpose is to rehabilitate. Instead, we would view the correctional system as having a different function—namely, to isolate and to punish. It is a measure of our confusion that such a statement will strike many enlightened readers today as cruel, even barbaric. It is not. It is merely a recognition that society at a minimum must be able to protect itself from dangerous offenders, and to impose some costs (other than the stigma and inconvenience of an arrest and court appearance) on criminal acts; it is also a frank admission that society really does not know how to do much else. (1975, 172–73)

In 1976, Franklin Zimring, after noting that the criminal justice system was under attack by diverse segments of the population, detected an emerging consensus as to the preferred direction of reform—"reducing discretion and the widespread disparity that is its shadow, abolishing parole decisions based on whether a prisoner can convince a parole board that he has been 'reformed,' and creating a system in which punishment depends much more importantly than at present on the seriousness of the particular offense" (1976, 13). As Zimring saw it, the reformers include many more concerned with the implementation of the principle of "fair and just punishment" than the utilitarian goal of crime control and community protection. A leading "justice as fairness" viewpoint was introduced by David Fogel. He advocated flat sentencing, the abolition of parole, and the abolition of the "fortress prison."

Fogel rejected parole because he thought it unjustifiably plays a more important role in sentencing than courts; it is a decision making process that is not adversarially based and "rarely reversible" (1975, 176). Essentially, he argued that indeterminate sentencing is inimical to both rehabilitation and justice because it is basically ruleless. According to Fogel,

> Prison life is largely a product of the anomie of sentencing and paroling. Like both, it too is effectively ruleless. How could it be otherwise with 95% of its prisoners unable to calculate when they will be released or even what is demanded of them for release candidacy by parole authorities. (1975, 199)

As Fogel saw it, a new conception of sentencing was needed, one based on the premise that "a penal sanction should only mean a temporary deprivation of liberty." Correlatively, the prison should be responsible "for executing the sentence, not for rehabilitating the convict." Prisoners should have all the volitional rights of any free citizen, including the right to select their own treatment program.

To support his conception, Fogel advocated replacing indeterminate with determinate sentencing. Felonies would be classified by seriousness and a series of fixed or flat sentences imposed, "with a narrow range in mitigation or aggravation allowed around that definite figure to permit adjustments either for the facts of a particular case or for the seriousness of the offense as compared to others in the same class" (Fogel, 254). To provide prisoners with an incentive for good behavior, Fogel would include provision for good-time credit.

Although his ideas on determinate sentencing parallel Fogel's in most respects, Andrew von Hirsch's reform measures stress the theme of punishment based on "just deserts." According to von Hirsch, sentencing and corrections have been based on four different notions: rehabilitation, incapacitation, deterrence, and desert. He emphasizes the last on the assumption that it is "the fundamental requirement of justice." The principle, he says, is based on two implicit postulates: the more serious the crime, the more severe the punishment; and crimes equally serious should receive the same punishment. The two measures of seriousness are the amount of harm done or risked and extent of individual culpability.

As with Fogel, von Hirsch prefers that sentences be flat and determined only after trial. But he and his colleague Kathleen Hanrahan assert that they are less concerned with who or what imposes sentence than that sentences be based on explicitly detailed standards.

While von Hirsch and Hanrahan believe that parole "in its present form" should be abolished, they think that parole boards should be retained. Echoing Fogel, they reject parole because parole decisions do not necessarily entail due process and because the ability to predict the probability of recidivism and accurate assessment of a prisoner's rehabilitative progress—two basic parole board functions—are "beyond our present capacities" (1981). Nevertheless, they grant the parole board a reprieve because it performs the important function of modifying sentence length, especially in instances where an unrealistically long sentence has been imposed.

Von Hirsch and Hanrahan think the future of determinate sentencing hinges on the quality of the sentencing guidelines devised by legislatures or their designated agents (e.g., a sentencing commission). Two states with commissions (whose members include judges, prosecutors, defense attorneys, other public officials, and private citizens) that have developed guidelines in a similar format and that von Hirsch and Hanrahan approve of are Minnesota and Pennsylvania.

In both, the guidelines are based on the identification of criteria for scoring offense seriousness and offenders' criminal history. The scores form the vertical and horizontal axes of a two-dimensional matrix. The cell where the two scores intersect contains the prescribed sentence. According to von Hirsch and Hanrahan, the cell may recommend a range of prison time. When this occurs, judges are free to select any term within the range they deem appropriate. Moreover, if the cell does not prescribe incarceration, the sentence of choice should not be imprisonment. In all instances, however, judges are free to modify the prescribed sentence if they believe mitigating or aggravating circumstances are involved.

The sentencing schemes of Minnesota and Pennsylvania approximate what von Hirsch and Hanrahan refer to as a *modified desert model*; that is, the commensurate desert principle is modified depending on the emphasis placed in sentencing on rehabilitation, incapacitation, or deterrence. They prefer a *strict desert model*, one that does not permit deviation from sentencing based on the seriousness of the offense committed. Nonetheless, modified forms were adopted in the first states to adopt determinate sentencing: California, Indiana, Illinois, and Maine. They were joined later by Alaska, Colorado, Connecticut, Florida, Georgia, New Jersey, New Mexico, New York, North Carolina, Oklahoma, Oregon, South Carolina, Washington, Wisconsin, and the federal government.

Michael Tonry (1987, 78–9) has identified three general categories of determinate sentencing laws. The first is one that abolishes parole release but does not establish new standards for guiding judicial sentencing. Maine is the only state that fits this category.

The second category is one that specifies sentencing standards. California and North Carolina are prominent examples. In both states, *presumptive* sentencing is the standard. That is, for all offenses, not only is a presumed sentence specified, but also a presumed sentence when there are certain mitigating or aggravating circumstances. In both states, the standards are specified by the state legislature. Determinate sentencing laws in the third category involve "only very general" sentencing standards (Illinois, Indiana, and Arizona). According to Tonry,

> the move towards statutory determinate sentencing seems now to have ended, perhaps because ten years' experience suggests that presumptive sentencing guidelines developed by a sentencing commission are a much more effective means for establishing and enforcing comprehensive system-wide sentencing standards. No jurisdiction to my knowledge, has adopted a statutory determinate sentencing law in the last few years. Several jurisdictions, including South Carolina, Wisconsin, New York, Maine, and the federal system have established sentencing commissions." (1987, 79)

The U.S. Sentencing Reform Act of 1984 authorized the creation of a commission to develop sentencing guidelines. Since November 1, 1987, federal offenders have been sentenced under commission guidelines based on offense seriousness and offender criminal history. As Douglas McDonald and Kenneth Carlson describe it,

> Under the guidelines Federal prisoners are no longer released from prison to parole by the U.S. Parole Commission. Instead, judges impose prison sentences that are served in full, except for time off that prisoners earn for good behavior. Offenders are supervised following their release from prison only if a judge requires it as a part of the sentence. (1992, 1)

Whatever its form, the general pattern has been for determinate sentencing to be associated with an increase in the number of offenders sentenced to prison and a decrease in imposed sentence length. Determinate sentencing has not, as some of its early advocates said, led to a reduction in the size of prison populations. To the contrary, for prison overcrowding is a general condition in the United States, and it is as prevalent in jurisdictions with determinate as indeterminate sentencing.

A major reason for the stalling of the movement from indeterminate to determinate sentencing has been the need to retain a paroling authority as a safety valve to alleviate prison overcrowding. Jurisdictions generally have responded to the public pressure to punish offenders more severely by increasing the frequency of prison sentences, including *mandatory* sentencing. As one notes in Box 10.2, *mandatory* sentencing is not determinate sentencing. Drug offenses have been those most often given mandatory sentences, and prison overcrowding is more often than not attributed to a rapid increase in the number of mandatory-sentenced drug offenders nationwide.

To summarize, if the goal were to increase sentence severity, to institute "just desert" sentencing, it was (is) as effectively accomplished by indeterminate as determinate sentencing. As Michael Tonry reasons,

> Prison populations have increased substantially since 1980 both in states that have revised their sentencing institutions and those that have not. My view—which is no more than a guess—is that prison population increases have resulted much more from changes in public and officials' attitudes about appropriate punishments than from changes in sentencing laws and institutions. (1987, 4)

Box 10.2 Sentencing Glossary

Indeterminate sentences—usually provide a minimum and a maximum term, either of which may be reduced by "good time" (time credits gained by inmates for good conduct or special achievement) or by a decision of the paroling authorities. The maximum sentence may be set as a range (for example, 5 to 10 years) rather than a specific number of years.

Determinate sentences—usually provide a fixed term that may be reduced by good time or parole. Judicial discretion may be available to grant probation or suspend the sentence. Sentencing laws generally provide a maximum (or a range) for sentence duration. Determinate systems are usually based on a definite length for a sentence that can be increased or decreased for aggravating or mitigating factors or on guidelines that define sentence lengths, deviations from which must be justified by sentencing judges.

Mandatory prison sentences—are defined by law and must be given upon conviction; the judge is not permitted to grant probation or to suspend the sentence. Most States apply a combination of sentencing strategies. Many States may have a pedominant orientation toward one strategy (for example, indeterminate) and require another strategy (for example, mandatory sentences) for specific offenses. The strategies utilized by States are constantly evolving, thus complicating overall classification.

Source: *Report to the Nation on Crime and Justice*, 2nd ed. (Washington, D.C.: U.S. Department of Justice, Bureau of Justice Statistics, 1988), 91.

The Death Penalty

The trend toward harsher sentencing included renewed interest in the imposition of the death penalty. In 1972, in *Furman* v. *Georgia*, the U.S. Supreme Court ruled the death penalty in violation of the Eighth Amendment prohibition against the imposition of cruel and unusual punishment. Four years later, the Court approved the death penalty in states with capital crime statutes requiring consideration of aggravating and mitigating circumstances.

Currently, 38 jurisdictions (37 states and the Federal government) permit capital punishment. From 1977 through 1993, 226 individuals (121 whites, 53.5 percent; 87 blacks, 38.4 percent; 16 Hispanics, 7.0 percent; and 2 Native Americans, 0.8 percent) were executed. In 1993, 38 prisoners were executed, the largest number in any year since 1977. The average time served by these 38 individuals since receiving the death penalty was 9 years and 5 months.

As of December 31, 1993, 2,716 prisoners were being held on death rows in 34 states and the Federal prison system. According to the Bureau of Justice Statistics, among those sentenced to death 2 in 3 had a prior felony conviction; nearly 1 in 10 had a prior homicide conviction. About 2 in 5 inmates sentenced to death had a criminal justice status when they committed their capital offense: About half of these were on parole and half included persons with charges pending, on probation, in prison or escaped from prison. (Stephan and Brien, 1).

In 1993, the minimum age eligible for capital punishment ranged from none specified (in eight states) to age eighteen (eleven states and the Federal system). Seventeen states have a minimum age under eighteen (age 10 in one state, age 14 in two states, age 15 in one, age 16 in nine, and age 17 in four).

The preferred methods of execution are lethal injection (22 states), electrocution (12 states), lethal gas (7 states), hanging (3 states), and firing squad (2 states). Some states authorize two forms of execution. In Utah, for example, the offender may choose between lethal injection or a firing squad.

Table 10.5 identifies the number of individuals executed by jurisdiction between 1930 and year-end 1993.

Capital punishment is among the most enduring debatable social issues. Those who favor it invariably invoke the Old Testament principle of an "eye for an eye." Those opposed tend to object to all killing, and are content to impose life sentences on convicted killers (for a provocative discussion of the different Christian positions on the death penalty, see Sister Helen Prejean's, *Dead Man Walking*). Some oppose the death penalty because they believe it to be practiced in a racially and economically discriminating manner. A disproportionate number of those executed tend to be poor and black. All too many of those on death row had to rely on a public defender or a court appointed attorney to defend them. The low quality of legal defense is reflected in the number of death sentences overturned by state appellate courts or the U.S. Supreme Court. Between 1973 and 1993, 1,785 of 4,984 convictions (36 percent) were overturned (Stephan and Brien, 1994, 12). The O.J. Simpson murder trial is interesting for a number of reasons, not the least of which are its economic and racial elements. If Simpson had not been an affluent celebrity, it is highly doubtful that the prosecution would have declined to seek the death penalty. That he is black and put on trial in a highly racially sensitive city must also be considered to be an imporant mitigating factor. Had he been poor as well as black, one would predict that he would receive a death penalty conviction in relatively short order.

Intermediate Sanctions

Propelled by a continuing rise in both the nationwide prison population and rate of serious crime, contemporary sentencing reformers advocate expanded

Table 10.5
Number of Persons Executed by State, 1930–93

State	Number Executed: Since 1930	Since 1977
U.S. Total	4,085	226
Georgia	383	17
Texas	368	71
New York	329	
California	294	2
North Carolina	268	5
Florida	202	32
Ohio	172	
South Carolina	166	4
Mississippi	158	4
Louisiana	154	21
Pennsylvania	152	
Alabama	145	10
Arkansas	122	4
Virginia	114	22
Kentucky	103	
Tennessee	93	
Illinois	91	1
New Jersey	74	
Missouri	73	11
Maryland	68	
Oklahoma	63	3
Washington	48	1
Colorado	47	
Indiana	43	2
Arizona	41	3
West Virgina	40	
District of Columbia	40	
Nevada	34	5
Federal system	33	
Massachusetts	27	
Connecticut	21	
Oregon	19	
Iowa	18	
Utah	17	4
Kansas	15	
Delaware	15	3
New Mexico	8	
Wyoming	8	1
Montana	6	
Vermont	4	
Nebraska	4	
Idaho	3	
South Dakota	1	
New Hampshire	1	
Wisconsin	0	
Rhode Island	0	
North Dakota	0	
Minnesota	0	
Michigan	0	
Maine	0	
Hawaii	0	
Alaska	0	

Source: *Capital Punishment 1993*. Bureau of Justice Statistics Bulletin. Government Printing Office (Washington, D.C., December 1944), p. 11

use of what they refer to as *intermediate* sanctions. By intermediate is meant sentences between the extreme of probation at one end and imprisonment at the other.[2] Intermediate sanctions include house arrest, intensive probationary supervision, boot camps, electronic monitoring, split sentences, day reporting centers, fines, and community service orders. According to James Byrne *et al.* (1992, ix), the ostensible aims of intermediate sanctions are to reduce sentencing costs, improve community protection, deter crime, and rehabilitate offenders. Citing Morris and Tonry (1990), Byrne and colleagues add that their unstated purposes include creating the appearance of correctional reform, creating a means for maintaining and expanding probation and parole, and providing a means for correctional administrators to counter the punitive orientation of the general public.

Box 10.3 Probation

The word "probation" is derived from the Latin *probare*, which means to test or prove. In the legal sense, the OED defines probation as "a system of dealing with...persons found guilty of crimes of lesser gravity, and especially with first offenders, wherein these, instead of being sent to prison or otherwise punished, are released on suspended sentence during good behaviour, and placed under the supervision of a probation officer, who acts as a friend and adviser, but who, in case of the failure of the probationer to fulfill the terms of his probation, can report him back to the court for the execution of the sentence originally imposed."

The first statute authorizing probationary sentencing was enacted in Massachusetts in 1878. It provided for the hiring of a probation officer to identify and supervise those "who may reasonably be expected to be reformed without punishment."

The origin of probation in Boston can be traced to 1841 and the exemplary efforts of one John Augustus, a local cobbler. While attending a session in Boston's police court, Augustus offered to stand bail for a man charged as a drunkard. The court granted the request but required the defendant's reappearance for sentencing in three weeks. At his reappearance, he evidenced such a positive change that instead of being sentenced to the House of Corrections, the usual penalty, he was fined one cent and required to pay court costs. This was merely the first of Augustus's many successes. Over the next several years, he vouched for and aided nearly 2000 men, women, and children charged with a variety of offenses.

But even after successful initiation, probation took time to establish and spread. After the enactment of the first statute in Boston, another thirteen years elapsed before probation became a statewide practice in Massachusetts. Juvenile probation in every state was not available until 1925. And adult probation did not exist in every state until 1956. The federal probation law was passed in 1925. In the absence of indisputable precedents, judges and lawyers found it difficult to reconcile probationary sentencing with established practices and concepts. Nevertheless, the principle prevailed, and despite its many critics, probation continues to be a, if not *the* major, sentencing component of the criminal justice system.

To a limited degree, intermediate sanctions have been long employed. What contemporary sentence reformers are calling for is their expanded use and systematic integration in a comprehensive sentencing plan combining elements from both determinate and indeterminate sentencing. The aim is to create a balance between punishing offenses (via the principle of "just deserts" or neoutilitarianism) and correcting offenders (to deter crime and protect communities by sentencing which promotes constructive binding ties between the offender and the community).

Box 10.4 Types of Intermediate Sanctions

Boot Camps: Programs lasting from 90 to 100 days generally for younger male and female felons, stressing discipline, physical conditioning, counseling, and basic education.

Community service: Unpaid public-service orders given to both "street" and white-collar offenders for a number of reasons, but especially restitution and rehabilitation.

Electronic monitoring: The use of devices, frequently located on the wrist or ankle, for maintaining contact with released offenders and checking on their behavior.

Fines: Fee payments as a form of public restitution and victim compensation.

House arrest: Confinement to one's home for limited periods, such as evening hours after work or around the clock.

Intensive probationary supervision: A form of probation requiring more frequent contact with offenders and the monitoring of required terms.

Split sentences: Combinations of incarceration and probation or parole.

The most comprehensive intermediate punishments rationale to date has been proposed by Morris and Tonry. They advocate a sentencing scheme based on the *interchangeability* of punishments, the notion that different punishments should be regarded as equivalent "just deserts." They acknowledge the difficulty of precisely establishing equivalency of different punishments but believe the effort is necessary if both sentencing justice and fairness are to be served. "A comprehensive sentencing system must harness," they say, "the tension between the requirement of fairness that there be general standards that apply to all and the requirement of justice that all legitimate grounds for distinguishing between individuals be taken into account when decisions about individuals are made" (Morris and Tonry 1990, 42). The basic elements in their vision of an effective and just comprehensive sentencing system include a range of punishments, a clearly defined sense of interchangeable punishments, and the application of presumptive sentencing structured by guidelines developed by sentencing commissions.

A basic criticism of the use of intermediate sanctions is that instead of being used as sentencing alternatives for those who would normally be punished, they are applied to those who would otherwise be treated more leniently. In other words, instead of being used to treat a traditional offender population, intermediate sanctions may be used to "widen the net" of those subjected to formal punishment. Morris and Tonry acknowledge the danger of "net widening" but argue that

> For judges and prosecutors who must decide what punishments should be imposed, the creation of a new program offering an alternative to incarceration may allow a judge to avoid doing nothing in cases in which, for whatever reasons, incarceration seems too severe. In the mind of that judge, sentencing an offender to the alternative program is not an inappropriate extension of state power over an offender who would otherwise not have been incarcerated; it is the imposition of nontrivial punishment on a person for whom this is the appropriate punishment. (1990 228–29)

Summary and Conclusion

With prison populations continuing to rise, it will be difficult to avoid increasing use of intermediate sentencing and broadening sentencing discretion. Added fuel for movement in this direction is the need to control spending the increasingly stretched public treasury on the expansion of existing and the construction of new prisons.

The pressure to enlarge sentencing discretion and alternatives compromises the deterrent power of determinate sentencing. Discretion to impose intermediate sentences would appear to mitigate both the certainty and severity of punishment, two cornerstones of deterrence-based determinate sentencing. Truly effective deterrence in a complex democratic society such as the United States is difficult to accomplish. Passing "tough" laws, such as the Rockefeller drug statute in New York State (it called for 15–year and even life sentences for drug pushers), deter their enforcement more than offenders. "As penalties get tougher," laments James Q. Wilson, "defendants and their lawyers have a greater incentive to slow down the process, and those prosecutors and judges who oppose heavy sentences for drug dealing may use their discretionary powers to decline indictment, accept plea bargains, grant continuances, and modify penalties in ways that reduce the certainty and celerity of punishment" (1983, 135).

Such an admission does not, of course, deter Wilson's commitment to deterrence theory and determinate sentencing. As he writes,

> Does the experience under the Rockefeller law disprove the claim that deterrence works? Not at all. If we mean by "deterrence" changing behavior by increasing either the certainty or swiftness of punishment, then the Rockefeller law, as it was administered, could not have deterred behavior because it made no change in the certainty of punishment and actually reduced the swiftness of it. (1983, 134–35)

But Wilson does not proceed to examine the essential prerequisites to increasing the certainty and celerity of punishment. To do so would inevitably entail advocating massive enlargement of policing, the creation of a police state and the virtual demise of democracy. Instead, Wilson opts for incapacitation, taking more active, but particularly the most active, offenders out of circulation more often by increasing prison sentences. This is what has occurred and contributed to nationwide prison overcrowding without any significant reduction in either the amount or the rate of serious crime.

What is to be learned here is that there is no simple fix to the crime problem. Certainly sentencing reform based on either indeterminate or determinate theory is not up to the task. Crime is at bottom an expression of basic societal and cultural ills. Invariably, proposed solutions entail ideological commitments rationalizing vested interests. As liberal critics Cullen and Gilbert put it,

> it is illusory to believe that progress in the administration of justice can be secured—particularly in a conservative social climate—through such easy remedies as determinate sentencing. The intimate link between crime, punishment, and society means that true crimi-

nal justice ultimately awaits true social justice, and that meaningful improvements in a criminal justice system located in an inequitable society are only attained through concerted efforts that guard carefully against the corrupting influences of prevailing interests. (1982, 185)

References

Adams, Thomas F., Gerald Buck, and Don Hallstrom.1974. *Criminal Justice Organization and Management.* Santa Monica, Calif.: Goodyear.

Barnes, Harry Elmer and Negley K. Teeters. 1959. *New Horizons in Criminology.* Englewood Cliffs, N.J.: Prentice-Hall, Inc.

Bowers, W.J. 1984. *Legal Homicide: Death as a Punishment in America,1864–1982.* Boston: Northeastern University Press.

Byrne, James M., Arthur J. Lurigio, and Joan Petersilia, Eds. 1992. *Smart Sentencing: The Emergence of Intermediate Sanctions.* Newbury Park, California: Sage.

Chambliss, William J. 1969. *Crime and the Legal Process.* New York: McGraw-Hill.

Chiricos, Theodore G., and Gordon P. Waldo. 1975. "Socioeconomic Status and Criminal Sentencing: An Empirical Assessment of a Conflict Proposition." *American Sociological Review* 40 753–72.

Cullen, Francis T., and Karen E. Gilbert. 1982. *Reaffirming Rehabilitation.* Cincinnati, Ohio: Anderson.

Clarke, S.H., and G. Koch. 1976. "The Influence of Income and Other Factors on Whether Criminal Defendants Go to Prison." *Law and Society Review* 11 57–92.

Clayton, Obie.1983. "A Reconsideration of the Effect of Race in Criminal Sentencing." *Criminal Justice Review* 8 15–20.

Eisenstein, J., and H. Jacobs. 1972. *Felony Justice: An Organizational Analysis of Criminal Courts.* Boston: Little, Brown.

Fogel, David. 1975.*We Are the Living Proof.* Cincinnati, Ohio: Anderson.

Frankel, Marvin E. 1972. *Criminal Sentences.* New York: Hill and Wang.

Gaudet, F.J. 1949. "The Sentencing Behavior of the Judge." In *Encyclopedia of Criminology* edited by V. Brandom and S. Katash. New York: Philosophical Library, 449–61.

Greenfeld, Lawrence A. 1992."Prisons and Prisoners in the United States." Washington, D.C.: U.S. Department of Justice, Bureau of Justice Statistics.

Hirsch, Andrew von and Kathleen J. Hanrahan.1981. "Determinate Penalty Systems in America: An Overview." *Crime and Delinquency* 27 289–316.

Hogarth, John.1971. *Sentencing as a Human Process.* Toronto: The University of Toronto Press.

Hood, Roger. 1962. *Sentencing in Magistrates Courts: A Study in Variation in Policy.* London: Stevens.

Howard, Joseph C. 1975. "Racial Discrimination in Sentencing." *Judicature* 59 120–25.

Jones, David A. 1979. *Crimes Without Punishment.* Lexington, Mass.: Lexington Books.

Klein, John F.1978. "Inducements to Plead Guilty: Frontier Justice Revisited." In *Readings in Criminology* edited by Peter Wickman and Phillip Whitten. Lexington, Mass.: D.C. Heath, 333–47.

Low, Peter. 1970. "The Sentencing Structure." In *The Criminal in the Arms of the Law* Volume 2 edited by Sir Leon Radzinowicz and Marvin E. Wolfgang. New York: Basic Books, 525–39.

Maguire, Kathleen and Timothy J. Flanagan. 1991. *Sourcebook of Criminal Justice Statistics 1990.* U.S. Department of Justice, Bureau of Justice Statistics, Washington, DC: Government Printing Office.

McDonald, Douglas C. and Kenneth E. Carlson. 1992. "Federal Sentencing in Transition, 1986–90." Bureau of Justice Statistics Special Report. Washington, D.C.: Government Printing Office.
McGuire, Matthew F. and A. Holtzoff. 1940. "The Problem of Sentencing in the Criminal Law." *Boston University Law Review* 413 724–33.
Morris, Norval and Michael Tonry. 1990.*Between Prison and Probation: Intermediate Punishments in a Rational Sentencing System*. New York: Oxford University Press.
The National Advisory Commission on Criminal Justice Standards and Goals. 1975. *A National Strategy to Reduce Crime*. New York: Avon.
The President's Commission on Law Enforcement and the Administration of Justice. 1967. *The Challenge of Crime in a Free Society*. Washington, D.C.: Government Printing Office.
Powers, Edwin.1973. *The Basic Structure of The Administration of Criminal Justice in Massachusetts*. Boston, Mass.: Massachusetts Correctional Association.
Prejean, Sister Helen. 1994. *Dead Man Walking*. New York: Random House.
Reid, Sue Titus. 1976. *Crime and Criminology*. Hinsdale, Ill.: The Dryden Press.
Report to the Nation on Crime and Justice. 1988. Washington, D.C.: U.S. Department of Justice, Bureau of Justice Statistics.
Schrag, Clarence. 1971. *Crime and Justice: American Style*. Rockville, Maryland: National Institute of Mental Health.
Sellin, Thorsten. 1935. "Race Prejudice in the Administration of Justice." *American Journal of Sociology* 41 212–17.
Smith, Alexander B. and Harriet Pollack. 1980. *Criminal Justice*. New York: Holt, Rinehart and Winston.
Stephan, James and Peter Brien. 1994. "Capital Punishment in 1993." Bureau of Justice Statistics Bulletin. Washington, D.C. Government Printing Office.
Tonry, Michael H. 1987. *Sentencing Reform Impacts*. U.S. Department of Justice, National Institute of Justice. Washington, D.C.: Government Printing Office.
Uniform Crime Reports. 1992. Washington, D.C.: Government Printing Office.
Waldron, Ronald J., Jagdish G. Uppal, Chester L. Quarles, R. Paul McCauley, Hilary Harper, Robert L. Frazier, James C. Benson, and John R. Altemose.1980. *The Criminal Justice System*. Boston: Houghton Mifflin.
Weinreb, Lloyd L. 1977. *Denial of Justice*. New York: Free Press.
Wilbanks, William. 1987.*The Myth of a Racist Criminal Justice System*. Monterey, Calif.: Brooks/Cole.
Wilson, James Q. 1979. "Changing Criminal Sentences." In AnnualEditions, *Readings in Criminal Justice 79/80*. Guilford, Conn.: Dushkin.
———. James Q. 1983. *Thinking About Crime*, Revised Edition. New York: Basic Books.
Zimring, Franklin E. 1976. "Making the Punishment Fit the Crime." *Hastings Center Report* (December).

Notes

[1]. *Sourcebook of Criminal Justice Statistics—1992* (Washington, D.C.: Department of Justice, Bureau of Justice Statistics, Government Printing Office, 1993), 492.

[2]. Most offenders under correctional supervision in the United States are on probation. In 1990, 61 percent (2,670,234) of the nation's total correctional population (4,350,000) was on probation; the nation's prisons contained 745,157 inmates, U.S. Department of Justice, Bureau of Justice Statistics, *Probation and Parole 1990*, Washington, D.C.: Government Printing Office, 1991, 5.

Chapter 11

Prisons, Punishment, and Correctional Processes

> Being in a prison is like living a life of opposites, all at the same time. You know you gotta help yourself, but you can't give in to the bulls. . . . . You wanna do your own time, but they never let ya'. Some days you get tested every minute and all you're thinkin' is, "How can I stay out of trouble?" Sometimes you need to be tough, even when you know it will only mess ya' up. Like, you can be angry, scared and sad, all at once. . . . Even living with 700 other guys, you get lonely and have no one to talk to. . . . You wanna be on the outside and you know you're scared of what will happen when you get there.
>
> —A jailed inmate, California, 1993

Turmoil—sometimes visible, often silent—has always been present in America's prison institutions. At the individual level, turmoil is manifested in the form of a personal dilemma on how to reconcile the contrasting demands of the official rules of prison life and the powerful norms of the inmate subculture with personal needs of autonomy and self-identity. Within the inmate society itself, constant struggles among inmate groups—some based on race and ethnic identity, others on sexual activity and "prison ideology"—compete for power and advantages within the prison community. Even more visible is the intrinsic tension between the inmates and prison management, which, notwithstanding penal philosophy about corrections and rehabilitation, takes the form of an adversarial relationship between the "keepers" and the "kept."

Yet, if there is turmoil within the prison community, so too has this been true in the society at large. As early as the colonial period, jails and prisons at times have been center stage for an ongoing public debate about how to deal with those who violate criminal laws and how prisons fit into the solution. Should prisons punish, rehabilitate, or accomplish some combination of both? Some have argued for harsh treatment, including corporal punishment, accorded to convicted criminals as just compensation for their harm to victims and for the damage caused to the social order. Others have pleaded for prisons that operate with humanity and promote rehabilitation of inmates on grounds that it is "morally right" and ultimately more cost-effective. Still others have argued that the prison system should be dismantled altogether, in favor of other forms of confinement, punishment, treatment, and rehabilitation.

Although there are countless positions and dimensions in this historic debate, never has there been a clear winner. While those favoring philosophies of harsh punishment have probably held the upper hand over much of the past two centuries, neither have they been immune to the arguments nor unaffected by the influence of movements seeking prison reforms. In reality, prison institutions in America have evolved as a combination of forces—philosophical, ideological, social, political, and economic. However removed and isolated traditional prisons may seem from the mainstream of community life, prison institutions nevertheless are influenced by the public mood, by community opinions about and tolerance of crime and criminals, and by public views about how they should operate. Collectively these forces create the circumstances by which prisons have changed over the years, including how institutional tension and turmoil are played out.

This chapter explains how prisons have changed historically over the years and offers readers a discussion of four major topics: (1) the organization and structure of modern correctional institutions, including treatment approaches and rehabilitation programs; (2) parole and community-based corrections (3) the crisis of HIV/AIDS in correctional institutions; and (4) the social organization of the inmate society.

American Prisons in Historical Perspective

Although the development of large prisons serving wide geographical areas, such as regions or states, and the concept of mass imprisonment are distinctly American inventions, the evolution of the U.S. prison system has its roots in England. Before the Revolutionary War, the colonies had common jails similar to those in England (Gillin, 1935). Both in England and in the colonies, the earliest jails served primarily as centers for detaining prisoners awaiting trial, rather than as a form of punishment per se. Capital and corporal punishments—death, mutilation, branding, and flogging—awaited those convicted of crimes. Many of the corporal punishments borrowed by the colonies, such as chains or shackles, the bridle or gag, the ducking stool, or the pillory and stocks (which involved affixing the offender's head, feet, and hands to the pillory), had been practiced in England for decades or centuries. Such practices persisted throughout the colonial period, but began to be curtailed somewhat after the Declaration of Independence (Tappan 1960, 601–3).

The autonomy gained by the successful revolution was conducive to the rejection of traditional forms of punishment practiced in England. For example, a revulsion to "cruel and unusual punishment" was clearly articulated in both the federal and state constitutions. In addition, Enlightenment thought challenged fatalistic conceptions of human behavior, such as that of the Calvinists, who believed that everything was predetermined by God; nothing essential could be changed. Eighteenth-century "Enlightened" thinkers in Europe and America were guided by the possibilities, not the limitations of human beings. It was the Age of Reason, and a "rational and scientific approach to religious, social, political, and economic issues promoted a secular view of the work and a general sense of progress and perfectibility" (Harris and Levy 1975, 877). Humankind was thought to be progressing toward a greater use of reason. A rationally ordered universe under human control was postulated to be inevitable.

Americans thought the first thing to be done was to change the criminal codes. "Armed with patriotic fervor, sharing a repugnance for things British and a new familiarity with and faith in Enlightenment doctrines, they posited that the origins and persistence of deviant behavior would be found in the nature of the colonial criminal codes" (Rothman 1971, 59). The crime problem was held to be a product of the imposition of antiquated and unreasonable laws. It was argued that lenient laws would prevent crime when "the mind of man is once more accessible to the mild influence of reason and humanity" (Rothman 1971, 61). The idea was to develop a treatment plan that would encourage criminals to reflect on their own behaviors, not the arbitrary expectations and actions of others.

Prison Reform

The first vigorous effort to abolish corporal punishment began in Pennsylvania and West Jersey during the later part of the eighteenth century. Headed by the Quakers of Pennsylvania, together with the Anabaptists and other dissident sects, reformers advocated isolated individual confinement, rather than corporal punishment, as the way to generate rational self-analysis. For example, in 1785 William Paley observed that isolation from "the society of his fellow prisoners, in which society the worse are sure to corrupt the better, is calculated to raise up in him reflections on the folly of his choice and to expose his mind to such better and continued sentence as may produce a lasting alteration in the principles of conduct" (Orland 1975, 20).

Reforms by the Quakers in Philadelphia were mostly instigated through the efforts of the Philadelphia Society for Alleviating the Miseries of Public Prisons. Founded in 1787, the society included among its members prominent Quaker names, such as Benjamin Franklin, William Rush, and William Bradford, as well as members of the American Philosophical Society. Within a year after its formation, the Philadelphia Society recommended to the legislature a system of solitary confinement and hard labor as a way to achieve reformation and public profit (Tappan 1960, 603–6). Later the efforts of this group led to the Act of Assembly of April 5, 1790, by which the old Walnut Street Jail, built in 1776, was transformed into the first American penitentiary. All convicted felons in the state, except those sentenced to death, were henceforth housed in this new institution.

The Walnut Street Jail

Covering more than two acres, the Walnut Street Jail functioned as both a prison and a workhouse. An elementary prisoner classification scheme was used. Witnesses and debtors were separated from felons. The sexes were segregated, as were the more hardened criminals of both sexes. Serious offenders were placed in solitary cells, measuring 6 feet by 8 feet, that contained inner iron and outer wooden doors. Other inmates were housed in large rooms.

Although offenders in solitary confinement did not work, others worked together in shops and earned small wages. Silence was enforced at work and meals, but quiet conversation was allowed at night in the dormitories. The rules of silence did not apply to women prisoners.

From all accounts the Walnut Street Jail was seen as a model prison in the 1790s. Prison officials from Europe and from other states frequently visited the facility, studying its cellular design and work programs. Other jurisdictions opened facilities patterned after the Walnut Street Jail, such as Newgate Prison, built in New York City's Greenwich Village (1796), and Charlestown Prison in Massachusetts (1804), as well as state prisons in New Jersey (1797), Kentucky and Virginia (1800), Vermont (1809), and Baltimore (1804).

The success of the Philadelphia experiment, however, was not long-lived. By the turn of the century, increased convictions produced a crowded prison and an overworked staff. Industrial activities became virtually impossible; discipline had degenerated; and prisoner riots became commonplace (Tappan 1960). The problem was that the city, like the rest of the Eastern Seaboard, was beginning to feel the effects of accelerated industrialization; it was growing and changing faster than was anticipated and could be managed. Between 1800 and 1830, Philadelphia's population nearly doubled—from 41,200 to 80,400. In New York City, the change was even more dramatic—from a population of 60,500 in 1800 to 202,500 in 1830 (an increase of 235 percent). This population explosion, which brought higher crime and more convicted felons, hastened the demise of the Walnut Street Jail, which was abandoned in 1835, after other prisons had opened in Pennsylvania.

The Pennsylvania System

Although the Walnut Street Jail was in operation for less than half a century, it established the concept of solitary confinement, wherein inmates could contemplate in solitude their wayward past and develop a resolve to change their behavior. Known as the "separate" or "Pennsylvania" system, this philosophy of penology became the basis for the reconstruction of the Western State Penitentiary (1826), located near Pittsburgh. A few years later construction of the Eastern State Penitentiary (1829), situated at Cherry Hill near Philadelphia, was completed, making it the first prison architecturally configured to the principles of the Pennsylvania, or "separate," system.

At the Eastern State Penitentiary all prisoners were thoroughly isolated from one another. Before entering the institution, the prisoner was blindfolded and taken to his cell; this prevented him from seeing anyone else as well as the lay of the prison. The facility had seven cellblocks emanating from a common center. Each block had two floors; the cell on the first floor had attached exercise yards, each 8 feet by 20 feet, and contained by a nearly 12-foot wall. On the second floor, an adjoining inside cell served as the place of exercise.

The prisoners worked, ate, and slept in their confined spaces. They were allowed contact only with prison officials and authorized visitors. Prisoners could neither post nor receive mail, in effect excommunicating them from outside influences.

Although a few other states temporarily adopted solitary-confinement principles in their prisons, the Pennsylvania system never gained widespread acceptance in the United States. But it proved to be very appealing to Europeans. Delegates from nations worldwide studied its construction plans, many recommending its adoption in their home countries.

The Auburn Silent System

Because of a growing penal population, other states were also driven to prison development and reorganization. Borrowing the single-cell concept from the Walnut Street Jail, the New York State Prison at Auburn constructed a new design in one of its wings, opening in 1823. Unlike the Pennsylvania system, Auburn confined inmates in tiers or banks of inside cells, each cell measuring 7 feet by 3.5 feet. Because these side-by-side cells did not attach to perimeter walls of the building wing, this architectural arrangement did not offer prisoners direct access to exercise yards (Tappan 1960).

During this period, the New York State Legislature required a three-grade system of prisoner classification. In grade 1 were the hardened criminals, who were kept in their cells and not allowed to work, much like circumstances in the Pennsylvania System. This was meant to compel them to reflect on the error of their ways. Grade 2 contained those defined as less incorrigible. They served a portion of their time in solitary confinement; they were required to work, but more for recreational than for punitive purposes. Grade 3 was composed of the most hopeful, those least likely to be recidivists. They worked together during the day, but were kept in separate cells at night. Due to the treatment given this third class, the program became know as the "silent," or Auburn, system.

While they worked and ate together, grade 3 prisoners were required to maintain silence. Interaction could lead to corruption, and this was to be avoided. As O.F. Lewis stated, "If granted communication with each other, they become a force for evil and an ever-present source of insurrection and riot. Hard work," said Lewis, "was productive, healthy, and taught the inmates the principles of self-support against the time when they should be discharged from prison" (Lewis in Gillin 1935, 277).

Silence and industry were strictly enforced at Auburn. An observer of the system, the Reverend Louis Dwight, described the daily regimen as follows: "There is the most perfect attention to business from morning till night, interrupted only by the time necessary to dine. . . . At the close of the day, a little before sunset, the work is all laid aside, at once, and the convicts return in military order, to the silent cells where they partake of their frugal meal. . . . After supper, they can, if they chose, read the Scriptures, undisturbed, and can reflect in silence on the error of their lives. . . . The men attend to their business from the rising to the setting of the sun, and spend the night in solitude" (Dwight, cited in Gillin 1935, 281; see also Box 11.1.)

Box 11.1. Prison Discipline circa 1870

According to a 35-year veteran correctional officer at a Massachusetts institution, "Prison discipline just isn't what it used to be when I first began work here. I wish we could skip the 1990s and go back to the *old* ways of doing things!" Many "hard-liners" on discipline would agree: prisoners today enjoy rights and privileges that were unimaginable decades ago.

Strict prison discipline was a cornerstone of institutional life in the eighteenth century. Elam Lynds, Auburn's warden circa 1825, established discipline principles that were recognized more than a century later. In fact, vestiges of "the old prison discipline," which assumes that prisoners could never be reformed until their spirits were broken, live on, even today. According to Howard Gill (ACA 1983), this is what prison discipline meant:

—Hard labor, ranging from "making little ones out of big ones" to organized prison industries.

—Deprivation of everything, other than what was needed for a spartan existence.

—Monotony, with no variation in daily routine or diet.

—Mass movement or "mass everything," including mass dining, mass living in the cellblocks, mass recreation, and even mass bathing. Individual identities could not be allowed.

—Degradation, by housing inmates in cages, requiring nondescript attire, and denying even courteous contacts with prison guards. Once again, individual identities could not be allowed.

—Subservience, to rules and more rules!

—Corporal punishment, including the whip, paddle, sweat box, and the infamous "boot."

—Noncommunication, absolute, complete silence or solitary confinement, including deprivation of mail, family visits, and other outside contacts.

—Recreation, none whatsoever at first, and later only an hour of "yard time" daily.

—No responsibility whatsoever! Prisoners were stripped of every social, civic, economic, domestic, and even personal responsibility.

—Isolation, up to 16 hours a day.

—Absolutely *no* fraternization with guards, which precluded efforts to solve everyday problems through staff-inmate contacts.

Source: Adapted from American Correctional Association 1983.

All the shops where inmates worked were ringed by a gallery permitting them to be seen by guards "without being seen by them." Those who deviated from the rules were whipped. Auburn's Warden Elam Lynds regarded "whipping as the most effective and at the same time the most humane punishment, for it never injures the health and forces the inmate to live an essentially healthy life" (Pierson 1938, 208). By means of a rawhide whip, or "cat," with six strands of wire, Lynds was reported to have lashed stripped prisoners as many as 500 times. As to the reformative possibilities of his manner of treating prisoners, Lynds was unequivocal. When asked by Tocqueville if he believed in reform, Lynds said: "I do not believe in complete reform (except for juvenile delinquents). . . . My opinion is that a great number of former convicts do not relapse into crime, and they even become useful citizens, having learned a trade in prison. . . . There's the only reform that I have ever hoped to produce, and I think it's the only one which society can demand" (Pierson 1938, 209).

Lynds and his deputy, John Carey, together with Gershom Powers of the Board of Inspectors, devised a plan of employment wherein prisoners could work in congregate, industrial shops under a code of strict silence (see Box 11.2). Elam's work program was implemented when a manufacturer secured a lucrative contract to operate a factory inside Auburn, paying prisoners very low wages. Within a few years, Auburn became an efficient industrial prison (Tappan 1960, 609), involving coopering, tailoring, shoemaking, weaving, toolmaking, and rifle manufacturing. Thus, in addition to the virtues of hard labor as a circumstance of punishment, the goal at Auburn was to make the prison not only self-supporting but also profitable.

The Auburn method of employing prisoners was soon copied in most states. But in the 1830s serious objections to convict labor began to be voiced. Critics were motivated less by humanitarian concerns than by economic self-interest. Groups of free laborers charged unfair competition, and envious businessmen claimed bias in the allotment of contracts. By the 1870s, most states had enacted legislation aimed at restricting the use of convict labor and the marketing of prison-made products.

Box 11.2. Lock-Step and Corridor

Probably no institutions in American history personified the classic regimen of prison life more than New York's Auburn and Sing Sing prisons. In the 1820s Auburn Warden Elam Lynds' deputy, John Cary, inaugurated a system of marching inmates to and from their work stations and dining facility in lock-step in order to make it easier to observe and supervise them during movement through corridors and across the prison yard. Prisoners were required to form a line. Placing their hands on the shoulders or beneath the armpit of the man ahead of them, they marched in military order to their destination, shuffling their feet in step so that they barely left the ground. The rules of the lock-step required that each man keep his eyes on nearby guards at all times, and a strict code of silence was imposed. Although prisoners cleverly developed a technique of "talking out of the side of the mouth" to evade the watchful eyes and ears of prison guards, violation of the lock-step and silence policies could bring a punishment of flogging or worse. At Sing Sing, the lock-step was retained until 1900 and at other institutions well into the 1900s.

The prison garb devised at Auburn and later initiated at Sing Sing conjures up a classic stereotype of the "jailbird." Fashioned in so-called prison stripes, these uniforms, which included a matching cap, first appeared at Auburn in 1815. The idea was to increase visibility of prisoners within the institution, enabling institutional authorities to identify a prisoner's custody classification by the type of uniform worn, and to make it easy to identify them if there was an escape to the outside. Striped uniforms also functioned to reinforce the disciplined and isolated circumstances of prison life and to degrade and stigmatize prisoners by further stripping them of individual identities. Striped uniforms did not disappear from prisons until the 1950s, replaced in modern times by denim outfits that some inmates call "prison blues."

Sources: Tappan 1960; American Correctional Association 1983; Gillin 1935.

Nevertheless, in the late nineteenth century prison factories developed across the nation. They were an integral part of prison programs until the 1940s. In October 1940 a federal act banned nearly all state-prison-made products from interstate commerce. Despite the exemption of certain articles (farm-related products and items made for state public-sector use), this legislation spelled the end of the prison factory as a viable activity. Employment had become "busy-work" rather than meaningful skill training.

Of related importance is the fact that cruel and exploitive employment of prisoners continued well into the present century. Most noteworthy in this respect was the widespread leasing of prisoners to private contractors for work outside prisons. Prisoners were used in quarrying, agriculture, mining, roadwork and bridge building, turpentine camps, and sugarcane plantations. The lease system was not abolished in every state until 1936.

The Reformatory System

Despite emphases on solitude, silence, and hard work from the Pennsylvania and Auburn systems, a philosophy of treatment began to emerge by the middle of the nineteenth century. Some penologists believed that some forms of criminality were expressions of conditions, such as psychological problems or an upbringing in unfortunate social environments, over which the criminal had little control. This viewpoint gave rise in part to the development of reformatories, which placed more emphasis on reform rather than on purely punitive programs (ACA 1983).

The reformatory era in American corrections, which began around 1870 and ended into the early part of the 1900s, owes much of its impetus to ideas borrowed from Australian Alexander Maconochie and an Irishman, Sir Walter Crofton. Maconochie can be credited with the idea of the "mark system," whereby inmates could earn release by hard work and good behavior. In contrast to fixed sentences, which carried no possibilities of release until the full sentence was served, the mark system placed the burden on the inmate. Thus, prisoners had to earn a certain number of "marks," which were awarded for completion of a determined and specified amount of labor.

Crofton reasoned that if prisons provoked prisoners into repentance, then there should be a way of releasing inmates when penitence had been achieved. His ideas and rationale created what was called the"indeterminate system," also known as the "Irish system," which involved releasing an inmate who had successfully progressed through a series of corrective stages. Once achieved, a conditional pardon, or "ticket-of-leave," could be earned by inmates who found outside employment. Crofton was the first to establish the rudiments of conditional freedom or parole (ACA 1983).

Both Crofton's and Maconochie's systems were adopted by American prison administrators and penal reformers at the National Prison Congress, which convened in Cincinnati in 1870. Since prison overcrowding was a continuing problem, these new programs could be best installed at institutions soon to be constructed. The first to implement these systems was the Elmira Reformatory in New York State, which opened in 1876. Similar in architecture to Auburn Prison, Elmira housed youthful, first-time offenders from 16 to 30 years of age. But, unlike Auburn, Elmira placed greater emphasis on positive reformation, academic education, trades and work training, military drills, even recreation in the form of organized athletics. The two most important features of Elmira were indeterminate sentences (with fixed maximum terms), parole if an inmate's record justified it, and a threefold classification system, wherein inmates were promoted according to their earned "marks" (ACA 1983). Between 1876 and 1913, seventeen states copied or adapted the Elmira Reformatory model, including Washington State (Monroe), Kansas (Hutchinson), Minnesota (St. Cloud), Colorado (Buena Vista), Wisconsin (Green Bay), Maine (South Windham), and Wyoming (Worland).

Contemporary Correctional Institutions

By the beginning of the twentieth century, the infrastructure of the American prison system was well established. As criminologist John Gillin (1935, 286) wrote in the 1930s, "To-day all States have adopted the Auburn system." By this he did not mean that nothing had changed since the 1820s, but that the American prison system was structured on the Auburn precedent. And while other types of penal institutions had emerged to accommodate special circumstances, such as minimum-security facilities, work camps, and farms housing inmates who did not require high custody, virtually every state had at least one large penitentiary that served as the centerpiece of the state's correctional system.

Gillin's (1935) discussion of the state of prisons in the first quarter-century demonstrates major differences in correctional philosophies from those practiced during the early years of the "separate" and "silent" systems: (1) segregation of male and female prisoners; (2) the establishment of separate institutions for young adults; (3) a modification in discipline (the substitution of privilege deprivation for corporal punishment); (4) the liberalization of communication with friends and relatives from the outside; (5) implementation of education and recreation programs; (6) sentence commutation by granting "good time" credit; (7) selection of prison personnel on the basis of competency rather than political considerations; (8) treatment prescribed on the basis of psychological and psychiatric examinations; (9) the establishment of university courses in sociology and psychology concerned with preparing students to "handle difficult personalities"; and (10) an emphasis on reformation (see Box 11.3). Many of the changes in twentieth-century prisons noted by Gillin merit special discussion, since they signal important trends in contemporary correctional philosophies and programming that offer insight into how modern prisons operate today.

Box 11.3. Opportunity
by
Sing Sing No. 65368

There's a chance for the fellow who tries;
There's a chance for the fellow who dreams;
There's many a chance if you look at the skies,
But chance is not what it seems.

Chance is never a dream of swift wealth,
Or vision of sudden found gains.
Chance, as you call it rests in self
And the taking of infinite pains.

Chance as you'll find it comes alone,
It wings but once to your door—
'Tis an arrow that strikes while many unknown
Have missed the target before.

Source: *Star of Hope* journal, circa 1917

The Competing Goals of Corrections

Certainly one of the hallmark features of correctional policy in the twentieth century is an emphasis on *rehabilitation* or *reformation* of criminals. Based on the positive assumptions that "people can change" and that treatment interventions can help redirect their lives, rehabilitation has come to be a major goal in contemporary corrections. Ideally, well-designed treatment programs provide circumstances that bring about positive changes in attitudes, motivation, and behavior that ultimately will allow offenders to return to the free community as law-abiding, independently functioning, and productive citizens.

During the Great Depression of the 1930s and throughout the World War II years, considerable attention was given by prison reformers to developing treatment interventions. By the 1960s and 1970s, efforts were made to tailor interventions to the specific needs of individual offenders. This included vocational and educational programs, psychiatric and social casework approaches, self-help programs for offenders with histories of alcohol and drug disorders, and even separate institutions for special offenders such as sex offenders and young adults.

Although this rehabilitation emphasis remains as a trend in modern correctional institutions, it has always been difficult to implement rehabilitation programming to a significant degree because of the competing goals of *retribution* and *deterrence.*

Retribution, or social retaliation, is based on the deeply ingrained principle of an "eye for an eye." Put another way, we believe that one who has committed a criminal wrong deserves to be punished in proportion to the harm done. Historically, law, custom, even religious beliefs have lent support to retribution as a legitimate reaction of the victim and the community. Thus, however indefensible it may be to progressive penologists, retribution as a community response is not likely to disappear.

The goal of deterrence is to prevent crime by inculcating fear of the consequences of illegality. "Presumably, the more unpleasant the incarceration, either in its conditions or its length, the greater will be its deterrent value" (Sommer 1976, 20). Thus the deterrent value of incarceration is measured by the extent to which the offender is dissuaded from further wrongdoing, and the potential offender is discouraged from initiating a criminal act.

The very nature of rehabilitation as a correctional goal is basically incompatible with retribution and deterrence. Indeterminate sentencing—a basic element in the rehabilitative response to crime—provides a good example. That is, "Any variation in the type or length of punishment for offenders convicted of the same crime undermines the retribution model which seeks an eye for an eye, not a tap on the wrist for one offender and twenty lashes for the next" (Sommer 1976, 26). Similarly, rehabilitation-motivated probationary sentencing may lessen the deterrent value of incarceration. As Sommer points out, "Advocates of deterrence maintain that it has not succeeded because imprisonment is applied infrequently, haphazardly, and in a discriminatory fashion" (1976, 21).

A further complication stems from the failure or inability to specify clearly the goal(s) of rehabilitation. To rehabilitate something is to restore it to a previous state—in this case, converting those in an offender status into a presumed previously held nonoffender status. Thus, to rehabilitate an offender in this sense, one must specify the exact meaning of nonoffender status desired and the means of effecting and measuring its attainment. Presumably, both the change agent and the offender would be provided with objective, or at least agreed upon, means of independently determining when rehabilitation occurs. In the absence of such means, the offender is likely to regard rehabilitation as a sham, myth, or excuse to accomplish something else (e.g., retribution). As noted earlier, ambiguity in rehabilitation goals is a major reason for abolishing indeterminate in favor of determinate sentencing.

Instead of restoration, the preferred terms associated with rehabilitation goals are *reform* and *corrections*. To reform something is to reshape it; to correct something is to "set it right" or put it "on a straight path." Both concepts stress reconditioning of behavior from a crime-violating to a law-abiding orientation. The social milieu of the prison has seldom been regarded as the most appropriate to effect the goal. As Sommer puts it: "Most inmates will acknowledge the legitimacy of reform as a social objective. . . . Their criticisms concern the practicality of accomplishing positive character change through immersion in a total criminal society; any reforming or reshaping under such circumstances would probably be in a negative direction" (1976, 24–25).

In sum, while rehabilitation or reformation constitutes a major goal in contemporary correctional policy and prison institutions, its coexistence with the aims of retribution and deterrence creates difficult social and political circumstances for implementing successful treatment programs. Despite the humanity, dedication, and skills of the many treatment professionals working in modern correctional institutions, it is very unlikely that the incompatibility of these goals will lessen in the near or distant future.

Growth of the Prison Population

The United States is second to none when it comes to prisons and prison inmates. As of December 1994, the U.S. Department of Justice, Bureau of Justice Statistics, counted 1037 state and federal correctional facilities that confined more than one million people, or approximately 400 inmates per 100,000 Americans. In fact, over the past several years the United States has been locking up a larger proportion of its people than any other nation. Only South Africa, which reported an incarceration rate of 311 per 100,000 residents in 1992 under its previous government, comes close to the matching American incarceration statistics (*Boston Globe* 1994).

This phenomenal growth in the American prison system traces back, of course, to the Walnut Street Jail, some 200 years ago. By the middle of the nineteenth century, large Auburn-style penitentiaries were firmly in place nationwide. Although America's population was steadily increasing, so too was the number of incarcerated inmates, in fact, at a pace well ahead of population growth. The growing number of convicted felons justified building more prisons, which in turn brought even more inmates.

Table 11.1 shows how prison populations have grown over the past 200 years. Notice a more or less steady increase in the incarceration rate over past 150 years.

Table 11.1
Prison Population Growth, 1840–1994

Year	Number of Prisoners	U.S. Population (millions)	Prisoners per 100,00 Population
1840	4,000	17	24
1850	7,000	23	30
1860	19,000	31	60
1870	33,000	40	83
1890	45,000	63	71
1900	57,000	76	75
1918	75,000	92	82
1925	93,000	106	88
1930	148,000	123	121
1940	174,000	132	132
1950	166,000	151	110
1960	213,000	179	119
1970	196,000	203	97
1980	321,000	227	142
1982	412,000	233	177
1990	740,000	249	292
1991	789,000	252	310
1993	948,881	260	351
1994	1,053,738	263	401

Sources: ACA (1983); Maguire/BJS (1992); *BJS* (1994); Stern (1995)

The vast majority of men and women now in confinement reside in state prisons. This has been true throughout American history. Although there have always been offenders sentenced for federal crimes, dating back to the signing of the Declaration of Independence, these inmates were housed in state or territorial prisons or in county jails until Congress authorized in 1891 a federal penitentiary system. The first institutions were opened in 1905 at Atlanta and at Leavenworth, Kansas; later, facilities were built at McNeil Island, Washington (1919), and at Alderson, West Virginia (1924), the last serving as a women's reformatory. Probably the most infamous institution within the federal system was Alcatraz Island, which in 1934 became a federal facility. Located off the coast of San Francisco, Alcatraz became too costly to operate, and in 1963 it was closed by the Federal Bureau of Prisons. Today there are 80 federal facilities in operation.

Types of Institutions

To bring some order to what Robert Sommer refers to as the "model muddle," the attempt to accomplish multiple and contradictory goals via imprisonment, correctional institutions have been constructed and organized to emphasize different degrees of security or custody. Three levels are distinguished: maximum, medium, and minimum security.

Maximum-Security Prisons. Maximum-security institutions house inmates convicted of the most serious felonies. They can be seen as fortress prisons—Bastille-like—in that they have massive walls, typically a "no man" zone separating interior structures from the outer walls, and all the other elements designed to minimize the possibility of escape. Sometimes called "The Big House" in vintage prison and gangster movies of the 1930s and 1940s, a maximum-security prison closely monitors the movement of inmates inside the facility, as well as exercise exceptional security measures to screen those who enter and leave the prison grounds. Many of the most infamous penitentiaries—Sing Sing and Attica in New York, Stateville at Joliet, Illinois, the Washington State Prison at Walla Walla, or San Quentin Prison in California—were built around 1900 utilizing the Auburn design, containing large cellblocks for housing inmates. Because of the architectural design, these massive structures, constructed with economy, isolation and security as guiding principles, are limited in the kinds of correctional programming they offer (see Box 11.4).

Box 11.4. A Day in a Maximum-Security Prison

Although daily routines vary by institution, there is a remarkable consistency in the events governing prison life. Here is a typical day in a maximum-security prison:

7:00 AM	Rise for the count. Wash and clean cell, making sure your bed is made. Also, stand at the door for the count.
7:20 AM	Breakfast
8:00 AM	Work call. If you are unassigned, you go to the TV block or stay in your room.
11:35 AM	Work for the morning is complete and the men come in from the shop, returning to their rooms to wash up for dinner and to stand at the door for count. This is the time to let the guard know if you do not want to go to the meal. This is so for each meal.
1:00 PM	Dinner over and this is the time for any announcements to be called, so listen for your name. You may be wanted to go to a hospital visit

	or the dentist. After any announcements, work call is again called, and if and when you are assigned to a job you are to go to it.
3:45 PM	The men return from the shops at this time. This begins your free time. On clear days, the yard is open and you can go out until yard time is called. At this time the library is open to take books out and return them.
4:20 PM	Count time is called again, this time for supper. When count is called, return to your room and stand at the door.
5:45 PM	Another count is called at this time, and this is when the mail is given out, plus any receipt for money, etc.
6:00 PM	Count is called complete and the evening activities are announced: gym, avocation and discussion groups, etc.
10:00 PM	Count is again called to return to your room for the night, so stand at your door until the guard passes it.
11:00 PM	Lights out.

Source: Adapted from "Prison Days and Nights," unpublished manuscript, NEMIC, Boston University School of Education, undated p. 8.

Especially in the 1950s, a variation on the Auburn institution came into vogue. Known as the "Telephone Pole" plan, it looks like a long telephone pole with spokes extending horizontally at right angles. This new type of Bastille retained all the custody features of its predecessors, yet the design permitted facilities to accommodate new treatment and work programs. This design featured a long central corridor with numerous branches: multitiered cellblocks, dormitories, dining, recreation, school and work facilities, and administrative office space. The Minnesota State Prison at Stillwater, which opened in 1914, was the first to utilize the telephone-pole design (Caldwell 1965). The prototype telephone-pole prison, however, is the Federal Penitentiary at Lewisburg, Pennsylvania, which was opened in 1932 and was designed by Alfred Hopkins. Others followed in the 1950s: the New Mexico Penitentiary at Santa Fe; Massachusetts Correctional Institution at Cedar Junction (South Walpole); Soledad, Tracy, and Vacaville in California; the Oregon Correctional Institution at Salem; and others in Ohio, Texas, and Ontario, Canada (ACA 1983, 203–5). Institutions built in the past few decades, however, have been able to create similar high-security environments by using state-of-the-art electronic warning and monitoring systems, rather than the imposing walls that are hallmarks of the Auburn architectural design.

Medium-Security Prisons. Medium-security institutions, typically fenced rather than walled structures, were introduced in the 1930s to reverse the emphasis from incapacitation to rehabilitation. These facilities house inmates committing less serious felonies or those seen as lesser custody risks, and movement inside medium-security environments is less restrictive. Generally fenced rather than walled, medium-security facilities sometimes feature dormitories and congregate living areas.

Among the first to use this design was the Norfolk Prison Colony (later renamed Massachusetts Correctional Institution at Norfolk), which had an open campus with dormitories and other buildings housing institutional services. Opened in 1931, it resembled a college campus because of its spacious yard and the architecture of its buildings. Today, virtually every state has at least one medium-security institution.

Minimum-Security Prisons. Minimum-security institutions are primarily a post-World War II development. Frequently constructed according to a "cottage plan," they tend to resemble a small college campus rather than a prison, and they contain no walls, fences, locks, bars, or guard towers. Inmates housed in these facilities are considered low security risks; for example, inmates convicted of white-collar and nonviolent crimes.

Variations on the minimum-security facility are work camps, ranches and farms, vocational training centers, and in some states even remote forestry stations. Such facilities bear no resemblance to traditional prisons, and only the most trustworthy of offenders are transferred to them. Among their many advantages is the fact that they are very cost-effective to operate, often producing income or saving tax dollars by providing a community with needed services at low cost.

Women's Prisons. It seems only natural to assume that separating men and women insofar as prisons and treatment are concerned would be one of the oldest and most established policies in correctional philosophy. In reality, the movement to separate institutions is a relatively new event in American corrections. Early jails in England and the United States were remarkably casual about separation policies, typically providing little more than an isolated wing in a male institution for housing arrangements. Historically, correctional services for women have been very sparse, at times nonexistent, and even those were supervised by male officers.

The first prison for women in the United States opened in 1873 in Indianapolis, and the first women's reformatory received inmates in 1877 at Framingham, Massachusetts, just four years after the opening of the Elmira (N.Y.) Reformatory for Men. Some thirty-five years later only three other penal institutions for women were opened: New York (1901), the District of Columbia (1910), and New Jersey (1913). Although the number of institutions exclusively for women climbed to seventy-one nationwide by 1990, many in the form of state farms and cottage colonies, some states continue to house women in special wings of maximum- and medium-security prisons for men (Tappan 1960).

Although there can be little doubt that blatant sexism accounts in some measure for the overall inattention to developing institutions for women and for investing in their treatment programming, the vast difference between the number of male versus female offenders also helps to explain this underdevelopment. Throughout history, both the crime and incarceration rates have been substantially higher for men than women. For example, in 1925 the incarceration rate for men was 149 (per 100,000 men in the general population) compared to 6 for women; by 1960 the gap had widened to 230 for men, compared to 8 for women. By 1983 it increased to 352 for men and only 14 for women. And though crimes rates for women have escalated dramatically in more recent years, the substantial disparity in incarceration rates for men and women continues (Maguire/BJS 1992; see also Box 11.5).

Box 11.5 Facts on Women's Prisons

—The rate of growth for female inmates exceeded that for males in each year since 1981. From 1980 to 1989, the male population increased by 112 percent and the female population by 202 percent.

—An estimated 41 percent of the female inmates in 1986 were in prison for violent offenses, nearly half of these serving sentences for homicide.

—More than two-thirds of women in prison are recidivists.

—More than a third of the women serving time for a violent crime have victimized a relative or intimate.

—An estimated 41 percent of the women in prison reported they had been previously sexually or physically abused. Women convicted of violent offenses are the most likely to come from abused backgrounds.

—More than three-fourths of the women in prison are mothers, two-thirds of whom have children under age 18.

Source: Adapted from Greenfeld/BJS 1991.

Notwithstanding sex differences in incarceration rates, nearly 50,000 women are now in confinement in state and federal facilities—a figure seven times higher than about twenty years ago, compared to a threefold increase for men during this period (Maguire/BJS 1992). Approaches to social and occupational programs for women continue to emphasize homemaking and domestic skills, food services, hairdressing and cosmetology, and secretarial or clerical work. However mundane this approach may seem, even this stands in stark contrast to the prison experience of incarcerated women in the nineteenth century, when virtually no programs were offered other than their daily chores of cleaning the institution. Neither were the facilities adequate, particularly those at adjunct buildings to maximum-security prisons for men. Rafter (1985, 84) cites the case of a Missouri warden who, at the turn of the century, pronounced the "female cell building as a disgrace to the State." As B.C. Smith, chaplain at Auburn Penitentiary, wrote in 1832, "To be a woman in prison was 'worse than death'" (ACA 1983, 165).

While women offenders today share in common with men many of the same correctional needs, they are also far more likely than men to be the principal caretaker of children, often in single-parent circumstances. Thus, incarcerated women who are single parents face special hardships during their prison experience that potentially complicate their adjustment to institutional living and their participation in treatment programs (see Box 11.6). In some states alternatives to traditional incarceration have been developed, some on an experimental basis, that enable women to enjoy frequent contact with their children, while serving their sentences in community-based correctional facilities. In past decades, rigid correctional policies dictated that women who gave birth while in confinement must send the infant home to relatives or friends within about six months of childbirth or, if unwanted, put the infant up for adoption.

Box 11.6 Drug-Involved Offenders in Women's Prisons

That alcohol and other drugs have dramatically changed the nature of crime today and the criminal justice system is obvious from the research findings reviewed in Chapter Two. Evidence reported by the Bureau of Justice Statistics (Harlow/BJS 1989), however, suggests that while men are far more likely than women to be sent to jail for drug offenses, such as possession of a drug substance or drug trafficking, the proportion of jailed inmates who have used drugs regularly is somewhat higher forwomen. Data reported by the BJS in 1989 found that approximately 77 percent of men in jails said they had used drugs at one time and about one in every four indicated they were under the influence of drugs at the time of their offenses. Among women, 84 per cent indicated they have used drugs and nearly 40 percent reported they were under the influence at the times of they committed crimes. In addition, over half (55 percent) of women in jails also reported they had used drugs in the month before their criminal offenses. The trends noted by the BJS suggest that the number of drug-involved women sent to jails and prisons is on the increase (Harlow/BJS 1989).

Although these data underscore the importance of treatment programming for drug-involved offenders in women's institutions, they also raise special concerns about pregnant drug-addicted women who are sent to jails and prisons. Since most prisons do not have extensive medical facilities, correctional officials are faced with the special challenge of assuring proper prenatal care and of safeguarding drug-free births. This is absolutely critical, inasmuch as drug use at any point during the pregnancy period carries high risk of passing along a drug dependency to the infant and of birth deformities. For women who have contracted the deadly HIV (human immunodeficiency virus), which eventually leads to AIDS (acquired immunodeficiency syndrome), through needle-sharing during intravenous drug use or from other risk behaviors, the need for proper health-care services becomes even more critical. From an institutional standpoint, this situation can also become a very complex public health problem.

Corrections departments in all states have had to develop policies and acceptable arrangements to handle the special health-care needs of pregnant women offenders. Some of the most creative programs, however, are those in which private community agencies work with women's prisons to provide perinatal medical care. In Massachusetts, for example, Social Justice for Women (SJW), an organization dedicated to advocacy on women's issues and to providing a full range of services for women involved in the criminal justice system, developed a unique program that not only enhanced the quality of health care delivered to women at the Massachusetts Correctional Institution in Framingham, but also promoted support systems to help women to reintegrate into the community after their prison release.

Funded by a federal grant from the Office of Substance Abuse Prevention, SJW provided pregnancy (and optional HIV) screening of all women at Framingham. SJW health-care and case-management staff worked with pregnant mothers willing to participate in their program, providing them perinatal health services. Women with substance abuse histories also participated in special treatment groups that dealt with drug recovery issues. Case managers, who coordinated various social and health services for each client, worked with these women to prepare them either for parole or for a negotiated early release. Some women returned to independent living circumstances, using SJW services on an outpatient basis. Others were placed in SJW's community-based facility for pregnant women, Houston House, where they received family counseling and substance abuse recovery services, as well as perinatal medical care. To date SJW has been successful in facilitating hundreds of drug-free births and in assisting these mothers to reintegrate into their home communities.

One of the most unique features of the program was a "community mom" concept, in which women who lived in their home communities were linked to a community volunteer who served as an advocate for and trusted friend to the SJW client, in addition to teaching infant care and parenting skills. Overall SJW programs have been able to substantially reduced recidivism among female offenders participating in their programs.

The Jail System. The American jail system has its origins in English jails, which housed arrestees awaiting criminal trials. In the United States the jail system has grown to more than 3500 facilities. Based on a report by the Bureau of Justice Statistics, it is obvious that these jails do a steady business:

1. In a 1992 jail census nearly 450,000 men and women were housed in jail facilities.

2. American jails operate at 99 percent of rated capacity.

3. Among the nation's largest jails, the average occupancy was 114 percent of rated capacity (Beck et al., 1993).

Jails, which are operated locally by counties and cities, contain a diverse population; in fact, so diverse that many reformers label them as dumping grounds! Over the years they have housed the mentally ill and alcoholic derelicts, along with youthful first-time offenders mixed with dangerous sex offenders and violent criminals awaiting trial. The Cook County Jail in Chicago and the Manhattan House of Detention in New York City, better known as "The Tombs," are among the most infamous of American jails. In the Los Angeles County system, which operates nine jails, recent data show that nearly 23,000 inmates are housed on any given day, making it the nation's busiest jail system (Beck 1993; see also Box 11.7).

Jail facilities provide custody for five types of inmates: (1) persons convicted of misdemeanors; (2) pretrial defendants who have been denied bail or who have not posted bail; (3) protective-custody inmates who have not been convicted of crimes per se but have exhibited behaviors that make them dangerous to themselves or to others, such as psychotics or the alcohol/drug-intoxicated; (4) convicted felons awaiting sentence or transfer to prisons; and (5) convicted felons who have been sentenced to jail instead of prison. With the exception of the last category, jails have relatively rapid turnover of their populations, ranging from a few hours of detention to upwards to twelve months, depending on local circumstances. Prison overcrowding has also impacted local jails, sometimes lengthening jail time, since convicted felons are can be temporarily stationed in jails because of overcrowded conditions in some prisons.

Although jails perform an important role in the American criminal justice system, the vast majority have minimal facilities and provide few, if any, programs. Older, traditional jails lack space or resources for recreation and exercise. And because jails are typically designed to be economical, utilizing a minimum of staff, almost all of whom are custodial, vocational training, education, and related programs are not available. In many ways this outcome is ironic in that social profiles of those in jails tend to show that they are among the most in need of assistance. The lack of programs, however temporary jail residents may be, makes for a tense environment, which may provoke emotional despair and sometimes violence. Assaults, institutional riots, and even suicide are potential outcomes of poor and inadequate conditions.

Box 11.7 Who's in Jail

Data obtained from the Annual Survey of Jails, conducted by the Bureau of Justice Statistics, U.S. Department of Justice, provide rather detailed information about the nearly 500,000 inmates confined in jails. Some of these findings are very thought-provoking. What conclusions do they invite?

Using the census day as an anchor point, on any given day:

1. Nearly six of every ten inmates are African American or Hispanic.
2. African Americans constitute 44 percent of the jail population.
3. Hispanics represent 15 percent of the jail population.
4. Approximately 2500 juveniles are housed in adult jails.
5. From 1970 through 1992 the rate of incarceration in the nation's jails jumped from 79 to 174 inmates per 100,000 U.S. residents.
6. Approximately eight of every ten jail inmates are located in only 503 jurisdictions.

It should be pointed out that there is great variation in jail facilities across the nation. While some have inadequate living arrangements and a paucity of programs, still others are modern, utilize state-of-the-art security systems, and offer a range of activities and programs. For example, many county jails, typically operated by the county sheriff or by the police in some of the largest cities have developed public works programs. Public works crews, such as one operated in Norfolk County, Massachusetts, provide valuable community service to cities and towns in the county such as repairs to public buildings, street maintenance, and construction projects in city or county parks. Work-release programs in which eligible inmates leave jail for community jobs and return each night, have also been implemented. Typically these arrangements involve payments by work-release inmates to the institution to defray costs of their confinement, as well as allocating earnings to support family members. Education programs are also increasingly common. These usually operate either as in-house schooling, such as preparation for the high school equivalency exam (GED), or through educational-release programs, wherein inmates attend classes at local community colleges or vocational schools.

Whether or not jails sponsor special programs, virtually all jails are expensive to operate. At least ten states have enacted statutes requiring inmates to reimburse local governments for their room and Board. For example, in Strafford County, New Hampshire, where the per-inmate cost of housing was $23,000 in 1995, inmates are required to pay rent on a sliding scale. Still other states have opted for a flat fee to defray jail costs. Although charging inmates rent or fees is controversial, there appears to be strong public support for these statutes (Gaines 1995).

Although building new jails and renovating antiquated facilities will not solve all the problems faced by county and city jails, substantial attention has been given to a new concept in jail architecture, management, and operation, known as "new-generation" jails. Initially developed by the Federal Bureau of Prisons, new-generation jails are configured into a podular design, which from the exterior looks almost like a college dormitory complex. Although there are variable floor plans—some with a central lobby with living units and facilities around the perimeter, others with a central lobby/surveillance area with linear wings extending outward—the overall look of a new-generation jail has little resemblance to its traditional jail counterpart. This architectural configuration appears to yield numerous advantages in structuring inmate movement and in creating a livable environment that has a positive impact on interpersonal contacts. At the same time, the podular design permits correctional officers to exercise constant surveillance from a central point, and in some designs facilitates officer-resident contacts that make officers more than just security personnel. They also enable officers to use direct supervision techniques to create a safe and secure environment. In fact, direct supervision is seen as the hallmark of new-generation jails (Zupan 1991).

Although new-generation jails have been criticized by hard-liners as "too soft" or "like a country club with taxpayers footing the bill," these facilities make no compromise on security. Instead of bars, guard towers, and other traditional symbols of jails, the new-generation approach uses standard building materials suitable to the task, closed-circuit monitors for movement in and outside of units, and state-of-the-art devices and security measures on the outside perimeter.

Many new-generation jails are now in operation nationwide; some are newly constructed facilities, and others were created by renovating existing jails. Since three federal Metropolitan Correctional Centers were built in New York, San Diego and Chicago, dozens of county facilities have opened, such as ones in Pima County, Arizona; Spokane, Washington; Las Vegas and Reno, Nevada; Dedham (Norfolk County), Massachusetts; and Richmond (Contra Costa County), California (Direct Supervision Institute 1992).

Although criticisms remain about the direct-supervision approach, results to date have been impressive. Not only have these institutions succeeded in developing constructive programs and services with the potential to impact the lives of residents, but they have also managed to substantially reduce institutional problems, such as violent assaults, homosexual rapes, and even vandalism to institutional property.

Rehabilitation and Treatment: Facilities and Programs

Rehabilitation and treatment begin with reception, diagnosis, and classification. Some systems have independent reception centers for diagnosis and classification. In most instances, however, these functions are done by the institution to which the individual is sentenced. Wherever conducted, diagnosis and classification are generally influenced by all of the following: social background, criminal history, physical examination, psychological testing, psychiatric evaluation, vocational aptitude and skills, educational background, religious preference, and the prisoner's first reactions to imprisonment.

Classification and Diagnosis

Ideally, classification involves specifying a carefully planned program of treatment and assignment to an institution best capable of realizing its goals. In fact, some have argued that classification is primarily a device for assisting the administrative management and control of prisoners: "Most correctional classification schemes in use today are referred to as classification systems for treatment purposes, but even a cursory analysis of these schemes and the ways in which they are used reveals that they would more properly be called classification systems for management purposes" (National Advisory Commission 1975, 492).

Whatever its primary functions, classification is generally accomplished by a committee composed of the institutional superintendent (or warden), a work supervisor, chaplain, educator, psychiatrist and/or psychologist, and perhaps a social worker. Committee work includes deciding whether or not another institution might best meet the needs of the offender, the most appropriate custody level (maximum, medium, or minimum), work assignment, academic program, recreational program, and psychiatric and psychological counseling.

Information gathering is typically done through interviews, records, and testing over a matter of weeks. The time period, as well as the specific information gathered, varies by correctional system. Computer technology is also extensively used in some systems. First developed in the federal system, computerized classification can be used to screen incoming inmates as to their risk for violent or aggressive behavior and emotional instability, as well as for classifying their social skills, learning abilities, and other factors considered in the federal classification scheme.

Vocational Training and Work

Vocational training is a pervasive feature of prison systems nationwide. The rationale underlying vocational training programs is simple: Men and women leaving prison with strong vocational skills increase their opportunities to secure meaningful employment after release. And since postrelease employment is a key factor in reducing the risk of recidivism, these programs should be seen as very cost-effective. Although some institutions have poor training facilities, mostly because of insufficient funding, vocational programs make important contributions to rehabilitation programming in prisons. Civilian shop supervisors, vocational counselors, and teachers are often employed to organize work and to develop programs.

Through vocational training programs inmates can develop and maintain skills in automobile repair, plumbing and electricity, radio and television repair, welding and sheetmetal work, woodworking and cabinetmaking, masonry, landscaping, beautician and cosmetology trades, sewing and tailoring, and secretarial work. Through cooperation with private industries, some institutions sponsor training in computer technologies, such as keyboarding and data entry skills, literacy in various software packages, and computer maintenance and repair. Although the federal system is by far a leader in vocational training, many state institutions, including county jails, have made great strides in developing vocational training programs by liaisons with local community colleges and universities and by encouraging community volunteers and local industries to get involved in prison programs.

Prison labor and industrial programs, which are occasionally linked to vocational training, also permit inmates to acquire marketable work skills after release, as well as to earn wages and develop solid work habits. Some programs also produce goods and services that have economic value to the institution and the state, such as printing; auto and equipment maintenance; production of automobile licenses, tags, and road signs; and manufacture of institutional clothing. In addition, a growing number of prison systems have agreements with private corporations to hire and compensate inmates to produce goods and services while inside the institutional facility. During the Middle East crisis in 1990, inmates in the federal system were used in the assembly of parts for jet fighters. During World War II and the Korean war, prisoners in both state and federal systems played major roles in producing goods used in the war effort. Although agreements with private enterprise involve only a limited number of inmates, this trend in prison industries can lead to employment experience that will enhance inmate qualifications in locating jobs following release.

Although prison labor programs have some value, they are criticized for a number of reasons. Many, if not most, of the jobs are boring and monotonous. Moreover, they pay low wages to "captive laborers" who become trained in jobs that do not truly exist on the outside! Much of the problem lies in how the goods and services from prison industries can be used. In 1929 antiprison industry efforts of business and labor led to the passage of the Hawes-Cooper Act (which prohibited the shipment of prison goods to states banning their sale) and the Ashurst-Sumers Act in 1935 (which made the shipment of prison goods into states banning their sale a federal offense and required the label of prison goods involved in interstate commerce). Such laws led to the state use of prison goods, that is, the distribution of items produced in prison to other state institutions, such as hospitals, colleges, universities, and state institutions. Consequently, much of the training associated with the goods and services produced in prisons is virtually worthless as occupational preparation. As Gordon Hawkins observes: "It seems odd to expect prisoners... after being subjected to a regime designed to render work offensive, unrewarding and distasteful, to be motivated to adopt it as a means of obtaining a livelihood" (Hawkins 1976, 110).

Academic Education Programs

Literacy and communication skills are absolutely essential to living in modern society. They are involved in virtually every dimension of daily living, including job performance, family life, and even social adjustment to everyday problems. Education shapes, if not determines, how these essential skills are acquired and developed. Thus it is not surprising that many correction professionals regard education as among the most important programs for the men and women in prison, precisely because low educational attainment among inmates is so prevalent. According to the Bureau of Justice Statistics, better than six of every ten inmates who enter federal and state prisons are primary or secondary school dropouts. In fact, nearly 20 percent have an eighth-grade education or less. Overall, the median level of educational attainment is the eleventh grade (Maguire/BJS 1993).

Basic education for prison inmates is in most states a matter of correctional policy or legislative mandate. Ultimately the goal is to have inmates complete a high school equivalency curriculum, earning a GED (general education diploma). Some programs are operated and funded by local school districts; still others, by the state's department of corrections. In most institutions, basic educational services are under the immediate supervision of a school principal or educational director.

Although educational curricula vary by institutional setting, typically they emphasize basic literacy and mathematics to raise reading, writing, and quantitative skills to a satisfactory level. Subjects such as social studies, history, and civics are also included. In many institutions volunteer tutors provide private instruction to inmate students. Because many prisons and jails have a substantial number of Latino inmates (currently about 17 percent nationwide), some lacking proficiency in English, English as a Second Language (ESL) programs make an important contribution to prison educational services.

Virtually all major prison systems also sponsor higher education programs, many leading to college degrees. Usually funded by the state department of correction (and occasionally using grant funds from federal or private sources for special or experimental programs), local community and senior colleges, including private institutions, are contracted to provide on-site courses. Inmates transferred to other prison institutions because of changes in their custody status can continue their education when courses are offered systemwide. Although graduation rates from higher education programs are not high, many offenders continue their degree programs after release. In systems that place eligible inmates in prerelease centers, that is, state-contracted or operated community-based living facilities where inmates reside during the latter months before parole release, educational-release provisions are sometimes permitted. Thus, inmates attend classes on a local campus, returning each night to their prerelease center.

Particularly in the past three decades, many states have developed very extensive prison higher-education programs, involving multiple colleges: California, New York, Minnesota, and Michigan, among others (Jones et al. 1991). In Massachusetts, a state especially known for its many academic institutions, inmates at Massachusetts Correctional Institutions enjoy programs provided by several colleges and universities. From 1972 until 1995, the University of Massachusetts at Boston administered the Higher Education in Prisons Program, in which college courses (as well as a GED curriculum) were offered throughout the correctional system. During the 1970s and 1980s, many continued their education on the Boston campus, commuting from community-based prerelease centers. Although the program underwent numerous changes over a two-decade period, ultimately closing in 1995 because of restrictive scholarship policies, nevertheless it was successful in providing hundreds of inmates with a college-level curriculum, many of them earning undergraduate degrees.

Community colleges have also been involved in prison educational services, providing lower-division courses and some vocational programs. In the Massachusetts system, private institutions have also played important roles. For example, Boston University, where faculty teach courses at prison facilities as a form of community service, offers a curriculum leading to a bachelor's and master's degree in liberal studies.

Comments from participants in these programs offer insight as to how prison education can affect the personal lives of prisoners:

> "When I began my first course, I figured it was a way of doing easy time, and by the end I couldn't get enough courses."

> "It turned out to be my ticket to get into a college and make something of myself."

> "I think it helped me think about myself and helped me get some positive attitudes."

"I really feel proud of what I've accomplished!"

The question is, while education programs may have intrinsic value to inmates, do they have an impact on recidivism? Are participants in prison education programs less likely than other inmate groups to be repeat offenders? Numerous studies have addressed these questions, most reaching similar conclusions. Garrett and Bryant (1986), for example, tracked a population of male inmates who had participated in the Massachusetts Higher Education in Prisons Program. Only released inmates who had completed at least three or more courses during their incarceration were included in the study group. Using a three-year follow-up period, the researchers examined the postrelease records of college men and compared them to a similar group of men who had not participated in the program. The results showed that at by end of the first year following release, college men were significantly less likely to be recidivists than the comparison inmate group. By the end of the second year, differences between the two groups widened even further; by the end of the third year, only 15 percent of the total number of college men could be classified as recidivists, compared to nearly 50 percent of the comparison group (Garrett and Bryant 1986). Although the figures vary in similar studies, overall findings generally show that educational programs have a positive impact on recidivism.

Despite this evidence, prison education programs are typically not well-funded in correctional institutions. Frequently they operate with poor classroom facilities, rarely have access to computer and educational technologies available on college campuses, and seldom enjoy the advantages of an adequate library. Moreover, they are among the most vulnerable programs for elimination or downsizing in times of budgetary problems. Sometimes they are singled out by "hard-liners in corrections" as providing inmates with undeserved privileges at taxpayers' expense. Efforts to restrict inmates' eligibility for basic scholarships to pay for tuition, fees, and books have also threatened the viability of some higher education prison programs, since most of these programs must be self-supporting. Nevertheless, prison education programs survive and continue to make important contributions to rehabilitation objectives.

Treatment Interventions

The analogy of the prison as a hospital and the prisoner as a patient with a disease to cure by treatment developed in the late nineteenth century. But a serious and concerted effort to implement the concept was not mounted until after World War II.

During the late 1940s, the view of crime as an expression of mental illness became especially important. To treat the mentally ill criminal, various forms of therapy were prescribed. The fact was, however, that psychiatrists and clinical psychologists were in short supply. They were also too expensive to attract to public employment in adequate numbers. Group treatment was the natural alternative. As Lawrence Bennett and his colleague tell it: "Group therapy became more widely used following World War II when practical needs dictated that some method be developed to use the available professional talents more efficiently... that is, group treatment approaches were substituted for individual ones on the basis that in a given hour of a professional's time eight to ten more clients could be seen" (Bennett et al. 1978, 11–12).

California led the way. During the 1950s, a variety of people were trained as group counselors (vocational instructors, correctional officers, tradesmen, work foremen, clerical workers, academic teachers). By the late 1950s, more than half of the state's inmate population was involved in some form of group counseling.

Group treatment proliferated elsewhere. By 1966, group methods were used in 70 percent of the nation's correctional and penal institutions (Bennett et al 1978). At the same time, the ethics of prison therapeutic programs came under severe criticism. Before discussing the nature of the critical reaction and its consequences, it is useful to describe some of the different group treatment approaches used.

Transactional analysis (TA) has been widely adopted, mainly because it was designed as a group method and because of its comparatively uncomplicated language and its practical goals. Developed by Eric Berne, its starting point is the assumption that mental problems are the result of an inability to overcome distresses encountered in early childhood. Berne's conceptual scheme for psychological analysis is based on the premise that humans have a multiple nature. Each of us is said to be simultaneously parent, adult, and child. The parent is internalization of all the rules and expectations the young person has heard from parents and observed in their behaviors. Simultaneously, the child develops from what the youngster sees and hears. Lacking vocabulary during the earliest years, the child develops, not conceptual notions, but feeling and impressions. Most of the feedback from parents comes in the form of "don't do this." But it is in the adult that the hope for change—the possibility of resolving problems that arise in the child and parent sides to personality—resides. The goal of transaction analysis is to effect a cure by liberating the adult from the troublesome influences of the parent and child. The means to the end is the application of the conceptual scheme to the analyses of transactions. "The transaction consists of a stimulus by one person and a response by another, which response in turn becomes a new stimulus for the other person to respond to" (Harris 1967, 55).

Transaction analysis also assumes that transactions take different forms—some that deal directly with a problem and others that serve as ruses, defenses, or "games." Games are common in prisons; they permeate many staff-resident interactions, including those concerned with impression management. For example, staff involvement in therapy with inmates may be less motivated by humanitarian concerns than the opportunity to make a favorable impression on superiors and earn a promotion. Among inmates, participation in therapy may be motivated less by a desire to solve important psychological difficulties than to make a favorable impression on staff toward the end of gaining earlier release. Although there are many barriers to effective treatment in a prison, transaction analysis, by deliberately seeking to identify interaction "games," has been more effective than most therapeutic approaches in being able to confront obstacles such as "game playing" directly.

Reality therapy, developed by psychiatrist William Glasser, assumes that anyone who requires psychiatric treatment suffers from one basic inadequacy: the inability to fulfill essential needs—the need to love and be loved and the need to feel that we are worthwhile to ourselves and to others. Not everyone is equally adept at satisfying these basic needs. When these are not met, all patients are said to manifest a tendency to "deny the reality of the world about them." Consequently, therapy that leads all patients toward reality, toward grappling successfully with the tangible and intangible aspects of the real world, might accurately be called a therapy toward reality, or simply reality therapy (Glasser 1975).

Instead of conceiving of patients as mentally ill, the reality therapist conceives of them as "irresponsible." The goal is to help them take responsibility for solving or dealing with their own problems (i.e., gratifying basic needs). Thus treatment does not dwell on imparting understandings of past misfortunes that caused the "illness," but on helping patients perform in a better way now (Glasser 1975). As Bennett et al. comment about reality therapy in a correctional context:

> When used in juvenile halls and reformatories, it can become warped to justify a rather punitive, heavily disciplined approach to maintaining a quasi-military condition. When appropriately applied, however, this method can serve as a valuable tool for encouraging responsibility on the part of offenders (1978, 32).

Of the several group-treatment methods used in correctional institutions, none has been criticized more for its authoritarian and coercive elements than ***behavior modification***. It is based on the theoretical orientation and experimental techniques of behaviorists, such as B.F. Skinner and O.I. Lovaas. In this perspective, "anti-social (i.e., criminal) behaviors are learned in the same way social acceptable behaviors are. . . . This conceptualization...has several implications. . . . It implies that behaviors . . . are acquired through experience . . . and as such can be altered by changing the contingencies which maintain and control behavior" (Bennett et al. 1978, 34).

The working principle in behavior modification is that people are influenced by the consequences of their behavior. Further, it is held that the individual's current environment influences behavior more than past experiences, basic personalty, or deeply ingrained psychological traits and problems. Once important behavior-influencing stimuli are identified, they can be manipulated to emphasize positive rather than negative consequences. That is, the therapist can provide the individual with positive reinforcement or aversive stimuli (rewards and punishments). The technique is called ***operant conditioning.*** It is based on the premise that "behavior that is rewarded will increase in frequency and behavior that is extinguished (ignored) or punished will decrease in frequency" (Binder 1976, 151).

The use of behavior modification techniques in correctional institutions is controversial for a number of reasons. Of major concern is its potential use as a controlling rather than a strictly therapeutic device. If state employed, for example, the therapist may be put in the bind of having to decide whether the primary client is the inmate, the employer (a government authority), the particular institution in which employed, or society in general. Some attempt to avoid the controlling and manipulative aspects of behavior modification by the careful design of safeguards that will ensure the voluntary consent of participants. But in a "society of captives," the voluntary nature of consent must always be doubtful. Consent may be given, not out of desire to solve a problem, but to seek to please authorities in order to gain early release. And many volunteer to participate in the most dangerous activities for no other purpose than to break routine or as an escape from the boredom and tediousness of imprisonment. In addition to ethical complications, legal measures have restricted the use of behavior modification in all manner of institutional settings.

Social casework and counseling are also provided in most prisons. In the ***social casework approach,*** a professional social worker helps inmate clients, first, by developing a case history, inventorying problems that are obstacles to adjustment and rehabilitation, and providing them with a supportive climate in which to problem-solve. Issues vary from immediate problems in adjusting to incarceration to poor family relationships and concerns about the future. The caseworker helps the client form and implement plans or strategies to address these problems.

Counseling involves a one-on-one relationship between a counselor and an inmate. The relationship normally evolves through a series of stages, and if successful leads to mutual rapport so that issues can be disclosed and discussed in an honest and supportive atmosphere. The overall goal in counseling is to enable the client to gain insight into his or her problems. In its simplest form, counseling can be likened to having a "good friend"—albeit, one with effective interpersonal skills—who is willing to listen to your problems and engage in a discussion about them without casting personal judgments. As in social casework, rapport and trust between the counselor and the inmate is absolutely essential.

Sometimes called "boot camp" programs, ***shock incarceration*** is a relatively new approach used with newly convicted offenders. Since their inception in 1983, twenty-nine states, ten local jurisdictions, and the Federal Bureau of Prisons have implemented boot camps, and nine additional programs are designed solely for juveniles. To date New York, Georgia, Oklahoma, Michigan, Texas, and Maryland have the largest programs (MacKenzie et al. 1995).

Shock incarceration requires offenders to serve a short term in a prison or jail in a quasi-military program similar to basic training in military boot camps (see Box 11.8). Most state programs target young adult offenders convicted of nonviolent crimes who are serving their first prison terms. Those accepted into the program generally spend between 90 and 120 days in heavily regimented programs. Inmates who successfully complete shock incarceration are then released to community supervision; the intensity of this supervision varies by state and local jurisdiction. Those who drop out of the program or are dismissed, which quite often is a fairly large percentage, must serve out their sentences in traditional prisons or return to court for a resentencing hearing (MacKenzie 1993).

Box 11.8 A Day at Boot Camp

Upon arrival, male inmates have their heads shaved; female inmates are allowed to have short haircuts. Strict rules are enforced: At all times inmates are required to address staff as "Sir" or "Ma'am." Permission to speak must be requested, and inmates must refer to themselves as "this inmate." Punishments for even minor rule violations are summary and certain, often involving physical exercises such as push-ups, running in place, and "laps." A major rule violation can result in dismissal from the program.

Beginning with predawn reveille, days are long, typically 10–16 hours. Inmates dress quickly and march to an exercise yard, where they participate in an hour or two of physical training and drill. Following this, they march to breakfast in a dining hall, where they must stand at attention while waiting in line and move in a military manner when the line advances. Inmates are required to stand behind their chairs until commanded to sit and must eat without conversation. After breakfast, they march to worksites, where they participate in hard physical labor that frequently involves community service such as picking up litter in state parks or along highways. When the workday is over, offenders return to the compound, where they participate in more exercise and drill. Dinner is followed by evening programs that include counseling, life-skills training, academic education, or drug education and treatment. As their performance and time in the program warrants, shock incarceration inmates gradually earn more privileges and responsibility. A special hat or uniform may be the outward display of their new status. Those who successfully finish the program usually attend an elaborate graduation ceremony, with visitors and family invited to attend. Awards are often presented to acknowledge progress made during the program, and inmates may perform drill routines they have practiced in the boot camp.

Source: Adapted and reprinted in part from MacKenzie 1993, 22–23.

A survey of twenty-six programs indicated that rehabilitation and recidivism reduction were the most important goals of shock incarceration. Because many offenders in boot camps participate in substance-abuse treatment programs, it can also be an effective setting in which to deal with offenders with histories of alcohol and other drug problems. In addition to providing courts with another disposition option for convicted offenders, boot camps are also a way of reducing prison overcrowding (see Figure 11.1).

Figure 11.1
The Importance of Shock Incarceration Goals

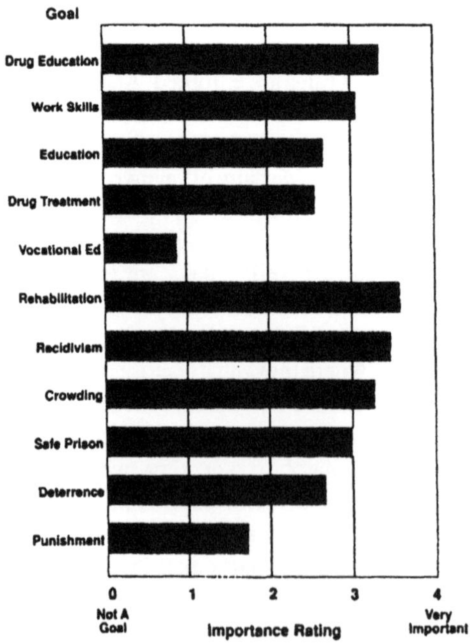

Source: MacKenzie 1993 23.

To date, the impact of shock incarceration has not been fully evaluated. Preliminary results suggest that some goals of shock incarceration are met, such as drug education and treatment, while others are not. Evidence indicates that from 8 percent to as many as 50 percent of boot camp participants fail to complete the program. In a multisite evaluation program, MacKenzie (1993) reports that boot camp inmates—regardless of the camp's orientation, therapeutic or work-oriented—had positive feelings about their participation in the program. Compared to institutionalized inmates, boot camp participants were more likely to agree that their experiences promoted self-discipline, positive changes in self-attitudes, and maturity, whereas institutionalized offenders saw little positive outcomes from their incarceration experience. (MacKenzie 1993)

As for the impact of boot camps on recidivism, there is no consistent evidence showing that shock incarceration approaches significantly lower recidivism rates. After studying programs in eight states, MacKenzie and associates (1995) did not find consistently lower recidivism rates across states for boot camp graduates in constrast to comparison groups, such as boot camp dropouts and conventional parolees. In two states, for example, there were no significant differences on recidivism measures between boot camp graduates and other groups. In two other states, boot camp graduates and dropouts did not differ on recidivism and both groups were lower than conventional parolees. In sum, the effectiveness of boot camps ln lowering recidivism rates seems to vary by program.

Substance-abuse treatment programs are also important components in the rehabilitation of incarecrated offenders. Over the past three decades, the number of alcohol- and drug-related offenders has placed an extraordinary strain on the criminal justice system. Although the relationship between alcohol, drugs, and crime has been analyzed in Chapter 3, it is also important to appreciate the sheer quantity of alcohol- and drug-involved offenders coming before the courts in a single year. For example, drug testing of arrestees in 1991 found that nearly six of every ten nationwide tested positive for at least one drug substance. In some cities, this percentage runs even higher. While not all of these offenders may be drug-addicted, data on the proportion of arrestees who self-report a need for alcohol or drug treatment is very high. For example, the National Institute of Justice found that in at least four cities—Philadelphia, Los Angeles, New York, and Birmingham—four of every ten male arrestees reported a need for substance- abuse treatment (Visher 1990). The net result is that American courts are clogged with offenders who need substance-abuse services. Unless these offenders receive adequate treatment, they are almost certain to become recidivists.

Either in or outside prison, there is no single treatment for those with alcohol and other drug-abuse problems. This is especially true of criminal offenders, who not only must confront chemical dependency but also deal with social and legal issues surrounding their criminal behaviors. Instead, substance-abuse rehabilitation approaches include a variety of programs and interventions. Depending on the setting, treatment programs include: (1) self-help and other social support programs; (2) drug counseling; (3) drug education; (4) individual and group psychotherapy; (5) education and vocational services; and (6) relapse prevention. Pharmacotherapy, that is, the use of stabilizing medications such as methadone, a synthetic substitute for heroin, or other medications that neutralize the effects of the addicting substance, are also used with drug-involved offenders. Though controversial, this approach has been used in community-based residential programs and at outpatient clinics. Urine testing is also an important tool in assuring drug-free living habits by inmates in prerelease and community-based facilities.

Self-help approaches are the most commonly found in prison and jail settings, not only because they launch an important step in the recovery process but also because they are virtually cost-free. Alcoholics Anonymous (AA), Narcotics Anonymous (NA), and Cocaine Anonymous are among the most known of these, each functioning as autonomous groups. These self-help organizations are predicated on a twelve-step philosophy that begins with admission that one is dependent on alcohol or drug substances and members helping one another through the recovery. AA/NA chapters exist in or near virtually every community in the United States, offering inmates a continuity in their recovery efforts after their release from prison. Other self-help and inmate-sponsored groups are occasionally formed in prisons that address substance abuse recovery and the problems faced by men and women with felony records.

Drug counseling and education are also common components in both prison and community-based treatment programs. Counselors trained in substance-abuse recovery work with clients to promote insight into their drug problems. Drug education classes or groups are also used in prisons, jails, and especially at community-based facilities. Sometimes independent and sometimes part of inmate self-help groups, drug education carries the rationale that it reinforces sober lifestyles; provides relevant information about the effects of alcohol, drugs, and recovery issues; and potentially affects both attitudes and behavior concerning the use of addictive substances. Drug education has been widely adopted in most boot camp programs, since many young offenders have histories of substance abuse.

Used in both prison- and community-based facilities, the ***therapeutic community model*** is the most comprehensive approach to substance abuse treatment. It involves a twenty-four-hour, highly structured living arrangement for offenders who have extensive histories of drug abuse. Such programs differ from others, first, because they draw personnel atypical of those currently working in the prison community; and second, because they usually isolate the inmate from the general prison population in a separate wing or facility. Inmates in the therapeutic community have separate work assignments, schooling, and dining arrangements. Staff working in these settings usually are assigned to the program exclusively (Chaiken 1989).

Although therapeutic communities use a structured living arrangement to deliver and control services, any number of program events can happen, depending on treatment preference. For example, in New York's Stayin Out program, located in dormitory units in a medium-security prison in midtown Manhattan, emphasis is placed on "tough love" methods of teaching individual responsibility, mutual trust, and self-discipline. In a program operated on the campus of Simon Fraser University near Vancouver, British Columbia, the primary approach stresses moral development through humanistic liberal arts education and recognizing alternative decisions. Daily routines can also differ by program, as well as actual therapeutic events. Thus, in Oregon's Cornerstone Program, located in a medium-security facility, much of the day is spent performing work duties by inmates who function like "family clusters." They attend seminars and discuss their interpersonal problems at individual and group counseling sessions. At Lantana, Florida, emphasis in on drug and group counseling, vocational training, community service activities, and work (Chaiken 1989).

Although the approach is currently popular in dealing with offenders who have histories of drug abuse, therapeutic communities are not without controversy, especially because of the "encounter group" and "controlled living" methods used in many operating programs. Moreover, evaluation results indicate that while this approach can be successful in helping offenders achieve drug-free lifestyles and staying out of crime, they also require full participation for extended periods of time, including following release. At the Stayin Out Program, offenders who were in the program for at least nine months had lower parole violations than others. In the Oregon program, 51 percent of the program graduates had no repeat offenses after three years, compared to only 11 percent of the dropouts (Visher 1990).

Because they are costly and difficult to operate inside prisons, only a limited number of therapeutic communities are in operation. But interest remains high in this approach, especially in federal correctional circles. Because hard-core drug abusers continue to increase in significant numbers in prison populations, further development of this approach is likely (Visher 1990).

Parole and Temporary Release

Among inmates currently sentenced to American prisons, from 97 to 99 percent will *eventually* be returned to the community. Some offenders will regain freedom by mandatory release, that is, by sentence expiration. The majority, however, will earn parole.

Parole

First used in Boston in 1846, parole, which today accounts for approximately three of every four releases, is a form of conditional release from prison. In 1991, nearly 5500 men and women were paroled from federal facilities. According to the Bureau of Justice Statistics, 287 of every 100,000 adults in the general population were on parole from a state or federal institution (Maguire/BJS 1992).

Although the decision to grant parole depends on a variety of factors, such as statutory eligibility, prison overcrowding, and public sentiments concerning the crime committed, parole is now so common that both inmates and institutional staff consider it to be routine. Nevertheless, as Travis and O'Leary point out, "It is generally considered at least a qualified 'act of grace' by the state and not a right of the inmate" (1984, 105).

From the standpoint of rehabilitation, parole can be seen as an effort to provide help and supervision to inmates in reintegrating them into their communities. Sometimes confused with probation, which constitutes an *alternative to incarceration* rather than a form of release from prison, parole is often criticized as an act of leniency that jeopardizes community protection. In reality, however, parole is a conditional release; that is, it "has strings attached." Here is how it works:

1. Barring any statutory restrictions on parole eligibility, all offenders are eligible for parole consideration. ***Eligibility*** refers to the earliest possible date for parole consideration, which carries no guarantees that it will be granted.

2. Determination of eligibility hinges on accumulated "good time"; that is, the number of days deducted from the sentence based on "good conduct,"and quality and quantity of participation in prison programs, such as job, education, and other institutional activities. Five states do not award good time. Among those that do, including the federal system, the application of "good time" varies widely. In some jurisdictions a fixed rate or formula is used to calculate good time (e.g., three days deducted for each month of good or meritorious conduct); in others, this determination rests with the discretion of prison officials, usually with a statutory cap on what proportion of sentence can be reduced through good behavior. Regardless of the procedure, good time must be earned by the inmate; consequently, it can also be taken away as a form of discipline when prison rules have been violated.

3. The next step is the ***parole hearing*** before the ***parole board*** or committee, which involves a presentation and review of the parole candidate's record. The parole board has the authority to review and select inmates for parole, as well as to conduct hearings and take action on cases involving parole violations. The organization and authority of parole boards differ by state, as well as how members are selected. In some jurisdictions, parole board members are experienced professionals in crime and corrections; in others, members are selected at the pleasure of the governor, who may or may not use political considerations as a basis for appointments.

4. At the parole hearing, the case is reviewed, using reports and other supporting materials included in the inmate's dossier. The inmate as well as institutional staff attend and are invited to speak. Once concluded, the case is discussed and a decision is reached. Parole boards enjoy a freedom to exercise wide discretion in reaching their decisions, since the courts have supported the position that inmates are not entitled to due process considerations (Parker 1984). Apart from an inmate's record, other factors, such as the nature of the crime and public sentiments, including those of the public prosecutor, can be and often are considered in determining parole selection. Thus, offenders convicted of heinous crimes, such as the brutal Manson family cult murders in California, are unlikely to receive parole for many years, if at all, because of strong community sentiments concerning these crimes.

5. Parole requires that a parolee comply with parole policies and stipulations. These conditions are similar to those used in probation. One set of stipulations, known as ***reform conditions***, specifies expectations of compliance with laws, maintaining employment, and refraining from illicit drug use. ***Control conditions***, in contrast, have to do with reporting to and cooperating with the parole officer and notification procedures concerning change of residence or employment. Many states continue to change these conditions, dropping some (e.g., regulation of alcohol usage or association with undesirables) and adding others (e.g., compulsory reporting if arrested or compulsory treatment and drug/alcohol testing) (Parker 1984).

Finally, parole discharge can occur in different ways; statutes concerning parole release vary by state. Parolees are automatically discharged when they fulfill the maximum or full sentence. They can also be discharged by the parole board when they have served some minimum percentage of the parole period. Commutation of sentence or executive pardon by the governor is also possible.

Temporary Release

Temporary release provisions are adopted by almost all state correctional systems, including the federal system, that permit inmates to leave prison or prerelease facilities for short periods of time for special purposes. Education- and work-release programs have already been discussed; both allow inmates to attend school or work at jobs outside the prison facility.

Home furloughs are also possible. Although states differ on eligibility criteria, furloughs permit inmates to leave the prison for home visits for specified periods of time to reestablish family ties and to make contacts in the community that will facilitate satisfactory adjustment after prison release. Home furloughs can also be granted for special purposes, such as attending a funeral or special family event.

Community Corrections

From 1950 to 1966, over one hundred riots and other major disturbances occurred in American prisons, one of the most infamous being at the State Prison of Southern Michigan in 1952. Then came the uprising at the Attica Correctional Facility in New York on September 1971—still considered a benchmark in the struggle for prisoners' rights. Although other riots were to follow, such as the bloody riot at the New Mexico State Prison that claimed the lives of thirty-three people, the Attica riot came to symbolize how ineffective prisons were in achieving the goals of corrections. In sum, it was the prison turmoil of this era that gave a strong impetus to the development of community-based correctional programs.

Scoring prisons for their dehumanizing qualities and failure to reduce crime, the National Advisory Commission on Criminal Justice Standards and Goals recommended shifting "correctional emphasis from institutions to community programs." The commission pointed out that its position was not based solely on the negative features of incarceration, which included high cost and ineffective results, but the positive values of community-based programs. From its standpoint, "The wide variety of correctional programs that are available—or could be made available—in the community allows a court to select one that is suited to the needs of an individual. . . . A youth, for example, may be sentenced to probation under varying conditions, such as the requirement that he make restitution to the victim. . . . Or he may be sentenced to partial confinement (sometimes called halfway houses) under supervision during hours when he is not working. . . . An adult may be required to live in a similar facility, working during the day and returning to the halfway house at night" (National Advisory Commission 1975, 440).

Ultimately the commission called for a moratorium on the construction of new facilities, recommending that no new adult prisons be built for ten years (and then only after convincing evidence of imperative need) and the phasing out of all state juvenile institutions for a five-year period. Any residential facility, it felt, should be located "in or close to a city." The commission acknowledged that public resistance to such thinking was inevitable and that corrections officials should be prepared to allay all fear and doubt as to the validity of community-based treatment.

The rationale underlying the movement toward community-based corrections is that while serious and violent offenders are best placed in institutional confinement, many others do not pose a major threat to the community.

Moreover, since the vast majority of offenders ultimately return to the community by way of parole or sentence expiration, rehabilitation strategies that utilize community influences can make this reintegration process more successful. The intent of community corrections is not to empty prisons, but to exercise effective rehabilitation strategies appropriate to offenders on both ends of the spectrum: diverting nonserious offenders from prison and serving incarcerated offenders when they are judged to pose no serious risks to the community.

This approach also carries valuable dividends. Not only is it cheaper on a per-capita basis to operate community-based facilities or to use alternatives to incarceration, but it also helps to reduce prison overcrowding. This in turn lessens the demand to build more prisons, saving valuable tax dollars. Latessa (1985) makes a persuasive case for the economy of community corrections compared to traditional incarceration. Latessa examined cost data for 240 diverted offenders in Lucas County, Ohio (i.e., offenders who were not sentenced to traditional incarceration). He concluded that it saved the state more than $900,000 over a seventeen-month period. Moreover, his preliminary analysis suggested that nearly 2500 offenders in a five-county district could have been diverted at an estimated savings of $9.2 million over a five-year period.

Overall evaluations of many community-based programs also point to lower recidivism rates among these offenders. This, too, adds to the cost-effective value of community programs, since the criminal justice system is spared the cost of reprocessing them on repeat offenses.

Many states have well-planned and well-developed community-based correctional programs. In 1973 Minnesota enacted the Community Corrections Act, making it the first state to take legislative action that encourages community-based correctional programming (Carney 1980).

Community corrections actually involve a variety of approaches. Some are directed at special offender groups, such as alcohol- and drug-involved offenders, youth, or young adults. Used as an alternative to incarceration, community-based facilities, such as halfway houses or "group homes," offer courts options in sentencing young or first-time offenders to programs that are more suitable to their correctional needs.

Community-based facilities also utilize different living arrangements, as well as employing a variety of therapeutic philosophies and program events. Whatever these differences, all programs or activities are located in community settings, permitting residents to interact with and utilize community resources.

Residential Centers

Residential centers are used to prepare inmates for release into the community. Criteria that must be met before an inmate can be assigned to a residential center vary by correctional system. Whatever the criteria, residential centers enable eligible inmates to return to the community under preparole arrangements. Many are operated by private organizations dedicated to helping ex-offenders under contract to the state's department of correction.

Although clinical and in-house programs operate in many of these centers, inmates also interact with community programs, such as schools or colleges, human service organizations, and state agencies pursuant to their needs. Thus inmates are able to work on their behalf by securing a job, continuing their education, and for some establishing eligibility for entitlement programs. Residential centers also enable inmates to reestablish ties with family and relatives more easily than is possible from prison facilities.

Halfway Houses

The first halfway house in America opened in 1917 as a temporary refuge for destitute released offenders in Massachusetts (Wilson 1985). Today it is the most familiar concept in community correctional approaches. Similar to prerelease centers, halfway houses are privately operated living centers that sponsor a variety of programs and services for men and women on parole. In many states, they serve as an alternative to incarceration for first-time and youthful offenders.

Halfway houses differ vastly as to their administrative and correctional philosophies, as well as in the offenders they will or will not accept as residents. Typically, living arrangements are governed by "house rules," such as curfew hours, signing in/out procedures, permissible conduct, everyday house chores, and similar details. Virtually all halfway houses operate individual and group counseling programs, assist residents in securing jobs and utilizing relevant human service agencies within the community, and work closely with state parole officials to assure resident compliance with parole stipulations. During their period of residence, house members are expected to pay their way from job earnings and/or entitlement benefits. Almost all halfway house programs place limits on how long residents can remain in the program.

Evidence of the value of halfway houses was reported in one evaluation, pointing out that they (1) are as effective in reducing recidivism as other alternatives to incarceration; (2) are successful in assisting their residents locate employment, though not necessarily in keeping it; (3) are probably less costly to operate per resident than placing offenders in prisons; and (4) do not reduce real estate property values in communities where they are located (Samaha 1991).

Ironically, halfway houses and other community-based programs are very vulnerable to political criticism, especially during periods of media-dramatized crime events. Neither are neighborhoods eager to accept them, despite vigorous attempts by halfway houses to contribute to and otherwise "fit into" the community. Commenting on the closing of an unusually creative and well-designed correctional center in Anchorage, Alaska, due in part to a relentless local media campaign, criminologist John Irwin (1970, 174) explained it in this way: "In general, the public will not allow convicted felons to live at a level of luxury or privilege above the lowest classes in society."

The Assessment of Rehabilitation Efforts

The effectiveness of rehabilitation programs has been measured primarily by comparisons of recidivism rates (as indicated by parole violations, arrest for a new crime, and recommitment) of those who have and have not undergone certain treatment (e.g., group counseling, vocational training, etc.). In 1971 Robison and Smith described the results of a study conducted by Kassebaum and associates to determine the effect of group counseling on the postrelease behavior of 968 individuals who had been inmates of a medium-security institution. Some of these inmates were assigned to small groups and others to larger groups. Still others, called the "control group," were given no counseling whatsoever. The results did little to boost the value of group counseling, in that the researchers found no significant differences in outcomes among the three groups (Robison and Smith 1978).

The most authoritative study to date on the subject was conducted by Robert Martinson. It was initiated in 1966 at the request of the New York State Governor's Special Committee on Criminal Offenders. The committee wished to know whether rehabilitation programs had "worked" anywhere in the world! "The committee," says Martinson, "was organized on the premise that prisons could rehabilitate, that the prisons of New York were not in fact making a serious effort at rehabilitation, and that New York's prison should be converted from their existing custodial basis to a new rehabilitative one" (1977, 3).

Martinson and his coworkers began their task by identifying all reputable studies of rehabilitation programs published in English between 1945 and 1967. To be selected for detailed analysis, a study had to meet the following requirements: It had to be concerned with evaluating a treatment method, and it had to involve a control group, that is, a comparison of treated and untreated subjects.

A total of 231 studies met the requirements. They dealt with a variety of measures of improvement in offender behavior: recidivism rate, adjustment to life in prison, successful employment, educational success, change in attitude and personality, and general community adjustment. In terms of recidivism, generally regarded to be the single most important indicator of the success or failure of rehabilitation programs, Martinson reported that "with few and isolated exceptions, the rehabilitative efforts that have been reported so far have had no appreciable effect on recidivism" (1977, 5).

Education, vocational training, individual and group counseling, modifications in the institutional environment, medical treatment, psychotherapy, and other basic treatment methods were found to have no appreciable influence on offender adjustment. In Martinson's (1977, 27) words: "This is not to say that we found no instances of success or partial success; it is only to say that these instances have been isolated, producing no clear pattern to indicate the efficacy of any particular method of treatment.

In an incisive critique, Ted Palmer argued that Martinson's "rather sweeping conclusion" was based on an implicit, excessively demanding criterion for assessing the effectiveness of treatment methods. That is, Palmer claimed that Martinson's judgment of a treatment method was whether or not "it worked" in nearly all tested instances. Thus, Martinson's standard for judging the success or failure of a treatment method was so stringent, so narrowly conceived, that the result of his analysis was predictable. He underrated the positive by overemphasizing the negative. But the fact is, some methods did work under certain conditions with some offenders. Thus, from Palmer's standpoint: "Rather than ask 'What works—for offenders as a whole?' we must increasingly ask 'Which methods work best for which types of offenders and under what conditions or in what types of setting'" (Palmer 1977, 825). In Palmer's view, the reasons for imprisonment are complex and require diverse treatment. Therefore, instead of seeking a serum to solve the problem, he advocates searching for many sera to treat many problems.

Appraisals of the effectiveness of rehabilitation have been heavily influenced by idealistic criteria. The tendency has been to conclude that since treatment methods have not solved problems, that is, appreciably lowered recidivism rates, they are a waste of time and energy. This conclusion seems to have been reached as often by inmates as evaluation researchers. As John Irwin points out, when new treatment programs were introduced in the 1950s in the California prison system, inmates participated in them wholeheartedly. This changed in the 1960s. "After years of embracing rehabilitation's basic tenet, submitting themselves to treatment strategies, and then leaving prison with new hope for a better future, they discovered and reported back that their outside lives had not changed" (Irwin 1981, 181). Certainly Martinson's study seems to confirm that treatment made little, if any, difference.

Nevertheless, due to a host of factors, including the overselling of the curative possibilities of different treatment methods in order to have them instituted, much more came to be expected of rehabilitation than it could realistically be expected to accomplish. In the words of one prison administrator: "One has to consider that the institution is supposed to be the end-all and correct a whole lifetime of errors, beginning with the family. . . . It's asking a bit much of an institution to completely rehabilitate a person whose history goes back to a long stream of failure" (Irwin 1981, 215).

Unrealistic expectations in regard to the postrelease behavior of offenders have also contributed significantly to critical assessment of prison rehabilitation programs. Many who believe that they have "straightened up their hand" have been returned to prison for reasons having less to do with the commission of a serious violation than an inability to appreciate the fact that "criminal ex-felons...live in a manner unacceptable by conventional people" (Irwin 1970, 181). Irwin provides the example of E., who was released from prison after serving 18 months for marijuana possession. E. returned to his family home and went to work for his father as an apprentice plumber. Within the first week after being released, E. was visited by a former friend, who offered him some marijuana cigarettes. According to E., he accepted the cigarettes but did not smoke them. Instead, after the friend departed, E. stashed them in his room. Some few days later, and apparently after E. had forgotten about the matter, policemen came to the home with a search warrant. They searched his room and found the cigarettes. The friend had been arrested for possession and told the police that he had given some marijuana cigarettes to E. Subsequently, E. was recommitted on a second possession charge (Irwin 1970).

It would seem naive to expect released offenders to avoid all past associates and to start a new life in a totally different or unfamiliar environment—at least without detailed prerelease planning (especially job placement) and postrelease assistance. Ex-offenders may get into further difficulty not so much because they have not changed but because of their social backgrounds, where they reside, past friendships, circumstantial dilemmas, the stigma of having a criminal record, and any number of equally important factors. The community treatment alternative to imprisonment has not realized the hopes of its advocates for such reasons. This explains in part why American corrections in the 1990s has shifted its policy emphasis in favor of more traditional correctional practices.

Correctional Institutions and the Crisis of HIV/AIDS

Acquired Immunodeficiency Syndrome, or AIDS, constitutes one of the serious health crises in modern times. Caused by the deadly Human Immunodeficiency Virus, more commonly called HIV, AIDS is a disease that undermines the human body's immune system, making its victims susceptible to a range of opportunistic infections, malignancies and other diseases that would not ordinarily be life-threatening to people with healthy immune systems. Although its highest incidence is currently found in certain "risk groups," the highest being intravenous (IV) drug users and among men having sex with men, epidemiological studies on the prevalence of AIDS and HIV infection show that it is on the rise in the larger population, including women and teenagers. African American and Latino populations have been especially vulnerable to high infection rates.

But, if AIDS is a public health crisis in the free society, it is even more so in prison communities, partly because prison populations have disproportionate numbers of inmates who have engaged in risk behaviors, such as IV drug use, many of them already HIV positive. What makes this health crisis all the more alarming is that prisons are essentially "closed communities," where *any* infectious disease can spread rapidly. Thus, by mutual consent or by force, men who have sex with other men in prison are at definite risk of passing along or contracting HIV.

Survey data collected from state prisons and jails nationwide show that 2.2 percent of all inmates who reported the results of their HIV test said they were HIV-positive. Thus, this percentage is based only on those who revealed the results (51 percent) and does *not* include those who did not, had never been tested, or who did not know the results of the HIV test (see Box 11.9).

Box 11.9 Factoid on HIV infection in Prisons and Jails, 1991

Of all prison inmates, 55.9 percent said they had been tested after the most recent admission to prison.

Of those inmates who were ever tested for the HIV *and* reported the results:

—Women (3.3 percent) were more likely than men (2.1 percent) to test HIV-positive.

—3.7 percent of Latino inmates and 2.6 percent of African American inmates tested HIV-positive, compared to 1.1 percent of white/non-Latino inmates.

—Latina women (6.8 percent) had higher HIV-positive rates than non-Latina white women (1.9 percent). African American women had a positive rate of 3.5 percent.

Drug users and those who had shared needles had higher positive rates than other inmates.

—For inmates reporting test results, 2.5 percent of drug users, compared to 0.8 percent of other inmates, reported that they tested HIV-positive.

—The percent of HIV-positive was higher among inmates who *(a)* used drugs in the month before their offense (2.8 percent); *(b)* used needles to inject drugs intravenously (4.9 percent) and shared needles with other drug users (7.1 percent).

Source: Bureau of Justice Statistics 1993.

Other data reflect how the AIDS epidemic is growing in American prisons. For example, the Bureau of Justice Statistics (1993) reported that in 1991, 28 percent of the 1863 prison inmate deaths in American correctional institutions were AIDS-related. New Jersey (69 percent) and New York (66 percent) were highest; Florida (44 percent) and Maryland (33 percent) followed. Moreover, AIDS-related mortality can be expected to grow in the 1990s, since the most recent data available show 9 percent of known HIV-positive inmates had confirmed AIDS.

Apart from the tragedy of those victimized by HIV/AIDS, this epidemic has created a policy crisis in correctional systems. Among the issues of greatest importance are protecting uninfected inmates and staff from infection, cell or housing policy, medical liability for care of HIV-infected inmates, and balancing health care for AIDS patients with custody obligations. To date, most of the court cases revolving around these issues have brought decisions that generally supported the position of correctional authorities.

The Inmate Society

Although correctional administrators and custodial staff are responsible for running a prison, presumably exercising an authoritarian system with strict rules that control every feature of institutional life, in reality an inmate society emerges in every prison community that is even more authoritarian and strict. In this sense, prisoners are as much responsible for maintaining the social order as administrators and guards. Some would even argue that the mark of an effective administrator is knowing what rules and policies will be tolerated by inmates, as well as how rigorously they are enforced. In sum, there is a delicate balance between the official authority of the staff, on the one side, and the collective power of the inmate society to determine how its members will be governed, on the other.

For several decades, the inmate subculture has been an object of fascination by sociologists, who have spent considerable time studying why it evolves and how it functions to bring cohesion to the inmate society. Among the first was Joseph Fishman's study, *Sex in Prison* (1934). Though addressing the features of the subculture only indirectly, Fishman identified two categories of men who have sex with other men: the passive group, made up of what inmates themselves call "punks," "girls," "fags," or "pansies"; and the active role, such as "wolves" and "top men." His observations led him to believe that prison life socialized men into these roles, making them homosexual "turn-outs" as heterosexual life fades away (see Box 11.10).

Box 11.10 Prison Sex roles: Inside Sing Sing

There are several main styles of homosexual adjustment. The jocker-commissary punk arrangement is probably the most common. Jockers are referred to in the joint as "daddies," "studs," the "old man," and "jockos." I seldom met one who wasn't a conceited son-of-a-bitch and a taker. Lots of times jockers are ex-punks who have got a lot of muscle lifting iron and are a little con-wise from being overlong in the joint. . . . Some hep cons see the jocker as being as weak as his punk. But their outward appearance is one of toughness and savvy. . . .

The commissary punk is the most common feminine figure in the joint. Most likely he is a young, "pretty," naive, and inexperienced inmate who is cajoled, forced, or socialized into homosexuality by an older, wiser con. . . . Maybe the kid will come back from dinner and find a carton of butts and a case of Hershey bars laying on the end of his bunk. . . .

Poor kid! In a little while he looks up and there's this stud leaning up against the bars with a shit-eating grin on his face. By this time the kid has consumed several of the candy bars and is chain-smoking the cigarettes. "Hey kid," says old jocko, "you take care of me, I take care of you! You know what I mean? Now, I'm going to send my runner up here with some more goodies that will make your fishtank time easier to do. What about that!" . . . What determines the strength and bravery of [the commissary punk] is past history and present motivation. If a punk desires material goods bad enough, and has no legitimate possibilities for obtaining them, he will often give in and go along with the program. If he doesn't need goods, or doesn't want them bad enough to compromise, he might be able to stand up against the pressure and survive without undergoing sexual assault. Of course, sometimes a kid is forcibly raped or gang-shagged by three or four roving jocks. . . .

Queens are feminine males, sometimes evolving from the kid role. Although queens are rarely transvestites, they are consider to be "she's," "girls," "bitches," "broads," or "ladies." They are outwardly feminine in appearance and mannerism, and to some various extent tend to have a psychological set toward femininity. They shack up, fall in love, get married (to jockers), become wives, and exhibit jealousy. . . . After you been in the joint a while, some of them boss bitches really get to resemble women.

In the homosexual life of the joint, the pervert or fag is considered to be at the end of the line. Sometimes guards are identified as perverts... who are considered by the cons to be "natural" in their roles. Usually the faggot is an older con, completely socialized and satisfied in prison life. They are often very secretive and withdrawn. . . .

Almost all homosexuals, both jocks and punks, are the result of being made that way inside the joint. A few are that way on the bricks, especially queens, but not many. Usually the guards and administration know what's going on, but they often refrain from taking preventive measures 'cause they have some kind of stake in the inmate structure remaining essentially the same, or they plain don't give a damn.

Source: Reprinted from Rettig, Torres, and Garrett 1977, 100–102, by permission of the authors.

Hans Reimer's (1937) paper on socialization into the inmate society identified various social types according to how closely they adhered to the inmate social code. Hayner and Ash (1936) also examined inmate activities, focusing on "conniving" or sub rosa activities to gain hard-to-get goods and services. Donald Clemmer (1940), a sociologist and later Director of Correction in the District of Columbia, contributed the first hallmark study on male prison subcultures. More than any other, Clemmer's work charted details of the prison subculture, such as the inmate social code, the underground economy of contraband, sexual activities and sexual roles, and the adversarial relationship between staff and inmates, around which much of prison subculture revolves. His concept of *prisonization* is especially important because it chronicles how inmates become socialized to the formal and informal social systems in prisons. Clemmer's work in this respect carried important practical implications, since he maintained that once inmates became "prisonized," that is, once they internalized the norms of the prison subculture, they became highly resistant, if not immune, to traditional values of the larger society, embodying what many people call the "hardened criminal." This form of treatment-resistant inmate does not bode well for the triumph of rehabilitation.

Clemmer's work begins what has come to be a rich tradition of sociological studies of the inmate social system and subculture. Building on the earlier work of sociologists, Schrag (1971) during the 1940s refined a typology of inmate social types, using inmate argot that precisely conveys the social roles these men played in the Washington State Penitentiary: the "right guy," the "square john," the "politician," and the "outlaw."

Gresham Sykes (1958) undertook a three-year study of the New Jersey State Prison at Trenton. In what is surely a masterpiece of cogent description, Sykes provides a detailed account of the prison subculture. He identifies prison argot, the "insider" words that develop around everyday events and social roles: rat, squealer, center man, merchant, fish, ball buster, and many more. The convict code, he observes, conveys the behavior expectations of how inmates *must* behave. It contains five prohibitions: (1) "don't interfere with inmate interests"; (2) "don't lose your head"; (3) "don't exploit inmates"; (4) "don't weaken"; and (5) "don't be a sucker." Sykes concludes that inmate subculture emerges as a response to the pains of incarceration: the loss of autonomy, freedom, dignity, security, and especially sexual relationships. Thus, this perspective assumes a deprivation model in explaining the emergence of prison subcultures. The more cohesive the prison society, the more effective it becomes in reducing the pains of imprisonment for its members (Sykes 1958). Others, however, have argued that an "importation model" better explains the prison subculture, which is much more than a response to deprivations; instead, criminals bring with them to prison values, norms and a social code (Thomas and Peterson 1975).

Although research on the inmate subculture in women's institutions also dates back to the early 1900s, the most in-depth studies were conducted since 1960. Heffernan (1972), for example, provides evidence that the social organization of women's prisons also embodies distinct social types: the square or noncriminal type; recidivists, made up of the prostitute, shoplifter, or drug user/dealer; and the "cool," who is a professional from organized crime. Giallombardo (1966) and Ward and Kassebaum (1965) delineate sexual roles, such as the "butch" and the "femme," noting that unlike the male inmate subculture, the social organization of women's institutions evidence "families" or pseudofamilies, wherein one member acts the role of father, mother, brother and sisters. Thus, families tend to serve as a form of emotional security and especially protection in times of crisis.

"Prison Days and Nights"

Correctional institutions always have rules! Many of these rules serve security needs, while others impose order and regimen on the inmate population so that the routine business of running and living in a prison can be done as conveniently and as efficiently as possible. This regimen also makes it possible to stand guard over a large population with a minimum of personnel.

Because rules are very important to prison life, new inmates learn about them even before they become settled into institutional life. Contrary to vintage Hollywood movies about life in the "big house," where "convicts" are called to the warden's office for eye-to-eye hardtalk, new inmates are usually briefed about prison rules of conduct during initial processing or during orientation and classification.

Inmates have established other rules and codes of conduct to keep order among themselves. Rarely are these written down, although one enterprising group of inmates actually prepared a booklet for inmates entering a maximum-security institution in Massachusetts, which gives their version of how to do prison time. Funded by the New England Materials for Instruction Center at Boston University, excerpts from this booklet offer a window into the inmate social structure and how inmates try to accommodate the rules of their keepers, and simultaneously get along with fellow inmates. It is the inmate version of "prison days and nights."

> In introducing this booklet, the first and foremost point we want to state is that every word has been compiled and written by inmates. It has been written specifically to familiarize new men with the prison surroundings here. It contains information that we feel will give you an overall (but not exact) picture of prison life here, and what we have found to be the smartest and quickest way back out that front door. Only you can decide how your time will be served. We only ask that you consider what is written in this booklet (much of which has been learned the hard way) before you decide. . . .
>
> Today you enter upon an entirely new experience, one we truly wish you could be spared. Hopefully, you will soon re-enter the "outside world"—most men do sooner or later. . . . It will depend to a great extent upon you—and you alone—which category you become: a "sooner" or "later."
>
> Your earliest concern should be to determine exactly what your parole date is, as well as your "good time" release date. Don't rely on the opinion of other cons... their views are just that—opinions. The administration can provide you with the best source, and it is their duty to do this. One word of caution, though: Doublecheck everything even though it stems from the administration. . . .
>
> If you are fortunate enough to have a friend here—and we mean a real friend—he will be in a position to ease your entry into the institution considerably. He can "grease the skis" and guide you in your efforts at survival. . . .
>
> There are many ways to "do time"—the hard way, in trouble most of the time; the solo way, which is safe but lonely, and what we will propose as the "smart way."
>
> As to the "hard way"—you can't win! They have plenty of manpower and plenty of lockup space. All we can say is use your head, play it smart and destroy the system by getting out as fast as possible. If there are no cons, there can't be any prisons.
>
> The "solo way" . . . is lonely. And if being a solo brands you as an oddball, it can be very unsafe. Cons are probably the most completely conforming group in the country. Anything unusual immediately calls attention to the individual and this is frowned on. Also, the most harmful part of this solo role is that it wastes the time you have to serve. . . .
>
> We're assuming that you've decided to at least try the "smart way" and make the best possible use of your time. You'll find that cons will

> be antisocial toward you and perhaps the best explanation for this is a lack of trust. Any feelings of fear or uncomfortableness that you have are the very same ones that other cons have for you. . . .
>
> Now we come to the problem that will make or break your stay here: the "screw" or officer. Your very survival will from now till you're released depend on these men. Some cons will tell you to hate them all. Our message is simple: you'll have to at least get along with the bad ones and don't take advantage of the good ones... as in the future it might be one of these men who will give you a break when a situation arises.
>
> During your first few days you'll probably feel you're walking on eggs. The administration will be trying to find out what kind of a con you're going to be as they're just as unfamiliar with you as you are with them. After they figure you out (or think they have), they'll act accordingly. . . . As a rule, they won't go out of their way to harass you unless you first give them reason to. On occasion, some of the more hostile ones will issue orders in a tone that invites a reaction from you. Here again, stop and think before you react—don't play the game their way! They lose nothing; you wind up losing "good time," visits from your family and all the things you now value in prison. . . .
>
> There are a few cardinal rules (inmate rules) which you should know and learn quickly:
>
> 1. Minding one's own business: It's best to make friends slowly if you don't know anyone as you could place yourself in situations where the consequences to you could be disastrous.
>
> 2. Do not gape into other people's cells: The reason for this is because there have been cases of theft in the past and men have been accused of just such acts on evidence as weak as this. This could lead to serious consequences for you, so take a word of advice and don't gape into other guys' rooms.
>
> 3. Don't weep about your sentence: Talking about your time doesn't do anyone any good. By this it is meant that no one is happy with the time they have and they don't want to sit around listening to a weeper! If you do feel that you have a legitimate beef, there are a few good men who are qualified and familiar with... criminal law to help you. Again, ask the block runner who knows their law; you can always get word to the guy no matter where he is.
>
> 4. Stealing from another inmate: Stealing from another inmate is the lowest of the cardinal sins that a man can commit. For a little material gain, a man may pay a great price—so just think about it! (NEMIC undated, 2–7)

Summary and Conclusion

This chapter has focused on correctional institutions and correctional processes. Considerable attention has been given to the history and evolution of prisons, identifying two major types of prison architecture and penology: the *Pennsylvania system*, which emphasized solitude and isolation, and the *Auburn system*, which came to be the dominant system of prison construction used in the United States. By the turn of the century, an infrastructure of large, fortress-like, Auburn-style prisons was in place nationwide. The impact of the Auburn system continues to operate today, housing inmates in large cell blocks and emphasizing a philosophy of discipline and participation in institutional programs.

Yet, as the chapter has pointed out, the evolution of the American philosophy of correction has shifted over the centuries, moving from a platform of discipline and punishment to a modern perspective emphasizing rehabilitation as a correctional goal. At the same time, it is clear that the American correctional system has had a difficult time in integrating traditional punishment and retribution objectives with efforts to rehabilitate prisoners. Nevertheless, evidence of a commitment to rehabilitation programs common to many prison systems has been reviewed, including job programs, prison labor and industries, vocational training, prison education, and counseling and substance-abuse treatment programs. Though subject to ever-changing public politics, community correction offers courts options for diverting offenders from the prison system, as well as serving needs of offenders exiting from prisons. In combination with parole and probation, community corrections has played an important role in shaping the correctional system during the 1960s through the 1980s. However, national trends in the 1990s show that American corrections is shifting its policy emphasis in favor of more traditional forms of confinement.

References

American Correctional Association. 1983. *The American Prison: From the Beginning*... Washington, D.C.: American Correctional Association.

Beck, Allen J., et al. 1993. *Jail Inmates 1992*. Washington, D.C.: U.S. Department of Justice, Bureau of Justice Statistics.

Bennett, Lawrence A., et al. 1978. *Counseling in Correctional Environments*. New York: Human Sciences Press.

Binder, Virginia. 1976. "Behavior Modification: Operant Approaches to Therapy." In *Modern Therapies*, edited by Virginia Binder, Arnold Binder, and Bernard Rimland. Englewood Cliffs, N.J.: Prentice Hall.

Boston Globe. 1994. "U.S. Inmates in '93 Soar to a Record 948,881." *Boston Globe*, June 2 1994, 26.

Bureau of Justice Statistics. 1993. *Survey of State Prison Inmates, 1991*. Washington, D.C.: U.S. Department of Justice.

———. 1994. *U.S. Prison Population, 1993* (press release). Washington, D.C.: U.S. Department of Justice.

Caldwell, Robert. 1965. *Criminology*. New York: Ronald Press.

Carney, Louis B. 1980. *Corrections: Treatment and Philosophy*. Englewood Cliffs, NJ: Prentice Hall.

Chaiken, Marcia R. 1989. *In Prison Programs for Drug-Involved Offenders*. Washington, D.C.: National Institute of Justice.

Clemmer, Donald. 1940. *The Prison Community*. New York: Holt, Rinehart and Winston.

Direct Supervision Institute. 1992. *Detention Facilities*. Denver: Direct Supervision Institute.

Finn, Peter, and Andrea K. Newlyn. 1993. "Miami Drug Court Gives Drug Defendants a Second Chance." *National Institute of Justice Journal*, November, 13–20.

Fishman, Joseph. 1934. *Sex in Prison*. New York: National Library Press.

Gaines, Judith. 1995. "Crime-and-punish Rent," *Boston Globe* (August): 1, 6,

Garrett, Gerald R. and Kathleen Bryant. 1986. "Looking for 'Mr Goodboy': Do Prison Education Programs Really Work?" Paper presented at the annual meetings of the Academy of Criminal Justice Sciences, Orlando, Fla.

Giallombardo, Rose. 1966. *Society of Women: A Study of Women's Prison*. New York: Wiley.

Gillin, John. 1935. *Criminology and Penology*. Rev. ed. New York: D. Appleton-Century.

Glasser, William. 1975. *Reality Therapy*. New York: Harper & Row.

Greenfeld, Lawrence. 1991. *Women in Prison*. Washington, D.C.: U.S. Department of Justice, Bureau of Justice Statistics.

Harlow, Caroline W. 1989. *Drugs and Jail Inmates, 1989*. Washington, D.C.: U.S. Department of Justice, Bureau of Justice Statistics.

Harris, Thomas A. 1967. *I'm OK—Your're OK*. New York: Harper & Row.

Harris, William H., and Judith J. Levy. 1975. *The New Columbia Encyclopedia*. New York: Lippincott.

Hawkins, Gordon. 1976. *The Prison*. Chicago: University of Chicago Press.

Hayner, Norman, and Ellis Ash. 1939. "The Prisoner Community as a Social Group." *American Sociological Review* 4 (June):362–69.

Heffernan, Esther. 1972. *Making It in Prison: The Square, the Cool, and the Life*. New York: Wiley.

Irwin, John. 1970. *The Felon*. Englewood Cliffs, N.J.: Prentice Hall.

———. 1981. *Prisons in Turmoil*. Boston: Little, Brown.

Johnston, Norman. 1973. *The Human Cage*. New York: Walker and Company.

Jones, R., Silva, W., and Williford, M. 1991. "A Bibliography Project for Prison Higher Education," presented at the Prison Higher Education Caucus of the National University Continuing Education Association, Miami (April).

Latessa, Edward. 1985. "Community Corrections as Diversion: Saving Money and Reducing State Commitments." In *Probation, Parole and Community Corrections*, edited by Lawrence Travis. Prospect Heights, Ill.: Waveland Press.

MacKenzie, Doris Layton. 1993. "Boot Camps in Prisons in 1993." *National Institute of Justice Journal*, November, 21–28.

———, Robert Brame et al. 1995. "Boot Camp Prisons and Recidivism in Eight States." *Criminology* 33 (August): 327–357.

Maguire, Kathleen, et al. 1992. *Sourcebook of Criminal Justice Statistics, 1992*. Washington, D.C.: U.S. Department of Justice, Bureau of Justice Statistics.

Martinson, Robert. 1977. "What Works? —A Comparative Assessment." In *Crime and Justice*. vol. 3. Edited by Sir Leon Radzinowicz and Marvin E. Wolfgang. New York: Basic Books.

National Advisory Commission on Criminal Justice Standards. 1975. *A National Strategy to Reduce Crime*. New York: Avon.

New England Materials for Instruction Center (NEMIC). Undated. *Prision Days and Prision Nights*, unpublished manuscript, Boston University.

Orland, Leonard. 1975. *Prisons: Houses of Darkness*. New York: Free Press.

Palmer, Ted. 1977. "Critique of Martinson." In *Crime and Justice*. vol. 3. Edited by Sir Leon Radzinowicz and Marvin E. Wolfgang. New York: Basic Books.

Parker, William. 1984. "Highlights of Parole." In *Probation, Parole, and Community Corrections*. 3rd ed. Edited by R. Carter et al. New York: Wiley.

Pierson, George Wilson. 1938. *Tocqueville and Beaumont in America*. New York: Oxford University Press.

Rafter, Nicole Hahn. 1985. *Partial Justice: Women in State Prisons, 1800–1935*. Boston: Northeastern University Press.

Reimer, Hans. 1937. "Socialization in the Prison Community." *Proceedings of the American Prison Association*.

Rettig, R., M. Torres, and G.R. Garrett. 1977. *Manny: A Criminal-Addict's Story*. Boston: Houghton Mifflin.

Robison, James, and Gerald Smith. 1978. "The Irrelevance of Correctional Programs." In *Justice and Corrections*, edited by N. Johnston and L. Savitz. New York: Wiley.

Rothman, David J. 1971. *The Discovery of the Asylum*. Boston: Little, Brown.

Samaha, Joel. 1991. *Criminal Justice*. St. Paul: West Publishing Company.

Schrag, Clarence. 1971. *Crime and Justice: American Style*. Rockville, Md.: National Institute for Mental Health.

Sommer, Robert. 1976. *The End of Imprisonment*. New York: Oxford University Press.

Stern, Henry. 1995. "State, Federal Prisons Reach One Million inmate level. *Boston Globe* (August 10).

Sykes, Gresham. 1958. *Society of Captives*. Princeton: Princeton University Press.

Tappan, Paul. 1960. *Crime, Justice and Society*. New York: McGraw-Hill.

The President's Commission on the Law Enforcement and the Administration of Justice. 1967. *The Challenge of Crime in A Free Society*. Washington, D.C.: Government Printing Office.

Thomas, Charles W., and David M. Petersen. 1975. *Prison Organization and Inmates Subcultures*. Indianapolis: Bobbs-Merrill.

Travis, Lawrence, and Vincent O'Leary. 1984. "A History of Parole." In *Probation, Parole, and Community Corrections*, edited by R. Carter et al. New York: Wiley.

Visher, Christy A. 1990. "Incorporating Drug Treatment in Criminal Sanctions." *National Institute of Justice Reports* 221 (Summer):2–7.

Ward, David A., and Gene G. Kassebaum. 1965. *Women's Prisons: Sex and Social Structure*. Chicago: Aldine.

Wilson, George. 1985. "Halfway House Programs for Offenders." In *Probation, Parole, and Community Corrections*, edited by Lawrence Travis. Prospect Heights, Ill.: Waveland Press.

Zupan, Linda. 1991. *Jails: Reform and the new Generation Philosophy*. Cincinnati: Anderson.

PART IV

The Future Prospect

Chapter 12
The Future: Crime Rates and Effects

Given the amount of research and writing on crime, it might be assumed that considerable attention has been given to future patterns and trends. Such is not the case. What little one finds on the subject is generally written by journalists rather than professionally employed criminologists. This is somewhat surprising for any number of reasons, not the least of which is the growing worldwide concern with forecasting the possible political and economic repercussions of population growth, urbanization, and the ever intensifying competition for scarce natural resources. The words of the Club of Rome and the contents of journals such as the *Futurist* and *Futurology* attest to this fact.

The few who examine future crime trends generally couch their discussions in terms of factors that have an overriding influence on human behavior and social organization in the contemporary world. Thus, this chapter begins with an examination of the possible bearing on future crime of two such variables: population (composition, growth) and economic change (unemployment rates). This is followed by a discussion of the possible law-enforcement response to future crime. The last section examines the future of corrections in the light of the findings and implications of the preceding sections.

Forces of Social Change and Future Crime

The Demographic Factor

It is commonly assumed that certain demographic changes may have a profound effect on future crime rates. The major demographic trend in the United States has been a declining rate of population growth. Over the past three decades, the average annual rate of population growth declined from 1.31 percent in the 1960s, to 1.05 during the 1970s, and .94 percent during the 1980s. More specifically, the percentage of the population in the high-crime-prone ages of 15–24 steadily decreased from 1940 to 1960 (from 18.2 percent to 13.4 percent). On the strength of such evidence, Joseph Coates predicted "that over the next 25 years there will be a great diminution in the percent of the population in [the] crime-prone ages and, consequently, a real downturn in serious crime" (1972, 31). And in 1973 the National Advisory Commission on Criminal Justice Standards and Goals went so far as to say that "the pressures recently felt by the criminal justice system due to the unusually large numbers of youths resulting from the postwar baby boom will be substantially lessened during the 1970s and 1980s" (cited in Wollan 1976, 124).

Unfortunately, such predictions were not only overly optimistic but also largely incorrect. Throughout the 1960s the rate of serious crime (as measured by the FBI's annual Crime Index) steadily increased (rising from 1870 in 1960 to 3984 in 1970). Although fluctuating from year to year during the 1970s, the total Crime Index rate rose from 3984 in 1970 to 5950 in 1980. During the 1980s, it decreased steadily between 1980 and 1984 (from 5950 in 1980 to 5031 in 1984) but steadily increased from 1984 to 1990 (from 5031 to 5820). Across the decade, the total serious crime rate dropped from 5950 in 1980 to 5820 in 1990. Nonetheless, the 1990 figure was more than three times the 1960 figure of 1870. But, since 1991, the data show a consistent decline from 5898 in 1991 to 5483 in 1993.

Interestingly, the percentage of the male population in the high-crime-prone ages (15–24) increased steadily between 1960 and 1980 (from 13.5 percent in 1960 to 17.5 percent in 1970 and 18.7 percent in 1980). Between 1980 and 1990 the percentage of the male population in these ages declined from 18.7 percent to 14.9 percent. In other words, there appears to be a correspondence between these trends and those for serious crime rates. When the serious crime rate increased (between 1960 and 1980) so did the male population aged 15–24. And when the serious crime rate dropped (between 1980 and 1993), so did the proportion of the male population in the high-crime-prone ages of 15–24.

When the subject is violent crime (which usually accounts for about 10 percent of the Crime Index Total but is disproportionately committed by young males), the pattern does not hold. Despite the drop in the male population between 15–24 between 1980 and 1993, the violent crime rate increased from 597 to 746. There has been, however, a steady lowering in the amount of the violent crime rate increase. It increased 127 percent between 1960 and 1970, 64 percent between 1970 and 1980, and 20 percent between 1980 and 1993.

It should be pointed out that there were those in the 1970s who had a surer sense than others of what was to come. For example, Lauran Wollan, after citing the National Advisory Commission's prediction, claimed that others believed a downturn in serious crime would not become evident until at least 1981 and probably not until the 1990s, "since there is now an increasing proportion of urban minority youth with disproportionately higher propensities toward violent crime" (1976, 124). What particularly concerned Wollan was the commission's failure to consider the bearing on future crime trends of the well-documented different fertility trends and residential patterns of blacks and whites.

The U.S. Bureau of the Census defines the fertility rate as "the number of births that 1000 women would have in their lifetime if, at each year of age, they experienced the birth rates occurring in the specified year." The fertility rate of the black population has long been found to be higher than that of the white population. Since 1950, the highest fertility rates for both groups were attained in 1960: 4522 for blacks and 3533 for whites. In 1989, the last year for which data are available, blacks (2583) continued to evidence a higher fertility rate than whites (1885).

Correlatively, the percentage of the black population in the high-crime-prone ages has remained higher than that of the white population. In 1970, those between ages 15 and 24 represented 8.5 percent of the white population and 9.2 percent of the black population; and in 1980 the respective figures were 9.3 and 10.5 percent. Between 1980 and 1990, the percentage of those 15 to 25 declined in both populations: from 9.3 to 7.1 percent for whites and 10.5 to 8.6 percent for blacks. Nonetheless, the gap between the two groups consistently widened over the course of the past three decades—from .7 percent in 1970 to 1.2 percent in 1980 and 1.5 percent in 1990. Assuming a continuation of these trends into the near future and a correlation between them and the violent crime rate, the rate of violent crime should continue to decline, but the proportionate involvement in violent crime of black and white males should increasingly diverge rather than converge.

It is important to note that any attempt to predict or estimate future crime trends on the basis of demographic trends must be tempered by an awareness of intervening and overriding factors such as discrimination and economic recession. As Wollan reminds us, "the origins of [street] crime are in the conditions of poverty, ignorance, and discrimination" (1976, 125).

The Economic Factor

An overriding fact of recent years is economic recession, a major indicator of which is a steadily increasing unemployment rate since 1989. At this writing some 9 million people (over 7 percent of the labor force) are unemployed. The question is, Is there a documented connection between unemployment and crime? If unemployment continues to rise, can we expect a concomitant rise in the future rate of crime?

At the outset, it is important to point out that since the 1960s, economists have taken an increasingly greater interest in the crime problem. Their work and theoretical orientation have shaped basic research on the relationship between labor force characteristics, including unemployment, and crime.

In classical economic theory, people in general are posited to be guided by a utilitarian motive, namely, a desire to maximize monetary and related forms of economic gain at minimum cost. The individual is a rational "actor" who decides to do something after weighing the costs and benefits of alternative courses of action. Considering the would-be offender, and as Nobel prizewinning economist Gary Becker puts it: "A person commits an offense if the expected utility to him exceeds the utility he could get by using his time and other resources at other activities" (1968, 176).

Following the economic model, one might predict a rise in crime when there is a decrease in legal and an increase in illegal opportunities for economic gain. Similarly, crime might be presumed to decline when the opposite situation occurs, that is, when there is an increase in legal and a decrease in illegal opportunities for economic gain. Interestingly, advocates of the economic model have favored a policy of crime rate reduction that emphasizes increasing the costs of crime (deterrence) rather than increasing the availability of legal economic opportunities (for example, government job creation). As Thompson et al. state: "One important cost—deterrence through the application of formal criminal sanctions (arrest, conviction and punishment)—is emphasized by economists to the virtual exclusion of the role of other factors, such as incentives deriving from improved employment opportunity" (1981, 37).

But the thrust of critical analyses of the model have been directed elsewhere, namely, at the need to test the validity of the theory by analysis of the everyday behavior of a properly selected cross-section of individuals in a given population. It seems certain, for example, that individuals make decisions to engage in illegal and other activity on less than objective appraisal and less than complete knowledge of all the means available to accomplish given ends, economic and otherwise. It is also true that behavioral decision making is guided as much as anything else by vaguely understood emotions. It is, then, one thing to assume that anyone is a potential criminal and another that all or most criminal behavior is either rationally contrived or economically motivated.

To conceive of crime as a rationally determined course of action by those with a variety of legal and illegal options to attain their ends would appear to require nothing less than consideration of all the behavioral factors that may influence decision making. At the least, it would be necessary to identify the actual conditions under which rationally decided upon, economically motivated crime occurs. Despite the lack of evidence on the specific factors that link the theory to the presumed effect, some economists, on the basic of statistical analyses of aggregate data, have drawn radical conclusions concerning the relationship between unemployment and crime. Economist M. Harvey Brenner (1976), for example, informed a congressional committee in 1970 that a 1.4 percent increase in unemployment was "directly responsible" for 1740 homicides and 7660 admissions to state prisons; and that a 1 percent rise in unemployment lasting for six years would be associated with about 3340 state prison admissions.

Subsequent research failed not only to support a high relationship between unemployment and crime but also gave rise to what Theodore Chiricos refers to as "a consensus of doubt." He reports that from the late 1970s many contend that aggregate level studies have failed to find a consistent and significant correlation between unemployment and crime rates.

Chiricos examined the results of sixty-three studies based on aggregate level evidence. Forty of the sixty-three studies were based on data collected during the 1970s, a decade marked by steadily rising levels of unemployment. Overall, Chiricos reports that the unemployment-crime relationship "is three times more likely to be positive than negative and more than 15 times as likely to be significant/positive as significant/negative" (1987, 192). Thus, he felt it "appropriate to argue" that the evidence supports "a positive, frequently significant U-C relationship," particularly for the property crimes that account for about 90 percent of the crimes included in the FBI's index of serious crime. In Chiricos' judgment, and despite the fact that "the relationship between unemployment and crime rates is less than perfect, it is sufficient to put jobs back on the agenda for dealing with crime" (1987, 203).

A major problem Chiricos found in assessing study results was the general absence of analyses of the connection between unemployment and crime rates for males and females by age. Acknowledging this important point, Allan and Steffensmeier (1989) examined the bearing of unemployment and underemployment on the property crime arrest rates of male juveniles aged 14–17 and young adults aged 18–24. For the juveniles, full-time employment was correlated with low arrest rates and unemployment with high arrest rates. For the young adults, the major finding was a correlation between arrest rates and the quality of employment; the lower the pay and number of hours employed, the higher the arrest rate. As Allan and Steffensmeier see it, "the more the youth labor market is characterized by adequate opportunities for work, the smaller the proportion of young people that may be susceptible to peer subcultures and to the attractions of illegitimate alternatives to the labor market" (1989, 118–19).

Hartnagel and Krahn's study of Canadian youth yielded results consistent with those of Allan and Steffensmeier. The 168 individuals (over 51 percent were male) in the sample had dropped out of school before completing the twelfth grade. The dependent variable was self-reported delinquency. The independent variables were current employment status, length of time employed since dropping out, and number of jobs held since leaving school. Consistent with previous study results, unemployment was correlated with property crime but not violent crime. The same was true of unstable work history. As number of jobs held since dropping out increased, so did the amount of reported property crime. Number of months employed had little measurable effect on the crime measures. Males were much more likely than females to report criminal involvement, police contacts, and court convictions. As Hartnagel and Krahn see it, "increased involvement in deviant behavior for unemployed dropout males may thus be a normal part of a somewhat marginalized world, a world where social controls of a job are absent, where peer group influences are strong, and where free time and boredom combine to increase the opportunities for and temptations to engage in deviant behavior" (1989, 440).

Race, the third variable of particular importance to disaggregate, was central to a study conducted by Simons and Gray. Controlling for race and lower- or middle-class socioeconomic status, they examined the relationship between perceived economic opportunity (employment and satisfactory job prospects) and self-reported delinquency. Those studied were a national sample of males in grades 7 through 12 from nine major cities. "Analysis," they state, "showed a moderate relationship between perceived occupational opportunities and delinquency for lower-class blacks but not for any of the other groups, including lower-class whites" (1989, 90).

Unemployment is, of course, related to poverty and poverty is related to race. Nonwhites are more likely than whites to be classified as living below the poverty level. There is some evidence (Patterson 1991) to indicate a connection between poverty status and violent crime, particularly murder (Crutchfield 1989). In a study based on self reported victimization in 57 small residential neighborhoods, Patterson found that "levels of absolute poverty, measured by the percentage of households with annual incomes below $5,000, are significantly associated with higher rates of serious violent crime" (1991, 769). Measures of relative poverty and income inequality were not related to violent crime rates. Demonstrating the greater influence of the financial status of residents than their racial and age composition was the finding that "the percentage of nonwhite population and the percentage of the population in the age range of 12 to 20 years are not significantly associated with rates of violent crime once the percentage of low-income households is added to the model" (1991, 769).

In brief, the evidence indicates that one would be well advised to keep a close eye on the unemployment rate as an important possible indicator of future crime rates, property crime rates most of all. The evidence also suggests that the impact of unemployment on crime is influenced by a number of intervening variables (age, education, gender, job history, place of residence, race). An intrusive factor of considerable potential influence, and one whose dimensions are difficult to measure, is the *underground economy.*

The underground economy is not only a complex subject but also a complex term. It is variously referred to as the black, clandestine, gray, hidden, informal, parallel, second, shadow, and subterranean economy (Feige 1990, 991). The underground economy includes all those lawful activities engaged in by all manner of people (the employed and the unemployed, the rich and the poor) toward the end of profiting and evading legal accountability. Unrecorded and unreported cash transactions typify the shadow economy. "Sole proprietorships" of various kinds are an outstanding example. According to Pennar and Farrell, "sole proprietorships—the corner stores, delis, selfemployed consultants, and the like—account for about $205 billion in unreported income yearly." Potential "shavers" of income include "the computer expert who hires out on a freelance basis as a tutor" and "the self-employed accountant who once held a middle-management position in a large company" (1993, 99–100).

Most analysts differentiate between the underground economy and the criminal underworld. Notwithstanding the fact that underground economic transactions invariably entail illegalities such as tax evasion, "they are," emphasizes Philip Mattera, "distinct from outright criminal activities such as drug dealing, prostitution, illegal gambling and other 'productive' underworld pursuits, as well as lawbreaking activities such as theft that involve the forcible redistribution of existing wealth" (1985, 11).

Legal underground activities are estimated to yield an annual income between $500 and $750 billion, roughly 10 to 15 percent the size of the reported economy. Pennar and Farrell suggest that the criminal underground (prostitution, drug dealing) accounts for another "$200 billion or so" in unreported income.

Of course, no one knows how much underground and underworld activities influence unemployment rates, but the impact must be presumed to be significant. In April 1982, the editors of *Business Week* concluded that national employment was about 4 to 5 million higher and unemployment about two percentage points lower than U.S. Department of Labor estimates. From the early 1970s to the early 1980s, Mattera (1985, 136) estimates the potential underground labor force (moonlighters, part-timers, the selfemployed, nonparticipants, the unemployed, and illegal immigrants) to have grown by some 26.1 million. In the wake of economic recession and continuing employment "downsizing," all these numbers have undoubtedly increased significantly from the early 1980s to the early 1990s. Available U.S. Department of Labor data, for example, indicates that in 1991 there were 8.4 million people unemployed, 20.3 million employed part-time, and 10.3 million self-employed. How many of these people added to the ranks of participants in the underground economy is not known. But the incentive was there. As Pennar and Farrell state, "in the 1980s, increased immigration, worsening income inequality, and a growing aversion to paying taxes all gave informal activity a big push" (1993, 99).

Most likely, unemployment will continue to be a problem, and an important consideration for one wishing to estimate the future rate of crime. Exactly how involvement in the underground economy influences unemployment and crime rates remains to be determined. Doubtless, however, involvement in the underground economy will continue to increase. Worldwide competition for increasingly scarce natural resources and markets militate against a rapid increase in the health of the general economy. Thus, one would be remiss not to predict that the impact of this involvement will grow and become of increasing public concern due to the loss of tax revenues and pressure to maintain and expand a variety of costly social services such as those involved in meeting the needs of the unemployed and caring for an aging population. What is difficult to estimate is the likely law-enforcement response to the problem. Will law-enforcement resources be redirected to confront the problem of "unorganized" underground white-collar illegality, or will they continue to be devoted toward the effort to combat street crime and organized crime? Technological innovations and their application will undoubtedly play an important role in the answer to such questions and the ability of law-enforcement agents to respond to the complex economic and demographic challenges that will confront them.

Policing in the Future

By most accounts, the future of policing appears to hinge on two estimable facts: economic instability and increasing population heterogeneity. What makes the two especially difficult to cope with is that they are the product of worldwide economic and political developments. This is not accidental, as the post World War II economic policy of the victorious Allies was aimed at lessening national isolation and increasing international economic trade. The success of the policy is evident in the fact that an economic upturn or downturn in a major segment such as the U.S. economy can be predicted to have immediate repercussions for all the others. Worldwide competition for scarce natural resources and access to certain labor markets now influence national economic well-being as never before. As the nations of the world are not political and economic equals, some are in a better position to rise to the occasion. Those with stronger economies attract the populations of those experiencing particularly high rates of unemployment and population growth. An outstanding example is the population shifts that occur between Mexico and the United States. But the United States, despite a weakened economy and public treasury to respond properly to the influx, has continued to attract even more immigrants from Asia and sizable numbers from other areas as well. Those concerned with the future of policing have been particularly sensitive to the need to anticipate the possible criminological effects of continuing business instability and increasing population diversity.

Canadian economist Kimon Vakaskakis traces the recent economic downturn to deep fiscal indebtedness (business, government, consumer) fueled by governmental policies and business practices of the 1980s. In his view, debt can be absorbed when an economy is growing, "but once the economy begins to contract, the pyramid of credit can easily be toppled, causing bankruptcies and massive financial failures" (1991, 260). The U.S. Savings and Loan experience is a good example. In addition to this "internal" condition, Vakaskakis thinks an "external" set of factors, from the possibility of another "oil shock" to the shift in economic power from North America to Asia and Europe, must be taken into account by the future forecaster. As he thinks the 1990s will most likely evolve into 1970s-like "stagflation," he forecasts more rather than less economic turbulence. For policing, Vakaskakis (1991, 260–61) envisions the future to include an increase in certain white-collar crimes ("unforeseen bankruptcies by a generation of Yuppies not used to economic hardship may tempt many into fraud, subtle embezzlement, tax evasion") and stress related crimes (from suicide to mass killings).

More generally, Valaskakis envisions some ominous possibilities due to the "uncoupling process," the growing trend toward the separation of technological change and labor demand. As he points out, recent technological advances in agriculture and industry suggest a demand for less rather than more human labor. The last few decades, Valaskakis tells us, have witnessed a steady rise in production and a steady decline in the demand for blue-collar employment. He traces labor displacement to both "classical mechanization" and "contemporary inforemediation" (from communication-enhancing technology to computerization and robotics).

Valaskakis believes the impact of "jobless growth" on crime rates to be dependent on "how the economic fruits of automation will be distributed" and "how surplus labor time will be absorbed" (1991, 263). As the two responses suggest considerable uncertainty, the message for policing seems unequivocal: "to determine the challenges that the police forces may have to face *in the future*, a close and continuous monitoring of economic (plus political, social and demographic) trends must be done *in the present*, not just on an occasional, once-a-decade basis, but as an ongoing annual activity of environmental scanning" (emphasis in the original) (Valaskakis 1991, 267).

Alvin and Heidi Toffler's estimate of the future of law enforcement parallels that of Valaskakis'. As they view it, the United States, since roughly 1955, has been undergoing a switch from a muscle-to a knowledge-driven economy. The immigrants who fueled the industrialization of the United States were sought not because of their knowledge but because of their muscle. As the Tofflers put it, the immigrants "actually entered the economy *before* [emphasis in original] they entered the culture" (1990, 3). Today's immigrants and youth must "enter into the mainstream culture *before* he or she can enter into the legitimate economy" (1990, 3). That many are not able either to acquire the prerequisite education for or obtain employment in the complex and rapidly developing technologically based economy is the problem. As with Valaskakis, the Tofflers foresee the future of street crime in terms of how well the growth of surplus labor is anticipated and constructively dealt with by socially responsible private and public decision making. And they too stress a connection between technological change and the emergence of new types of crime and criminals: "Breakthroughs in genetics, birth technologies, bizarre new materials, software, and a thousand other fields will shake up our economy yet again, dislocate additional millions, and provide new opportunities for creative criminals" (Toffler and Toffler 1990, 4).

Gene Stephens recently provided a thought-provoking glimpse into the near future of the possible implications of "the biotech revolution" on crime, criminals, and policing. He focused on three areas of biotechnological research in particular: the unlocking of the genetic code, organ replacement, and memory transfer.

Considering how much has been accomplished since Watson and Crick discovered the basic structure of the DNA molecule, Stephens thinks it not unlikely that we will soon be able to program life and death, to become immortal by controlling the aging process. Such a prospect raises a number of issues, for example, the proper punishment for the murder of an immortal. "If an immortal commits a murder, could society afford to sentence him to life imprisonment?" (Stephens 1992, 40). Alternatives include speeding up or slowing down the culprit's aging process or depriving one of antiaging drugs. For law enforcement, the possibilities include policing a blackmarket in antiaging drugs.

Organ-replacement research may lead to similar problems. As Stephens points out, it is quite possible that the foreseeable future will witness the emergence of a market in body parts. The rich may tempt the poor by offering to buy their organs for a price; parents may offer the sale of their childrens' body parts to the highest bidder. "Already," says Stephens, "parents have produced additional children as a source of bone marrow for transplants for themselves or their other children" (1992, 40). And even more likely than in the case of antiaging drugs, a black market in human organs may emerge, posing special problems for the law enforcement community.

In memory research, scientists have been able to transfer memory in worms and rats. As Stephens wonders, could the future include the ability to transfer the memories of master thieves and master detectives to designated others? As Stephens sees it,

> The next big step in the technological revolution will be the merging of biological and information technologies. Computers will ultimately be implanted into the human body to improve organic functioning and to simulate, increase, and enhance the capacity and capabilities of the brain. (1992, 42)

Of all recent technological innovations, none has had a greater impact on crime than the computer. Computer crime is a growing subfield of criminology. Because of its potentially devastating possibilities, computer crime is also a subject of considerable importance to law-enforcement administrators concerned with estimating its present and likely future dimensions.

Computer Crime and Future Policing

As with so many valuable tools, the computer's strengths are the source of its vulnerability. Its basic strength is an ability to carry out complex calculations of great value to people quickly and accurately. The computer is so good at doing what it does that people have come to depend on it and be in awe of it. This has reached a point where the computer has come to be regarded as an autonomous entity. When a billing error is made, for example, we blame the computer rather than the human agents involved. "In the past," says Donn Parker, "we would blame Mr. So-and-So at the bank for bank statement errors; then we shifted the blame to the bank; now we just blame the computer at the bank" (1976, 12). For this reason and others, Parker refers to computer abuse rather than computer crime. To him, computer abuse refers to "any incident associated with computer technology in which a victim suffered or could have suffered less and a perpetrator by intention made or could have made gain" (1976, 12).

Those who determine what a computer can do and when and how it does it, from systems designers to maintenance engineers, are well aware of the fear and respect evoked by the computer and the importance of their work. Not all have the ability to resist the temptation to use their expertise for illicit gain. And others, aware of the unique positions and abilities of computer experts, do not hesitate to bribe or coerce them to manipulate a machine for illegal purposes.

Unlike most white-collar crimes, computer-related violations tend to entail collusion. The collusion, as one might expect, tends to be between those who know how to manipulate the computer and those who know how and to whom to market the results. In effect, computer related crimes and criminals cover a broad and growing range.

August Bequai (1979, 196–99), a professor of criminal law, has identified eight categories of crime involving the computer: (1) *data crimes* (the stealing of a company's valuable computer tapes and their sale to competitors or other interested parties, including organized crime elements; (2) *theft of service* (the illegal use of a firm's computer facilities by employees); (3) *property-related crimes* (theft of important computer components, manipulation of computer programs to alter accounts or divert merchandise shipments); (4) *industrial sabotage* (the destruction of machines, tapes, and equipment by competitors); (5) *politically related sabotage* (the destruction of computer facilities by political activists and terrorists); (6) *employee vandalism* (the destruction of computer hardware and software by disgruntled or deranged employees); (7) *crimes against the individual* (fraudulent billing, the termination of computer controlled life-support systems); and (8) *financial crimes* (the modification of payrolls and accounts payable and receivable).

Bequai believes that the computer has opened a new avenue of exploitation for organized crime. He also thinks that it encourages unification among organized crime groups because computer crimes are often "too complex for one group to handle, especially those requiring a vast network of fences" (1979, 199).

Computer abuse is attractive to criminal elements not only because of the possibilities of great financial gain but also because of the difficulty of detecting the fact, source, and extent of certain acts. The fact, extent, and perpetrators of some computer abuse (e.g., vandalism and sabotage) may not be difficult to identify. But other abuse, invariably that involving the greatest potential economic cost (theft of property and financial crimes such as electronic fund transferring), may not, without a confession or a "leak," become detectable. And even after it has been determined that a crime has been committed and the perpetrator has been identified, the extent of wrongdoing (e.g., the amount and location of missing funds and goods) may not be specifiable. In brief, computer-related activity presents any number of opportunities for illicit gain.

Not surprisingly, then, computer abuse involves a diverse range of offenders. Donn Parker (1983, 106) identifies them as (1) *amateurs* (ordinary people, typically those without criminal records, employed in computer-related situations who take advantage of a position of trust to appropriate resources for a number of reasons (e.g., gambling or substance-abuse addiction); (2) the *deranged* (psychotics and others who attack and destroy computer equipment and facilities); (3) *system hackers* ("unauthorized system explorers" or "technological trespassers," typically high school and college students without criminal records); (4) *career* (repeat offenders committed to computer abuse); (5) *organizations* (from the systematic criminal efforts of a group or a firm to the intrusions of organized crime elements; (6) *extreme advocates* (those who engage in computer abuse in the name of a cause, political, economic, religious, and so on); and (7) *governments* (computer-related sabotage and espionage efforts by foreign power agencies).

Although each is important and of future concern, the one that has inspired the greatest concern to law-enforcement authorities is the *system hacker.* Hackers not only seek to obtain unauthorized access to computer information for their own purposes but also to destroy data and halt system operations. The hackers' means to the end are referred to as "malicious codes," for example, "viruses" (which destroy data) and "worms" (which cause system overload and shutdown). As former FBI Director William Sessions tells it,

> These products of computer criminal action have the potential for great harm, not only to large financial institutions but also to all citizens. Criminals who hack into a computer storing a doctor's patient and prescription information could, by electronically altering the drugs and dosages, inflict serious harm on patients. Criminals who hack into defense computers could compromise valuable

> intelligence information and possibly alter the world's balance of power. (1991, 14)

Some insight into the motives of the hacker has been provided by Bill Landreth. In 1985, he described himself as a nineteen year old caught by the FBI two years earlier. He had been convicted of computer fraud (for gaining unauthorized access to a GTE computer network in Virginia) and was serving a sentence of 3 years' probation. To the law-enforcement community, he was known as "The Cracker" and a leader of "a group of hackers" (by "invitation only") who called themselves "The Inner Circle."

Landreth describes the typical hacker as a young male in his teens or early twenties who is invariably a "fast learner," often "gifted," rather independent, and inclined to be "bored with school." He identifies five types of hackers: the Novice, the Student, the Tourist, the Crasher, and the Thief.

The Novice tends to be the youngest of the five ("maybe twelve to fourteen"). He is inclined to view hacking as "play, or mischief making," something attractive because it is "fun" and rather "naughty."

The Student is someone bright and bored with school. He is motivated by intellectual curiosity rather than maliciousness or material gain.

The Tourist seeks a new experience rather than an intellectual challenge. He is the one who must always "test himself" in a risky adventure. He aims not to exploit the system of another but to discover the means of gaining access to it.

The most dangerous of the five are the Crasher and the Thief. The Crasher is not rationally motivated; he does not have "a logical purpose." He is the kind of individual who simply enjoys making trouble. As Landreth describes him, the Crasher is analogous to the bully who takes pleasure in calling attention to himself by inflicting pain and suffering on others. He is the one out to destroy data and shut down systems just to cause others misery.

Landreth describes the Thief as "the rarest" of the five. The Thief is the computer criminal, the one motivated to hack his way into a system toward the end of acquiring data for illicit gain. He is analogous to the embezzler, the employee who takes advantage of his knowledge and position to appropriate company funds for his own purposes.

To be sure, computer crime may be committed for any number of reasons by those with a variety of aims and strategies. And while it is useful to identify certain computer crime, for example, vandalism, theft of information, burglary by modem (see Willis 1986, 43–5), it is important to keep in mind that computer applications offer seemingly unlimited opportunities for abuse by the deviously and criminally inclined. The future challenge to the law-enforcement community concerns the emergence of a new type of computer offender, the "cyberpunk," and the possible linkage of computer applications with advancing biological knowledge.

As Philip Dewitt (1993, 59) tells it, the term *cyberpunk* is derived from cybernetics ("the science of communications and control theory") and punk ("an antisocial rebel or hoodlum"). The two terms also denote *cyberpunk culture*, an outlook "that combines an infatuation with high-tech tools and a disdain for conventional ways of using them" (Dewitt 1993, 59). Dewitt contends that what sets cyberpunks apart from their hacker predecessors is their future orientation. He describes them as leading the way into the twenty-first century. "In the long run," says Dewitt, "we will all be cyberpunks" (1993, 61).

A key concept in cyberculture is *cyberspace*, the "data highway" that is the worldwide telephone network for person-to-person and computer-to-computer communication. Cyberpunks view the network from the inside; that is, they imaginatively project themselves into the operating system whose components become means of gratifying basic needs in the same manner as any human habitat.

In other words, the internal world of computers and their network links became a "virtual space," an open area, *cyberspace*, available to anyone with the means of access (a computer, modem, software). Cyberspace, as Dewitt points out, is a new medium, and one that thousands now enter any time of the day or night via Compuserve, Prodigy, and the Well (the 7000 member northern California based Whole Earth Lectric Link). According to Dewitt (1993, 62), the Well, a cyberpunk "magnet," recently held a debate that resulted in certain agreed upon cyberpunk "attitudes" such as the following:

1. *Information wants to be free* (computer hardware and software capabilities will be exploited by those interested and able to do so regardless of the wishes of law-makers and enforcers ("datacops").

2. *Always yield to the hands-on imperative* (cyberpunks "believe they can run the world for the better, if they can only get their hands on the control box."

3. *Promote decentralization* (society is rapidly breaking down into diverse subcultures and cults).

4. *Surf the edges* (the best way to stay ahead of social change is to lead events).

In a brief piece entitled "Surfing off the Edge," Richard Behar gives us an example of the latter "attitude" that illustrates something new about the participants in computer crime that has important immediate and future implications for the law-enforcement community.Behar tells the story of twenty-one-year-old Morty Rosenfeld, a cyberpunk serving an 8 month jail term for illegally accessing credit accounts in the computers of TRW, Inc.

Behar (1993, 62) states that Rosenfeld claims to have committed his first illegal hacking at fifteen when he "broke" into a NASA computer system. At the time he was a member of The Force Hackers, a cyberpunk gang.

Rosenfeld, says Behar, sometimes dealt with another cyberpunk gang, The Masters of Disaster. The MOD gang, as of early 1993, was scheduled to be tried for "hacking" their way into a number of computer systems (the University of Washington, Bank of America, ITT). Rosenfeld and the "modsters," it appears, do not conform to the stereotyped image of the hacker as an upper-middle-class suburbanite out for a good time. According to Behar,

> These cyberpunks are ethnically mixed (from blacks to Hispanics to Italians and Lithuanians), favor close-cropped hip-hop haircuts and live in urban, blue-collar neighborhoods. They fight rival gangs with cheap computers, not sticks or knives. Some are big drug users; most are simply addicted to what Rosenfeld calls the "adrenaline rush of computer power, which is better than sex, drugs or rock 'n roll." (1993, 63)

Considering the future possibilities from Gene Stephen's vantage point, it may soon be possible for cyberpunks to satisfy their addiction in a more personal and effective way. "Criminals," says Stephens, "soon may carry all the information they need for computer thefts in database implants in their brains" (1992, 42). As if this is not frightening enough, "a police officer of the next century will walk down the street and identify everyone he sees: Complete birth-to-death dossiers of all citizens, including criminal records and 'wanted' alerts, will be stored in the officer's computer-enhanced brain, and the officer will scan his implanted nanocomputer databank in fractions of a second" (Stephens 1992, 42).

As important as it seems for the law enforcement community to focus attention on the complexities of policing cyberspace and the possible implications of "the biotech revolution," its efforts to date have emphasized the problem of policing a population daily becoming more racially and ethnically diverse.

Population Diversity and Future Policing

The ethnic and racial diversification of computer hackers and cyberpunks is a reflection of the growing diversification of the nation's population. Over the past three censuses, the data indicate that European immigration has steadily declined while Asian immigration has steadily risen. From 1981 to 1990, some 7.3 million immigrated to the United States (a little more than 705,000, or 9.6 percent from Europe and 2.8 million, or 38 percent from Asia). Emigration from North America, South America, and Africa also has steadily increased. Within North America, the leading country of origin is Mexico, but significant numbers have also streamed in from the Caribbean (particularly Cuba) and Central America (El Salvador most of all). From Africa, immigrants from Egypt and Nigeria have led the way. As demographers anticipate continued relatively high rates of immigration from Asia and Latin America, the proportion of the white population is expected to decline steadily. "In consequence," says Paul Kennedy, "some demographers refer to the 'browning' of America by 2050 as Caucasians become a minority" (1993, 312).

A growing view of those concerned with the future of law enforcement in America is that policing must increasingly acknowledge and reflect the ethnic diversity of the population. To police their jurisdictions effectively, law-enforcement agencies are advised to institute systematic means of making themselves aware of their constituents' ethnic differences. As Police Commander Charles Bozza of Irvine, California, warns, "law enforcement needs to understand how to deal with people from other backgrounds in today's society or be prepared for the results of lack of understanding" (1992, 208).

Gary Weaver, a professor of communications, has dramatized, by critically assessing four commonly held assumptions regarding those of different cultural backgrounds, some of the possible consequences when law enforcement agents are insensitive to ethnicity. One assumption is that "*as society and the workforce become more diverse, differences become less important*" (Weaver 1992, 2). As Weaver states, simply juxtaposing people from different cultural traditions is less likely to promote harmony than misunderstanding and conflict. "Differences," says Weaver, "usually become more apparent and hostilities can actually increase during encounters between culturally diverse individuals" (1992, 2).

Another assumption is that "*it's just a matter of communication and common sense*" (Weaver 1992, 3). The problem with this assumption, notes Weaver, is that 90 percent of communication is nonverbal, or by means of facial and bodily gestures. He illustrates the point by means of a hypothetical scenario involving an officer who has stopped a Nigerian cab driver who has run a red light. As Weaver tells it,

> Before the police officer can exit the patrol car, the cabbie gets out of his vehicle and approaches the officer. Talking rapidly in a high-pitched voice and making wild gestures, the cab driver appears to be out of control. As the officer steps from his car, he yells for the cab driver to stop, but the cabbie continues to walk toward the officer. He does not make eye contact and appears to be talking to the ground. What began as a routine stop for a traffic violation culminates in charges of disorderly conduct and resisting arrest. (1992, 3)

But all was not as it seemed. While most citizens know that they should remain in their cars when stopped by an officer, "the Nigerian exited his cab because he wanted to show respect and humility by not troubling the officer to leave his patrol car" (Weaver 1992, 4). And while it is an American custom to make eye contact when conversing with another, "in Nigeria, however, people often show respect and humility by averting their eyes" (Weaver 1992, 4). It was the officer's ignorance, then, not the Nigerian cab driver's behavior that was the problem.

If officers of the law are to keep up with the technological and demographic changes occurring in contemporary America they certainly must become more broadly and thoroughly educated than has been the practice. Mandated basic police training of any kind was not a national pattern until after 1960. In a recent national survey, Cox and Moore (1992, 247) found that 400 hours, or ten weeks of training, was the national average.

But training in the elements of police work is not the only educational area needing improvement. Most states require only a high school diploma as the general educational requirement. Some college, typically at the community college level, is stressed by some departments, but very few require a four-year college degree.

College-level education for police officers has long been a controversial subject. A basic argument against it has been the premise that an average level of education is all that is needed to cope with average citizens. Another is the fear of elitism. As James Ahern observes, a highly educated and professionally trained police force "evokes visions of militaristic, super-efficient, semi-thoughtless automatons, marching in lock step to a set of 'police values' that are independent of democratic controls and backed up by tear gas and guns" (1972, 178). The years since these words were published witnessed an unprecedented rise in concern with law and order and increased support for more rather than less formal policing. Today, people worry hardly at all about the possible emergence of tyrannical policing and a great deal about the consequences of inadequate and incompetent policing.

Arguments for college-educated police officers include enhanced foreign language skills, greater tolerance and understanding of ethnic and racial differences, improved communication skills, and greater public respect. More important, as Cox and Moore point out, the twenty-first century police officer will not only have to be prepared to cope with undereducated offenders but also "the well educated whose greed leads to a criminal career which offers a greater opportunity for wealth at a more rapid rate than legitimate enterprise" (1992, 247). For them, "the question for the twenty-first century is not whether college education and increased training is needed for police officers, but rather *how much and how soon*" (emphasis in the original) (Cox and Moore 1992, 253).

The Future of Corrections

While precise predicting of the future of corrections (conviction rates, probation and parole populations, and so on) is not possible, estimates of patterns and trends can be made. If, for example, the rate of offending remains the same but the number apprehended rises due to more effective law-enforcement, the correctional population will increase. From the evidence examined above, it might well be hypothesized that the American public is more likely to support means of enhancing policing (adding more officers and equipping with the latest technological advances) than improving prison rehabilitation (advanced educational and vocational training). For the near future, one predicts a continued emphasis on apprehension and punishment and a relative neglect of rehabilitative programming. As Edward Rhine states, "get tough" sentencing policy "is likely to continue well into the 1990s" (1992, 27).

Even if policing efficiencies were to remain constant and the balance of resources allocated to rehabilitative efforts, one would expect the correctional population to continue to rise as major rehabilitative programs (e.g., psychological treatment in conjunction with social changes such as job access creation for ex-offenders) take time to implement and have measurable effects. In the immediate future, then, prison overcrowding can be expected to worsen, or in the words of John Dilulio, "there will be no escape from the greatly increasing number of citizens in prison" and "no escape from the need for more prisons and jails" (1991, 2–3).

According to John Conrad, "the annual cost of keeping all the nation's prisoners locked-up runs to nearly $14 billion" and "the national outlay for new facilities and renovation of the old was about $4,700,000,000" (1991, 5). As he states, alternatives will eventually have to be considered as "we can't go on like this" (1991, 5).

Pressure to alleviate prison overcrowding can be predicted to increase because of three apparent factors: (1) the declining availability of tax monies to build and staff new prisons; (2) fear of the destructive effects (human, political, material) of prison riots; and (3) continued application to imprisonment conditions the Eighth Amendment prohibition against the imposition of cruel and unusual punishment. Exactly when the combined effects of the three will result in lowered rates of incarceration as opposed to rises in parole and probation rates remains to be seen. In the short run, the number of offenders on parole and probation can be expected to continue to rise (see Table 12.1).

To reduce institutional crowding and costs, and to assure an acceptable degree of public protection, it is certain that emphasis will continue to be placed on certain "front" and "back" door diversionary efforts. "Programs of the former type," points out Michael Tonry,

> operate as diversions from prison and thereby notionally keep offenders from entering the prison's front door. Programs of the latter type offer early release from prison, on condition of the intense supervision of ISP [Intensive Probationary Supervision], and thereby notionally hasten prisoners' exist through the prison's back door. (1992, 245)

Table 12.1
Adults on Parole & Probation, 1985–1990

	Parole		Probation	
Year	Number	Percentage of Adult Population[a]	Number	Percentage of Adult Population
1985	300,203	.17	3,011,000	1.7
1986	325,638	.18	3,240,000	1.8
1987	355,505	.20	3,460,000	1.9
1988	407,907	.22	3,713,000	2.0
1989	456,803	.25	4,055,000	2.2
1990	531,407	.29	4,350,000	2.4

Source: "Probation and Parole 1990" *Bureau of Justice Statistics Bulletin* (Washington, D.C.: U.S. Department of Justice, November, 1991), 5.

[a]. The percentage of the total adult population of the United States.

Diversionary sentences and intermediate sanctions (those between imprisonment and traditional probation such as fines and community service orders; see Morris and Tonry 1990), particularly community corrections efforts (e.g., home arrest, with and without electronic monitoring and ISP) can be expected to be relied upon increasingly as implementation problems are reduced and new program efficiencies discovered. The same can be said for back-door programs such as shock sentencing and parole.

A fact yet to be reckoned with is the impact of increased reliance on community corrections on the public. Unless efforts are made to convince citizens that the correctional effort requires not only public acceptance but public involvement, negative reaction could prevent the growth and development of effective community programs. The task is exceedingly important if the basic aim of corrections is ever to be realized, that is, the reintegration of the offender into the community. Goal realization requires changes on both sides. The offender must be motivated to become law abiding and community residents must be willing to provide the necessary change resources (places of residence, family and emotional support, general educational and vocational training opportunities, and job access). To the extent that the public continues to view the offender as strictly a victimizer rather than both a victimizer requiring punishment and a victim needing rehabilitative assistance, corrections can be predicted to be an individual exception rather than the general rule.

References

Ahern, James F. 1972. *Police in Trouble*. New York: Hawthorn.

Allan, Emilie A., and Darrell J. Steffensmeier. 1989. "Youth, Underemployment, and Property Crime." *American Sociological Review* 54 107–23.

Becker, Gary S. 1968. "Crime and Punishment: An Economic Approach." *Journal of Political Economy* 76 169–217.

Behar, Richard. 1993. "Surfing Off The Edge." *Time* 141 62–3.

Bequai, August. 1979. *Organized Crime*. Lexington, Mass.: Heath.

Bozza, Charles M. 1992. "The Future of Diversity in America: The Law Enforcement Paradigm Shift." *Journal of Contemporary Criminal Justice* 8 208–16.

Brenner, M. Harvey.1976. *Estimating the Social Costs of National Economic Policy: Implications for Mental and Physical Health, and Criminal Aggression*. Report to the Joint Economic Committee of the House and Senate. Washington, D.C.: Congressional Research Service.

Chiricos, Theodore G. 1987. "Rates of Crime and Unemployment: An Analysis of Aggregate Research Evidence." *Social Problems* 34 187–212.

Coates, Joseph F. 1972. "The Future of Crime in the United States fromNow to The Year 2000." *Policy Sciences* 3 27–45.

Conrad, John P. 1991. "The Pessimistic Reflections of a Chronic Optimist." *Federal Probation* LV 4–9.

Cox, Barbara and Richter H. Moore, Jr. 1992."Toward the Twenty-First Century: Law Enforcement Training Now and Then." *Journal of Contemporary Criminal Justice* 8 235–53.

Crutchfield, Robert D. 1989. "Labor Stratification and Violent Crime." *Social Forces* 68 489–512.

Dewitt, Philip Elmer. 1993. "Cyberpunk." *Time* 141 59–63.

Dilulio, John J. Jr. 1991. *No Escape: The Future of American Corrections*. New York: Basic Books.

Feige, Edgar L. 1990. "Defining and Estimating Underground and Informal Economies: The New Institutional Economics Approach." *World Development* 18 989–1002.

Hartnagel, Timothy F., and Harvey Krahn. 1989. "High School Dropouts, Labor Market Success, and Criminal Behavior." *Youth and Society* 20 416–44.

Kennedy, Paul.1993. *Preparing for The Twenty-First Century*. New York: Random House.

Landreth, Bill. 1985. *Out of The Inner Circle: A Hacker;s Guide to Computer Security*. Bellevue, Washington: Microsoft.

Mattera, Philip. 1985. *Off the Books*. New York: St. Martin's.

Morris, Norval, and Michael Tonry.1990. *Between Prison and Probation: Intermediate Punishments in a Rational Sentencing System*. New York: Oxford University Press.

Parker, Donn B. 1976. *Crime by Computer*. New York: Scribner's.

———. Donn B. 1983. *Fighting Computer Crime*. New York:Scribner's.

Patterson, E. Britt. 1991. "Poverty, Income Inequality, and CommunityCrime Rates." *Criminology* 29 755–76.

Pennar, Karen and Christopher Farrell. 1993."Notes from The Underground Economy." *Business Week*/February 15 98–101.

Rhine, Edward E. 1992. "Sentencing Reform and Correctional Policy: Some Unanswered Questions." In *Correctional Theory and Practice* edited by Clayton A Hartjen and Edward E. Rhine. Chicago: Nelson-Hall.

Sessions, William S. 1991. "Computer Crimes: An Escalating Crime Trend." *FBI Law Enforcement Bulletin* 60 12–15.

Simons, Ronald L., and Phyllis A. Gray. 1989. "Perceived Blocked Opportunity as An Explanation of Delinquency among Lower-Class Black Males: A Research Note." *Journal of Research on Crime and Delinquency* 26 90–101.

Stephens, Gene. 1992. "Crime and The Biotech Revolution." *The Futurist* 26 38–42.

Thompson, James W., Michelle Sviridoff, and Jerome E. McElroy. 1981. *Employment and Crime: A Review of Theories and Research*. Washington, D.C.: Government Printing Office.

Toffler, Alvin and Heidi Toffler. 1990. "The Future of Law Enforcement." *FBI Law Enforcement Bulletin* 59 2–5.

Tonry, Michael. 1992. "Stated and Latent Functions of ISP." In *Contemporary Community Corrections* edited by Thomas Ellsworth. Prospect Heights, Illinois: Waveland.

Valaskakis, Kimon. 1991."Economic Trends and The Future of Policing: Whatto Expect from The Turbulent Nineties." *Canadian Journal of Criminology* 33 257–268.

Weaver, Gary. 1992."Law Enforcement in a Culturally Diverse Society."*FBI Law Enforcement Bulletin* 61 1–7.

Willis, Rod. 1986. "White-Collar Crime: The Threat from Within." *Annual Editions: Criminal Justice 87/88*. Guilford, Ct: Dushkin, 43–5.

Wollan, Laurin A. 1976. "Crime in Tomorrow's Society." *The Futurist* 10 124–34.

Index

www.ingramcontent.com/pod-product-compliance
Ingram Content Group UK Ltd.
Pitfield, Milton Keynes, MK11 3LW, UK
UKHW041103150926
475561UK00001BA/16

9 781882 289257